To Scale

How big is Moscow's Red Square in comparison to Tiananmen Square?

Why are there fewer public squares in Japan than in Italy?

What lessons might be found in the plan of Savannah, Georgia's historic district?

To Scale is a collection of plans of urban spaces drawn at the same scale to help answer these and other questions by providing a single and accurate resource of urban plans for architects, urban designers, planners and teachers and students in these fields.

The book contains one hundred figure-ground plans from seventy-eight cities around the world, describing an identical area (half a kilometer square) for each urban space. Accompanying each plan are photographs, diagrams and text that illustrate essential aspects of the plan or urban space for the designer. Rather than purely historical description, the text attempts to explore those lessons that might be found in the urban condition. This compilation is an excellent resource for helping to visualize, compare and reconceptualize urban design for those wanting to understand the lessons of existing cities and the making of urban spaces.

Eric J. Jenkins is Associate Professor and Assistant Dean in the School of Architecture and Planning at the Catholic University of America, Washington, DC, where he teaches design, analytical sketching and research methodologies.

To Scale

One hundred urban plans

Eric J. Jenkins

Simultaneously published in the USA and Canada
by Routledge
270 Madison Avenue, New York, NY 10016

First published 2008
by Routledge
2 Park Square, Milton Park, Abingdon, Oxon OX14 4RN

Reprinted 2010

Routledge is an imprint of the Taylor & Francis Group, an informa business

Typeset in Eurostile by Keystroke, 28 High Street, Tettenhall, Wolverhampton
Printed and bound in Great Britain by The Cromwell Press Group, Trowbridge, Wiltshire

Library of Congress Cataloging in Publication Data
Jenkins, Eric J., 1964–
To scale : one hundred urban plans / Eric J. Jenkins.
p. cm.
Includes bibliographical references and index.
ISBN 978-0-415-95401-3 (pbk : alk. paper) — ISBN 978-0-415-95400-6 (hbk : alk. paper)
1. Plazas—Designs and plans. 2. Measured drawing. 3. City planning. I. Title.
NA9070.J46 2007
711′.40223—dc22 2007006403

British Library Cataloguing in Publication Data
A catalogue record for this book is available from the British Library

ISBN10: 0-415-95400-2 (hbk)
ISBN10: 0-415-95401-0 (pbk)

ISBN13: 978-0-415-95400-6 (hbk)
ISBN13: 978-0-415-95401-3 (pbk)

To Adrianna, dancing in the piazza

Contents

Illustration credits ix
Preface xi
Acknowledgements xiii

Introduction 1
Scale 5

1 **Amsterdam** Dam Square 6
2 **Arras** Grande Place and Place des Héros 8
3 **Athens** Platia Syntagmatos 10
4 **Baltimore** Mount Vernon Place 12
5 **Barcelona** Barri Gòtic 14
6 **Barcelona** Eixample 16
7 **Bath** Queens Square, Circus and Royal Crescent 18
8 **Beijing** Tiananmen Square 20
9 **Bergen** Fisketorget and Torgalmenningen 22
10 **Berlin** Museumsinsel 24
11 **Berlin** Potsdamer Platz and Leipziger Platz 26
12 **Bern** Altstadt 28
13 **Bologna** Piazza Maggiore 30
14 **Bordeaux** Allées de Tourny 32
15 **Boston** Copley Square 34
16 **Boston** Faneuil Hall Marketplace and Quincy Market 36
17 **Brasília** Praça dos Três Poderes 38
18 **Bruges** Grand Place and Burg 40
19 **Buenos Aires** Plaza de Mayo 42
20 **Cairo** Midan al-Tahrir 44
21 **České Budějovice** Náměstí Přemysl Otakar II 46
22 **Chandigarh** Capitol Complex 48
23 **Chicago** Federal Center 50
24 **Cincinnati** Fountain Square 52
25 **Cleveland** Public Square 54
26 **Copenhagen** Amalienborg Slotsplads 56
27 **Cuzco** Plaza de Armas 58
28 **Denver** Civic Center 60
29 **Detroit** Campus Martius 62
30 **Dresden** Zwinger and Theaterplatz 64
31 **Dublin** Temple Bar 66
32 **Dubrovnik** Placa 68
33 **Edinburgh** St Andrew Square 70
34 **Florence** Piazza della Signoria and Palazzo Uffizi 72
35 **Genoa** Piazza de Ferrari 74
36 **Indianapolis** Monument Circle 76
37 **Isfahan** Maidan-i-Shah 78
38 **Istanbul** Yeni Cami and Misir Çarsisi 80
39 **Jerusalem** Western Wall Plaza and the Temple Mount 82
40 **Kraków** Rynek Główny 84
41 **Lisbon** Praça do Comércio 86
42 **London** Belgrave Square and Wilton Crescent 88
43 **London** Cavendish Square and Hanover Square 90
44 **London** Park Crescent and Park Square 92
45 **London** Trafalgar Square 94
46 **Los Angeles** Pershing Square 96
47 **Lucca** Piazza dell' Anfiteatro 98
48 **Madrid** Plaza Mayor 100
49 **Mexico City** Zócalo / Plaza de la Constitución 102
50 **Milan** Piazza del Duomo 104
51 **Montréal** Place d'Armes 106
52 **Moscow** Krasnaya Plóshchad 108
53 **Nancy** Place Stanislas, Place de la Carrière and Place Général de Gaulle 110
54 **New Haven** The Green 112
55 **New Orleans** Jackson Square 114
56 **New York** Bryant Park 116
57 **New York** Rockefeller Center 118
58 **New York** Stuyvesant Square 120
59 **New York** Times Square 122
60 **New York** Union Square 124
61 **New York** Washington Square 126

62 **Oslo** Rådhus Plassen, Kronprincess Märthas Plassen and Eidsvolls Plass 128
63 **Paris** Palais Royal 130
64 **Paris** Place Charles-de-Gaulle/Place de l'Etoile 132
65 **Paris** Place des Vosges 134
66 **Paris** Musée du Louvre 136
67 **Paris** Place Vendôme 138
68 **Paris** Voison Plan 140
69 **Philadelphia** Rittenhouse Square 142
70 **Portland** Pioneer Courthouse Square 144
71 **Prague** Staroměstské Náměstí 146
72 **Rome** Piazza del Campidoglio 148
73 **Rome** Campo dei Fiori 150
74 **Rome** Piazza Navona 152
75 **Rome** Piazza San Pietro in Vaticano 154
76 **Saint Petersburg** Dvortsóvaya Plóshchad 156
77 **Salamanca** Plaza Mayor 158
78 **Salzburg** Domplatz, Residenzplatz and Kapitalplatz 160
79 **San Francisco** Union Square 162
80 **Santiago** Plaza de Armas 164
81 **Savannah** Historic District 166
82 **Seattle** Pioneer Square 168
83 **Seville** Plaza del Triunfo, Patio de los Naranjos and Real Alcázar 170
84 **Siena** Piazza del Campo 172
85 **Stockholm** Slottsbacken and Stortorget 174
86 **Tallinn** Raekoja Plats 176
87 **Telč** Náměstí Zachariáše z Hradce 178
88 **Tokyo** Asakusa Nakamise Dori 180
89 **Tokyo** Hachiko Square 182
90 **Torino** Piazza San Carlo 184
91 **Trieste** Canal Grande 186
92 **Tunis** Medina 188
93 **Vancouver** Robson Square 190
94 **Venice** Piazza San Marco and Piazzetta di San Marco 192
95 **Verona** Piazza delle Erbe and Piazza dei Signori 194
96 **Vienna** Ringstrasse 196
97 **Vigévano** Piazza Ducale 198
98 **Washington, DC** Dupont Circle 200
99 **Washington, DC** Grand Plaza, Woodrow Wilson Plaza and Daniel Patrick Moynihan Place 202
100 **Washington, DC** Judiciary Square 204

Plan sources 207
Bibliography 217
Index 223
Plan index by country and city 227

Illustration credits

Diagram Credits

Page	
xi	Angelo Uggeri, Edifices de la Décadence, 1809
48	Dhiru Thadani
52	Michael McCann for Cooper Robertson
62	Rundell Ernstberger Associates
140	Artists Rights Society

Photo Credits

Page	
6	Ronald F. Boisvert
8 all	Richard Birkby
10	Cory George
14 bottom	Dreamstime
14 top left	Robert Lindley Vann
14 top right	Dreamstime
16	Raúl Deamo
18 bottom	John Yanik
18 top	Dreamstime
20	Khawar Z. Ahmed
22	Dreamstime
24	Lothar Willmann
26 all	Veit Kaestner
28	Karl DuPuy
30 left	Olivier Schneller
30 top right	Philip Barber
30 bottom right	Giovanni Sighele
32	Aéro Photo Industrie www.api- Photo.net
34	Robert J. Lee
36	Robert J. Lee
38 left	Zel Nunes
38 middle	Preston Grant
38 right	Thomas J. Karsten
40 top	Travis Nelson
40 bottom	Timothy Brighton
42	Dreamstime
44	Yuji Nakamura
46	Dreamstime
48 top	Jiat-Hwee Chang
50	Robert Lindley Vann
56	Thomas L. Schumacher
58 all	Patrick Rog
60	Bi Yue Xu
62 bottom	Rundell Ernstberger Associates
64 left	Dreamstime
64 right	Marcel Moré
66 right	Grafton Architects
68	Dreamstime
70	Anne Johnstone
72 left	William Putnam
72 right	Dreamstime
74	Doriano Zaccherini
76 all	Keith Clark
78 all	Nicolas Hadjisavvas
80	William Bechhoefer
82 left	Dreamstime
82 right	Sarah Lehat
84	Dreamstime
86	Dreamstime
88	Mario Stagliano
92 right	James Donohue
92 left	Alex Gilletti
94 left	Visitbritain
94 right	Tony Dabruzzi
96	Pictometry
100 left	Vítor Ribeiro
100 middle	Robert Lindley Vann
100 bottom	Joel Oppenheimer Odom

102 right	Ben Smedley
102 left	Luis Fernando Franco Jiménez
104 left	Dreamstime
104 right	George Steinmetz
106	Viki Fong
108 all	Dreamstime
110 top	Aurélien Schvartz
110 bottom	Jean-Francois Chargois
112	James R. Anderson
114	Richard Loosle Ortega
116	Beau Wade
118	©2006 Rockefeller Center Archives
120	Pictometry
122 left	Matthew Evans
122 right	Ian Lewis
124	Nasozi Kakembo
126 all	Nasozi Kakembo
128 left	Tom Severns
128 right	John Watne
130 all	Richard Ortega-Loosle
132	Dreamstime
134 all	Vincent Marqueton
136	Dreamstime
138	Justin Choulochas
142	James Sanderson
144 all	Tara Hanby
146 left	Allister Taggert
146 top right	Ryb Chen
146 bottom right	David Bjorgen
148	William Putnam
150	David Shove-Brown
152	Sylvan Miles
154 all	Dreamstime
156	Dreamstime
158 top	Daniel M. Karlsson
158 bottom	Antonio García Rodríguez
160	Ryan Emanuel
162	Amber Kendrick
164 top	Anita Maria Veoso
164 bottom	Jackson Brustolin
166	Pictometry
168	Beth Somerfield Seattle Department of Parks and Recreation
170 left	Dreamstime
170 top right	Luis Boza
170 bottom right	Richard Ortega-Loosle
172 top left and right	Dean Hutchison
172 bottom	Dreamstime
174 left	Richard Melkerson
174 right	Jill Shih
176 all	Daoyong Liu
178 all	Janos Korom
180 top left	Julie Murphy
180 top right	William Putnam
182 all	Alasdair Milne
184	Gianluca Garelli
186	Derick Williamson
188	Michael Whitehouse
190 top	Jacee Weidong Tan
192	Dreamstime
194	Dreamstime
196	Adrian X. Whitehead
198	Thomas Walton
202 left	Pictometry

All other photographs and diagrams © Eric J. Jenkins

Preface

Architectural education, or any design education for that matter, is often a series of seminal moments. Sporadic, sometimes personal and seldom connected moments mark design epiphanies along a circuitous educational journey: these internal realizations are often the response to external, even unintended forces. A marginal sketch in a distant land, an instructor's peripheral comment, an unintentional slice or tear in a model or even a single image can prompt heightened awareness and intensified curiosity. Instructors that are aware of these seminal realizations in education will often use metaphors or analogies to help spur the architecture student into relating what is known to the unknown and, perhaps, prompt seminal moments. If the student is fortunate, the provocative metaphors lead to surprising insights as they establish connections that, until that moment and for them, did not exist.

Much of the idea behind this book comes from an early seminal moment prompted by a visual analogy depicted in a single image. During a freshman History of Architecture survey lecture, my professor projected a slide of Angelo Uggeri's iconic, side-by-side, same-scale comparison of one pier of Michelangelo's Basilica San Pietro in Vaticano with the entire plan of Francesco Borromini's San Carlo alle Quattro Fontane. Well aware of this image's power, I am sure my instructor was pleased by the sound of our gasps as most of us suddenly realized or at least visualized the basilica's immensity.

Since then, I have had an unrelenting curiosity regarding frame-of-reference and its role in understanding architecture and urban design. In my own teaching career, I have often asked students to find their own frame of reference. By drawing or modeling something with which they are familiar (plans of their bedrooms to existing curtain walls) the architectural analogy can inform their design process. The hope is that they could come to understand their work in relation to a physical and mnemonic context and, likewise, engage in a conversation with precedent. This book is a collection of analogies or metaphors from which design students might come to understand and design the built environment.

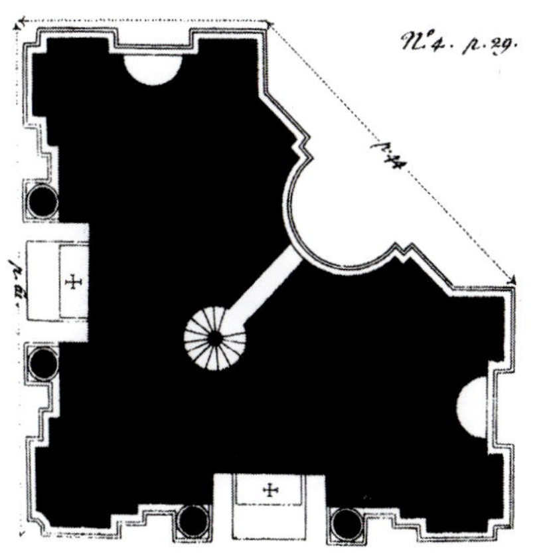

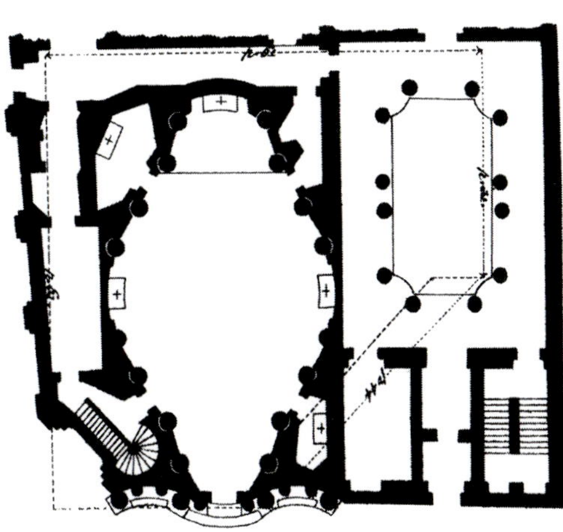

Comparison of the size of a pier in Basilica San Pietro in Vaticano and San Carlo alle Quattro Fontane

As in any metaphor, this book accepts a certain conceit of making and using metaphors and, specifically, in using abstract plans or maps to represent reality. The conceit is that we are well aware that plans represent reality all the while knowing that they are inherently inaccurate, biased and apocryphal. In his book, *The Sovereign Map: Theoretical Approaches in Cartography throughout History* (2006), Christian Jacob begins with a simple question: "What is a Map?" The answer, of course, is less simple. A map can be many things: physical artifact, ephemeral tool, semiotic system, political statement, social mediator and even omniscient vantage point. Above these physical or metaphysical definitions, he observes that:

> A map is defined perhaps less by formal traits than by the particular conditions of its production and reception, and by its status as an artifact and a mediation in a process of social communication. In a problematic mixture, it combines the transparence of referential illusion with the opacity of a medium that materializes the geographical image.
>
> (Jacob 2006: 21)

When we use the plan or any other representation, we embrace the conceit that it is reality made present. Within this accepted representation, we establish frames of reference and, in turn, materialize other realities. I can only hope that this book will allow designers to gain additional reference points and, possibly, prompt a seminal moment in their design education.

Acknowledgements

To the many friends, colleagues, former professors and former students – many of whom are now dear friends and colleagues – who helped make this book possible; the author is solely responsible for its shortcomings.

Thanks to the many trustworthy friends throughout the world who photographed their home towns: Robert J. Lee in Boston, Jacee Weidong Tan in Vancouver, Tara Hanby in Portland, Nasozi Kakembo in New York, Sarah Lehat in Jerusalem and James Sanderson in Philadelphia. Special thanks to Amber Kendrick, whose initial drawings for this project started the book and who contributed photographs of San Francisco.

I would like to thank those colleagues who shared their insights into urban history and theory: Nigel Hiscock on London, Jaan Holt on Tallinn, Hans Kühn on Dresden, Veit Kaestner on Berlin, Walter Ramberg on Tokyo, Stanley Hallet on Tunis and, finally, Todd Ray and Susan Piedmont-Palladino for their insightful musings and provocative conversations. Thanks to Dean Randy Ott and my colleagues at the Catholic University of America's School of Architecture and Planning for their support and patience. I am grateful to architect, urban designer and friend Terrance Williams, who offered new insights into New York and Isfahan and to urban design that can be both of our time and urbane.

To those Catholic University of America students for their "on assignment" photographs: Harry Paul Ross, William Putnam, Sylvan Miles, Craig Martin, Patrick Rog, Deanna Kiel, Terence Heron, Dean Hutchison and Derick Williamson.

Other assistance came from friends and associates who helped out when needed most, including Laura C. Jenifer, Petr Hlavácek, David Shove-Brown, Gregory K. Hunt, Thomas J. Bucci, Merrill St. Legier-Demian, Richard Ortega-Loosle, Deane Rundell, Joe Pikiewicz, Eddie Rangel, Seska Ramberg, Felix J. Malinowski, George Bott and Anna-Maria Correa. For their diligence, research assistants Joanna Beres, James Malone, Megan Shiley and Lindsey Vanderdray. Heartfelt thanks to Christine Cole and William Putnam for their patience and diligence as they helped refine the drawings for publication.

To those who allowed me to use their photographs yet are acknowledged only in the photography credits: your graciousness was inspiring.

I would like to thank the staff at the Library of Congress Geography and Map Reading Room for caring for and retrieving the maps and atlases from the library's extensive collection. Thanks also to curator Cynthia Frank at the University of Maryland Architecture Visual Resource room for access to the school's vast slide collection and the librarians at the Catholic University of America libraries.

Also, thanks to David McBride and Caroline Mallinder of Taylor & Francis. Acknowledgement goes to the Catholic University of America's Vice Provost, George Garvey, and the grant that helped fund the book's completion. Special thanks to my professors, especially William Bechoeffer, Karl DuPuy, Michael Hays, Mark Jarzombek, Roger Lewis and Thomas Schumacher, each of whom inspired, through analysis, the significance of urban fabric.

Sincerest thanks to my supportive parents George and Betty, who encouraged faith and good works. Finally, my deepest appreciation is to my wife, Adrienne, without whose patience and endless support this project would not have materialized.

Introduction

The idea for this collection is exceedingly straightforward: Collect accurate urban plans and redraw them at the same scale using the same graphic convention so that students might establish a frame of reference for their design work. This is not an altogether unique or astounding idea; however, since 1990, in both academia and practice, it is one that colleagues, architects, urban designers and students have found of interest.

As a design instructor, I find that students often have difficulty conceptualizing the scale or size of their project's program, sites or precedents. Frequently they go about their design comparatively unaware of the project's actual scope. To help, I suggest that they draw something with which they are familiar at the same scale as their design project or site. Though varying depending upon the student or project type, I usually suggest their house, apartment or apartment building, the School of Architecture and Planning building or urban spaces. Occasionally, the object relates to their past experience. For a retired US Navy commander who embarked on a graduate architecture education, I suggested he draw his old destroyer.

The outcome of this exercise is manifold. First, there is an immediate awareness of their project, site and the object's true size and that, more often than not, surprises students with a realization that what they knew, or thought they knew, was much smaller or much larger than imagined. Through measuring and drawing the familiar, students can link the past or present to their design project and the future. The drawn frame of reference transforms both the unknown and the apparently known into the reality that they inhabit.

This, in turn, creates a framework or frame of reference for their own work that allows them to see their work as part of a continuum in the design environment, in other words, it places their work in the historical and physical context.

The frame of reference is a type of metaphor or analogy that helps link what is known to the unknown, thus allowing for comprehension of new situations, conceptualizing unfamiliar forms and, moreover, solving problems based on semantic relationships. Often, it is metaphor that helps activate or prompts sudden insight. Commonly known as a "Eureka! moment", epiphany or "ah-ha" moment, this insight is the sudden and emotional recognition that there are relationships previously isolated and unrelated semantic elements. That these suddenly recognized connections occur in the context of visual media, problem solving – and even the realm of "getting" jokes – is no accident. Recent studies have shown that insight, understanding metaphor and semantic processing occur in the same temporal area of the right hemisphere of our brains. It is also the same part as the understanding of jokes (Jung-Beeman et al. 2004). It is critical, therefore, that in the learning process, students be exposed to the unfamiliar in relationship to the familiar so that they might make unconscious and then conscious leaps to reconceptualize their own work. It is hoped that this can lead to the unfamiliar or the design of things yet to be realized. As Jung-Beeman et al. conclude, "the nature of many insights [is] the recognition of new connections across existing knowledge" (Jung-Beeman et al. 2004).

Moreover, the urban precedent helps establish a conversation between the past and the future. Unlike a monologue, this temporal dialogue is one in which the past and future inform one another. It makes precedent tangible. Though precedent can sometimes hinder reconceptualization, an informed architect can move through a series of design ideas and relate them to a greater historical and theoretical context. Access to varied plans allows the student to consider and examine a range of spatial patterns. Examining patterns, such as street hierarchies, ground plan dimensions or path–room relationships, helps develop the differences between formal ordering and actual movement in the space.

A need for compilation

While accurate architectural plans are readily available, the same cannot be said for urban plans. Published in journals and books or amassed in typological collections, architectural plans are often easy to find. Examples of this include Roger Sherwood's *Modern Housing Prototypes* (1978), Werner Blaser's *Drawings of Great Buildings* (1983) or Richard Weston's *Key Buildings of the Twentieth Century* (2004). In contrast, urban plans are generally not highlighted in architectural or urban planning journals. Moreover, there are no corollary urban plan compilations. Compounding this deficiency are the inaccuracy, inconsistency and variability of plans published in many books and journals.

Inaccuracy is, oddly enough, quite common as plans often vary in dimension and geometry. This was underscored a few years ago, when a student showed me her research on Piazza San Pietro in Vaticano. Though garnered from three reputable urban design books, each plan differed in dimension, geometry and cardinal direction. At first, I thought her unmatched collection was an anomaly; however, it turned out to be more common than I imagined.

If accurate plans are, indeed, found, many architects and urban designers usually draw them using varied conventions over many years, to serve various needs. The drawing conventions seem consistent only in their differences. While it is easy to accommodate varied line weights and poché, the most common variation is in cardinal direction. While "North up" is a common convention today, it was less so in the past. If that convention was followed, it was rarely consistent. Some specific cities are oriented in one cardinal direction, despite that other contemporaneous city plans are drawn – often by the same architect – with North up. This is especially true for Bordeaux, which is commonly delineated so that the riverfront urban spaces open to the bottom of the page. Even in design practice, sheet composition or design concept often overrule cardinal direction.

Like architectural plans, urban plans are drawn at a variety of scales. Owing to their size, urban plan scales vary extensively and are more easily affected by drawing conventions. The range and types of scales encountered while compiling this book have included 1:1250, 1cm=200m, ³⁄₈″= 500′ not to mention US, French, Russian, Polish and other pre-modern or regional measuring systems. Though a graphic scale is common, they are often published with a written scale, the most common of which is the ratio or representative fraction. While that ratio may be the actual scale, if the drawing was reduced or enlarged even slightly, the stated scale is irrelevant. Even the drawing tools themselves start to affect the representation at smaller scale maps. Maps smaller than 1:5000 (as the ratio increases, the scale becomes "smaller") quickly become inaccurate as an ill-advised line thickness or flick of a pen nib can mean a serious setback to a city's dimension.

Accurate urban plans are often limited to specific regions. Western European urban plans are readily available while Asian urban plans are quite rare. While this might be attributable to a specific architectural or urban canon or western bias, it is more likely based on differences in conceptual and on representational traditions of the urban fabric. Regardless of western or non-western differences, it is moderately difficult to find a wide range of cities even within the western hemisphere. As a result, comparison of one French city to another French city is challenging but the comparison between cities in different regions or hemispheres is nearly impracticable.

Two collections that ameliorate the dearth of city plans are Wayne Copper's Cornell University urban design thesis "The Figure/Grounds" (1967) and Robert Auzelle's *Encyclopédie de l'urbanisme* (1947). Copper's thesis was originally a portfolio of thirty-seven figure-ground and figure-ground reversed plans drawn at various scales on 8 ½″ × 11″ unbound sheets. This collection was further edited, redrawn and inserted in the *Cornell Journal of Architecture* (Copper 1982). Although the journal plans are of high quality, there are only thirteen predominantly pre-modern, western cities and, like the thesis, are drawn at different scales. Moreover, many of Copper's plans were based on Baedeker guidebooks due to the "deficiency of city planning documentation in major libraries" (Rowe 1996: III, 17). A second, more comprehensive collection is Robert Auzelle's *Encyclopédie de l'urbanisme*. This three-volume, unbound collection provides a broad spectrum of urban spaces throughout the world, including miscellaneous post-World War II suburban housing and shopping centers in the United States and Europe. Each folio sheet contains a plan, several photographs and a brief description. Though drawn with relative consistency, they are at varied scales and are often with little context beyond the spaces themselves.

Of course, this criticism may be leveled against any collection – and this collection is no exception. While I have made every effort to find accurate plans and delineate them consistently, to maintain this rigor is extremely difficult and it is expected that more than one plan may be contested.

Methodology

The process for this compilation was fairly straightforward: Collect plans from authoritative, primary sources and redraw them at the same scale using identical graphic conventions. By "authoritative" I mean those plans published or commissioned by government agencies that, in turn, are used and distributed for official, legal purposes including planning, building or historical documentation. While "authority" does not guarantee accuracy, it increases the likelihood. In contrast, maps published by a tourist agency, even those of a government agency, are usually composed, simplified and otherwise edited for the tourist trade.

The majority of the plans came from the Library of Congress Geography and Map Division in Washington, DC. This vast collection includes original folios and atlases from foreign and domestic sources. Adding a bit of intrigue to this collection are the once top secret, now declassified, maps drawn by the Central Intelligence Agency or captured by the War Department during and after World War II. The second most common sources were hard copies from individual city planning offices or equivalent digital versions now available on many city websites. Satellite imagery websites, such as TerraServer© and GoogleEarth©, helped verify and update older urban plans.

Since cities are constantly changing, the plans in this collection are usually an amalgamation of several plans. For example, parts of London have changed dramatically since World War II but combining pre-World War II Ordnance Survey Maps, web-based maps and published building plans, I was able to make a somewhat up-to-date plan. All plans were scanned into Photoshop©, re-sized, edited, overlaid and then traced into figure-ground. These amalgamations were then transferred into vector AutoCAD© drawings.

Drawing type

The figure-ground plans in this collection are what might be called "modified Nolli" plans. Similar to Giambattista Nolli's 1748 plan of Rome that delineated important, semi-public interior spaces along with exterior public spaces, in this collection, plans delineate areas that are generally open to the public or are considered part of the urban experience. For example, the Piazza del Campidoglio's colonnade is part of the urban space and included, but the interior of the Palazzo dei Conservatori and Palazzo Nuovo that are considered "public," but are secured at night, are not delineated. In all spaces, there was a practicable effort to represent colonnades or arcades. There are, more than likely, circumstances where several important loggias, slots, alleys or other areas that may be crucial to the spatial experience were excluded for practical reasons or simply inadvertently excluded.

The horizontal cut in these plans is approximately one meter above the ground; however, this does vary to some degree. Again, at the Piazza del Campidoglio, Michelangelo's piazza is several meters above the Piazza d' Aracoeli at the base of the Cordonata stepped ramp yet is delineated as if it was at the same level. Of course, this exposes one of the problems with the figure-ground in which everything is delineated as if it were flat. As Wayne Copper notes in his own collection, "It would be absurd, for example, to attempt to analyze midtown Manhattan with only one level of plan . . . although in Rome it would not" (Copper 1982: 44). So much for the sensibility of this collection that includes four plans from Manhattan.

Included and excluded plans

The most frequent questions by colleagues, friends and critics concerned what plans should be or should not be included in the collection. Why, for example, are there fourteen squares from Italy but only one from Turkey? Why are there fifty-seven European spaces and only nine African and Asian spaces combined?

Familiarity played a role in plan selection. Students and faculty need to identify with a space or know it through experience in order to establish the frame of reference. I tried to include spaces that a range of people may have visited or were aware of in their education. It would not help, in many cases, to focus on obscure albeit interesting spaces, as a wide audience would not know them. There was a bias to include important, frequently visited and populated cities. A plan of Tallahassee, a planned city similar to Philadelphia and of interest for its urban form and transformation, was not included in favor of plans more familiar to a larger population.

The spaces are primarily secular, public, open-air, identifiable figural void spaces. That is, the spaces are identifiable rooms in a city defined by a clear contextual perimeter. The context is dense and the void or room of the square or space is correspondingly solid. Ambiguous spaces could have been included, but I opted, especially in this first attempt at an urban plan compilation, for those spaces that were recognizable rooms in the city. Perhaps other authors will follow with a more complete collection of ambiguous urban spaces.

Though the focus was primarily on secular spaces, it was not always easy to disengage civic from sacred space. Activities in spaces change throughout the day or, for some cultures, civil and secular activities are more fully integrated. In many Islamic countries, for instance, the mosque complex is a gathering space for civic rallies, socializing and even a market. Identifiable rooms in the city are more common for cultures that have a greater tradition of social, open space. Societies with less of a tradition of urban squares, such as the Japanese, are, of course, less likely to have public squares and, for that matter, are less likely to design and draw them. Sometimes the public gathering space is not a figural void but a street, park or identifiable non-physical place based on temporal rather than spatial perimeters.

More often than not, determining the collection's contents came down to what was available. The smallest scale plan used for the collection were plans, less than fifty years old, drawn at 1:5000, though I preferred 1:4000 and larger, and that delineated building outlines. If a space met several criteria listed above but were available only from a secondary or tertiary source, they could not be included in the collection. A common problem seems to have been government bureaucracy and the political relationship of the United States government with nations behind the Iron Curtain. For example, while I hoped to include Havana, Budapest and Sofia, there was little access to large-scale plans available to me in those countries and none at the Library of Congress.

Accompanying all plans is a brief commentary, most of which are illustrated with diagrams. The fundamental intention of these descriptions is to raise, albeit briefly, design related issues and opinions for a student's consideration. Rather than being purely historical, which I defer to more qualified authorities, these descriptions hope to describe why a space might be important to study. Historical highlights are incorporated simply to place the space in the historical context that affected the space's design and morphology.

Ultimately, it was difficult to select sites. The nature of squares, their importance to the society that built and used them, their tradition or lack thereof in any given culture makes any uniform criteria leading to a definitive collection nearly impossible. That there could be no one set of criteria reveals that the concept of public space varies greatly from country to country and from region to region and that is a strength in understanding urban form throughout the world. Though there was no uniform criteria, several issues helped select the sites and make any collection possible. As it was frequent, it was as difficult to answer. Answers delved into representational tradition, historical canon, familiarity and even political bias.

Representational bias

Before deciding to use or review this collection, it is important to recall that there are several inherent problems with the figure-ground drawing. While Wayne Copper (1982), Peter Bosselmann (1988) and others more fully elucidate this topic, it should be briefly noted that, like any representation, the figure-ground represents reality in an abstract, often oversimplified fashion. The black and white figure-ground is especially reductive as it differentiates only inside and out, solid and void with little literal regard for section material or time. While these are accepted limitations, they are limitations nonetheless. Like a plan, section, digital model, scale model or other representational method, they are narrow, reductive glimpses of reality. Subtleties can be found in the plan but it requires additional information such as photographs or sections and the experience to know that the thickness of building can be understood as a particular building type. This, of course, raises the extent or capacity of the figure-ground to delineate space or space in the twentieth and twenty-first centuries. As building technologies transform building envelopes and as the urban realm becomes less black and white, the figure-ground drawing begins to lose meaning. The most regrettable aspect of the figure-grounds is that they sometimes remove the interiors, materiality and other textures of a plan. The strength of the figure-ground as a diagram, however, outweighs its inherent limitations but only as long as the student or architect is aware of the limitations. It can be an excellent tool as it quickly and clearly delineates the spatial patterns of the voids and solids in the urban fabric.

Lastly, all representations reveal bias. There is no such thing as an objective, accurate and unbiased drawing. A plan, section, perspective, scale model, digital fly-through or any representation of reality involves decisions of representation that help to communicate ideas or, in some cases, to augment reality. From a fourteenth century city-state's map that overemphasized its domain to Saul Steinberg's "View of the World from Ninth Avenue" graphic representation shows the authors' depiction of their reality.

While I attempted to be accurate, there were times when the plan should be cut to retain the convention for accuracy or convention for clarity. I chose clarity as it best communicated the book's intentions. For example, if Le Corbusier's Voison Plan was cut one meter above grade, the drawing shows the building's piloti. While that would have been accurate, I felt that the more informative cut would be one story higher. It is true that Le Corbusier intended that the ground floor appear and surface of the earth move beneath the buildings and the mass float above the ground plane, but as an architect, I felt that the mass would be more revealing.

With this admitted bias, I strove for accuracy, yet I am sure there are errors and omissions. I welcome any suggested corrections or additions and, for that matter, welcome any large-scale, accurate, authoritative city plans for this evolving collection.

Scale

The scale used for every plan is:

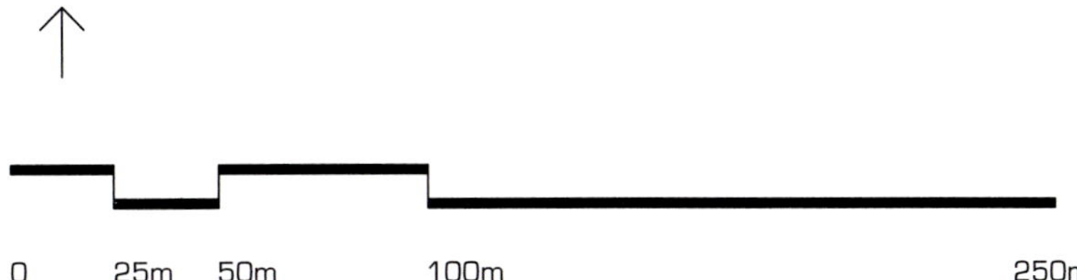

Amsterdam

1

Dam Square

Most notable for its picturesque beauty, Amsterdam's tree-lined canals and distinguished brick houses gracefully conceal their utilitarian original function as an expansive and efficient mercantile port. Founded at the mouth of the Amstel river as it flows into the Ij basin and the sea beyond, Amsterdam's canals are a comprehensive docking system dating to the thirteenth century. Beginning with the construction of a sluice dam, built near the site of the current Dam Square, that controlled the water flow between the river and the sea, and two subsidiary diversionary channels, the city itself transformed into a rational and functional berthing system. The concentric, gently curving canals, with quays and warehouses on both sides, allowed ships to arrive, dock and depart without rotating once inside the port (Braunfels 1988: 102). Each canal is four lanes wide: two lanes for quayside docking and two lanes for two-way ship traffic. The ships would enter at one end of the canal, move along the quays and exit at the other end. Over the course of several centuries, additional concentric canals were added to accommodate as many as several thousand ships at one time.

Amsterdam still retains much of its original form, though in the nineteenth and twentieth centuries several canals were filled to make wide commercial streets (A. Morris 1994: 164). Moreover, until the construction of an artificial island to accommodate the train station, the canals and city connected directly to the Ij and the sea – a connection that is no longer apparent.

View from the east

The canal system offers two unique spatial experiences: one of moving along the linear, concentric canals and the other of moving across the canals' grain along the radial streets. The long-grain experience is spatially dynamic as the curved canals obscure the horizon and thus provide a sense of discovery that contributes to the city's picturesque quality. Though the houses along the canals themselves are repetitive, they provide a pleasing rhythm with intermittent cross streets and bridges. In contrast, the movement along the grain is a rhythmic spatial sequence alternating between buildings and across canals.

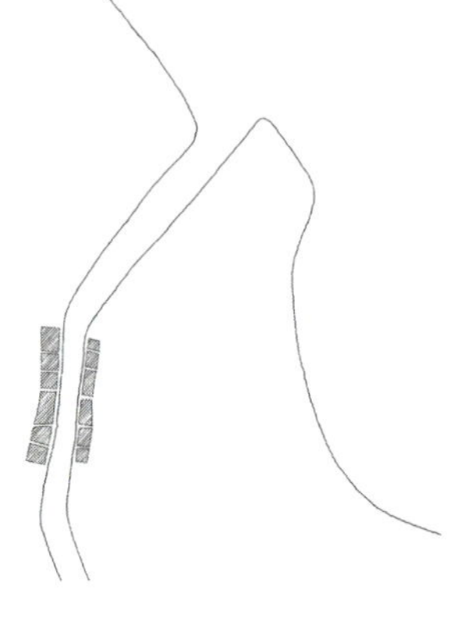

Amsterdam's original configuration before the sluice dam

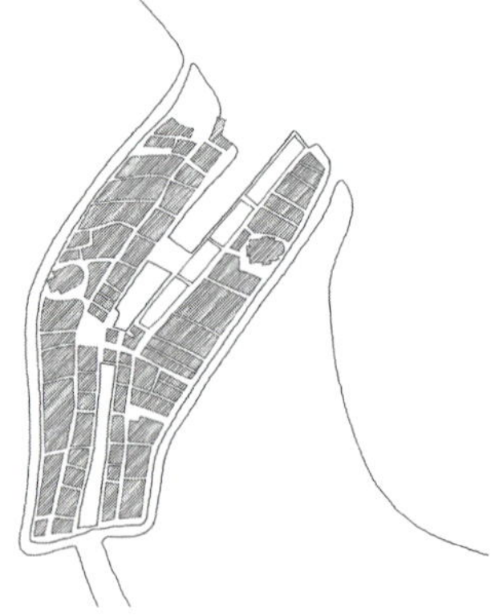

Amsterdam's configuration after construction of the sluice dam with two canals

Dam Square

Arras

2

Grande Place and Place des Héros

Since the twelfth century, Arras' interconnected central squares have accommodated specific aspects of daily civic life and are examples of what urban historian Paul Zucker describes in his book *Town and Square* (1966) as closed and grouped squares. "Closed" in that they are well-defined, regularized spaces often with uniform walls and "grouped" in that they are part of a spatial and functional ensemble within the town (Zucker 1966: 11).

Each of Arras' squares plays its particular role in the civic, commercial and religious life of the city. The larger Grande Place, originally a monastery courtyard, is generally for public festivities. The smaller Place des Héros, formerly the Petite Place but renamed to honor executed World War II French Resistance fighters, is dominated by the Gothic town hall, Hôtel de Ville, and continues as the city's market place.

Weaving the squares together both spatially and architecturally are the moderately uniform façades and ground level arcades. Much of this regularity emerged from Arras' seventeenth century zoning ordinances that dictated conformity of decoration, material, height and number of stories and form of gables. The façades have remained unchanged since that time and were even entirely recreated following the town's utter destruction during World War I artillery bombardments. Spatially, the links between the two squares and the city are lateral pathways. Paths move along edges and under arcades so that the pedestrian experience is along the square's edges without actually entirely engaging the squares' interior. As a result, pedestrian and vehicular traffic does not disrupt the space and activities within, but remains on the outer edges.

Though lateral paths are common in many squares, in Arras it contributes to a dynamic, if unintended, spatial experience. Since the Grande Place and Place des Héros are at nearly right angles to one another and abut at the corners of their short edges, the sequence from one space to another is a dynamic spatial shift. For example, movement along the Grande Place's elongated, northwestern edge toward the Place des Héros is a protracted experience with views through the arcade and across the square to the southeast. As the two squares meet there is a slight spatial compression followed by an expansion in the opposite direction to the northwest along the short edge and down the Place des Héros' long axis. This one path not only unifies the spaces but also offers a distinct experience alternating from width to breadth and left to right.

Arras Town Hall

Grande Place

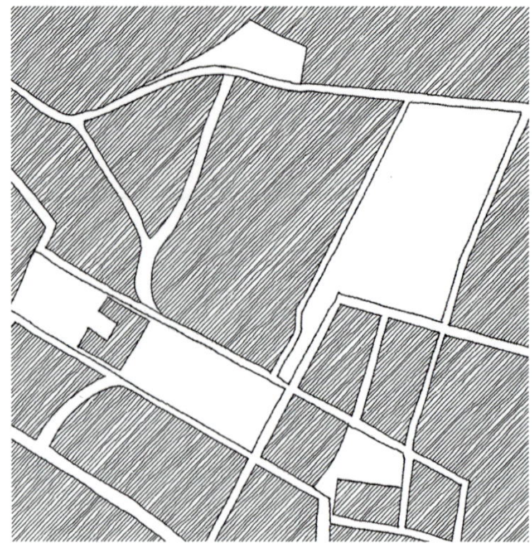

The lateral pathways along Arras' squares

Grande Place and Place des Héros

Athens

3

Platia Syntagmatos

Platia Syntagmatos, or Constitution Square, is a center of activity in modern Athens and represents nineteenth-century attempts to reinstate Greek civilization within Greece itself and, in a broader sense, recapture the ideals of classical architecture and urban form throughout the world. For Greece itself, as Eleni Bastéa observes, Athens' nineteenth-century urban design conciliated the Greek nation's "yearning for acceptance in the family of civilized, modern European nations; yearning for internal political and cultural unity and national definition; and yearning for a strong connection – if not identification – with the classical past" (Bastéa 1994: 112). Accordingly, the city's plan and the Platia Syntagmatos synthesized and idealized the classical past into a nineteenth century city.

After nearly four hundred years of Ottoman rule, the city of Athens was in near ruin and its transformation and gradual return as Greece's capital required extensive urban revitalization and planning. In accord with the Peace Treaty, rule of Greece fell to Otto von Wittlesbach, son of King Ludwig of Bavaria and thus introduced nineteenth-century German urban planning ideas to Greece.

The plan, originally proposed in 1833 by Stamatios Kleanthes and Eduard Schaubert but revised not long after by Leo von Klenze, is three boulevards forming a triangle. The apex of the triangle points north, away from the Acropolis, while its hypotenuse is a major east–west boulevard running through the Ottoman town and parallel to the Acropolis to the south. Where this boulevard and the triangle's northeastern boulevard meet is the Platia Syntagmatos and the Royal Palace designed by Friedrich von Gärtner, today's Parliament Building. Defining the square today are six- and seven-story residential and commercial buildings on the northwest and northeast with the Parliament Building and the National Park to the southeast.

While Kleanthes and Schaubert's plan attempted to recapture Greek civilization through an urban plan, it remained an academic abstraction. The city's overly formal, geometric plan with radiating boulevards aligned with Greek revival buildings reveals how western trained architects in the nineteenth century abstracted Greco-Roman tradition into formalized, geometric pattern making. Both Edmund Bacon and R.E. Wycherley note that ancient Greek cities were, in fact, a matter of interlocking spaces whose compositions were based more on movement and topography (Bacon 1967: 53). Athens' Agora and Acropolis, for example, grew, albeit gradually, from the diagonal Panathenaic Way and framed views. Even the Greek colony of Priene with its gridiron plan accommodates the topography and movement. The steeply sloped site transforms the grid into a series of terraces with streets moving laterally along public spaces rather than formally or axially. Wycherley remarks that Greek public spaces were "involved in the street system, and was not exclusive or segregated from the rest, but vitally linked with it" adding that "varied streams of energy flowed freely in" so that the space becomes part of a journey rather than a static destination (Wycherley 1976: 78).

Platia Syntagmatos toward the Parliament Building

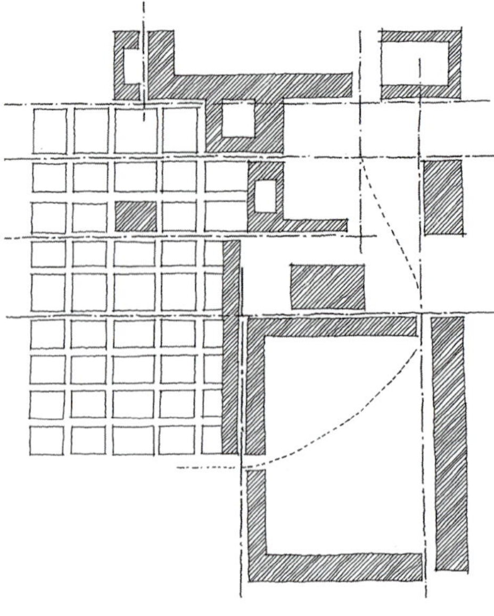

Lateral movement and edge alignments in Ancient Greek spaces

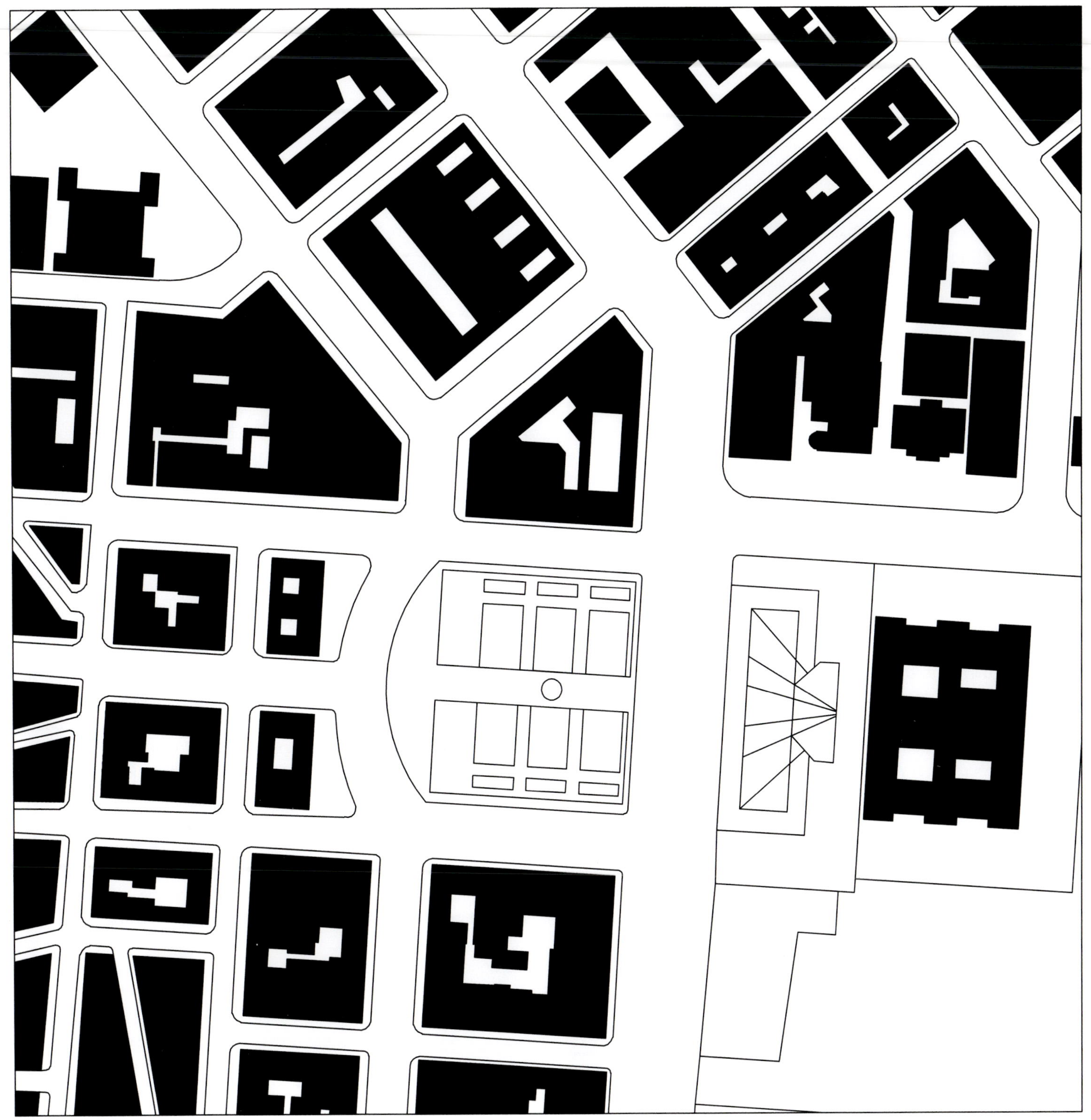

Platia Syntagmatos

Baltimore

4

Mount Vernon Place

Described by Paul Zucker in *Town and Square* as the most "dignified and gracious a city square as one can find," Mount Vernon Place is a cross-shaped square at the crest of a small rise just north of Baltimore's business distinct (Zucker 1966: 247). At its center is the neo-classical George Washington Monument. Designed by Robert Mills in 1815, it is similar to Nelson's Column in Trafalgar Square. The square was the centerpiece of a land development by the family of revolutionary war hero John Eager Howard. When conceived in 1827, Mills' column was in undeveloped countryside north of downtown but the design used it as a starting point so that, twenty years after it was laid out, the square's arms and the column would align with the city's street grid (Howland and Spencer 1953: 108).

The square's plan appears uniform and equilateral however; in much the same way that Palladio's Villa Rotunda in Vicenza is deceivingly equilateral, the symmetrical Mount Vernon square gives each leg its own distinct spatial identity and experience that take advantage of topography, landscaping, orientation and surrounding buildings.

Each of the four arms has a unique character. As illustrated in the diagram, each leg is somewhat unique despite the nearly symmetrical plan. The square's northern leg and southern leg is Charles Street – Baltimore's fashionable street that begins from the center of Baltimore and continues north to the more picturesque settings of the Baltimore Museum of Art and Johns Hopkins University. While Charles Street continues through both visually and spatially, the greater insets of the street edges just beyond the square to the east and west give a sense of enclosure to those two legs. The Walters Art Gallery, the Peabody Conservatory and four-story apartment buildings border its southern leg, which slopes approximately fifteen feet from the downtown side of the site. The low-scale landscaping is intermixed with cascading fountains and small sculpture terraces. The northern leg, which is relatively level, has higher six- to ten-story apartment buildings and one side of Mount Vernon Place Methodist Episcopal Church. Its landscaping is similar to the southern leg with the exclusion of cascading fountains. The east leg slopes approximately fifteen feet from St. Paul Street and is fronted by the portal of Mount Vernon Place Methodist Episcopal Church and lined with Greek Revival and nineteenth century brownstone row houses similar to those in Boston's Back Bay and New York's Upper East Side. The west leg, like the north leg, is relatively flat but is bordered by brick Georgian townhouses on its south side and larger six-story apartment buildings on the north. Both the east and west legs are landscaped with deciduous trees.

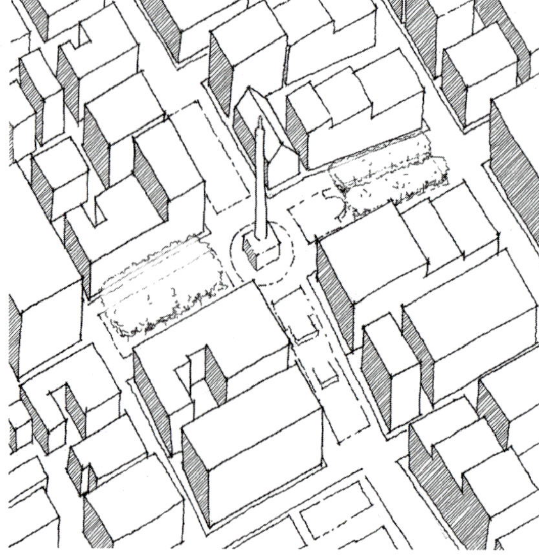

The sectional and massing change around Mount Vernon Place

Mount Vernon Place from the south

This square can be compared to small-scale residential squares in London; however, unlike many residential squares, Mount Vernon Place is surrounded by a variety of building types including a college, museum, hotels, a retirement home, churches, single family houses and apartment buildings. Because of this, the space remains relatively active with a variety of people throughout the day.

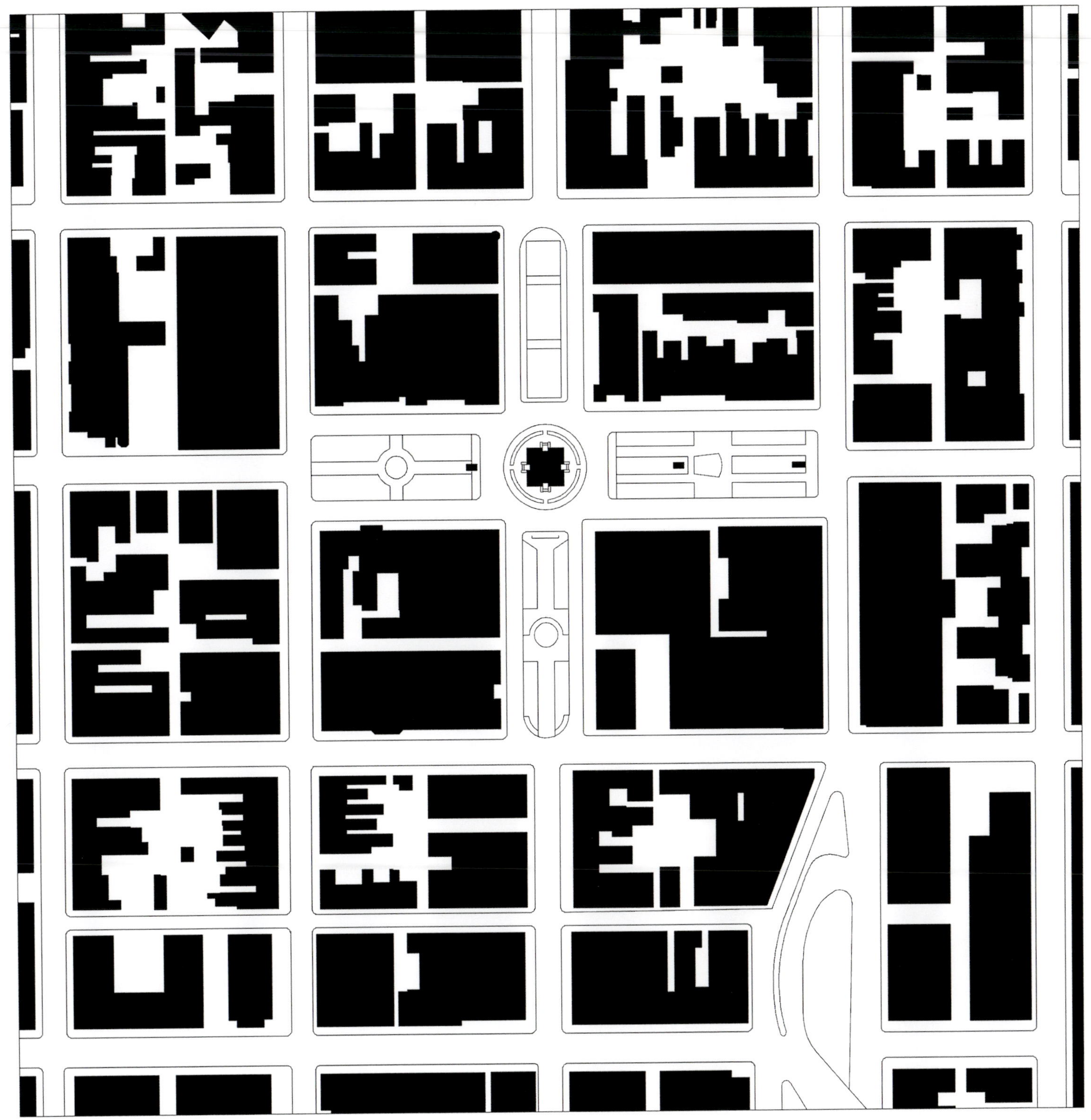

Mount Vernon Place

Barcelona

5

Barri Gòtic

The Barri Gòtic, or Gothic Quarter, is at Barcelona's center and is distinguished by its dense, pedestrian scale streets and spaces. Movement through the quarter from the cathedral, the cloister of which is at the upper right in this plan, to the Ramblas, the broad street to the west, is along tight streets and through a series of small squares. On the east is the Plaça de la Catedral, which is an active forecourt to the Gothic Quarter where, on Sundays, worshipers dance traditional Catalan circle dances called *sardanas* that have their roots in village squares. Moving south along the cathedral's flank leads to a series of narrow streets and smaller squares including the Plaza de San Jaime, dominated by the Provincial Council Building and the Town Hall. This square marks the beginning of Carrer de Ferran, an east–west street that bisects the quarter and leads, ultimately, to the Ramblas. Just before the Ramblas, however, is the Plaça Reial. Designed by Francesc Daniel Molina and built between 1848 and 1856, this serene, fully enclosed Royal Square was once the site of a convent but, following anti-monastic laws imposed in 1835, was transformed into a public square.

Entry into the Plaça Reial

The southern end of the Ramblas

This well-ordered space with its uniform, four-story, well-proportioned façade and ground-level arcade stands in great contrast to its Gothic Quarter context. Access to the square is from several points, most of which are from beneath covered streets and galleries into the encircling arcade. Until the 1980s, the square was known more commonly as a place of ignominious activities and automobile parking. Renovated in 1982, with some controversy, by architects Federico Correa and Alfonso Milá, the designers opened the square by removing elements that had accumulated over the decades and added a discrete grid of slender palm trees set in a nearly continuous paved floor.

From the Plaça, to the west through the one access point that is open to the sky, is the Ramblas, Barcelona's famed street used primarily for leisurely strolls yet open to vehicular traffic. Once the center of the small stream that defined the thirteenth-century fortifications of Barcelona, the Ramblas was designed by Juan Martin Carmeno in 1776 in order to move goods from the harbor on the south to the city's gate to the north (Bosselmann 1988: 26–28). Contributing to the street's success is its contrast from the Gothic Quarter's tight fabric. As Allan Jacobs notes in his book *Great Streets*, the Ramblas' "placement in the city and in the Gothic Quarter, its grand scale in relation to its narrow, winding surroundings, the people-welcoming nature of its design, and the quality of the buildings that lines its edges make it a street for everyone to come to and know" (A. Jacobs 1993: 93).

Plaça Reial

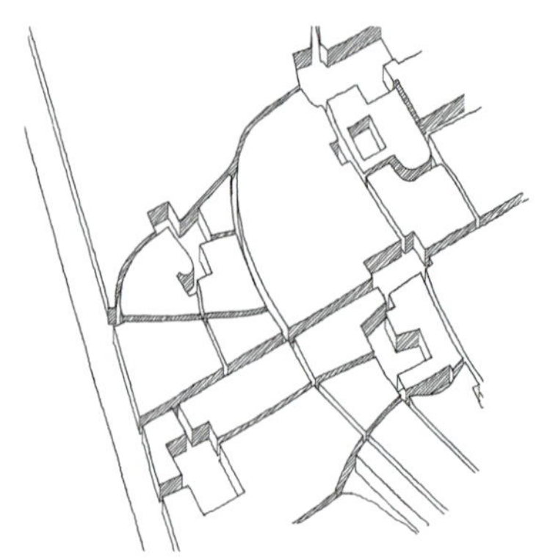

The fabric of the Barri Gòtic and spatial sequence of plazas to streets

Barri Gòtic

Barcelona

6

Eixample

Barcelona's Extension, known as the Eixample in Catalan and the Ensanche in Spanish, is the distinctive grid pattern surrounding the city's Barri Gòtic. Designed by engineer Ildefons Cerdá, the plan anticipated both Barcelona's rapid growth and possible industrial age social and economic turmoil. Cerdá's design was part of nineteenth-century urban renewal projects that, like Georges Haussmann's Parisian urban renewal project, Daniel Burnham's City Beautiful Movement and Ebenezer Howard's Garden City model, attempted to ameliorate urban dilemmas resulting from industrial age urban growth.

By the mid-nineteenth century, Barcelona's population was almost entirely within the Barri Gòtic making it one of the most densely populated cities in Europe. As a result, it suffered from unsanitary conditions, disease and a degree of social unrest. Anticipating controlled growth, Barcelona's city council sponsored an 1859 competition and ultimately, though not immediately, selected Cerdá's proposal. His gridiron plan of 550 uniform square blocks with chamfered corners – angled to ease the flow of traffic through the intersections – would extend Barcelona around the old district and across the alluvial plain between the hillsides to the north and the sea to the south. Overlaid on this grid were several diagonal avenues that would link the Gothic Quarter through the new town to smaller settlements on Barcelona's outskirts (Hughes 1992: 272–275; Bosselman 1988: 30–34).

In 1867, nearly a decade after the design competition, Cerdá published the *General Theory of Urbanisation and the Application of its Principles and Doctrines to the Reform and Expansion of Barcelona* to explain his doctrine of rational, scientific urban design. The work, while published after the planning and initial implementation, helped clarify his ideas and more than likely helped perpetuate the plan's execution (Cerdá 1999: 34–35). In the book, Cerdá explicates the interrelationship of social, hygienic and spatial ideas of the urban design. One idea to make the city responsive to these issues was to propose limiting construction to two opposing sides of each block and to a specific height leaving the center residents' garden. The two built edges would be set in alternating patterns to help transform the two-dimensional and nearly monotonous grid into a more three-dimensionally dynamic experience. The result, he hoped, would be a low density, green city. Within a decade, however, these strictures were ignored with all four perimeters built up and center courts filled. By the end of the nineteenth century, the height was increased to sixty-five feet. Today, the Eixample is an extensive and dense mix of housing, office blocks and hotels, most with ground floor retail, restaurants and cafés with enough variety in building masses and articulation to prevent monotony.

The Eixample from above

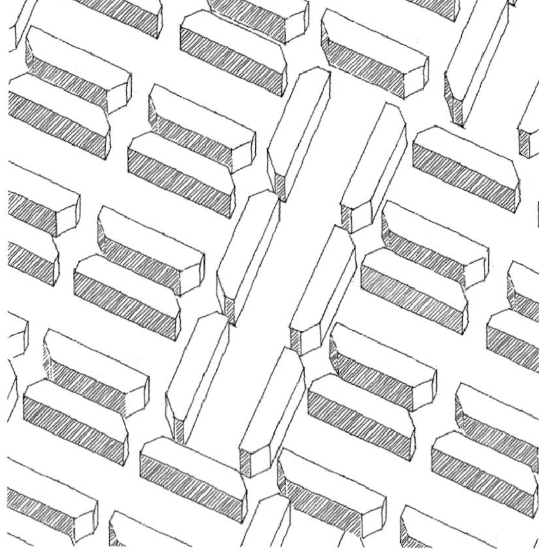

Cerdá's original intention of blocks lined on only two sides with center garden courts

Eixample

Bath

Queens Square, the Circus and the Royal Crescent

7

This area of Bath was part of a real estate venture by the Earl of Pulteney to both profit from and accommodate the increasing number of wealthy visitors to Bath for recreational and health reasons. Established just north of Bath's old town, the fifty-year-long project began under the direction of architect John Wood Sr. but completed by his son John Wood Jr. The development extended northward from Queens Square, at the bottom right in the plan, and culminated at the Royal Crescent, to the upper left. Like Place Vendôme in Paris, the Woods' uniform façades were constructed in stages while individual investors or owners would complete a house's rear at a later date.

The project is a series of discrete residential squares that contribute to a spatial sequence from dense urban fabric to open park. With Bath's roots as a Roman colony, the Woods interwove Roman building archetypes of the forum, imperial gymnasium and circus into urban and landscape spatial composition. Wood's initial urban space, Queens Square (1730), connects the old Roman town to a new development by its rectilinear form and establishes the architectural tone for the forthcoming development. Each of the square's four sides are stately four-story townhouses that appear, owing to their unified façade, as one palace.

Leading from Queens Square to the north is Gay Street that, like the square, is lined with uniform façades behind which are individual row houses. This relatively narrow street provides a spatial compression that is released only at the cylindrical Circus (1764). Again, the uniform yet rhythmic façades give continuity to the space and overall sequence that is even further orchestrated by only three streets punctuating its sides. From the Circus to the northwest is Brock

The Royal Crescent

Street. Like Gay Street, it is a narrow street with uniform façades at the end of which is the final and more expansive spatial release of the Royal Crescent (1775). Opening to the park to the south, the Crescent is a definite culmination with the architecture that remains rigorous and uniform with the crescent's curvilinear form allowing an appropriate conclusion and counterpoint to the landscape.

An important lesson of Bath is that urban spaces are not merely patterns but have topographical and spatial roles (Zucker 1966: 204). Rather than sprinkling arbitrary forms, the Woods selected specific spatial archetypes and placed them in specific areas in the landscape in order to make a unique spatial experience. Second, despite its small scale, the project required a great deal of discipline and patience. The project took over half a century to complete during which time it may have been easy to alter plans and façades. This sort of disciplined and rigorous framework that is open to change is difficult to establish and more difficult to maintain. As Lewis Mumford notes, Bath's excellence demonstrates "the advantage of a strict discipline, when it is supple enough to adapt itself to challenging realities, geographic and historic" (Mumford 1961, Graphic Section III: Plate 37). This is probably true for many projects that are easily weakened by either too much or too little discipline.

The Circus

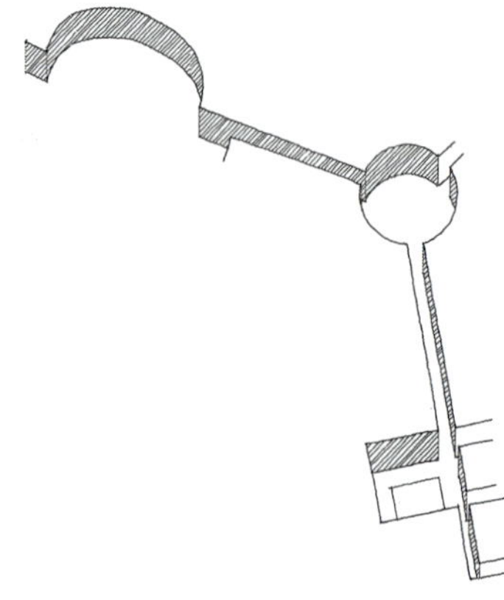

Spatial sequence of Queens Square, the Circus and the Royal Crescent

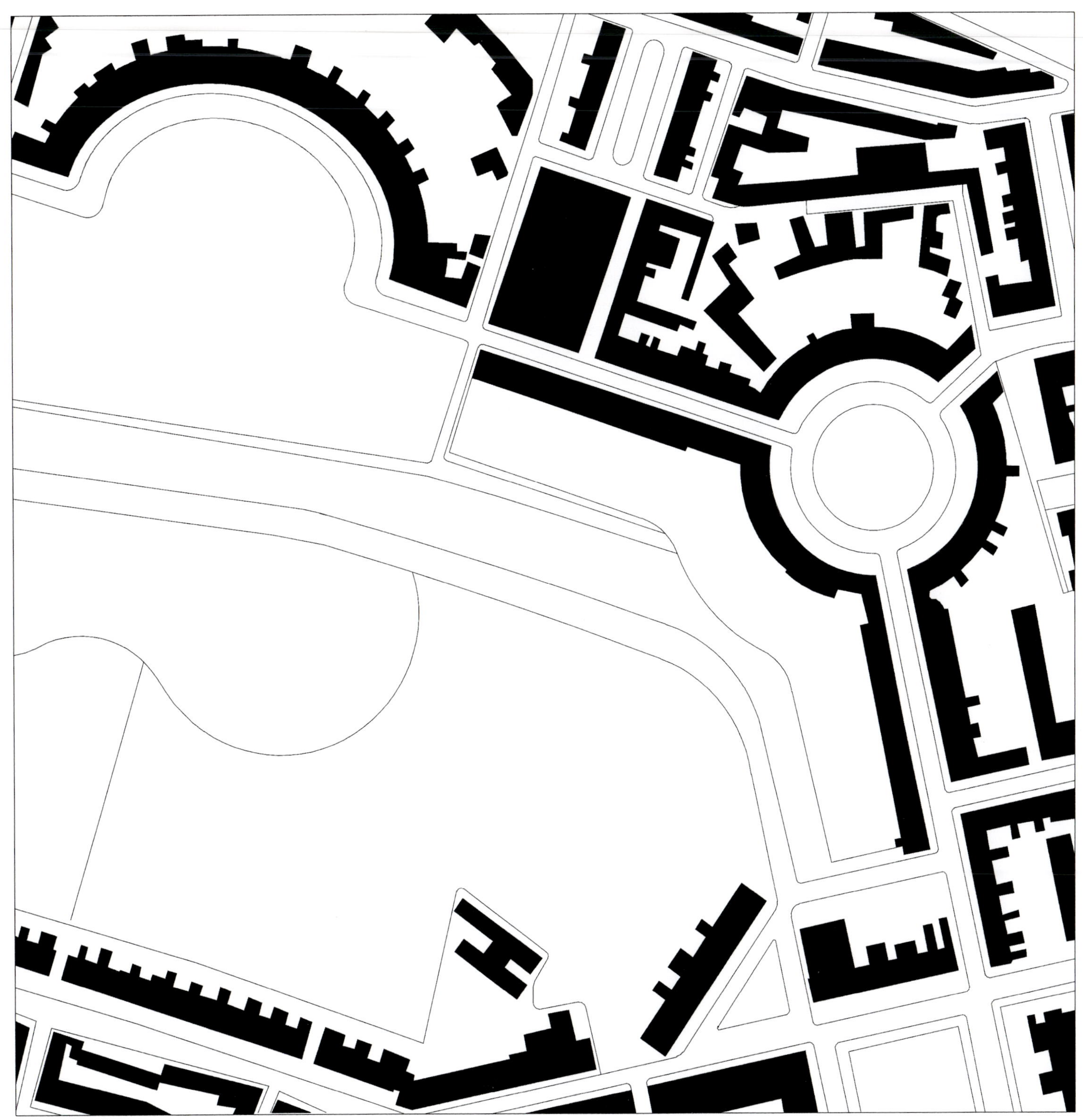

Queens Square, Circus and Royal Crescent

Beijing

8

Tiananmen Square

Tiananmen Square is most notable for its political significance rather than its spatial or urban qualities. It is worthy of examination, however, because it represents how political ideologies often shape urban space to adequately reflect those ideals.

Directly south of the Forbidden City in central Beijing, it is named after the area it displaced that led to the imperial palace called Tiananmen, or Gate of Heavenly Peace, which is actually several gates along a central axis. Until 1959, the area just before the main gate was a much smaller square in front of the Forbidden City but was enlarged for the tenth anniversary of the 1949 revolution. Surrounding the square are immense cultural buildings: the Museum of the Chinese Revolution to the east and the Great Hall of the People to the west and the mausoleum of Mao Zedong to the south. At its center is the Monument to the People's Heroes. The square continues as the venue for choreographed political rallies as well as family outings.

The square is immense even by totalitarian regime standards. Interestingly enough, it is nearly the same size and proportion as Albert Speer's Grosseplatz for New Berlin. Despite its size, it does in fact fit the nation. With a population over one billion and commensurate political demonstrations, China simply has to have an appropriately scaled space in order to accommodate a representative percent of its population. Anything smaller would both be insufficient for the anticipated numbers and possibly reflect poorly on the government.

Tiananmen Square looking south from the Forbidden City

The square is a product of communist political culture and not part of the Chinese tradition of public space. Unlike Occidental societies and cultures, Oriental cultures have little tradition of a public square that is separate from either temple precincts or imperial complexes that were, strictly speaking, off limits to the general population. Though public parks and plazas can be found in Asian cities, most have been introduced since the 1950s or are transformations of traditional religious grounds.

Tiananmen is a space of spectacle rather than public interaction. This, of course, is why Tiananmen Square is also infamous as the setting for the military's suppression of democratic reforms. In May 1989, nearly one million people from various segments of Chinese society filled the space to protest corruption within the communist government and call for democratic reforms. In early June, the government ordered troops to remove the protesters; this resulted in many deaths, injuries and detained individuals yet the incident is officially denied by the Chinese government. The square remains highly monitored by security cameras and police in the name of security.

Unfortunately, this type of monitoring is increasingly prevalent in other countries as democratic and totalitarian governments alike install cameras, set up barriers, station police officers and alter a space's layout to dissuade unacceptable assembly that may or may not be a security risk. Public space provides the framework for social life and it represents a society's ideals. Used for celebration and protest or for spectacle and intimate interaction, the shape, use and freedom to use a space reveals the nature of a society and a country. Unfortunately, in many countries security concerns may trump the civic life of public spaces and slowly castrate their significance as expressions of freedom and democracy.

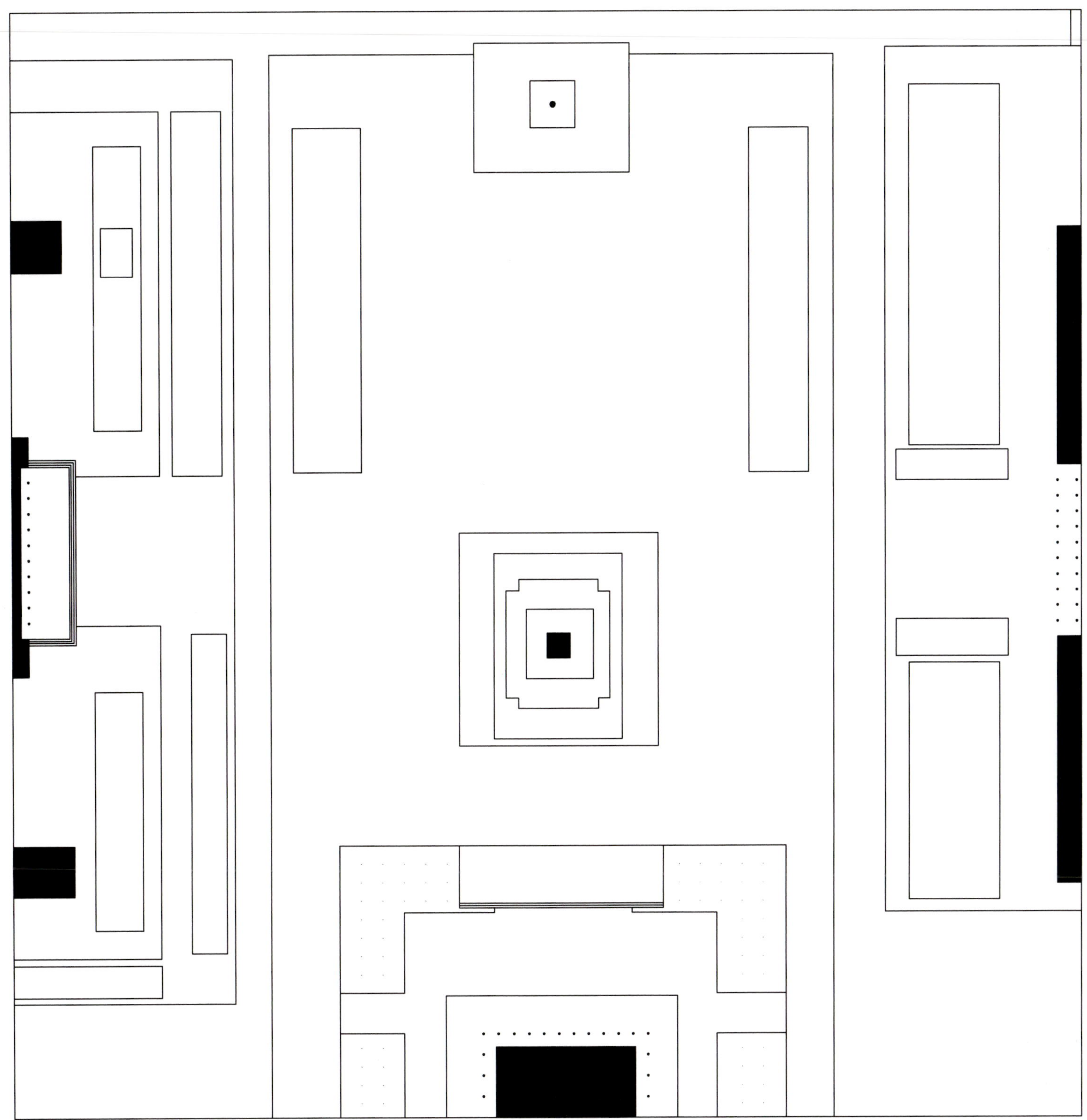

Tiananmen Square

Bergen

9

Fisketorget and Torgalmenningen

Bergen is centered on the Vågen, a small, yet deep harbor that was once along a major sea-based trading route between Norway and Europe and access to North Sea fisheries. Today, the harbor is more for small fishing and recreational craft and its quay more for recreation and tourism. Combined with its topography and a wood building tradition, the town's form is a series of narrow streets following the contour with a series of wider common corridors cut through the city to prevent the spread of fire.

Bergen is set within a basin between the foot of Mount Flørien to the north and a small peninsula to the south. Established in the late eleventh century by Norwegian King Olav Kyrre, the city became a base for German traders and then the German Hanseatic League, a German commercial federation, from the middle of the fourteenth century until the seventeenth century. The town remained an important trading post until the rise of Oslo in the nineteenth century. Much of Bergen's current economic health is based on the North Sea oil industry, its university and tourism.

The town is organized linearly along both sides of the Vågen. On the south is the Nordnes peninsula and on the north side is the Bryggen or German Quay. This northern tract, as its name suggests, was the German traders' settlement and is now the site of the last *gärder* or rows of gabled wood houses. The main streets of the city paralleled these districts and converge at the Fisketorget or Fish Market (Gutkind 1965: 367).

Besides its harbor, Bergen's most distinctive urban features are the perpendicular fire corridors, or *almenningen*, that divide the city's neighborhoods. Following devastating fires in the sixteenth, eighteenth and the early twentieth centuries, the city cut and then widened these corridors to limit the spread of fire through the town. The most distinctive corridor is the Torgalmenningen, the central large square just south of the Fisketorget that took its current shape after the fire of 1916. Today, it is a pedestrian-only zone lined with five-story neoclassical buildings with retail on the ground floor and businesses and housing above.

The lesson of Bergen is stated by the architects Terje Kalve and Arne Smedsvig of the firm Next to Nothing, A.S., responsible for the renovations of Fisketorget and Torgalmenningen in the 1990s. Kalve and Smedsvig react against the tendency of filling urban spaces with terraces, amphitheaters, fountains, ticket booths, cafés and sculpture. Instead, they feel that urban spaces should find "the balance between rehabilitation and new construction, between emptiness and fullness" (Kalve and Smedsvig 2002b: 115). They add that urban spaces "should be filled with people, and should therefore not be crowded with obtrusive street furniture. Urban places should resist emptiness while at the same time coming to terms with the daily and seasonal reality of the city" (Kalve and Smedsvig 2002b: 115). While Norway and the culture of Bergen may allow this to occur, it is a good lesson for urban designers and landscape architects who tend to inundate, program and overdelineate urban spaces, leaving no room for the space itself.

Bergen from the surrounding hillsides

The *almenningen* fire corridors

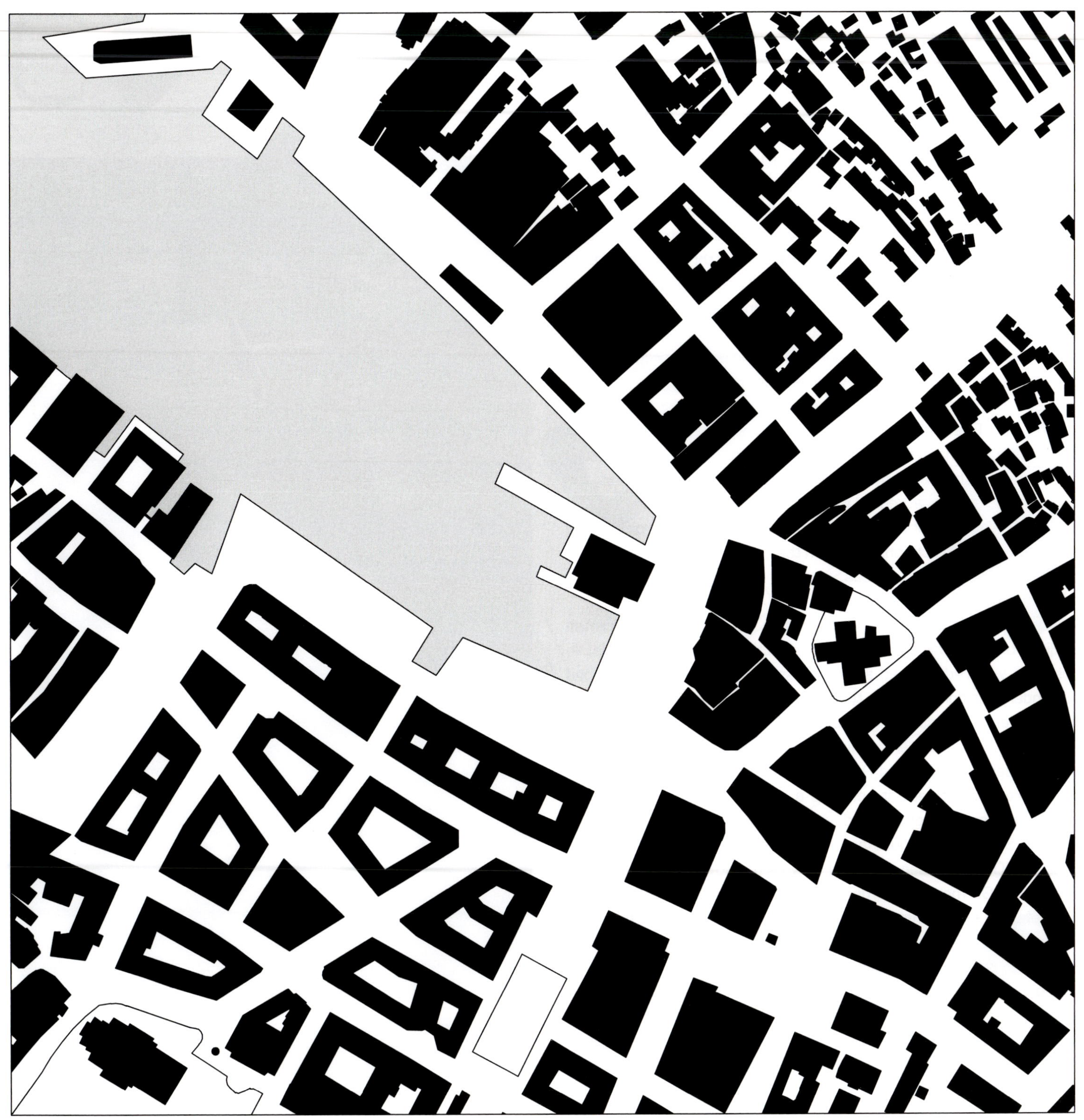

Fisketorget and Torgalmenningen

Berlin

11

Potsdamer Platz and Leipziger Platz

After the reunification of East and West Germany in 1990 following decades of physical, social and spiritual division, the major revitalization efforts of Berlin centered on Potsdamer Platz. Essentially the intersection of five streets, and paired with the octagonal Leipziger Platz, Potsdamer Platz represents, for many Germans, a rebirth of the country's commercial and cultural power.

Until World War II, the area had been a thriving commercial and popular culture node in Berlin. During the war, however, the entire area was completely destroyed leaving few buildings and nearly indistinct street outlines. Compounding this condition, the area became the dividing line between East and West Berlin with the actual Berlin Wall separating Potsdamer Platz from Leipziger Platz. As a result, the area remained undeveloped and for nearly fifty years was an overgrown vacant land.

Today, Potsdamer Platz and Leipziger Platz are nearly rebuilt and nearly all physical references to the Wall eradicated. Despite the construction's rapidity, it is difficult to recall the area's condition as it appeared as recently as the mid-1990s. Based on urban design and architectural guidelines established through an international competition, awarded to German architects Heinz Hilmer and Christoph Sattler, Potsdamer Platz and Leipziger Platz have developed into a series of corporate office buildings, dominated by Sony and Daimler-Benz, intermixed with public interior and exterior spaces, entertainment and shopping complexes. The nearly 120 acre (nearly 50 hectare) area maintains a degree of architectural unity as individual designers, such as Helmut Jahn, Arata Isozaki, José Rafael Moneo, Renzo Piano and Richard Rogers, adhered to established guidelines regarding height, material and building profile.

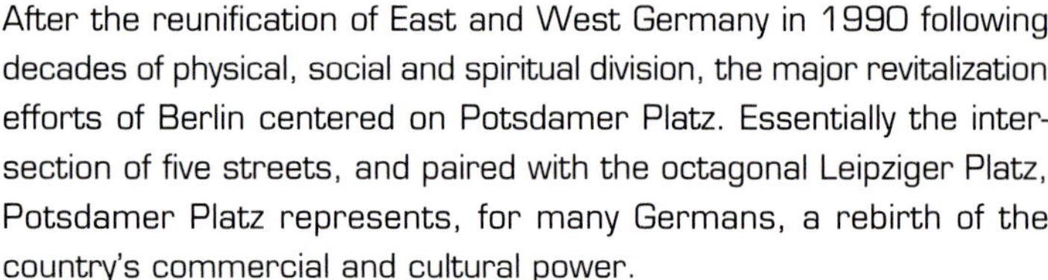

View of Leipziger Platz under construction

Potsdamer Platz is divided into several individual blocks interconnected with a series of pedestrian-only spaces and streets. While much of Potsdamer Platz has adopted spatial configurations for the twenty-first century, Leipziger Platz retains its octagonal, nineteenth-century form. In all, both squares connected Berlin's Mitte to the post-war Kulturforum that includes Hans Scharoun's Philharmonie and State Library as well as Mies van der Rohe's National Gallery of Art.

The area is often the target of criticism for the dominance of corporate buildings and their apparent control of public space. This argument tends to overlook a more European attitude in which there is an ambiguous division between private and public property and use.

Interior court of the Sony Center, Potsdamer Platz

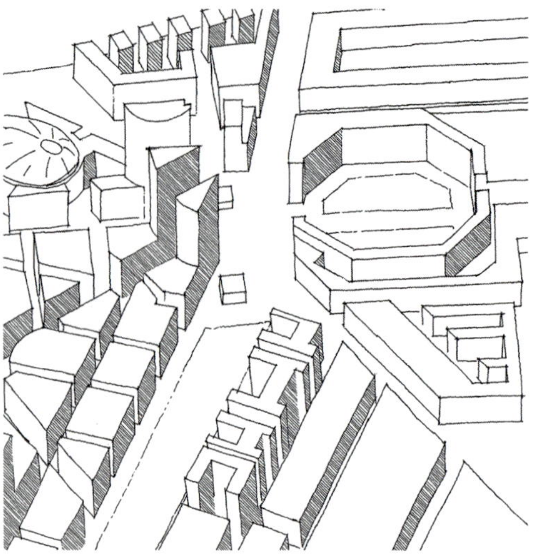

The overall expected massing of Potsdamer Platz and Leipziger Platz

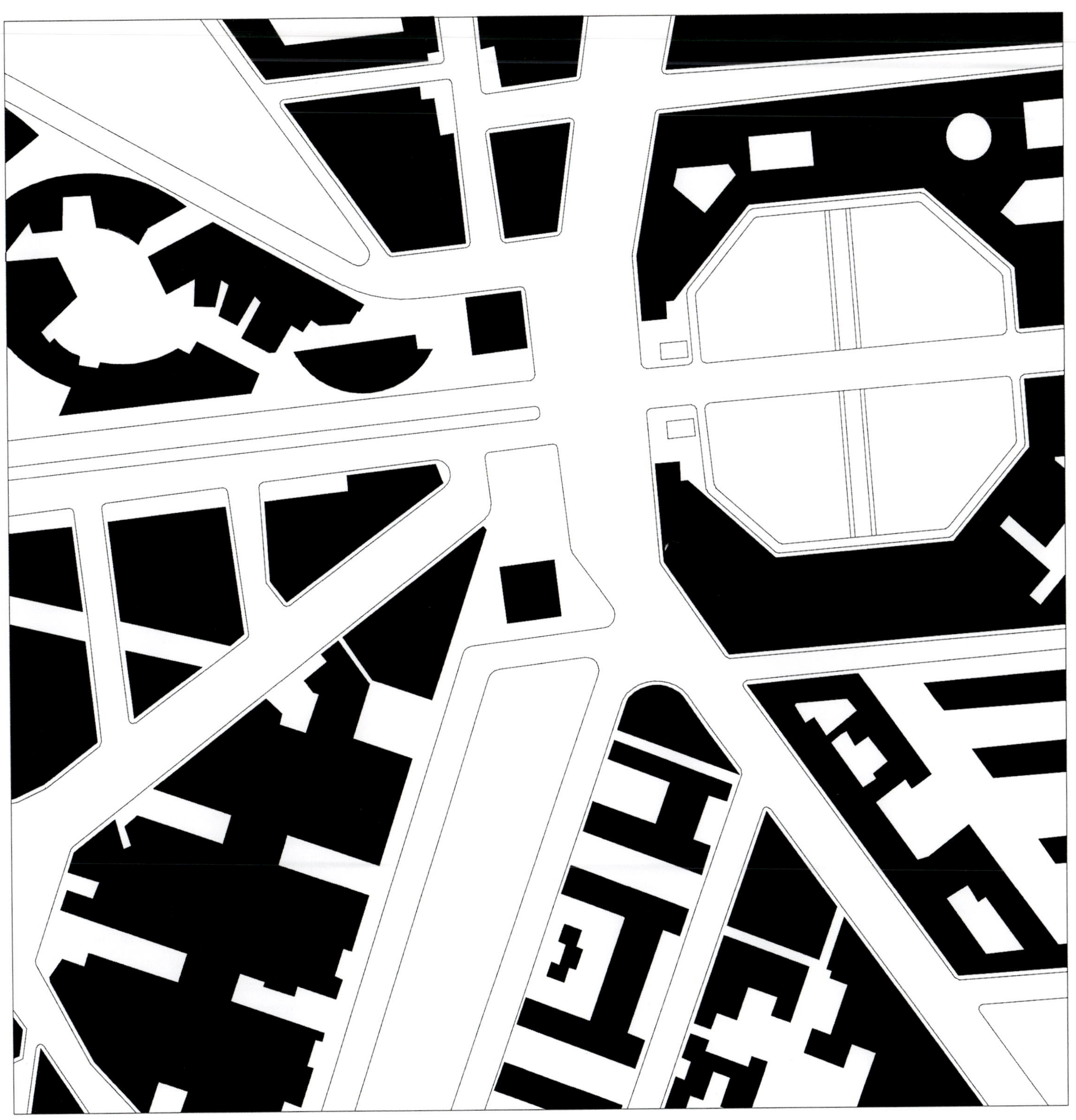

Potsdamer Platz and Leipziger Platz

Bern

Altstadt

12

Bern is an important medieval town in Switzerland because its form was derived primarily from the function of a market system. As such, its resemblance to a market hall, even to Quincy Market in Boston with rows of vendors, is no accident. Established in 1190, the city is set along the ridge of an elongated meander – a nearly 180-degree turn – in the River Aare. This had the effect of making a linear town with a natural moat on three sides while the fourth side was the only side needing fortification. The plan is similar to Craig's New Town in Edinburgh in that the main axis was placed along a ridge while two parallel streets stepped down to either side. Unlike the two outer parallel streets in Edinburgh, Bern's secondary streets are enclosed on both sides (Braunfels 1988: 74–75).

The city plan followed the pattern of new towns founded by the Dukes of Zähringer between 1122 and 1218, such as Zurich and Breisach. This pattern included a main thoroughfare along its spine designated as the main market street with two secondary, parallel streets to either side. Since the town was primarily for exchange rather than religious or social life, there was little emphasis on public squares. In fact, squares did appear in Bern until the fifteenth century when the city developed to the west and, later, larger public spaces near civic buildings.

The blocks were divided into specific planning modules to ease property allocation and development (Morris 1994: 95). The city's ubiquitous *lauben* or arcaded walkways were originally limited to the main street but soon were on other streets as the houses extended over the street to create a protected walkway for markets and shops on the ground floor.

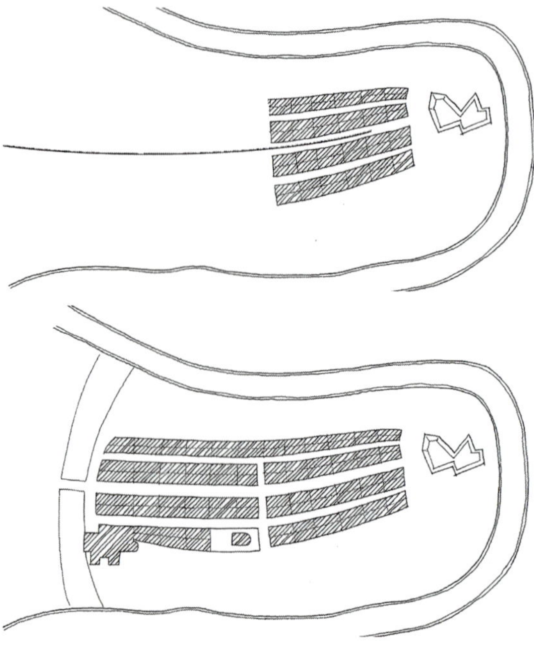

Development of Bern

Bern from above

The discipline of the nearly nine-hundred-year-old urban plan remains clear, yet due primarily to the site, has resulted in a dynamic spatial experience. As Erwin Gutkind notes in *Urban Development in the Alpine and Scandinavian Countries* (1965), Bern's arcades

> are the most characteristic features of this beautiful city, which belongs to the very small group of urban communities where all the ideas of city development were expressed in a mature language of form: organic growth without rigidity; creative adaptation to the terrain with slavish submission to the dictates of nature; instinctive feel for architectural harmony with theoretical narrowness; and spontaneous blending of the human scale with the grandeur of natural conditions without impairing either of them.
>
> (Gutkind 1965: 199–201)

Altstadt

Bologna

13

Piazza Maggiore

Enhancing the spatial sequence through the city are Bologna's ubiquitous arcades that offer protection from the elements and street activity. These arcades culminate at the Piazza Maggiore, the main public square in front of Bologna's cathedral that was not only a public gathering space but also a political statement. Like other Italian squares and cities, Bologna's urban plan and its piazzas did more than serve as commercial or social frameworks, but were interwoven into the citizens' political and social status (Tuttle 1994: 39; Gutkind 1969: 261–262). A piazza's location and dimension as well as the political institutions that surrounded it and the groups or individuals that sponsored and possessed it were important facets in the city's culture.

Originally a medieval market place, Piazza Maggiore was surrounded by palazzos of significant Bolognese citizens and was part of a prolonged redevelopment of Bologna's center between the fourteenth and sixteenth centuries. It was also a part of a Bolognese political demonstration to create a cathedral and urban space in tribute to the city's patron saint, Saint Petronio. As historian Richard Tuttle (1994: 42) points out, dedication to the city's patron saint "was a profession of faith in the history, prestige and autonomy of the free communal state." San Petronio, with the Palazzo dei Notai, dominates the square's south side. To the north is the Renaissance arcaded Palazzo del Podesta that creates an orderly, permeable edge to the space.

Looking north

Looking east

Bologna from above

On the west side is the Palazzo Communale and to the east is Vignola's Palazzo dei Banchi. Vignola's building is essentially a uniform arcade giving the piazza, as Tuttle (1994: 45) remarks, "a definitive boundary, dignified it with a uniform, modern prospect and, by masking a string of heterogeneous private building fronts, succeeded in making it wholly public." This idea of a continuous arcade was continued along the east side of the cathedral as the Pallazo dell'Archiginnasio. The main, north–south pedestrian movement to and from the southern part of the old city is along the east edge beneath arcades.

A smaller square, Piazza del Nettuno, with a large fountain topped by a trident-wielding Neptune, acts as the forecourt to Piazza Maggiore from the city's main east–west street, Via Rizzoli and receives the Via della Indipendenza from the north.

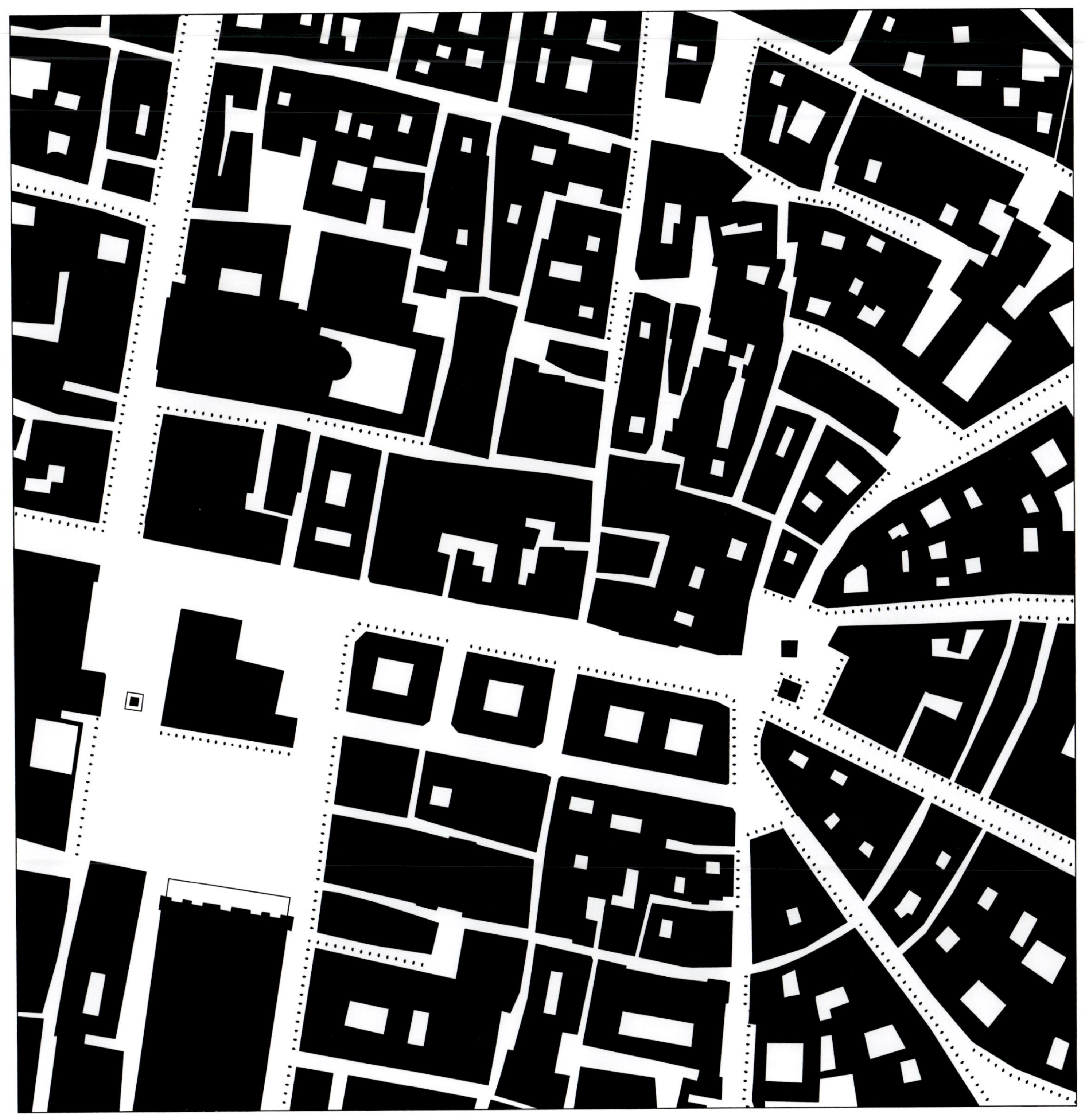

Piazza Maggiore

Bordeaux

14

Allées de Tourny

The Allées de Tourny is one of several boulevards and urban spaces in Bordeaux built in the middle to late eighteenth century at the high point of the French Baroque urban planning on the cusp of the French Revolution. Though Bordeaux's spaces were distinctly pre-revolutionary, the forms influenced nineteenth-century urban design especially Georges Haussmann's reworking of Paris.

Bordeaux's eighteenth century urban development was part of the city's expansion resulting from its wine production and of foreign trade afforded by its harbor along the Garonne river. Though the city suffered under the frequent European wars in the first half of the eighteenth century, during times of peace, its trade increased and the city prospered. The most significant development was under Louis-Urbain Aubert, the Marquis de Tourny, the King's Intendent in Bordeaux between 1743 and 1758.

The boulevards cut through Bordeaux's medieval center and in place of the city's former fortifications. These fortifications are, according to Steen Eiler Rasmussen, the source of the term "boulevard" (Rasmussen 1969: 109). Apparently it is a bastardization of the Nordic word *bulvirke* for bulwark of which these types of streets were generally associated. The Allées de Tourny is one of these boulevards and connects the city's ancient center via other boulevards and *rond-points* to the Place de Tourny at the eighteenth century perimeter.

Bordeaux from above

The Allées forms the northeastern edge of the Grande Hommes district, the center of which is the circular market: the Marché des Grandes Hommes. The Allées connects the Place de Tourny with the Place de la Comédie, which is also the site of the forum of the Roman colony of Burgdigala. For over several decades the Allées de Tourny was a one-sided boulevard with its northeastern edge open to the former Château Trompette fortress and the Garonne river beyond. Following a 1792 design competition, however, the semicircular crescent of the Place de Louis XVI eventually defined the expansive garden that opens to the river (Cleary 1998: 148–149). Today, the Allées, with four ranges of trees, is associated with fashionable shops and restaurants.

Bordeaux's urban pattern remains relatively obscure perhaps due to its appearance at the threshold of political upheaval and fading *Ancien Régime*. The city's Baroque boulevards coincided with the zenith of decadent imperial and subsequent political changes in the mid to late eighteenth century. Like those political and social infrastructures, Bordeaux's architecture suffers from being caught in political and social change (Brace 1968: 6–13).

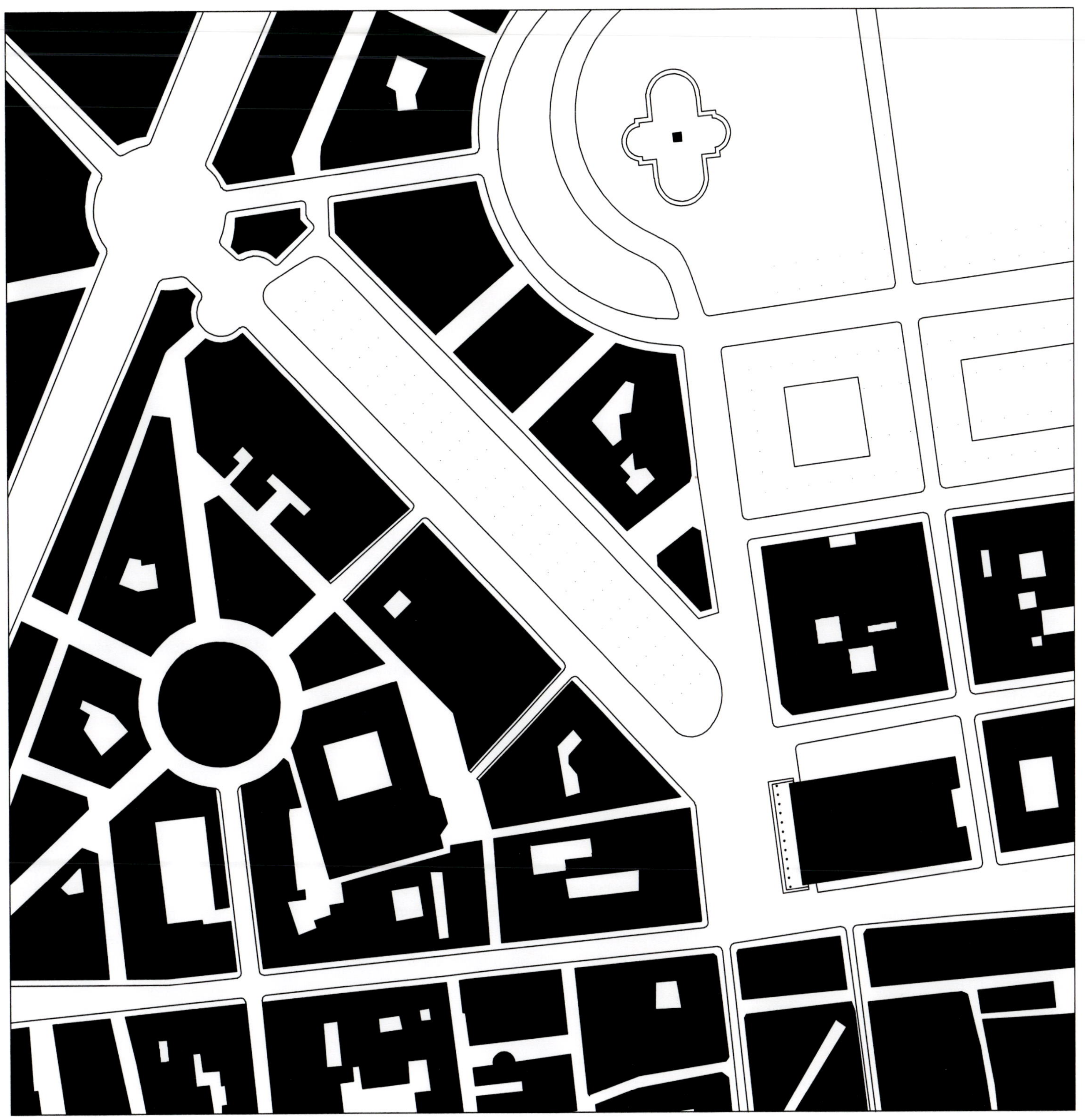

Allées de Tourny

Boston

Copley Square

15

Southwest of the Boston Common and Public Garden and on the south edge of the Back Bay, Copley Square is surrounded by several significant buildings including McKim, Meade and White's Boston Public Library (1895), H.H. Richardson's Trinity Church (1877) and Pei Cobb Freed and Partners' John Hancock Tower (1976).

Initially, the square was not a public space but evolved into that role over time as the space remained undeveloped. While implementing the Back Bay plan between 1857 and 1880, the area was a residual fissure at the intersection of new and existing streets where the Back Bay's grid met the South End's Huntington Avenue geometry. Though not overly complex, the resultant geometry was awkward enough to delay the site's sale and commercial development so that by 1883, the city purchased the open, undeveloped site and designated it for public use (Whitehill 1968: 172).

For nearly seventy-five years the square and surrounding fabric remained indeterminate. While the Boston Public Library's neo-Renaissance façade helped define the square's western edge, Trinity Church's romantic massing could not enclose its eastern side. The Copley Plaza hotel somewhat enclosed the south edge, but it could not help resolve the awkward geometry and massing of area between it and the library. Further exacerbating the indistinct edges, between the mid-1950s and mid-1960s, the area just south of the square was cleared to make way for the Massachusetts Turnpike.

The square itself remained unresolved and a formal plan was not implemented until 1968. Designed by landscape architects Sasaki, Dawson & DeMay, the square featured fountains and a sunken plaza offering refuge from the city. Unfortunately, this refuge also created a visual and spatial barrier from the surrounding streets which helped create an alienating space that quickly transformed into a convenient drug-dealing boutique. Within fifteen years, a group of concerned citizens formed the Copley Square Centennial Committee to help revitalize the square. To help set the revitalization's direction, this public–private organization surveyed Bostonians who, overwhelmingly, appealed for a street level square that incorporated a green lawn. With this information, the committee established a 1984 design competition program and selected the entry by Dean Abbot with Clarke and Rapuano, Inc. The design brought the plaza up to street level, removed the visual barriers between street and square and incorporated a one-acre lawn reminiscent of New England town greens (Miller and Morgan 1990: 164–165). Additionally, the designers resolved varied forces and created a series of varied and flexible spaces. Meanwhile, the

Copley Square from the Boston Public Library looking east

area surrounding the neighborhood and Boston as a whole started to change. By the late 1980s, the area's real estate boomed and buildings slowly filled vacant lots and air rights over the turnpike. The combination of internal resolution and external changes further enhanced the square's transformation from unidentifiable to distinct civic space.

As many urban designers and landscape architects know, American plazas have to be more than just an "open space" but must incorporate areas for quiet lunches, napping, markets and concerts. For example, Los Angeles' Pershing Square, San Francisco's Union Square or Cincinnati's Fountain Square have undergone similar changes to incorporate increased connection between sidewalk and plaza and accommodate for varied uses yet remain unified and identifiable.

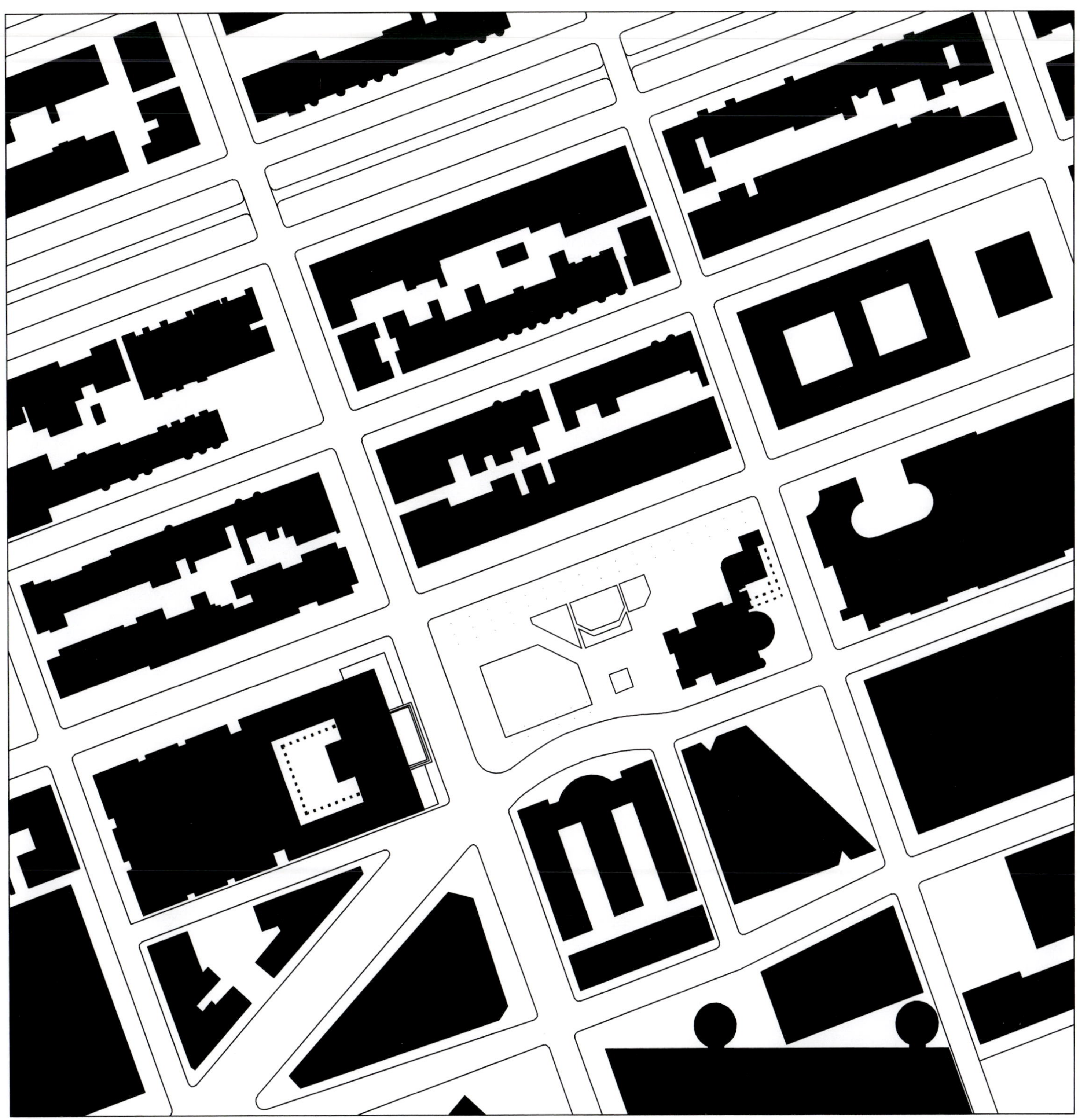

Copley Square

Boston

16

Faneuil Hall Marketplace and Quincy Market

The Faneuil Hall Marketplace and Quincy Market, a popular destination for tourists and Bostonians alike, is an example of sensitive urban revitalization that recognized a city's physical infrastructure could be preserved as a financial and cultural amenity. As an integral part of the city's redevelopment, this area connects the center of Boston back to the harbor and central Boston to the North End neighborhood.

The area proper is comprised of five buildings. At the west end is the historic Faneuil Hall that leads to three, parallel linear trade buildings toward the east. Along its center is the Quincy Market with vendors of fresh and prepared foods. To its north and to its south are two former warehouses that now contain retail shops and restaurants. When first built in the early nineteenth century, these three parallel buildings aligned with piers on the Boston harbor designed by Alexander Parris in 1825 (Whitehill 1968: 96). Like three fingers stretched eastward toward the harbor, they were practically part of the wharves that at one time extended into the harbor. In the late nineteenth century and into the twentieth century, the harbor's edge was slowly filled and shifted eastward away from the market. What was once the water's edge is now a small building with an apsoidal anteroom that funnels pedestrians into an arcade leading toward the harbor. Until recently, however, this passage led only to the possibility of the harbor. In fact, it culminated with the underside of the elevated Central Artery. This elevated highway, which eradicated much of the city's fabric when it was constructed between 1955 and 1957, fundamentally cut the city off from the harbor. Fortunately, after nearly fifty years, the connection was reestablished following the Central Artery's immense, complex, costly and long awaited burial. Beginning in 1991 and concluding in 2005, the city, state and federal government buried the highway and covered its right of way with parks and public buildings similar to the fortifications removed from Vienna's Ringstrasse. The park system now allows for movement from the city to the harbor and make the market district integral to the sequence of spaces through Boston: from the Back Bay, through Boston Common, through the City Hall plaza, around Faneuil Hall, along the market and onward to the harbor.

The original team that renovated the area in the 1970s included the Rouse Company, founded by James Rouse, and architect Benjamin Thompson. The team transformed Faneuil Hall, Quincy Market and the surrounding area by using the functioning, if dilapidated, amenity within the city's core (Miller and Morgan 1990: 68). Though it might be easily argued that Rouse sanitized and commercialized a once thriving and authentic market, the alternatives, especially in the late 1960s and early 1970s, were less than optimal. Just across the street is Boston's City Hall and the surrounding neighborhood, typical of that era in which it was common to raze the entire historic urban fabric in an effort to improve cities. In contrast, Quincy Market is a sensitive redevelopment that used the existing fabric rather than its wholesale removal. Through this approach, Rouse sought to improve the city financially and civilly by conserving and revitalizing existing systems (Thompson and Schmertz 2006: 46–51). The area is a vibrant space and influenced other urban redevelopments in the United States including those in New York, Baltimore and Norfolk.

Quincy Market from the east

The link between the City Hall and Boston's harbor

Faneuil Hall Marketplace and Quincy Market

Brasília

Praça dos Três Poderes

17

Designed to be a capital city, Brasília embodies the distinct albeit naive optimism of post-war modern architecture and urban design. Though Brazil had been an independent nation since 1822, it took well over 130 years for it to establish a new capital. From 1832 to 1936, the capital city was known only as the name of some future city somewhere in the interior. Finally, in 1936, the government designated a specific site 600 miles north of Rio de Janeiro in central Brazil. In 1957, the Brazilian government sponsored an international competition for the city and selected Brazilian urban designer Lúcio Costa to develop the master plan with Brazilian architect Oscar Niemeyer to design the government buildings. While the pace from national independence to winning competition was unhurried, the move from winning entry to completed government complex was rapid with many government buildings opening as early as 1960.

The intention of Brasília was threefold. First, it was to symbolize a modern Brazilian nation and prompt development of the nation's interior. Like other newly established capitals, such as Washington, DC, it was sited at the physical, if not populated, center of the country. As a modern capital it embraced modernist landscape, transportation and architectural concepts. As such, the automobile, seen as the independent transportation system of the future, dominated the city's form and scale. A second goal of Brasília was spatial exploration: Costa's and Niemeyer's designs are an examination of mid-twentieth century concepts of urban space, of landscape and the ideals of a "Functionalist City" outlined by Congrès Internationaux d'Architecture Moderne (CIAM). For CIAM, the city was arranged into functionally segregated zones with buildings arranged rationally and scientifically, yet often sculpturally, in "continuous space" woven together by elevated and recessed roads and highways. Finally, as anthropologist James Holston notes, Brasília embodied a critical social agenda in which the city and its architecture would ameliorate social injustices through "egalitarian and functional prescriptions" (Holston 1989: 41). With these good intentions and high aspirations, it was easy to understand why the city was easily, sometimes rightfully, criticized.

Edmund Bacon concludes his own analysis of the city that "the gift of Brasília is not primarily the form of its structures or the formal symmetry of its composition, but rather the reformulation of the vision of the city as a totality" (Bacon 1967: 227). In any discussion of Brasília, it is important to remember that it was designed to be a more ceremonial capital city like Washington, DC, Canberra or Chandigarh. Like these cities' monumental cores, Brasília's spaces were envisioned as a symbolic framework. For Brazil, the framework announced its international entrée onto the post-World War II political stage with a significant capital representative of a twentieth century nation. As such, it was never meant to be a typical city but a symbol in the Brazilian landscape. It is often derided by urban designers and architects many of whom, as Edmund Bacon observes, never visited it (Bacon 1967: 221). It is true that much of late 1950s and 1960s urbanism leaves much to be desired, with often boundless streets that lead to somnolent, uninhabitable plazas surrounded by single-use zoned buildings. This is a valid criticism of which Brasília is a representative vestige; however, abject rejection and subsequent reversion to traditional urban forms has the potential for a pessimistic, even cynical retreat to possibly unrealistic visions of late twentieth and early twenty-first century urban. This can lead to trends that embrace pre-modern urban forms or disguise contemporary needs behind schizophrenic masks. What is really needed is an urbanism that embraces the needs of human activity, life of the street and at the same time embraces contemporary building practices, social structure, economic system and information technologies.

Brasília

Looking down the Capital Mall toward the Congress Hall

The Congress Hall

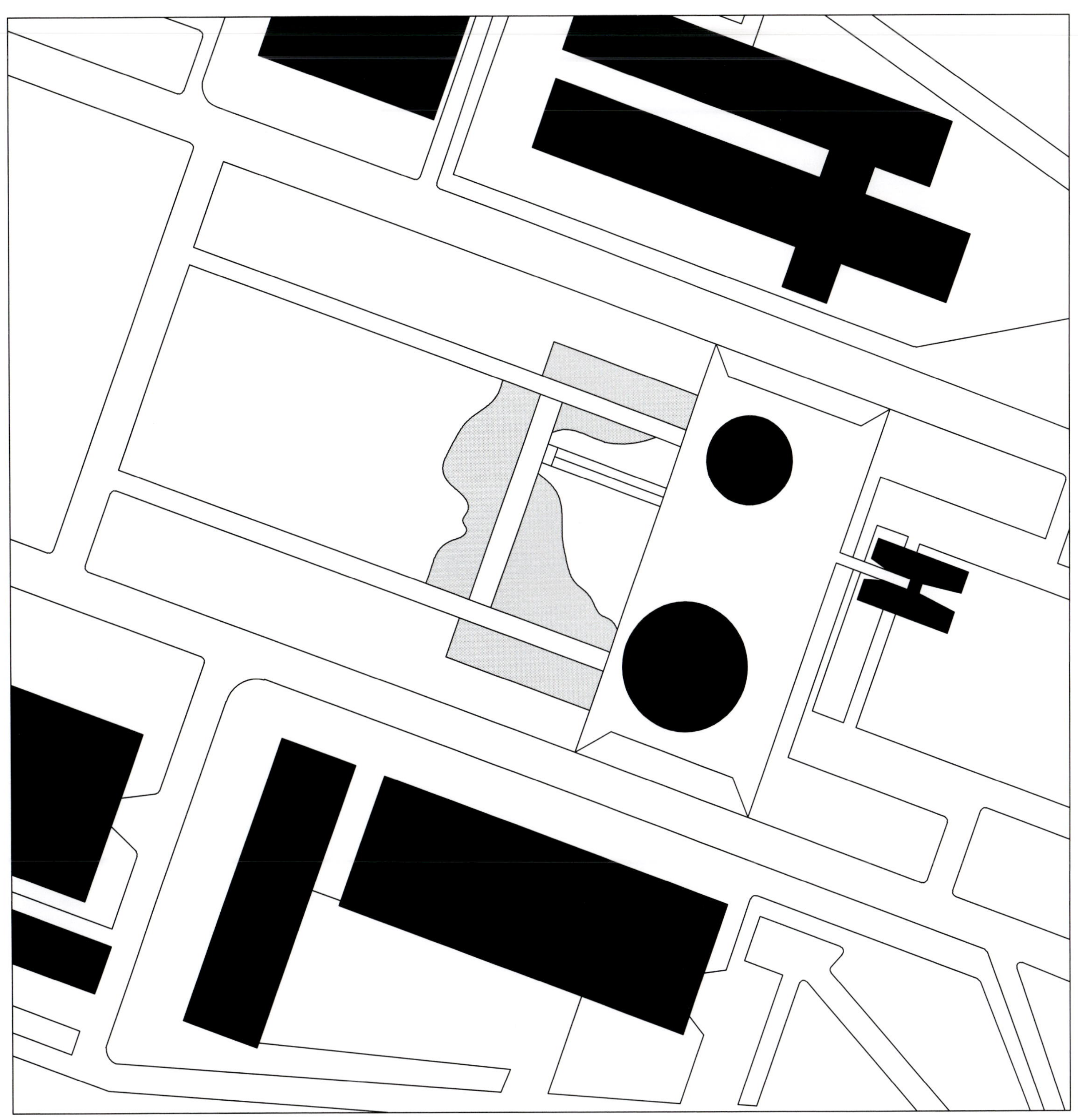

Praça dos Três Poderes

Bruges

18

Grand Place and Burg

Bruges is an example of a medieval town that evolved around a pair of grouped squares each with its own role in the city in which the power dynamic among the church, state and mercantile systems influenced its form. This expression is especially clear in Bruges, Arras or Venice and gave rise to systems of sacred, governmental mercantile spaces.

Bruges' urban fabric is comprised of small public squares interconnected with small streets, canals and alleyways. Its two primary squares are the Burg and the Grand Place. The Burg, once dominated by Bruges' cathedral, is now dominated by the Basilica of the Holy Blood, the town hall and the law courts. The Grand Place, also known as the Markt Platz, is surrounded by seventeenth-century gabled houses, provincial offices, post office and dominated on the south edge by the Belfry at the base of the Halle or market building. The bases of most buildings are restaurants and shops. With its urban form, Bruges was also one of the earliest towns to legislate urban zoning and building codes which include stipulations on fire resistant construction, street cleaning and publicly financed market buildings and infrastructure (Gutkind 1970: 374–384).

Originally, its river and canals led to a deep harbor that allowed Bruges to become a wealthy and prosperous mercantile center of Europe. This is evident in the civic Gothic architecture that included the Grand Place's bell tower, stock exchange, hospital, hospices and town hall built in the late fourteenth century. Beginning in the late fifteenth century and into the sixteenth century, however, the town slowly declined due to changes in markets, political structure and the silting of the canals and harbor. Though it remained relatively active into the late seventeenth century, it could not maintain its viability, did not acquire industry and thus preserved the town from eighteenth and nineteenth century development. By the mid-nineteenth century, it became important architecturally and urbanistically. With the increased interest in Gothic revival architecture prompted by John Ruskin and A.W.N. Pugin, the town's own citizens helped transform Bruges into an architectural destination and one of the earliest examples of a town anointed through historic preservation. The city's brick Gothic architecture (known as *travée brugeoise*) remained relatively intact into the nineteenth century and attracted the attention of scholars and architects who were inspired by it and sought to restore, conserve and perpetuate it.

Bruges remains an important artifact that many believe is locked in time. Its architecture, streets, squares and canals, when not filled with tourists, transport the visitor back to medieval times without, of course, the disease, superstition and other day-to-day realities of the thirteenth century. In reality, Bruges is more an artifice of restoration and preservation than of truth. Like other cities dependent on maintaining its image for its self and the tourist trade, the town was and continues to be revived to a medieval simulacrum. As historian Gavin Stamp observes, "Such is Revivalism, which can be a creative force. It can also be stultifying, by imposing a rigid, false image and by making history stop at a particular point so that an ancient city no longer appears as the consequence of centuries of continual change and growth" (Stamp 1989: 34). This is important today due to preservation that locks architecture in an acrylic block or trends in new urban development that pessimistically mimic the architectural styles and even spaces of the past.

The Burg

Belfry in the Grand Place

Grand Place and Burg

Buenos Aires

19

Plaza de Mayo

The traditional two-dimensional gridiron layout of colonial cities throughout the New World is easily recognized in Buenos Aires, starting at Plaza de Mayo or May Square, an integral public square since the city's founding during the Spanish colonization of South America in the sixteenth century. The city's original sixteen by nine quadros plan followed, like other Spanish colonies in the New World, the "Leyes de Indias" or Laws of the Indies. These laws prescribed specific methods, dimensions and, in general, the design rules for colonies. Derived by similar rules and practices of colonization within Europe and from a range of sources including Vitruvius, its critical stipulations included laying out the colony into square blocks on the cardinal directions with the center square designated as a plaza and focus of the town. The central plaza's size would correspond and allow for the town's ultimate expansion. Street widths were determined both by climate and the ability of the military to move easily through the city while surrounding buildings were lined with colonnades for protection from the elements (Broadbent 1990: 42–48).

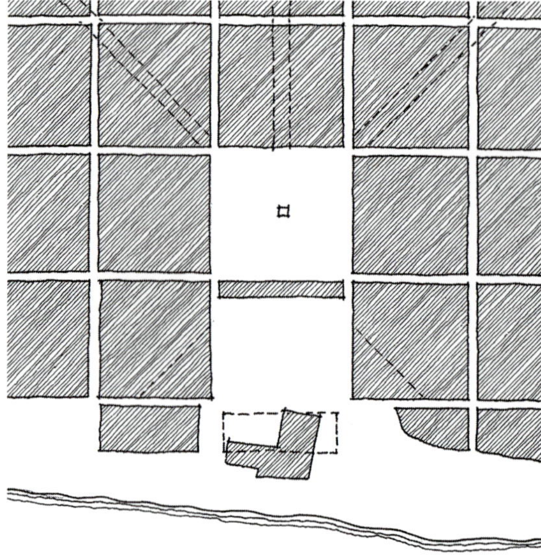

Original configuration overlaid with diagonal streets

As might be expected, the Laws of the Indies resulted in a nearly homogenous, two-dimensional gridiron layout of colonial cities regardless of topography and locale. The clarity and ease of the rules indirectly influenced colonization and city form throughout the New World that produced nearly identical towns throughout South, Central and some parts of North America.

Buenos Aires' layout by Pedro de Mendoza in 1535 remained similar and relatively unchanged for nearly three centuries. In the early nineteenth century, a market colonnade called the Recova divided the oblong square into two semi-independent quadros called Plaza Victoria (city side) and de Mayo (water side). The Recova, like the colonnade surrounding St. Peter's Square in Rome, allowed for enclosure yet provided a visual and spatial connection between the two spaces. As Fritz Rothstein points out in *Beautiful Squares* (1967), the Recova had the effect of creating two more intimately scaled plazas (Rothstein 1967: 184–185). In 1883, the city's urban renewal project razed the Recova and inserted the axial street Avenida de Mayo and the radial Avenida Presidente Julio A. Rocca and Avenida Presidente Roque Sáenz Peña. Unfortunately, while these avenues give a grander feel to the Buenos Aires center, with more automobile traffic around the square they decreased the enclosing edge of the square.

Plaza de Mayo looking east

Religious, civic and commercial buildings surround the square. At the opposite end of the Avenue de Mayo is the Casa Rosada (President's Palace). The palace became the focus of political and social protests. As author Michael Webb points out in *The City Square* (1990), the only effective protest of Argentine military rule were las Madres de la Plaza de Mayo or Mothers of the Plaza de Mayo, who gathered in the square to protest and seek answers to the missing "loved ones" (Webb 1990: 183).

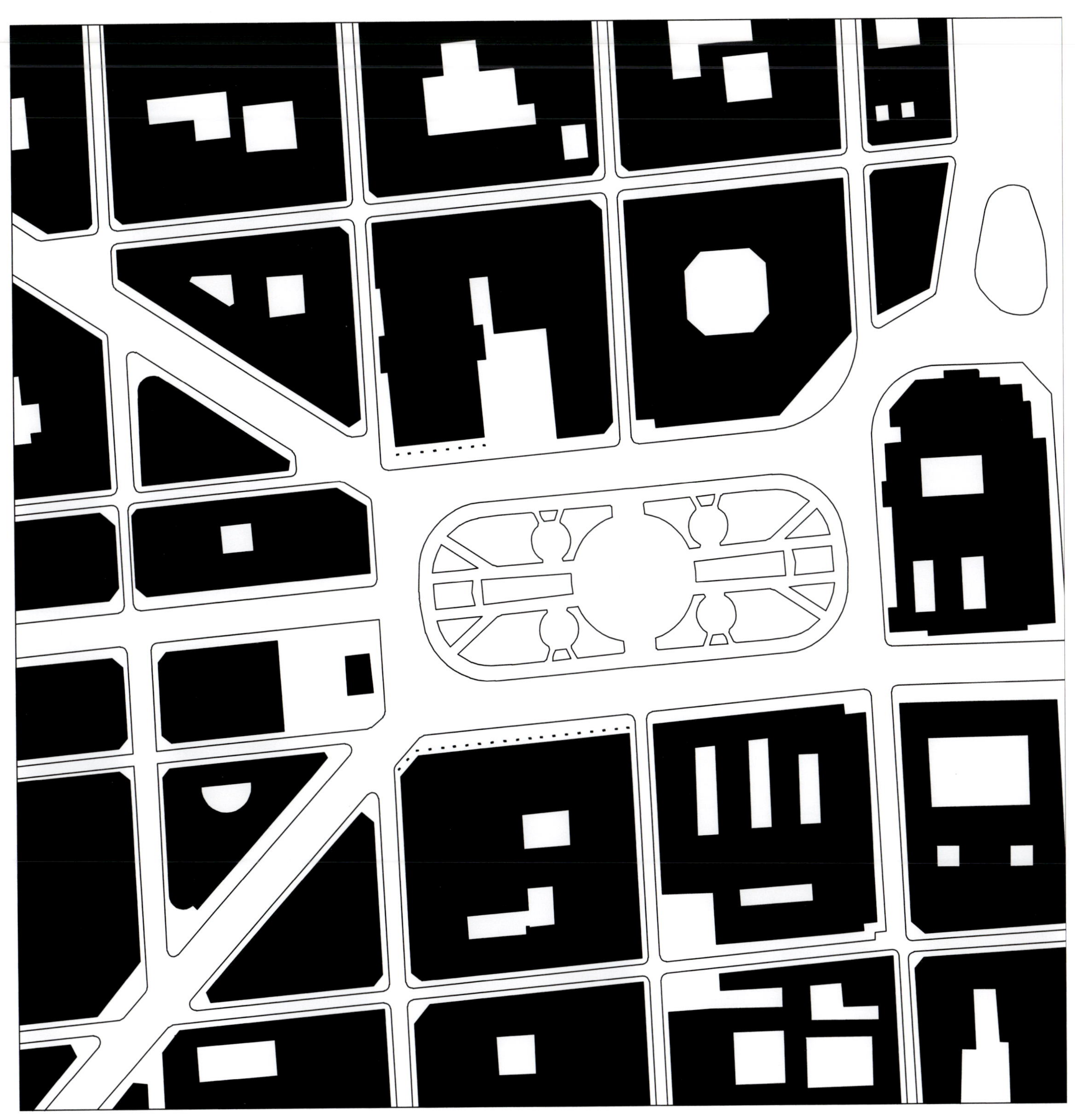

Plaza de Mayo

Cairo

Midan al-Tahrir

20

Midan al-Tahrir, or Liberation Square, is an intersection near Cairo's burgeoning commercial and residential district along the Nile. Fashioned on Parisian boulevards and streets, the Midan is not so much a square as a vast, billboard-girdled fissure in Cairo surrounded by financial, cultural and administrative institutions and, therefore, often the center of political and social turmoil.

Beginning in the early nineteenth century under the leadership of Mohammed Ali Pasha, Cairo underwent a series of urban revitalization projects to transform and extend the Arab city. What Mohammed Pasha began, his grandson, Khedive Ismail Pasha (1863–1879) continued and expanded. Following his return from the Paris Universal Exposition in 1867 where he befriended Georges Haussmann, Ismail Pasha moved quickly to bring about Cairo's modernization to coincide with the opening of the Suez Canal. Like Haussmann's plans for Paris that included boulevards through the existing urban fabric and new boulevards outside the city's center, designer Ali Mubarak proposed an extensive urbanism program that would both extend Cairo and revitalize its center. The extension was primarily westward from the old city to the Nile's edge across the low-lying area susceptible to the Nile's annual flooding (Abu-Lughod 1971: 100–107).

Ismail Pasha envisioned the new district between the old city and the Nile as a European district that would not only stimulate real estate and economic development but also transform Cairo into a more European city. The center of this district, known as Ismailia, was the Midan Ismailia, renamed Midan al-Tahrir in 1954. The square is, like a Parisian *rond-point*, an intersection of radiating streets that bring streets from east, north and south and direct them toward the Qasr al-Nil bridge across the Nile to the west.

By the late nineteenth and early twentieth centuries, the area became fully associated with English and French nationals and home to civic institutions such as government ministries, the Egyptian Antiquities Museum, American University in Cairo and art museums. Though several of the original nineteenth century buildings survive, today the square is formed by apartment buildings, hotels, the Arab League and office buildings, including the infamous Mugamma building, home to the Egyptian government's bureacracy (Beattie 2005: 198). Western fast food restaurants dominate the street level along with entrances to the metro system and underground passages. Like the rest of Cairo, the square is almost completely filled with automobile traffic that contributes to the overall pollution in the city.

While the subway and several changes such as a new park on the northwest side of the square help, it will be difficult to escape the impact of the city's unabated population growth. Cairo, like other burgeoning cities in developing nations, has been hit with a nearly uncontrollable influx of people from rural communities; it is suffering from nearly uncontrolled growth and the subsequent clash of rural tradition and modern urban life. As architectural critic Michael Sorkin notes, "Egypt is one the world's great battlegrounds between tradition and modernity" (Sorkin 2001: 84). If this is so, then Cairo's Midan al-Tahrir is a skirmish line in that battle. It represents how an urban square can illustrate the drive of an empire to project an image of modernization while at the same time have a nearly schizophrenic attitude toward it.

Midan al-Tahrir looking north

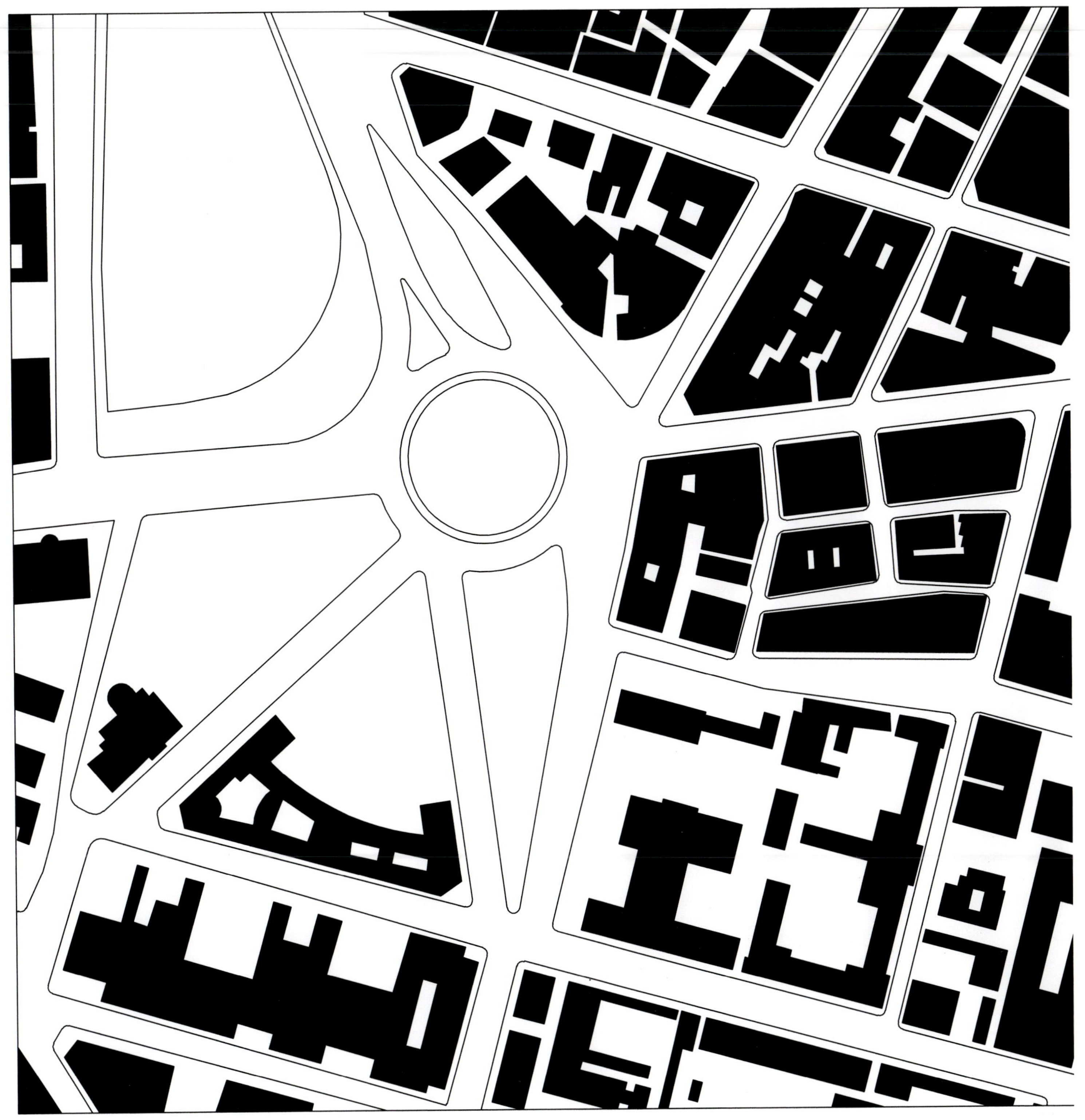

Midan al-Tahrir

České Budějovice

21

Náměstí Přemysl Otakar II

České Budějovice is an archetypal thirteenth-century Bohemian planned town that, despite fires and political and economic changes, has retained much of its medieval form. As such, it is a good example of medieval town planning, like Bern and Bergen, that was part of an extensive regional and even pan-European mercantile network. Founded as a royal colonial town under King Přemysl Otakar II in 1265 in southern Bohemia near the Austrian border, České Budějovice helped demarcate territorial boundaries along the Czech and Austrian border and exploit the economic potential of the surrounding region (Morris 1994: 93). Though established by Czechs, České Budějovice and other colonial towns grew increasingly populated by German merchants and craftsmen so that by the fourteenth century the town had lost its Czech identity.

České Budějovice was established near an existing village and the confluence of the Malse and Vlatava, which flows through Prague. Like other planned Bohemian colonial towns, České Budějovice was formed along a trading route and centered on a central, harmonious, arcaded square. Like any colonial town established in a frontier, it was an island of one culture set within a sea of another. As such, the town was a refuge surrounded by fortifications and laid out on a grid for easy allocation of property, for ease of construction and for regulated growth (Gutkind 1972a: 227). While the town's underlying architecture is Gothic, surrounding the square on four sides are mostly Renaissance and Baroque three- and four-story houses with shops beneath a continuous arcade on the ground floor. Though increasingly populated by tourists and tourist related services, it remains a day-to-day shopping and civic gathering space. České Budějovice, like many other Czech towns, survived relatively unscathed during World War II and post-war modernization due to the Czechoslovak economic and social system that focused on developing industrialized zones and building mass-produced housing blocks outside city centers. The town's medieval edge remains intact: its fortifications were removed, and like Vienna and Kraków, are used as green belts between the old city and outer development.

The square looking south

Though relatively large compared to squares in other Bohemian colonial towns, Náměsti Přemysl Otakar II demonstrates several distinctive architectural elements that help make it a layered spatial experience. These elements include its arcade, its floor and its entry. The arcades, which are single story, shallow vaults, allow for literal protection from the weather but also provide a perceptual refuge as they afford the pedestrian a more immediate connection with the shops yet are not entirely disconnected from the more public open area of the square. Correspondingly, the square's floor is, generally, continuous from the square into the arcade. This uninterrupted surface accentuates the spatial interweaving from outside to underneath the arcade. Lastly, the square's entries – like those of Arras' grouped squares, Prague's Staroměstské Náměsti or Florence's Piazza della Signoria – are lateral. Entry to the square is at its corners, keeping the square unrevealed until nearly inside it. These lateral entries allow the pedestrian to move along its edges and beneath the arcade without entering or fully engaging the square if engagement is undesired. In the end, the elements combine and allow for a dynamic spatial experience that is both inside and outside.

Náměstí Přemysl Otakar II

Chandigarh

22

Capitol Complex

Chandigarh reflects both the grand naive optimism and the unhappy inadequacies of post-war urban design. Designed by Le Corbusier, Pierre Jeanneret, E. Maxwell Fry and Jane Drew between 1951 and 1964, this state capitol complex in Punjab, India is representative of an era in which modern architects, urban designers and politicians attempted to create new capital cities for emerging nations. Like Louis Kahn's Dacca and Costa and Niemeyer's Brasília, Chandigarh's designers, for better or worse, attempted to make capitals suitable for emerging nations that came to power following post-colonial domination and World War II. As such, they were unique, somewhat visionary and, at times, overly idealistic and perhaps egotistical designs. But this was to be expected: Chandigarh, like the other capitals, was meant to be a deliberately different and distinct modern city (Evenson 1966: 6–7).

Chandigarh was established following the bloody partitioning of India and was to symbolize a new, twentieth century Hindu nation. As architectural historian Vikramaditya Prakash notes in *Chandigarh's Le Corbusier: The Struggle for Modernity in Postcolonial India* (2002), India's Prime Minister Jawaharlal Nehru wanted to avoid adapting an old city to the new nation, but sought, in his own words, to build a "new city, unfettered by the traditions of the past, a symbol of the nation's faith in the future" (Prakash 2002: 9). As such, Chandigarh reflects both modern and western ambitions linked with Hindu cosmology. The city derives its name from a shrine near the site dedicated to Chandi, the ubiquitous female principal in Hindu cosmogony. Though the shrine played a role, the goddess was particularly important because, as Prakash notes,

> Chandi is the enabling force of transformation and change. Her participation, in one form or another, is mandatory at all events of any significance. The inherent auspiciousness of her presence must surely not have escaped the Hindu official who picked the site.
>
> (Prakash 2002: 8)

Though not the city's original designer, Le Corbusier was chosen for the site simply because he represented the visionary post-war modern architect who might be able to provide the city of Nehru's dreams. Le Corbusier's design essentially uses a modular grid to demarcate an unending landscape. As such, the capital was not intended to be a city *per se* but an open ceremonial landscape. The grid was based on Le Corbusier's modular proportioning system with major buildings aligned and arranged on regulating lines. The capitol complex included an assembly hall, office building, governor's house and court building.

View from the Senate building to the north

The town, and especially the capitol complex, is placed in an abstract, landscaped plateau with Himalayan mountains to the north. As in Brasília, the primary means of movement in this modern townscape was to be, of course, automobiles.

A lesson of Chandigarh is that it was meant to be a ceremonial modernist landscape project separate from the past. As a new spatial idea for a new state and for a new nation, it reflected the deliberate breaking away from traditional, colonial India to a twentieth century, progressive India. It embodied a new spirit. Certainly Chandigarh, as a new, untested concept of landscape urbanism, is an easy target of critics. As many critics have noted, it is too open, desolate and somewhat alienating. Some critics have taken this as an opportunity to augment it into a city with blocks and with pedestrian-oriented streets. Unfortunately, this is like rewriting James Joyce's *Ulysses* so that it is more readable. That's not really the point. True, Chandigarh is not a book you can put down if you don't like it, but it was designed with the same exploratory modern ideals.

The Assembly Hall and relationship to the Himalayas on the horizon

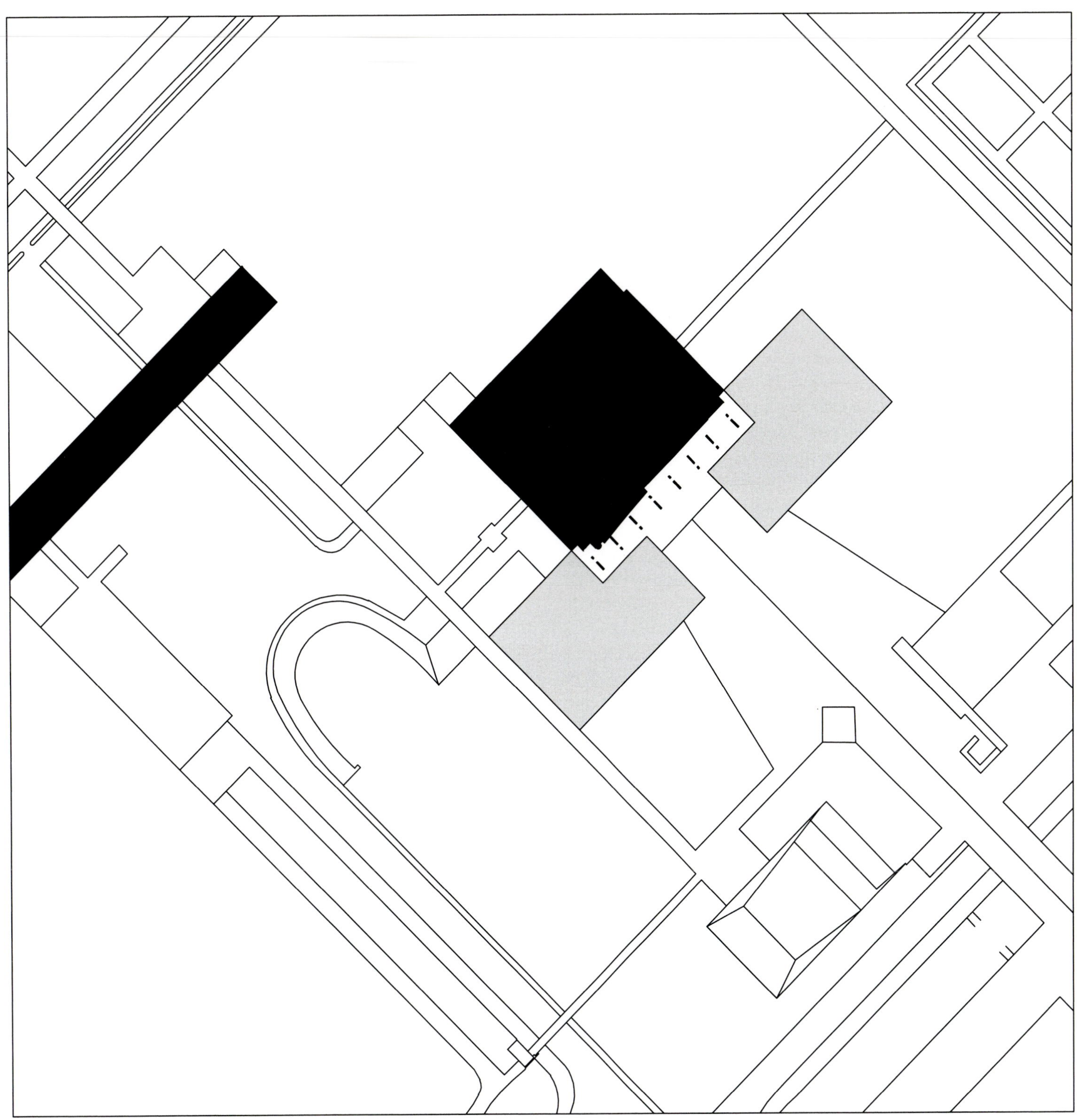

Capitol Complex

Chicago

Federal Center

23

More of a composition of objects in space, the Federal Center (1964–74) remains an important spatial idea of mid-century modern urban design and part of a series of open plazas in Chicago's loop. Though this type of urban strategy has been and continues to be questioned, its strengths lie in its context and its limits.

The Federal Center, designed by Mies van der Rohe, is a composition of three separate buildings: a post office, office building and courthouse on two sites. The forty-two-story Federal office building and the one-story post office occupy one block defined on the north and south by West Adams and West Jackson Streets and on the east and west by South Clark and South Dearborn Streets. This is also the site of Alexander Calder's bright red Flamingo stabile that acts as a sculptural and colorful contrast to the somber monotone buildings. Across Dearborn and on half the block is the thirty-story Federal Courthouse. The three buildings and the city's neutral ground plane become independent entities with their width, length and height arranged asymmetrically to create an ambiguous enclosure. At times the space is identifiable but upon moving through the space that sense changes to one of increased or decreased openness.

Rather than define space through definitive enclosing walls, it articulates space through the relation of buildings to one another. The spatial experience is not one of rest but one of change. Walking through Chicago and coming upon this space is not a matter of arrival, but a matter of encountering a civic landmark with overlapping and interpenetrating spatial views. This extension of the idea of spatial flow is reflected, literally, in Mies' façades. As architect and Mies pupil Masami Takayama notes, if a building's

> skin is a physical expression of infinity, then the ground floor can be viewed as a spatial expression of the same concept. In general, the ground floor is left open and transparent with no function other than as an entrance space.
>
> (Blaser 2004: 14)

A key to the Federal Center's success is that the elements are treated as monuments. As such, they are objects in the field or part of a sculptural arrangement that creates a pedestrian experience reminiscent of moving among a series of monoliths. Underscoring its success as a sculptural experience is its context of the hard-edged, somewhat austere building architecture in Chicago's loop that act as a counterpoint to the composition. Applying this strategy to entire cities or even to entire districts that lack the foil of a surrounding dense fabric or using varied building types, can result in undifferentiated, heterogeneous residual spaces. Unfortunately, this was often the case for many decades. As Thomas Schumacher notes in "Contextualism: Urban Ideals and Deformations," modern architects insisted "that this type of configuration be typical for all building types rather than special to particularly important building uses" (Schumacher 1971: 80).

View across the Federal Plaza

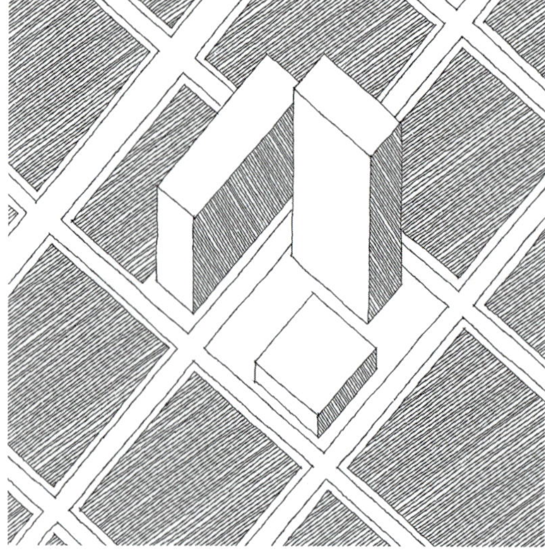

The concept of freestanding, sculptural elements within Chicago's grid setting

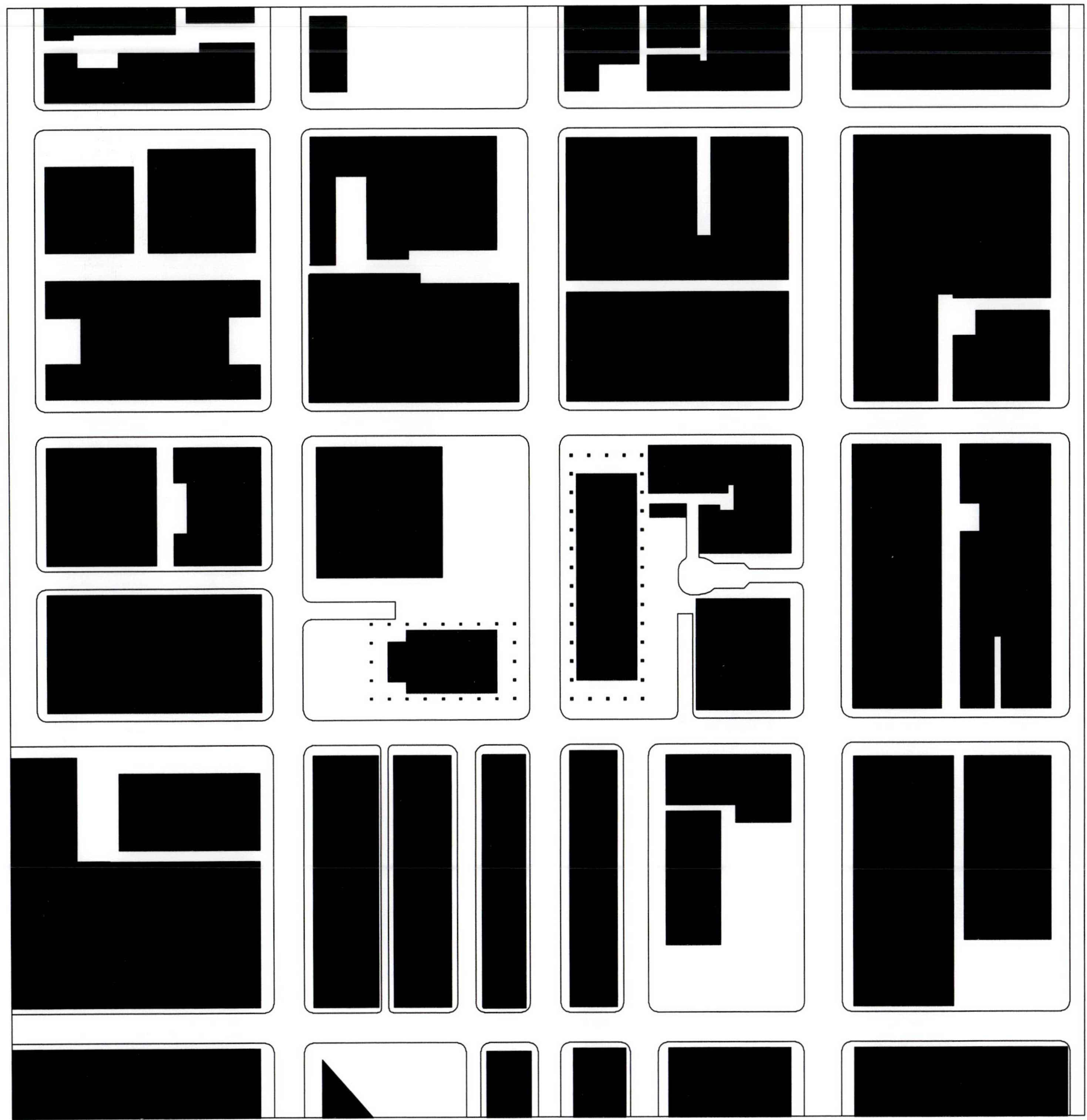

Federal Center

Cincinnati

24

Fountain Square

It seems that nearly every twenty years many American cities must redesign their plazas to accommodate changes in culture or taste but mostly to correct ill-conceived, if well-intentioned designs. Fountain Square is important urbanistically because it is at the crux of Cincinnati civic activities created in an effort to revitalize the downtown central business district in the late 1960s – an effort that continues as the square was reconfigured in 2006 mostly to correct issues of accessibility.

The square, the centerpiece of which is the Tyler Davidson fountain, is bounded by 5th Street on the south and Vine Street on the west. Its east side is dominated by the Dubois Tower built in 1970 and the northern edge defined by a bank and retail area and, until recently, a portion of the city's Skywalk system (Dorsey and Roth 1987: 17–18).

Cincinnati's gridiron plan was laid out by John Filson and Israel Ludlow in 1788 with the Fountain Square, conceived by William Tinsley in 1827, originally a two-block esplanade in the center of 5th Street between Vine and Main Streets. Its current configuration as a raised, pedestrian-only plaza is the result of early 1970s urban renewal and a need for downtown parking which was placed beneath its surface. This was first designed by RTKL in 1970 and then refurbished by Baxter, Hodell, and Donnelly & Preston in 1985. To achieve its current fundamental shape, the Dubois Tower was built into the existing 5th Street right-of-way. Penetrating 5th Street created the square configuration yet left the remaining eastern half of 5th Street somewhat isolated. This portion, now called the Government Square Terminal, is a city bus stop and remains ill defined and residual despite attempts to incorporate kiosks, trees and other amenities. Across 5th Street to the south is the First National Bank Center and Westin Hotel. While the first three floors maintain the street edge, the building's upper configuration is set back to allow sunlight to reach the plaza (Dorsey and Roth 1987: 22).

The 2006 redesign amended some of the problems created in 1970 and 1985. The corrections were both substantial and subtle. Elements on the plaza, such as the large concrete proscenium arch stage and stair tower leading to the below grade parking garage, were removed to open the plaza on all sides. A new, small café pavilion was added on the northwest corner of the square. The fountain, which had been closer to 5th Street and faced west, was moved to the north near the center of the space and now faces south. The skywalk system was removed to allow greater access to the retail development on the north side of the square. The most important change, however, is the plaza connection to the sidewalk. From its inception, the plaza was separated from the sidewalk with a series of landscaped terraces that both physically and psychologically separated the street from the plaza.

Revitalization proposal 2006

It is quite common for awardwinning civic spaces from the 1970s and 1980s to be torn out and replaced with brand new awardwinning designs. This is true of Los Angeles' Pershing Square, Boston's Copley Square and San Francisco's Union Square. Rather than a simple design that can accommodate a variety of functions (e.g. a lawn that can be a playground, market, performance space), designers often balkanize the squares into ultra-specific zones that can accommodate only limited functions. As such, when uses change, the squares are incapable of adapting to those changes. While it takes many years for a square to succeed, many redeveloped squares in Europe, in Barcelona for example, have limited divisions in favor of open spaces that can accommodate multiple uses.

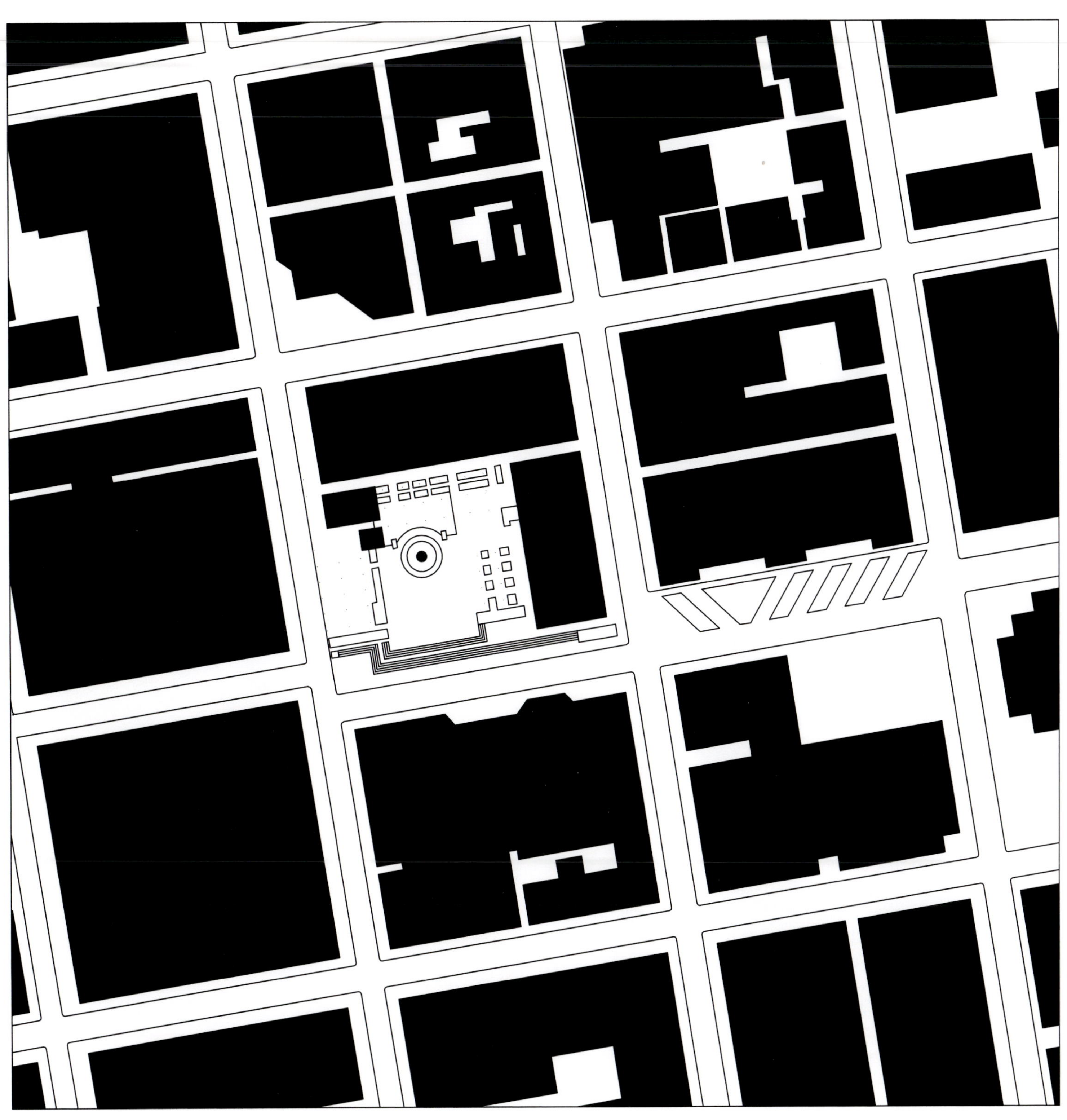

Fountain Square

Cleveland

25

Public Square

Cleveland is an example of eighteenth-century American frontier planning influenced by urban design in the eastern United States. Like many frontier cities, Cleveland rose to prominence in the nineteenth and early twentieth centuries, but began a steady decline in the mid-twentieth century and is only now beginning to recover. In the intervening years, many of these cities razed much of their fabric leaving somewhat empty downtown neighborhoods.

Cleveland, like other early Ohio towns and cities, has roots in New England owing to English colonies that claimed land to the west. Like many of the thirteen original colonies, the crown granted Connecticut land from the east coast westward between the forty-first parallel on the south and Massachusetts to the north with the Pacific Ocean as its western limit (Kolson 2001: 52). The area just west of Pennsylvania, therefore, was considered the Western Reserve and it is this area that, in 1795, the state sold as 3 million acres to the Connecticut Land Company. Though the federal government governed claims to the Western Reserve, the impact of the New England heritage was already evident in Ohio by the nineteenth century (Reps 1965: 230).

Laid out in 1796 by General Moses Cleaveland, the city's plan followed the familiar New England town plan, if not the Puritan ideals. Like New Haven, Cleveland – sans "a" – is laid out on a grid with 10-acre squares set aside for public use. Unlike New Haven whose Green is a middle square at the center of a nine square grid, Cleveland's plan is cruciform so that the center square is at the intersection of two major cross streets. This has implications on the space's use and continues to impact Cleveland's Public Square to this day. When laying out the city, General Cleaveland could have used two alternative layouts regarding the streets leading into the square. He could have stopped the streets so that traffic would move around the square's edge or, conversely, allowed streets to continue and move through the square's center. Unfortunately, he chose the latter so that Public Square is divided into four smaller, isolated parks.

For a time, this design move was relatively inconsequential since traffic was predominately horse-drawn vehicles. By the late nineteenth century the tree-lined streets and Public Square were considered by many, as Paul Zucker notes, a "most perfect expression of Victorian civic art in the country" (Zucker 1966: 252). Unfortunately, with the rise of industry and increase in streetcar, automobile and other vehicular traffic, the square or, rather, squares became isolated, median strips and separate from surrounding fabric.

Today, Public Square's periphery is several surface parking lots and, just to the north, Daniel Burnham's and the Cleveland Group Plan's Civic Mall. Though the three-block-long Mall includes important civic buildings including the City Hall, Public Auditorium, Convention Center, Public Library and Courthouse, its proximity and size diminish the uniqueness of the Public Square. These forces are significant hurdles to surmount if the city attempts to revitalize the downtown. Today, Public Square is dominated by the Terminal Tower building, combining a railroad terminal, office buildings, retail and hotels. When it opened in 1930, the Terminal Building, which included retail, a hotel and offices, helped refocus attention from the Civic Mall. It is hoped that efforts to bring housing and mixed uses into the downtown will once again bring focus back to Public Square.

The relationship of Public Square to the Civic Mall immediately to the north

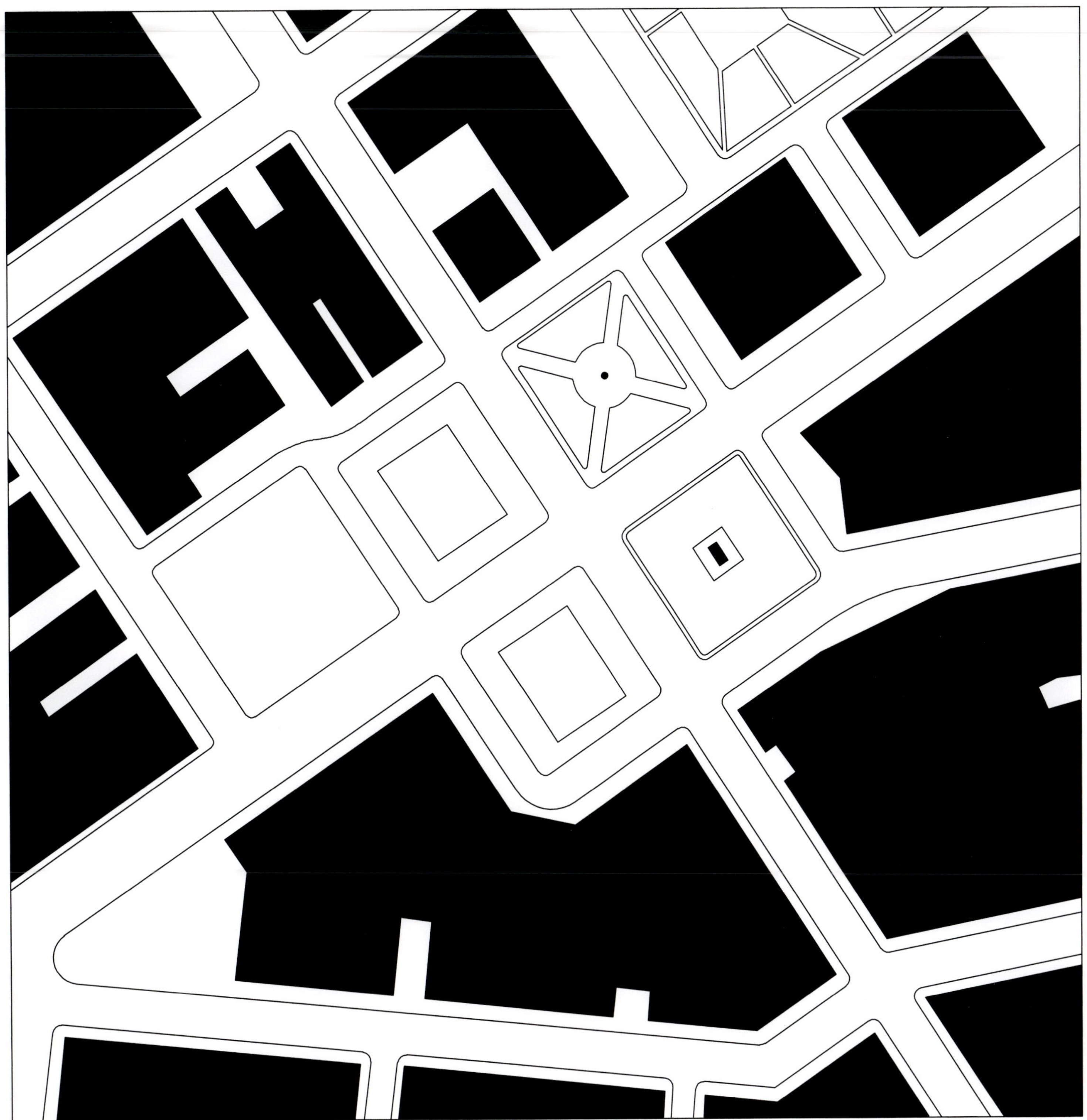

Public Square

Copenhagen

Amalienborg Slotsplads

26

Amalienborg Slotsplads, the octagonal urban square that is the centerpiece of Copenhagen's Frederiksstad district, illustrates how strong design can help spur development and how strength need not be simplistically uniform but can be a complex weaving of several elements into a uniform whole.

Designed in 1749 by Nikolai Eigtved under the direction of Denmark's King Frederik V and his steward, Adam Moltkein, the Amalienborg Square and the rectilinear Frederik Square were meant to help redevelop lands held by the royal family. The heart of this redevelopment district is a two-square design linked by a primary northwest–southeast axis along Frederiksgade Street connecting the water's edge to the Frederiks Kirke – an axial connection that today extends to the opposite shore to the city's new opera house. Between these is the octagonal Amalienborg Square with the equestrian statue of King Frederik V at its center (Rasmussen 1969: 128–129). Nobility initially occupied the four pavilions, but in the late eighteenth century, the palaces became home to the royal family. Today, they are primarily the winter residence of the Danish royal family though two of the palaces are public museums.

Though similar to the Place Vendôme in Paris, the Amalienborg Square's walls are less uniform and comprised of four, three-story palaces diagonal to the cross axes. Weaving these palaces together are two-story galleries with pavilions flanking the cross axes of main Frederiksgade and the more secondary Amaliengade. This irregular interior wall adds an alternating rhythm to the square's interior and, as Edmund Bacon notes, the "four buildings provide an ever-changing series of relationships with one another" creating a dynamic interior space (Bacon 1967: 157).

Initially, the square's interior surface was more differentiated. The two-story gallery was initially a single story that accentuated the palaces and flanking axial gates appear more like freestanding pavilions rather than a continuous building. Additionally, on the south gateway, a wood pavilion across the north–south axes encloses the square. Unlike Parisian squares with unvaried façades, the Amalienborg is a synchronized grouping of primary, secondary and tertiary elements.

From the harborside garden, the pedestrian pathway is slightly compressed between a short street. At the end of this street are two flanking pavilions that mark the entry to the Amalienborg Square. Across the square, the street is flanked by another gate leading to another narrow street that opens at the end to the quadrangle dominated by the Frederiks Kirke. Also known as the Marble Church, the Frederiks Kirke nearly fills the space defined by residential apartment blocks. Initially the church, which is approximately eighty meters high, was to be nearly four times the height of the surrounding buildings and thus be a final culmination to the spatial sequence (Rasmussen 1969: 128–129). Due to its diminished size, however, the Amalienborg seems to be more of a culmination.

Amalienborg Slotsplad reveals how an urban space can posses both uniformity and variety. Rather than the overly uniform façades of Place Vendôme, uniformity can be achieved through a disciplined composition of elements that contribute to a whole. The key part of this success, however, has to do with each element playing a particular role in the hierarchy of the composition. This is somewhat like Jefferson's University of Virginia that is defined by similar pavilions superimposed on a more regular, smaller scale colonnade.

View of Amalienborg Slotsplads to Frederiks Kirke

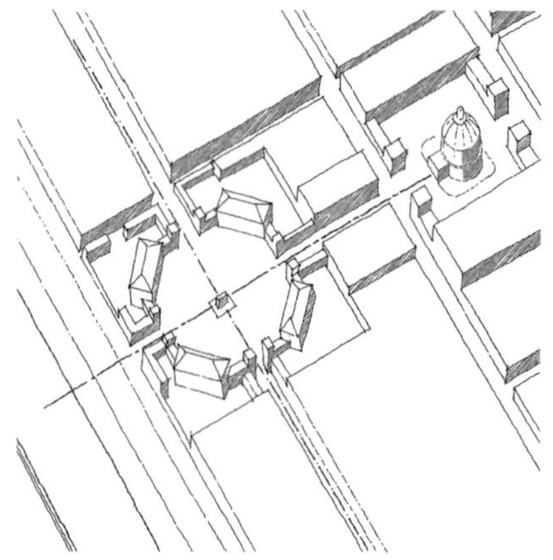

The relationship between the grouped squares

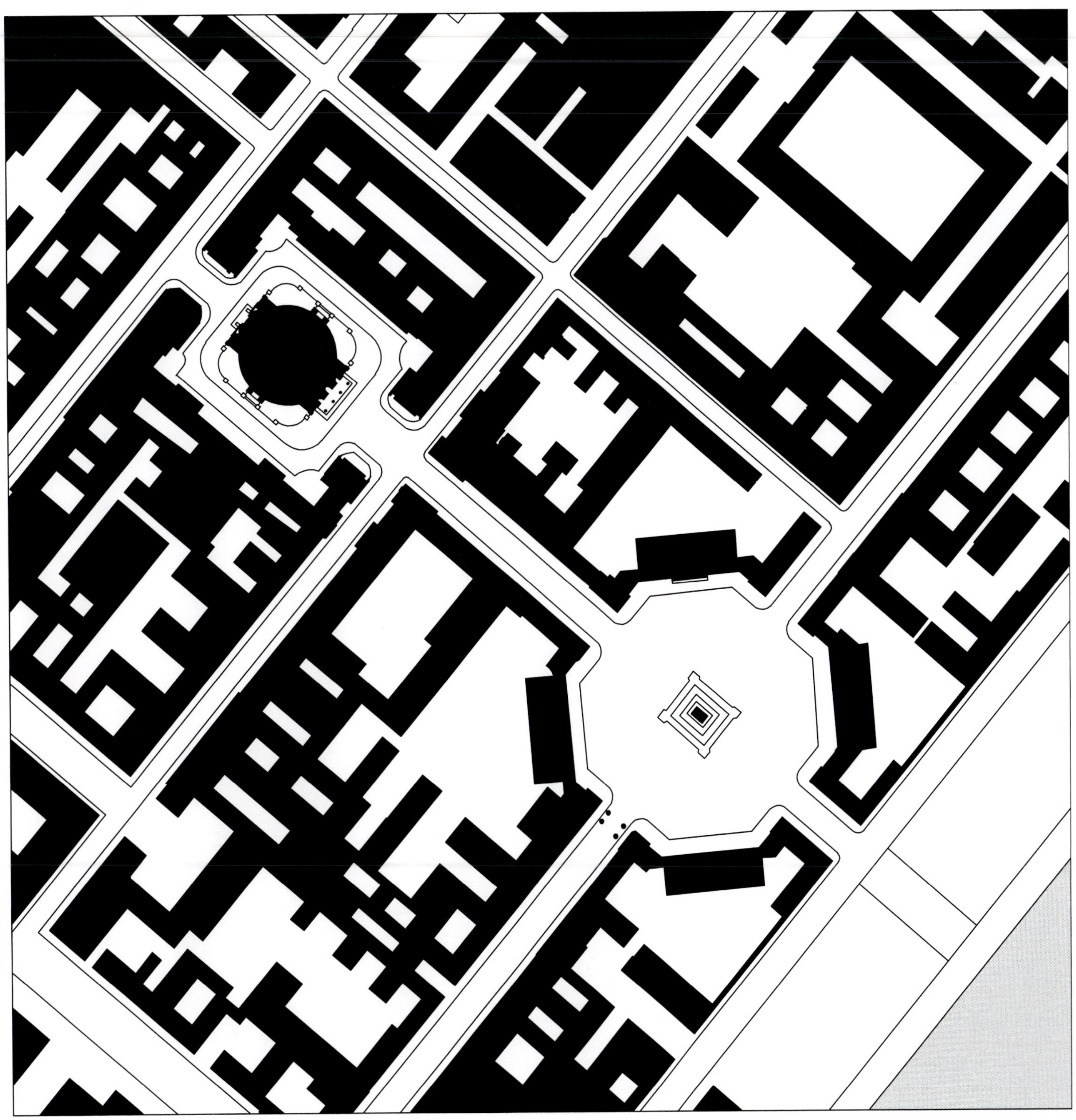

Amalienborg Slotsplads

Cuzco

27

Plaza de Armas

Cuzco, derived from the Quecha word *qosqo* or earth's navel, is the oldest continuously inhabited city in South America. It was founded in the fifteenth century as the political, administrative and religious center of the Incan empire that extended nearly 4000 kilometers along the Pacific coast. Set within the Andes mountains, 3400 meters above sea level at the confluence of the Tullumayo and Huatanay rivers, the city was probably the largest city in the Americas when the Europeans arrived in the sixteenth century (Beltrán 1970: 3–11). The center of the city was originally Hawkayapata Square, which may have been four times as large as the present day Plaza de Armas.

Beyond size the city's original plan more than likely used symbols in its design. As architect Jeanne-Pierre Protzen and anthropologist John Howland Rowe show, the city's original plan conforms to that of a puma in profile with the orthogonal grid adjusted to the contours. Additionally, the city and its monuments were organized on radial lines called *zeq'e*. These *ley lines* organized the location of sacred monuments and, more importantly, as Protzen and Rowe (1994: 238) note, "played an important role in how the city's residents perceived and understood [the city's] spatial organization and influenced the way they oriented themselves in it."

The layout and use of the immense Hawkayapata Square remains indeterminable due to devastation related to the Spanish invasion and subsequent transformations in the late sixteenth and early seventeenth centuries. What is known, however, has been pieced from Spanish accounts by historians such as Protzen and Rowe. From these accounts, it is estimated that the space was approximately two hundred meters square and likely corresponded to the city's overall political and physical magnitude. The square seems to have been subdivided into a section for religious ceremonies and another for military exercises.

Unfortunately, the Incan city lasted as the center of the Incan empire for just over one hundred years. In 1535, Francisco Pizarro and his troops arrived in Cuzco and, not long after, destroyed much of the urban pattern as they rebuilt the town based on Spanish colonial conventions. Despite the near obliteration, many of the Incan masonry stone walls remain and give a good indication of Cuzco's Incan design. Two imposing Baroque churches dominate today's Plaza de Armas: the cathedral finished in 1654, and La Compañia, former church of the seminary, now a parish church. The square remains an open center of the city and the narrow streets that lead to it are shaded. The transition from these streets to the square is a feeling of compression and release. Though it is a pedestrian gathering place, it is still partially used for vehicular traffic. The surrounding buildings, with arcades along the ground floor, are geared to tourism and much of the residential area is in the surrounding neighborhoods.

Looking southeast across Plaza de Armas

View from the side street leading into the square

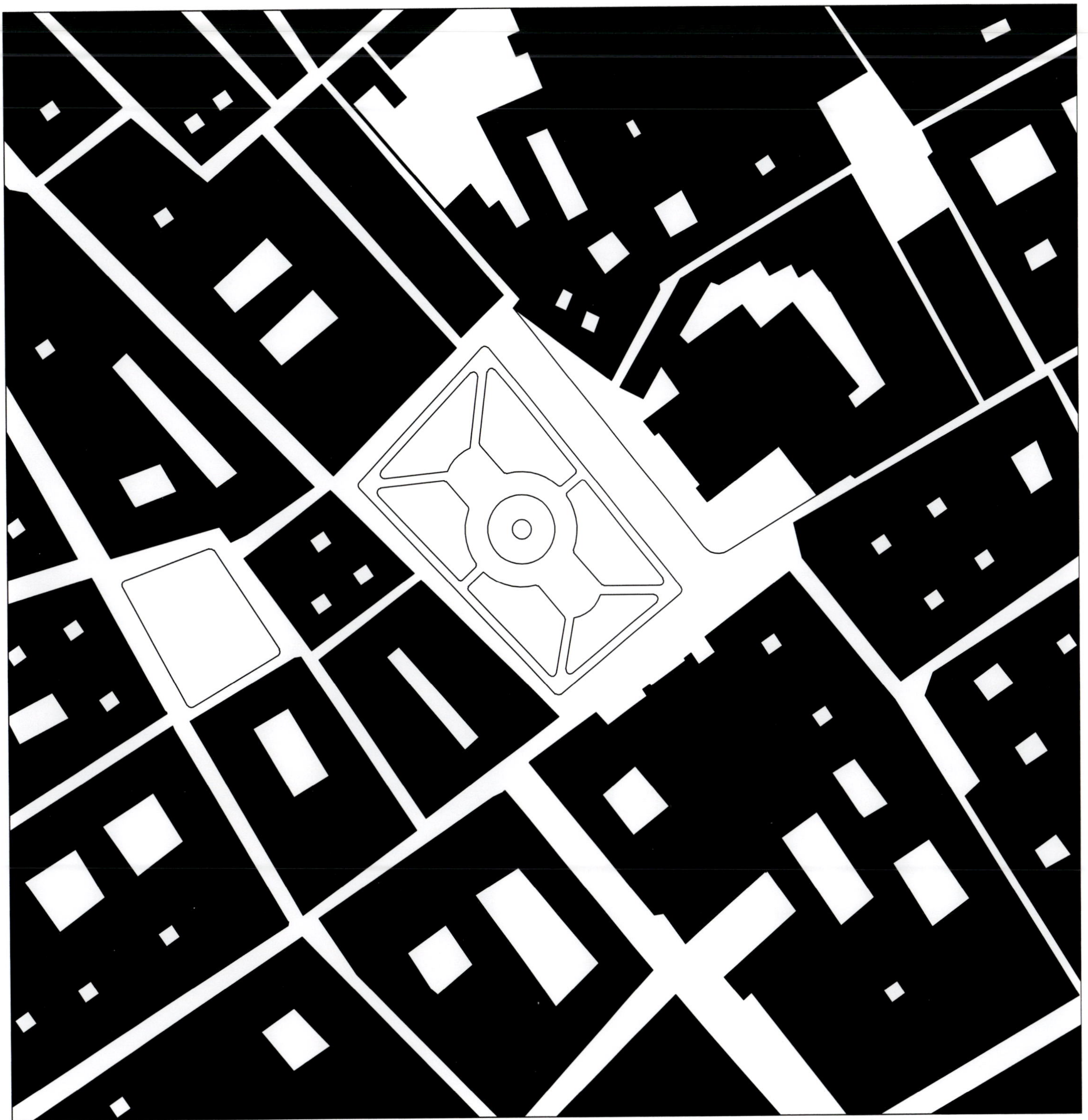

Plaza de Armas

Denver

28

Civic Center

Denver's Civic Center is an example of early twentieth-century urban space embodying the concepts of the City Beautiful Movement. Set along the axis of the State Capitol building and the City and County Building and surrounded by civic, cultural and commercial buildings, it represents Denver's transformation from boomtown to state capital.

Following the 1850s gold rush, Denver grew rapidly into a large metropolis at the foot of the Rocky Mountains. With its increased population, Colorado achieved statehood in 1876; five years later Denver was chosen as its capital and a new capitol building was started in 1883. Unfortunately, the city's gold-rush-origin uniform grid plan had little public space or amenities to match its new role in the state.

Inspired by the 1893 World's Columbian Exposition in Chicago, then Mayor Robert Speer proposed a grand public mall to front the new State Capitol building, as well as a new city hall and other public buildings. Beyond beautification, Speer hoped to bring some grace to the city, amalgamate city and state government agencies and, through the green spaces, contribute to the health and well-being of its citizens (Leonard and Noel 1990: 146–149). Several designers were involved including Arnold W. Brunner and Frederick Olmstead Jr.; however, Edward H. Bennett was responsible for the project that is seen today.

The Civic Center is bounded by the State Capitol to the east, completed in 1908, and the City and County Building to the west, completed in 1932. The central green space is bounded by smaller neo-classical pavilions. To the north is the colonnaded Voorhies Memorial Gateway and to the south is the outdoor Greek Theater. By World War II, the Civic Center and Park were essentially complete and remained relatively unchanged into the late twentieth century (Denver Foundation for Architecture 2001: 99–117). Beginning in the 1980s, however, there was a move to revitalize the space. To the south is the renovated Denver Central Library designed by Michael Graves and, to the library's west, the Denver Art Museum with a new wing designed by Daniel Libeskind.

Denver's Civic Center reveals a direct influence of not only the World's Columbian Exposition but also the City Beautiful Movement that later helped shape American civic space well into the late twentieth century. Led by architects Daniel Burnham and George McKim, this movement sought to improve America's cities through monumental civic spaces surrounded by classical architecture. The spaces and architecture springing from this movement, like those in Cleveland and Washington, DC, were grand, eloquent and especially needed in many American cities, such as Chicago, that were founded and developed for commerce rather than civic beauty. Ultimately, however, the City Beautiful Movement's formal and often immense urban spaces often resulted in alienating spaces and somewhat academic exercises that did not fully account for the day-to-day life or the future of the city. Denver's Civic Center remained somewhat governmental; however, recent developments in nearby neighborhoods that include housing promise to help invigorate the downtown.

View from the east

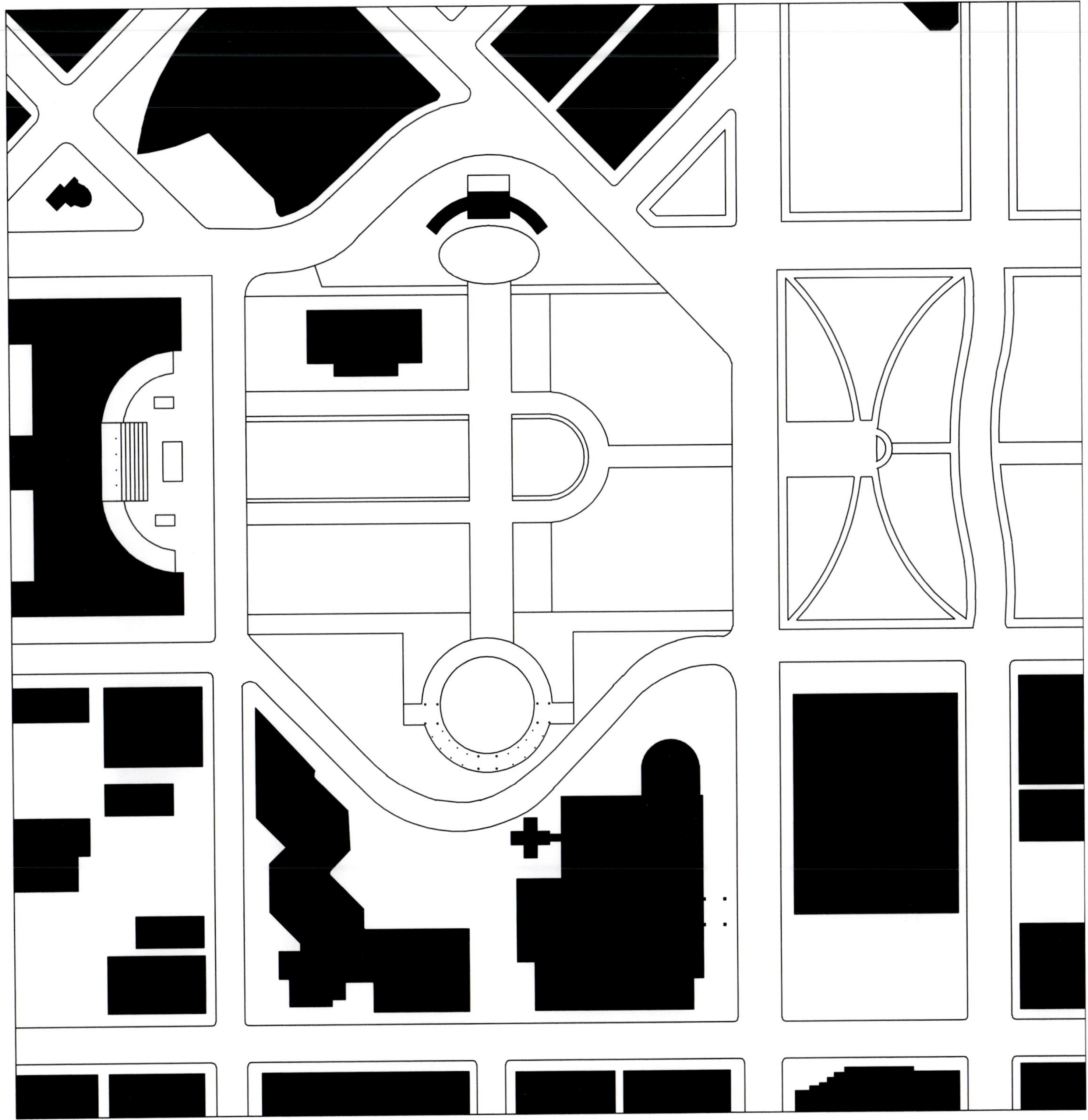

Civic Center

Detroit

Campus Martius

29

Since 1788, Campus Martius has served as a public space for the citizens of Detroit. Though it and its surroundings have undergone significant changes through the nineteenth and twentieth centuries, it has remained a symbolic center of the city, which should continue to be a spark for the city's redevelopment into the twenty-first century. Detroit, like other industrial cities such as Gary, Indiana and Toledo, Ohio, has suffered greatly since the mid-1950s with increased suburban flight; this led to the inner city's abandonment as the city lost nearly 40 percent of its population in as many years. Since the mid-1980s, much of the original manufacturing base has greatly diminished or departed. Likewise, neglect or ill-advised revitalization destroyed much of Detroit's parks and avenues. Fortunately, like other cities, Detroit has experienced a rejuvenation as cities, in general, have once again become popular places to live and work.

Founded by Antoine de la Mothe Cadillac, Detroit began as a French outpost in 1701. In 1805, it became the capital of the then frontier Michigan territory administered by Governor William Hull and three judges, Frederick Bates, John Griffin and Agustus Brevoort Woodward. It is Woodward who would make the most significant mark on Detroit. His arrival in Detroit nearly coincided with the fiery destruction of Detroit in early June 1805 and, not long after arriving, he was appointed superintendent of the city's redesign. A friend of Thomas Jefferson and perhaps even Washington's designer Pierre L'Enfant, Woodward was knowledgeable of Washington's plan. As John Reps notes, "among his possessions when he came to Detroit was a small notebook in which were pasted sections of a Washington map" (Reps 1965: 264). Unlike Washington, DC's plan that combined only a select number of radial streets superimposed with a grid street field, Woodward's plan, devised by surveyor Abijah Hull, inverted this hierarchy so that the plan was an extensive web of radiating avenues meeting at over two dozen primary and secondary nodes with only a limited number of orthogonal streets (Reps 1965: 264–266).

Detroit's downtown plan is a partial and restrained version of that plan with one primary node, the Grand Circus, to the north from which several radiating streets extended south toward the Detroit river. Nearly mid-way from the Grand Circus to the river is the Campus Martius and the "Point of Origin" for Woodward's plan. Originally a militia training ground, the Campus Martius is at the intersection of six streets; the northwest–southeast street is Michigan Avenue that becomes Cadillac Square on the Campus Martius' southeast side. To the north is Woodward Avenue that leads to the Grand Circus while to the south it extends to the waterfront.

View of Campus Martius as proposed

View of Campus Martius from the south

In 1997, then Mayor Dennis Archer and the Greater Downtown Partnership envisioned a new Campus Martius Park as a centerpiece to Detroit's downtown redevelopment. This vision was adopted by Detroit 300, a private organization, that hoped to revitalize the square to coincide with the city's Tri-Centennial. In 2003, the city approved the design of Rundell Ernstberger Associates which was completed in late 2004. The one and a half acre park is, like Washington, DC's Dupont Circle, at the center of a traffic circle yet is successful due to the greater urban context and its relatively straightforward design. Campus Martius' two lawns, fountain, café, and the Michigan Soldiers' and Sailors' Monument do not overburden the park. Since its opening, the park has become the focus of Detroit's revitalized downtown, hosting concerts, movies and ice-skating and the city's Christmas tree in the winter.

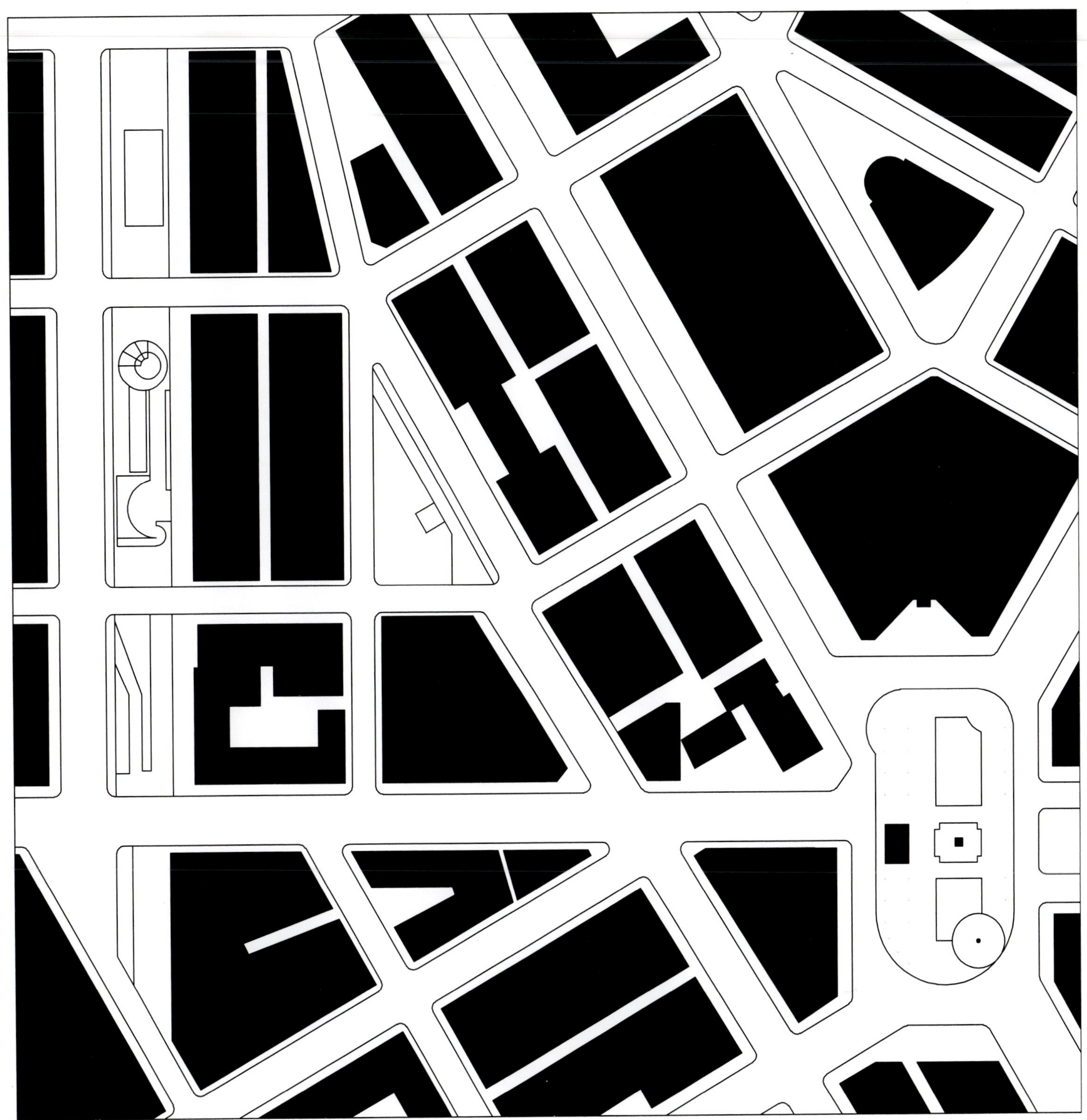

Campus Martius

Dresden

Zwinger and Theaterplatz

30

Considered one of the finest late Baroque spaces in Germany, the Zwinger and Theaterplatz are part of Dresden's series of composed spaces that are really less of an urban fabric but more of a landscape of theatrical space and buildings. Located on the south side of the Elbe river, the first half of this ensemble is the enclosed Zwinger initiated by architect Matthäus Daniel Pöppelmann and built between 1711 and 1722. The second half is the Theaterplatz, which is predominantly the work of Gottfried Semper, who was commissioned to complete the palace grounds in the early nineteenth century (Rothstein 1967: 160–163). The southeastern edge of this platz is the Catholic Church and the Schloss. Though designed as a private royal retreat, by the late nineteenth century it became an important component of Dresden's civic life.

The Zwinger was built near the existing palace's fortifications and takes its name from the German word *bezwingen*, meaning the area of the defeated or conquered. The moat of these original fortifications forms its southern boundary. The complex was intended to be primarily a kind of enclosed garden for royal festivities, tournaments and performances. As such, its boundary is appropriately ornate, gaudy and attenuated with its primary role of defining the inner garden. Flanking the Zwinger's square garden are two apsoidal spaces with light, two-story pavilions at their apex.

Originally, Pöppelmann's design extended the Zwinger courtyard to the river's edge. Semper initially attempted to perpetuate this idea by creating two galleries on either side of the axis toward the river with the northern gallery intersecting a new opera house (Zucker 1966: 220–221). Unfortunately, this concept was never implemented. Only Semper's opera house, whose form is derived more from internal functional organization than conforming to external civic space, was constructed as planned. Instead, Semper enclosed the Zwinger courtyard with a new painting gallery creating a strong façade for the Theaterplatz but disconnecting the Zwinger's garden from the river.

To the northeast is the Elbe river lined with the "Italian Village" that takes its name from the Italian craftsmen whose houses were once at that location. The river continues to play an interesting part in Dresden. Unlike most European cities such as Rome, London or Paris, Dresden never walled or channeled its river with a definitive edge. Instead, the river has a soft edge, sometimes sandy and muddy, sometimes grassy, that is used by Dresden's residents for recreation. Unlike Rome or Paris where the river is experienced only for a brief moment, the Elbe's attenuated edge plays a greater role in the urban experience.

Exhibiting the transition from space-dominated to building-dominated urban design, the Zwinger and Theaterplatz reveal the inverse of Semper's proto-functionalist architecture. Like his refinement of architectural language, Semper sought to form architecture based on the expression of the building's interior functions. Rather than mediating, even deferring the building's external form to the public space, the building expressed its internal functions primarily. As such, the buildings themselves become primary in urban space and become more objects in a field. Of course, other buildings foreshadowed this trend, but Semper's employed the functionalist argument to make an object in the space. Like modernist buildings in the twentieth century, Semper's theater takes a more dominant individual role in occupying the space rather than shaping it.

View of the Zwinger courtyard

View of the Zwinger entry pavilions

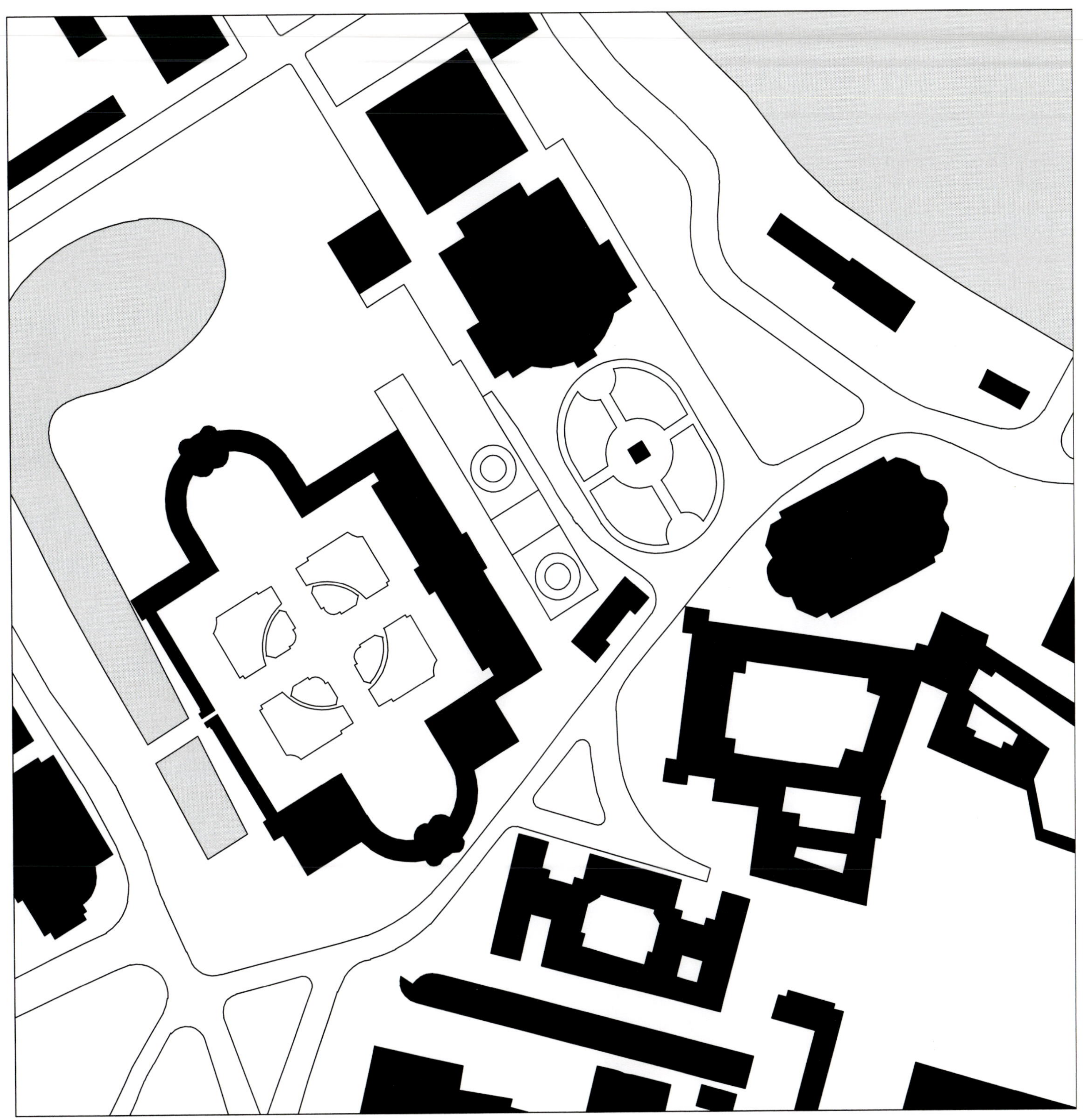

Zwinger and Theaterplatz

Dublin

31

Temple Bar

Temple Bar is a vibrant district between the River Liffey, to the north, and Dame Street, to the south. Its western edge is Parliament Street and the Bank of Ireland and Trinity College, with its expansive Parliament Square, to the east. The area takes its name from William Temple, a former provost of Trinity College, whose estate and that of other landowners including the Cramptons, Eustaces and Fownes helped form the entire district. The streets, which often kept the names of the original gentry, were laid out in the seventeenth century, often following the estates' garden designs. From the eighteenth century and into the twentieth, the area combined residences and handicrafts such as printing, bookbinding and gilding, and was also home to several theaters, meeting houses and warehouses (Lincoln 1992: 143).

By the 1970s, however, the area and its buildings had fallen into disrepair, were partially abandoned and were set for a comprehensive urban deletion. Fortunately, the area managed to survive due in part to a planned, yet delayed, bus terminal in the 1980s. The former state transportation company, Coras Iompair Eireann (CIE), purchased most of the land in Temple Bar in the hope of developing extensive transportation hubs in central Dublin. While the CIE planned the terminal and worked toward its implementation, it rented the dilapidated buildings at substantially discounted rates to artists, craftsmen and other bohemian and fringe groups. Locally owned pubs and restaurants quickly followed, which increased interest among architects and preservationists who sought to delay or derail CIE's terminal plans. Between the delay, economic difficulties and new street life, the area was quickly rejuvenated within a few years (Pearson 2000: 35–39).

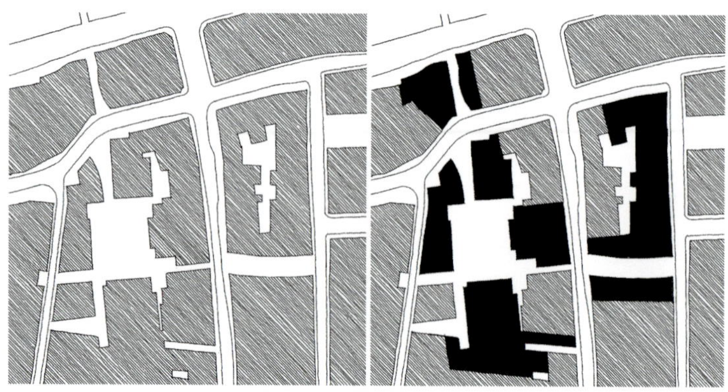

The composite buildings that deform to make civic space

Curved Street

Market Square

Today, the area is a vibrant tourist area and has suffered, to some degree, from too much rejuvenation. As its popularity rose, so too did the property values and rents. This has driven much of the fringe to other parts of the city. Moreover, some of the historic buildings that many had hoped to save have been eviscerated during well-meaning renovations. Overall, however, Temple Bar is an excellent example of how cities can be formed without reverting to neo-traditional garb. The transformations here weave sensitive yet distinct modern mixed-use buildings woven into the urban fabric. These include Meeting House Square and Temple Bar Square, designed by firms such as Group 91 Architects and James Kelly architects, which are intimate rooms defined within the district (O'Regan and Dearey 1997: 59–61).

Temple Bar exemplifies the unapologetically modern architecture appearing since the early 1990s that not only fits into the scale of the city but also contributes to the urban fabric. Some of the buildings are, as Colin Rowe and Fred Koetter describe in their book *Collage City*, "ambiguous and composite buildings" that take on mutated shapes by "engaging circumstance and rising above it" (Rowe and Koetter 1978: 168). The architecture and urban fabric of Dublin's Temple Bar is a synchronicity of architecture and urban fabric that is respectful without reverting to nostalgic architectural language. Unlike the majority of work generated in the guise of New Urbanism, the work of Dublin's contemporary architects is of our time without being historically derivative and thus serves as a model for building cities in the twenty-first century.

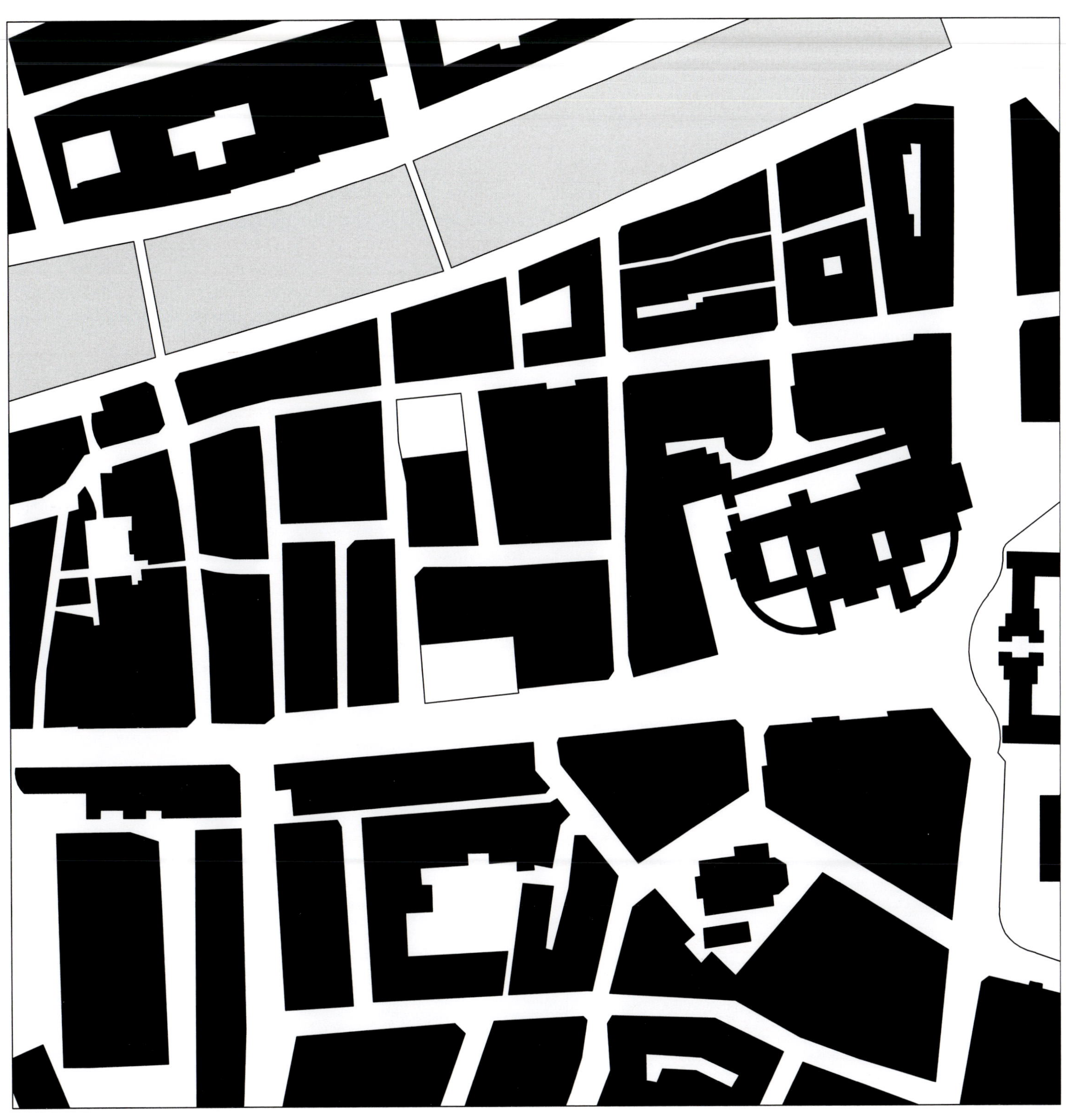

Temple Bar

Dubrovnik

Placa

32

A quick glance at Dubrovnik's plan reveals that the town has no singular square. What is noticeable is the slender east–west street known as the Placa that connects the western entry of the city to the harbor at the eastern side. Though a street and not what might be considered a square in the traditional sense, nevertheless it functions as the town's square for shopping, socializing and civic events.

Dubrovnik was a Dalmatian Coast trading center that began in the sixth century as a new settlement called Laus and later Ragusa on a small rocky island parallel to the east–west shoreline. The separating channel was filled in the twelfth century to form what is essentially the configuration seen today. The near untainted condition is owed in part to the fortifications started at the same time, beyond which are more contemporary residential neighborhoods.

The Placa marks the joint between the island and the shoreline. The reclaimed area is noticeable as the more regularized north-south streets run perpendicular to the Placa. Where the regularity ends on the southern half of the city demarcates the extent of the reclaimed land (Rothstein 1967: 56). The Placa also marks a significant change in the terrain of the city. While the southern half maintains a somewhat regular terrain consistent with a former rocky island – a slight rise then a slight fall to the south – the northern half is steeply sloped upward toward the northern walls of the city. The perpendicular streets that lead from the Placa north are stepped pathways with a grade change of approximately thirty meters. These narrow north-south streets across the contours offer a very different spatial experience than the east–west along the contours. As such they are appropriately sized. Stepped streets are more numerous and narrow to allow multiple access between the Placa and neighborhoods. The east–west streets that parallel the Placa are less numerous, yet wider for more commercial traffic.

This Placa itself remains the predominant space in that, like many squares and plazas, its success is rooted more in the urban, historical, cultural and social context rather than codified rules. The Placa is the main byway visually and spatially connects the city's western entrance to the harbor on the east. It is at the eastern edge and near the harbor as well as both the religious and governmental center of the town. The Placa is anchored at both ends by towers. These landmarks, one at the western gate of the city and the other at the eastern harbor gate, clearly demarcate the extent of the city and provide what urban theorist Kevin Lynch describes in *The Image of the City* (1960), as a sense of knowing where you are in the scheme of things. Accompanying the two towers at each end of the Placa are two small squares that act as forecourts to the spatial sequence through the Placa. From the western side, the promenade begins from the small space in front of a Franciscan monastery but is slightly compressed in the gap between the buildings. Then the Placa slowly widens toward the east and culminates at the town hall and Cathedral Square. The path, however, is compressed again through the eastern gate then reopens into the harbor basin.

The city plan is clear and straightforward, yet subtle in its spatial hierarchy. Like any subtlety, they become clear when they are removed. For example, by eliminating the slight angle of the Placa and transforming into a straight street, the Placa becomes a less dynamic sequence. The sequence along the Placa would probably be less spatially interesting as the tension created from the diverging walls is eliminated. This lesson is especially important in urban design that moves toward regularity but misses the opportunities for nuance.

View of the Placa from the west

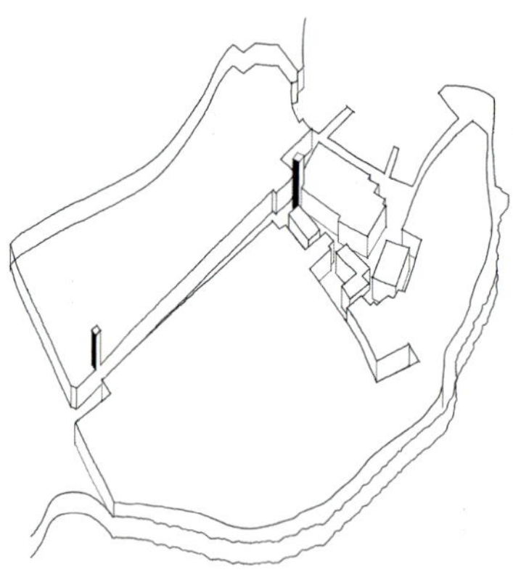

The landmarks that mark the Placa's ends

Placa

Edinburgh

St Andrew Square

33

The area surrounding St Andrew Square is part of James Craig's design for the eighteenth century development of Edinburgh. Considered the apex of Georgian urban design, the plan is both straightforward and subtle, earning the praises of many, including historian A.J. Youngson in *The Making of Classical Edinburgh* as an "entirely sensible, and almost painfully orthodox" plan (Youngson 1966: 71). Craig's winning entry in a 1766 design competition sponsored by the Edinburgh City Council, the "New Town," as it is called, was part of the city's growth north of the medieval city center.

The plan consists of three sets of primary, secondary and tertiary orthogonal streets. The primary set is three east–west streets: George Street, in the center, and Princes Street and Queen Street along the south and north respectively. Terminating each end of George Street are St Andrew Square to the east, shown in this plan, and Charlotte Square to the west. Seven north–south secondary streets divide the development into eight segments. Paralleling the primary streets are two tertiary inner-block streets that further divide the blocks into mews.

While the three main streets appear similar, they are quite different due to topography, orientation and connection to an amenity. The topography of the area upon which the New Town was built is a long, east–west ridge of a hill. Craig placed George Street along this ridge from which the topography slopes down to the North Loch and to a new park to the north. Princes Street and Queen Street are one-sided streets so that one side of the street is built up while the other side is park which slopes away from the street.

The New Town, like its contemporary Georgian urban design in Bath, is a taut spatial composition. In both cities, the designers used topography, hierarchy and the idea of spatial sequence to guide the design. More than a formal, planar organization, topography participates in the plan function and nuance. Unfortunately, after Edinburgh, Georgian planning became increasingly formalized, with sequence or topography taking a less important role. Developments north of Craig's New Town illustrate what Paul Zucker describes as design dependent on form without incorporating hierarchy, spatial sequence or topography (Zucker 1966: 205–206).

Edinburgh is an example of clear organization that overcomes its monotonous potential by differentiated street types and edges to create a complex urban plan. This design approach, sans squares, is most notably used in American urban development in the nineteenth and early twentieth centuries. For example, in the late nineteenth and early twentieth centuries, developers in Baltimore, Maryland used a similar hierarchical street system to supply a range of housing types corresponding to varied income levels. These developers saw the potential of offering multiple sizes and prices mixed within the same development. Primary streets were lined with larger, more expensive houses or used for commercial development, secondary streets were for medium priced homes and tertiary streets were allocated for low-income housing. This type of integrated mixed income development was nearly lost in the twentieth century but has re-emerged in late twentieth century urban redevelopment.

View north along George Street to St Andrew Square

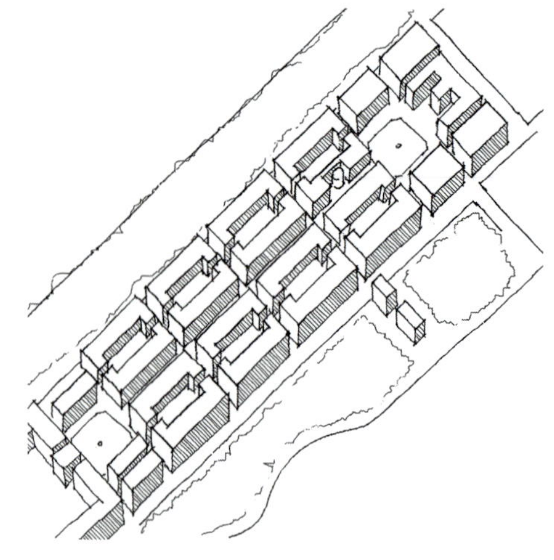

Craig's New Town and relation to the landscape edges

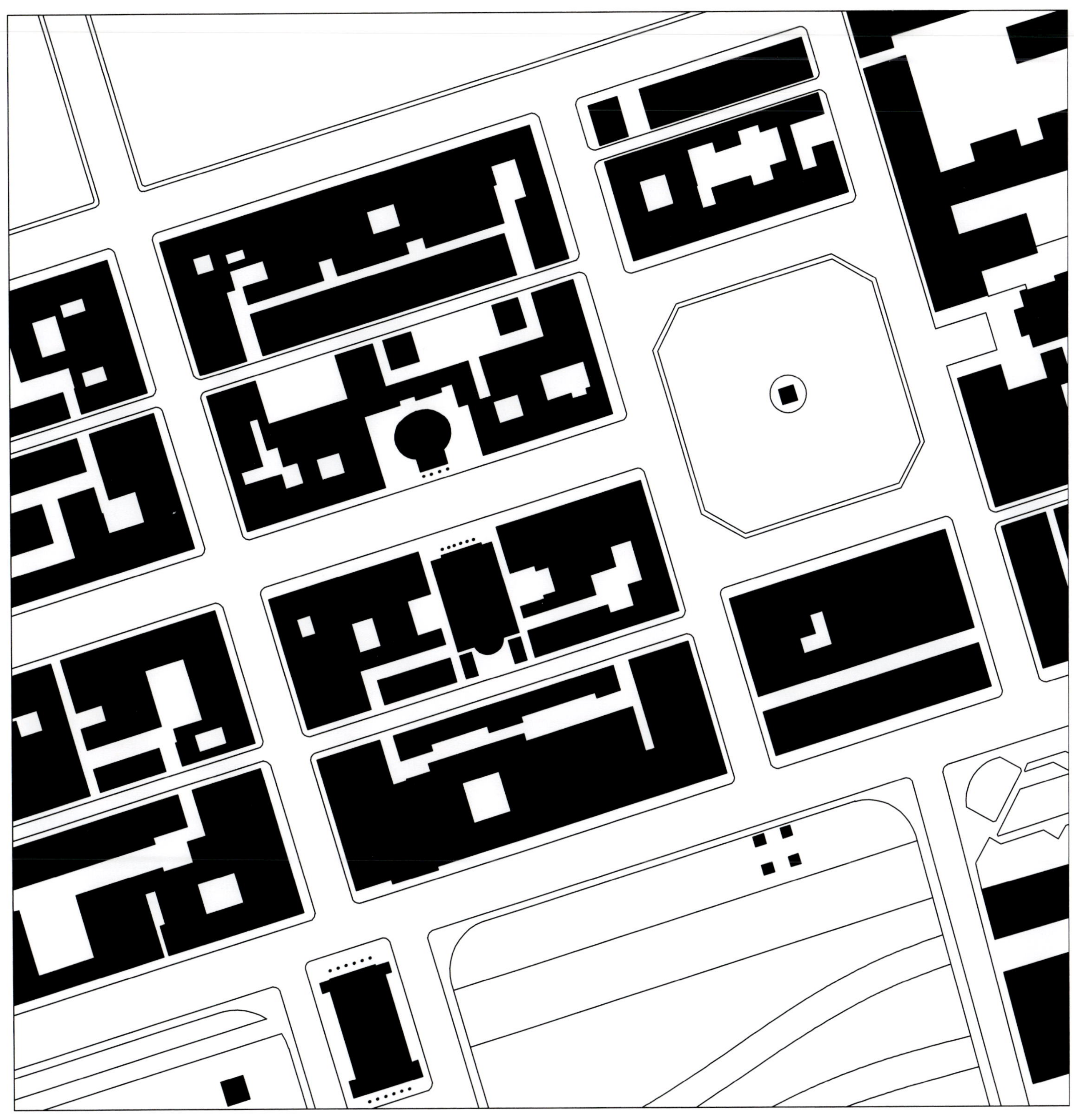

St Andrew Square

Florence

34

Piazza della Signoria and Palazzo Uffizi

The carefully choreographed urban sequence of Piazza della Signoria and Palazzo Uffizi takes urban design out of purely compositional terms and produces a spatial, three-dimensional and topographical assemblage. Formed predominately by background residential buildings, the Piazza della Signoria is dominated by the medieval Palazzo Vecchio (1288–1314), the Loggia dei Lanzi (1376) and, leading toward the Arno river, the Palazzo Uffizi Gallery (Giorgio Vasari, 1560–1574). The Piazza della Signoria itself could be seen as quadrilateral in plan with the Palazzo Vecchio superimposed to create essentially two squares. The resultant smaller square is further defined by the placement of a line of statuary that includes the equestrian statue of *Cosimo I* (Giovanni da Bologna), *Hercules and Cacus* (Baccio Badinelli), *Judith* (Donatello) and Bartolomeo Ammanati's *Neptune Fountain* and, finally, Michelangelo's *David*.

The monuments contribute to a deliberate spatial sequence that, as Edmond Bacon observes, "visually interrelates the ancient monuments, the Palazzo Vecchio, the dome of the cathedral, and the sculpture in the Piazza della Signoria, and fuses the perpendicular movement from the square onto the movement course of the Arno" (Bacon 1967: 85). The piazza, the buildings and its contents are part of a choreographed sequence from central Florence and the city's Duomo to the Arno river, on to the Ponte Vecchio and, ultimately, to the Borgesse palace on the river's south side.

The orchestrated steps are only slowly unveiled as each element along the path delineates the next stage and reorients the pedestrian. A common path through the space is from the Piazza del Duomo in the center of Florence south to the river. From the Duomo, movement is along a relatively straight street with only glimpses of an open area ahead with no view into the square's center. Rather, the view and entry are at the corners and, once inside, views are diagonal across the space. This lateral entry and view is part of what nineteenth century urban theorist Camillo Sitte codified in *On the Art of Building Cities*. Sitte notes that successful urban spaces allow for enclosure and passage without the sense of rigid confinement. There is no sense of formal movement but of a natural flow (Sitte 1945: 22–23). As individual elements in the deliberate composition, they act as a screen to help direct the eye and the path toward the Palazzo Uffizi Gallery.

Palazzo Uffizi from the south

The role of sculptural elements both in articulating and guiding movement through the square

While in the Piazza della Signoria, the Uffizi's role as a colonnaded street, however, remains unclear until the last moment. It is only after nearing Michelangelo's *David* that the arched passageway at its end frames the Arno river. Like the façade unifying the Piazza San Marco in Venice, the Uffizi façade acts as a unifying mask over irregular buildings behind. Similar choreographed spaces include John Wood Sr. and Jr.'s Bath, Nancy and, in some way, from Boston's City Hall, through Quincy Market to the waterfront.

The use of sculptural elements to guide the eye and path toward the Palazzo Uffizi

Piazza della Signoria and Palazzo Uffizi

Genoa

Piazza de Ferrari

35

Architect Eliel Saarinen writes in *The City: Its Growth, its Decay, its Future* that a "city is an open book in which to read aims and ambitions" (Saarinen 1965: ix). Italian, French, Japanese, American and other cities reveal the underlying framework of the respective social, cultural and political systems. The unique qualities that differentiate squares and housing types in Paris, London, Tokyo or Tunis indicate the underlying philosophies of each city.

While compiling this book, students and colleagues asked a frequent and legitimate question: "Why are there so many Italian cities and spaces?" A primary reason for their preponderance is a distinctly Italian cultural, social and political identity linked inextricably to urban form. As Erwin Gutkind notes, the city and the square played, and in many ways continue to play, an important role in Italy more so than in other cultures due to the long tradition of linking the literal definition of a city to an elevated social and legal status (Gutkind 1969: 261–262).

Gutkind observes that

> Genoa is an instructive example of the distinguishing social factors which were instrumental in the formation of urban communities in Italy in contrast to the countries north of the Alps. The city was respected as a space *sui generis* by the invaders, as a walled-in "container" with a special legal status superior to that of the countryside. The walls were the material and ideal symbol of civitas. It was, therefore, more than a mere expediency if a conqueror destroyed the walls of a city that had opposed him; it was a deliberate and official act of degradation, a meaningful humiliation by reducing the city to the status of a vicus, that it should be called a village.
>
> (Gutkind 1969: 261)

View of Piazza de Ferrari

With this status, Genoa's residents were ensured special legitimacy and rights. Correspondingly for anyone to assume responsibilities or rights, such as political leadership, economic leadership or other agreements, required residence in the city. This tradition of residence within a jurisdiction remains strong especially in politics but even unelected public officials or licensed professionals are often required to reside in the district.

Italian piazzas continue to be a part of Italian society and culture; however, like many important squares throughout the world, they are increasingly dominated and shaped by non-Italian tourists and by the tourism industry. As a result, these squares are not really "Italian" as much as they are idealized and romantic Italian piazzas. The original culture that shaped the square has been appropriated by new uses and new meanings. Examining and referring to specific spaces, especially those on tourists' agenda, as endemic to a particular culture may not be entirely accurate. More than likely they represent a past culture while the current culture uses other, possibly newer spaces or, due to technology, may not use a public space at all.

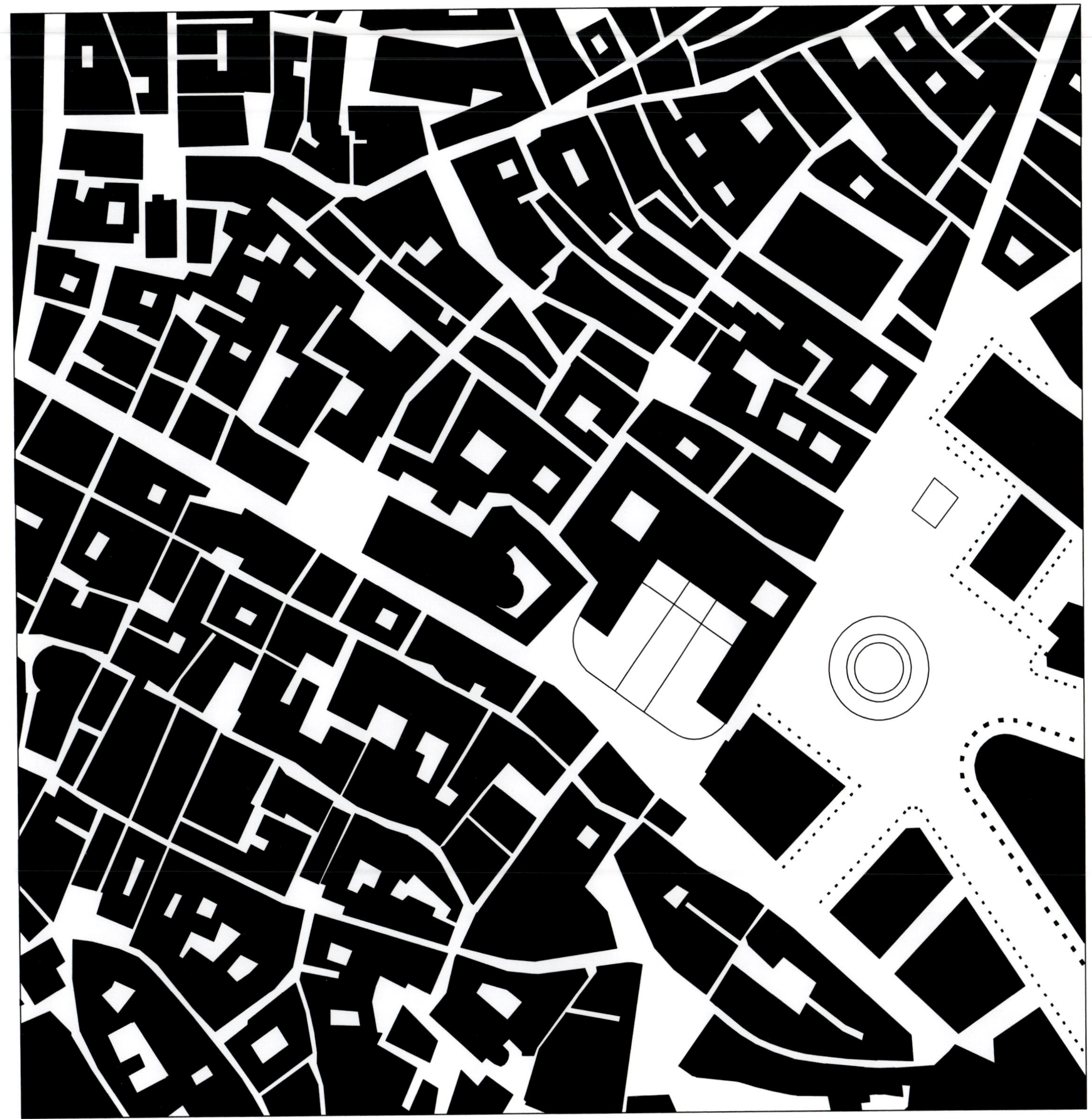

Piazza de Ferrari

Indianapolis

36

Monument Circle

Laid out in 1821 by surveyor Alexander Ralston with Elias Fordham, the new state capitol of the State of Indiana owes its plan, like Cleveland and Detroit, to the cities on the east coast. In this case, Ralston, who had served under Pierre L'Enfant in the survey of Washington, DC in 1791, takes much of its form from the nation's capital (Leary 1971: 12).

The main feature of the plan is a center circle with four radiating streets superimposed on a one-mile square street grid. Near the end of three of these diagonal streets were smaller squares reserved for churches. The center circle was originally set aside for the state governor's house with the surrounding area designated as Governor's Square. Though a house was built, it was never used as a governor's mansion and was ultimately razed in the mid-nineteenth century. Into the late nineteenth century the circle was known as Circle Park, but in 1902, the city unveiled the 300-foot tall Soldiers' and Sailors' Monument and renamed it Monument Circle (Reps 1965: 272).

A superimposed grid and radial system like Indianapolis would usually result in awkward building lots and urban spaces and streets. This was avoided in Indianapolis to some extent because, as historian John Reps notes, "Ralston had the good sense not to bring the diagonals together at the center but to terminate them some distance apart" (Reps 1965: 272). This "good sense" allowed the circle to have only four streets, the east–west Market Street and the north–south Meridian Street, rather than eight streets focused on the square. This allowed more building mass to form the square's walls and to give the circle a stronger sense of enclosure. Today, office buildings with retail at their base, a theater and the Christ Church Cathedral surround the circle (Davidson-Powers 1987: 34–39).

In addition to the central square, Ralston included two open areas to the east and west of the circle. Two blocks to the west were reserved for the State House while two blocks to the east were reserved for the courthouse with each of these reserves assigned space for a public market. These areas continue in this fundamental capacity with the State House on the western axis of Market Street and the city's market and courthouse on the north and south of Market Street respectively. The most recent addition, centered on Market Street to the east, is the Market Square Arena. Several blocks to the north forming the east side of Meridian Street is the University Plaza and the expansive, four-block-long Memorial Plaza dominated by the Indiana War Memorial.

View of Monument Circle from above

View from inside Monument Circle

Like other American cities, Indianapolis suffered from gradual loss of its economic manufacturing base and suburban flight between World War II and by the 1970s; it was known as, among other things, "India-no-place" (Tenuth 2004: 136). In the late 1980s, however, the city changed strategy and promoted Indianapolis as a center of professional sports and life sciences. The city invested heavily in several downtown sport venues, museums, a convention center, and retail including the Circle Center mall and other commercial development. While housing and mass transportation are needed, Monument Circle continues to be a focal point of Indianapolis civic life and the center point of the city's revitalization efforts (Tenuth 2004: 148–149).

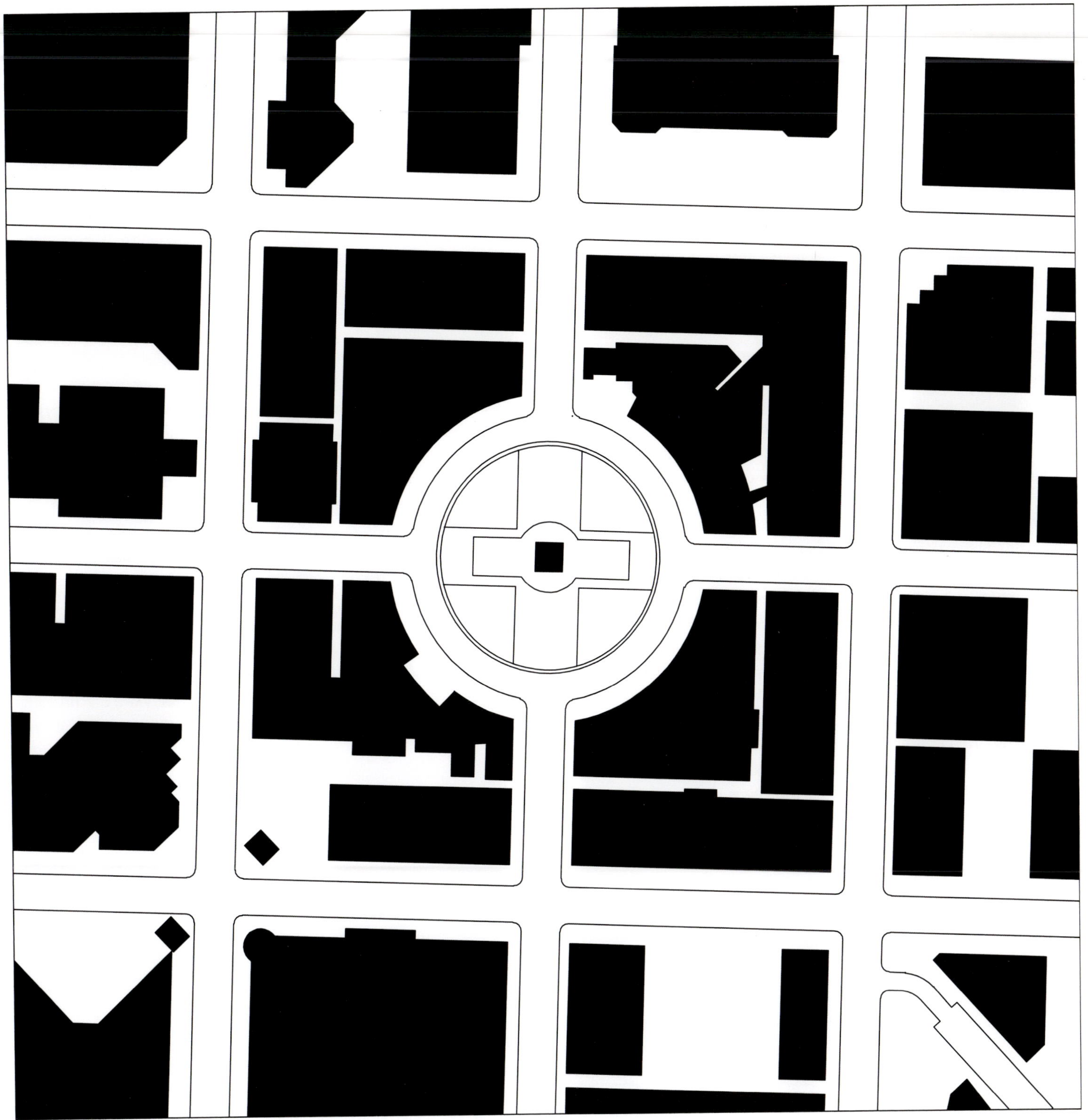

Monument Circle

Isfahan

Maidan-i-Shah

37

The Maidan-i-Shah, built by Shah Abbas I of Persia between 1599 and1627, is considered one of the most superb examples of Islamic architecture and urban design. It has attained this status because it is an overall complex that linked many functions into a unified whole and with unparalleled proportions, subdued architectural language and taut spatial composition (Herdeg 1991: 13). Though ostensibly a royal polo ground, the Maidan unified the Shah's mosques, bazaar, gardens and palace into a distinct whole. As it unified buildings and spaces, it also brought together streets and alleys leading to different parts of Isfahan. To the south is the Majid-i-Sah mosque while to the north is the bazaar through which is the street leading to Isfahan's Friday or great mosque. On the Maidan's east is the Sheik Lutfullah mosque across from which is Ali Qapu, the former pavilion that also marked the former entrance to the royal palace and gardens.

The Maidan emerged out of the Persian walled garden tradition that recalls Eden or paradise. This concept is manifested in the Maidan's most distinctive feature: a regular, two-story arcade that acts as a kind of datum or regulating screen for the mosques and markets. At one time, the second-story bays were individual viewing niches while the ground level arcade and niches, like many are today, have shops and coffeehouses (Blunt 1966: 63). This screen wall's height seems deliberate beyond its façade composition. While in the space, all but the tops of the mosques and the mountains on the horizon are seen while inside. This is probably not an accident as the top part of the arcade is actually a false wall or parapet that extends above the height of the surrounding buildings. While in the space in the midst of an urb or polis, the wall is a reminder of nature beyond.

All elements in the composition are subsidiary to the regular arcade. The mosques' entries and passage to the bazaar are subsumed into the arcade. This is usually common in arcaded Islamic courts in which the court remains primarily complete and whole. The exception and one that is unique to Isfahan is that the Ali Kapur extends above and into the Maidan.

The juxtaposition of the arcade's regular façade and the mosques beyond creates a dynamic between the pure world and the sacred world. Because the mosque's geometry shifts in accordance to their Quibla wall orientation, the mosques, most clearly represented by their domes, seem disconnected and disjointed from the Maidan – a juxtaposition that architect Klaus Herdeg compares to formal compositions in Persian art that use "an interplay between two-dimensional surface and three-dimensional mass and volume" (Herdeg 1991: 18). This interplay is heightened by asymmetrical axial organization. Though the Maidan's primary, longitudal axis is bilateral, its cross axis divides the space into two-thirds.

The hope for the Maidan is that it is brought back to its original state or at least cared for as a garden. For example, in the 1940s, a road was cut into the wall, allowing many automobiles to enter and park in the space. Like many public spaces in Europe that were car parks for many years, the Maidan could be turned into the gem that it once was.

View of Maidan-i-Shah from the south

View of the square from the north

View down the square's main axis

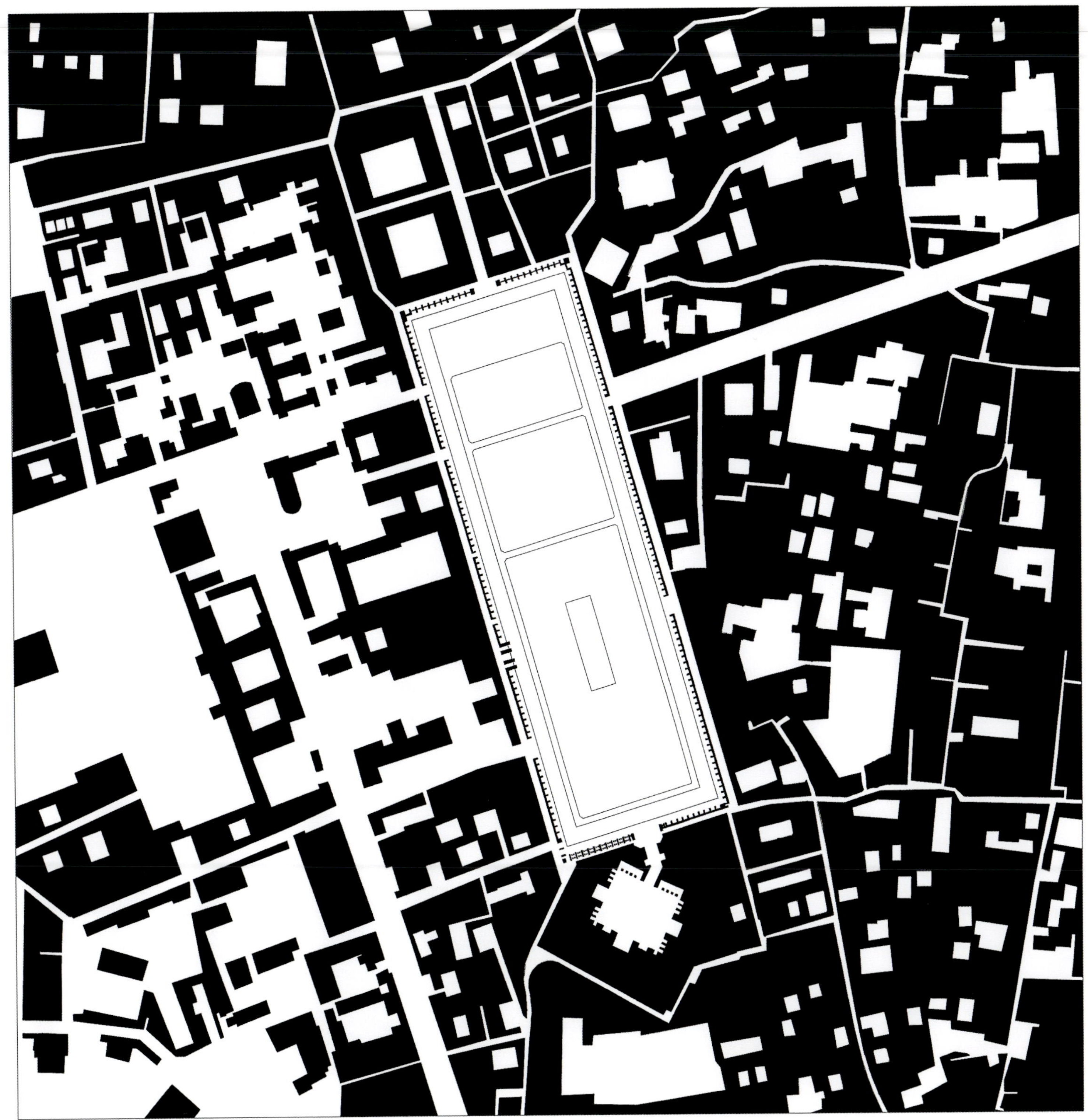

Maidan-i-Shah

Istanbul

38

Yeni Cami and Misir Çarsisi

First designed by Dalgiç Ahmet Çavus in 1603 and completed by Mustafa Aga in 1663, the Yeni Cami or New Mosque and the L-shaped Misir Çarsisi or the Spice Market and the area they define demonstrate that the success of an urban space depends largely on pedestrian movement and the mix of essential activities around it (Sumner-Boyd and Freely 1987: 21–22).

Located at the foot of the Galata Bridge that connects the Stamboul and Galata districts and alongside the Golden Horn that is lined with disembarking passenger ferries and fishmonger boats, the Yeni Cami complex is a hub of activity in Istanbul. Demarcated by a market building, the mosque and mausoleum, the interior market is predominantly spice vendors while the outdoor market hosts a range of vendors selling, among other things: vegetables, live animals and local specialties such as medicinal leeches.

This type of public outdoor space is relatively unique in Istanbul. The city does have public outdoor spaces, however, they are generally limited to mosque forecourts, enclosed bazaars and streets. There are also a number of late nineteenth century and twentieth century parks, such as those along the Bosphorus, attached to universities or gardens such as those between the Hagia Sophia and the Blue Mosque. Though unique, the mosque complex does keep in the tradition of an Islamic *külliye*, a self-sustaining, philanthropic development established and endowed with a *waqf* or bequest by a specific patron. *Külliye* generally include a mosque, school, bath, fountain, mausoleum, market and other buildings that served society's needs. The reason for these is the nature of Muslim society. Unlike the western tradition of distinct governmental, religious and economic entities with associated urban spaces, Islamic culture has little tradition of secular autonomous non-sacred systems and thus little secular squares. For the Muslim, the mosque was all things: it was the political and cultural center, law courts, market and school (Bianca 2000: 100). As such, *külliye* are districts that became nodes of urban life. Though the Yeni Cami's bath, school and other support buildings have been razed over the centuries, three of the *külliye* buildings – the market, the mausoleum and the mosque – remain standing and now define the exterior secular space.

Of note in this plan is the Golden Horn's waterfront north of the complex that has undergone extensive urban renewal since the mid-1980s. Like many urban waterfronts through the world, the water edge was cleared for road expansion. Eminönü, the district where the Galata Bridge touches the Stamboul waterfront, has been a vital and often chaotic quay for centuries and a problem of traffic control and resolution of bridge, waterfront and urban fabric for the past century. Beginning in the late 1980s, however, the quay was dramatically revitalized. Entire neighborhoods were removed for road widening and limited waterfront parks and promenades. This development, unfortunately, created a greater obstacle between downtown Istanbul and the Golden Horn as city planners created what amounts to a multi-lane highway in an attempt to ameliorate the city's growth.

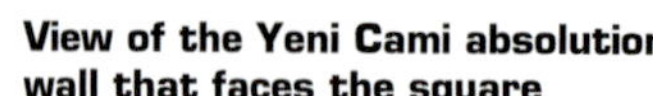

View of the Yeni Cami absolution wall that faces the square

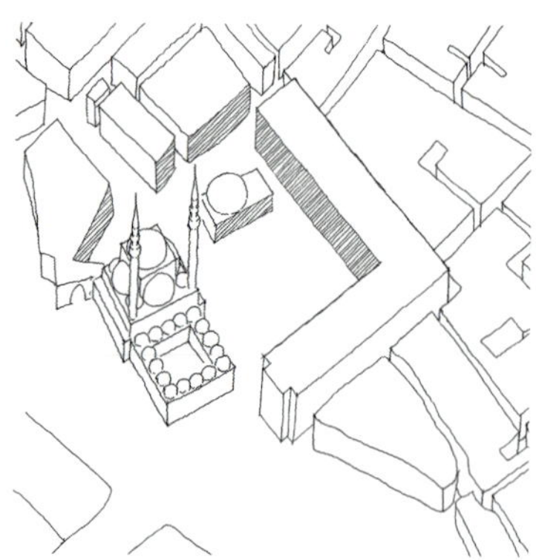

The Yeni Cami complex

View toward the gap between the Yeni Cami and the Spice Market

Yeni Cami and Misir Çarsisi

Jerusalem

39

Western Wall Plaza and the Temple Mount

The Western or Wailing Wall and Temple Mount are probably the most revered, most contested and, proportionately, the most adjacent sacred spaces in the world. Judaism and Islam and, with less zeal, Christianity hold the area as sacred so that while visiting the site, there is a strange sense of august holiness and, regrettably, underlying tension.

The Temple Mount is, fundamentally, an immense, rectilinear mass around which are the more compact quarters of old Jerusalem upon which was built the First and Second Temples of Jerusalem. The only remnant of these temples, destroyed in 586 BC and AD 70 respectively, is the massive stone foundation wall and platform upon which now sits the Dome of the Rock and Al-Aqsa mosque.

The open area in front of the Western Wall is where Jews pray or express their sorrow for the loss of the temples, hence its other name, the Wailing Wall. Until the late 1960s, this area was, like the rest of Old Jerusalem, fundamentally an Arab city with warrens of tight streets and courtyard houses. Access to the Western Wall was limited to a narrow and decrepit alley that ran along its base. Following the 1967 Arab–Israeli war and seizure of Jerusalem, the Israeli government razed the area to provide room for the expected increase of visitors to the wall by the Jewish faithful.

Unfortunately, the square is out of scale with the rest of the old city that is, in general, an overlay of Roman, early Christian and Islamic urban fabric in which one can sense the history through worn stone streets. As Michael Webb comments in his book, *The City Square*, the "area is a yawning vacancy on all but a few days of the year" (Webb 1990: 28). The experience of moving from the dark East Jerusalem into the square is a jolt. The unresolved plaza slopes like an amphitheater toward the Western Wall with the ancient stone wall as its focus. Attempts to complete and formalize the space, most notably those proposed by architect Moshe Safdie, remain undeveloped due to the reemerging controversies over possible defilement of sacred areas and the political and social tensions (Fisher et al. 1978: 106).

The Western Wall Plaza

Just above the Western Wall is the Temple Mount, the third holiest site in Islam. At the plateau's center, on a slightly raised platform, is the seventh century Dome of the Rock and, at the southern end, the Al-Aqsa Mosque. Since the plateaus are above most buildings in the Old City, these buildings are among pavilions, trees and fountains so that there is a sense of quietness and peacefulness mixed with tension.

The examination of this sacred space in Jerusalem is less an education about the shaping of a space but an understanding of the interaction of urban space, spirituality and political tension. The entire city emits an aura of overlapping civilizations but it is at the Western Wall and Temple Mount that this overlap and adjacency are manifested most clearly.

Illustrating the adjacency of the Temple Mount and Western Wall

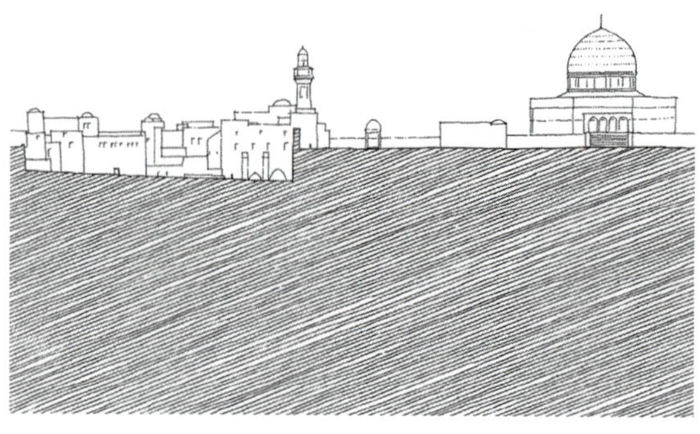

The sectional relationship between the Temple Mount and Western Wall

Western Wall Plaza and the Temple Mount

Kraków

40

Rynek Główny

Remaining relatively unchanged over the course of several centuries, Kraków, the former capital of Poland, is a planned thirteenth century colonial town that despite political and economic fluctuations has managed to maintain its historic core surrounded by parks and wide tree-lined boulevards.

Located just north of Poland's border with the Czech Republic, it was at the intersection of major trade routes across central Europe and became a major trading center and, later, a significant educational center in Poland. The city was laid out in 1257, just north of the Walwel Hill castle, in a grid plan with surrounding fortifications in accordance with the Germanic civil law of Magdeburg that governed both the structure of civic government and the town design (Dziewonski 1943: 29–30).

At its center is the Rynek Główny or Market Square that is now dominated by the Sukiennice, the arcaded medieval Cloth Hall. Remodeled in the late nineteenth century into the Palace of Commerce, the hall now sells mostly souvenirs and other trinkets. Until the nineteenth century, the square also contained the town hall and a food market. All main streets, except one, enter into and leave the main square laterally so that, like other medieval squares, traffic movement does not disrupt the activity in the space.

Kraków's urban design and its subsequent development is a distinct, three-zone pattern that emerged between the thirteenth and twentieth centuries. These zones include the inner core or old town, a green ring and, finally, an inner suburb that mixes green landscape with the urban fabric. This form owes itself to both the town's original charter and to political developments. The city's original charter granted common agricultural lands around the city just outside the fortification walls that had the effect of limiting the town's growth for several centuries.

The first major extensions of the city were in the fourteenth century when King Lasislas Lokietek and his son Casimir the Great deliberately established several small competing towns directly adjacent to Kraków's old town. These towns, initially meant to drain Kraków both economically and politically, ultimately helped make the city's development a series of small precincts around the city's center.

Beginning in 1822, the medieval fortifications were removed and replaced with a green park called the Planty. This green ring park, which remains a park today, is a buffer zone between the nearly intact medieval urban fabric and mid-nineteenth century urban fabric. Like Vienna, several civic buildings, including several university buildings and a theater, edge the park (Balus 2001: 25–27). Though new walls were built outside the Planty in 1846, these were razed in 1906 and cleared the way for Kraków's further extension. By 1910, the city's vision included extending Kraków into distinct zones but maintaining the somewhat pastoral qualities.

View of the Rynek Główny

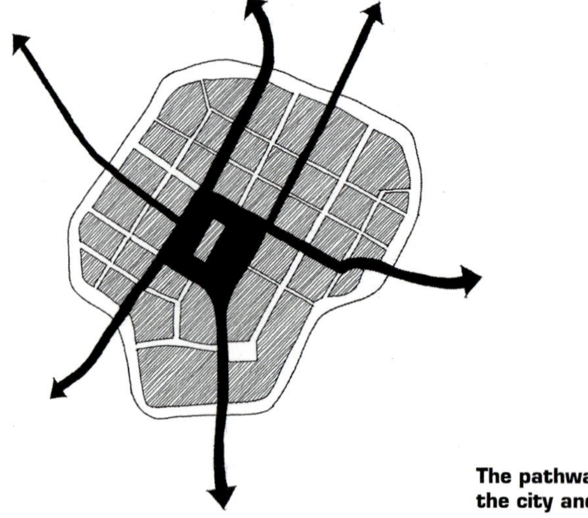

The pathways through the city and square

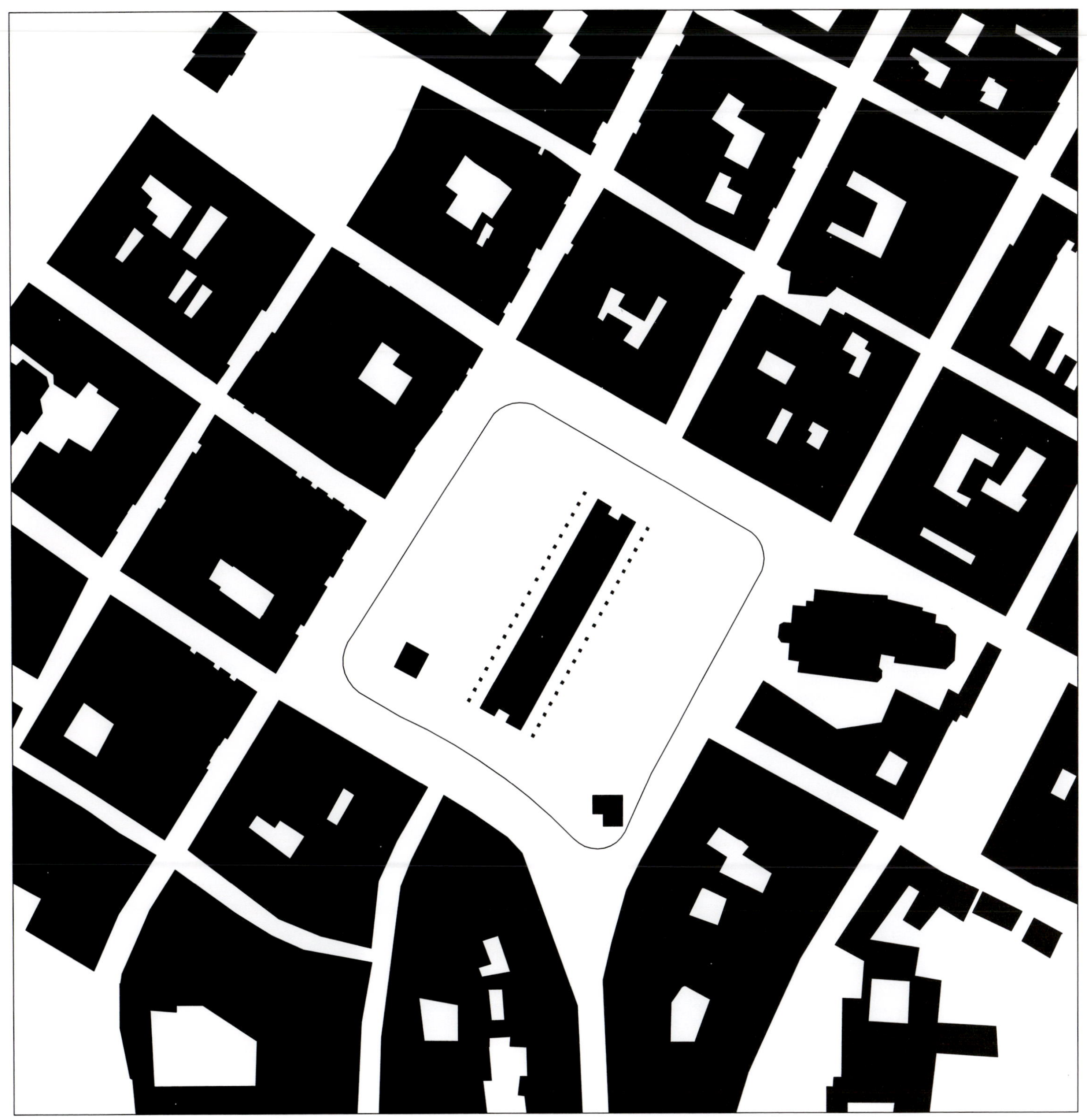

Rynek Główny

Lisbon

41

Praça do Comércio

Considered a gateway to the sea and representative of Lisbon's link to ocean commerce, the Praça do Comércio or Commerce Square in Lisbon's Baxia district is an orthogonal, highly ordered district that reveals how an urban space plays a role in forming an image of the city and how autocratic dictates influence urban space, architecture and living conditions in the city. Designed as the Baxia's focal point by Eugénio dos Santos under chief architect Manuel da Maia and the King's Minister Sabastiao José de Carvalho e Melo, the square is defined on three sides by uniform, arcaded three-story buildings housing governmental agencies with the Tejo river defining its fourth side. Arriving by boat, as was the custom for centuries, a visitor moves north through the square to a triumphal arch that marks the main axial street Rua Augusta. This street leads through the Baxia and ends at the Praça dem Dom Pedro IV more commonly known as the Rossio (Brückelmann 1996: 32–33).

The Baxia is the heart of Lisbon's reconstruction following the 1755 All Saints Day earthquake. The plan consists of a regular street grid set between two hills and the water's edge. Three north–south streets, the Rua Augusta in the center with Rua da Prata and Rua Aurea to the east and west respectively, lead from the water's edge into the northern parts of the city while smaller streets and a series of service alleys cut east and west. Both Praça do Comércio and Rossio were pre-existing squares but were regularized and connected with the street grid.

Like any reconstruction, the city also used it as an opportunity to introduce sewer systems, improve vehicular movement and increase daylight and ventilation to the streets. Additionally, the city mandated specific rules for the reconstruction including standardized block and housing types, allotted zones for specific trades, and limited the embellishment of façades in favor of an efficient and unified visage. As historian Lutz Brückelmann notes, "The subordination of the individual building to the configuration of the overall urban plan was a goal that was pursued for its own sake" adding that "the eminently pragmatic character of the project [became] unambiguously ideological" (Brückelmann 1996: 38). This architectural and urban homogenization helped assure the city's rapid reconstruction and perpetuation as well as a means of authority to dictate and leave the impression of power.

Praça do Comércio

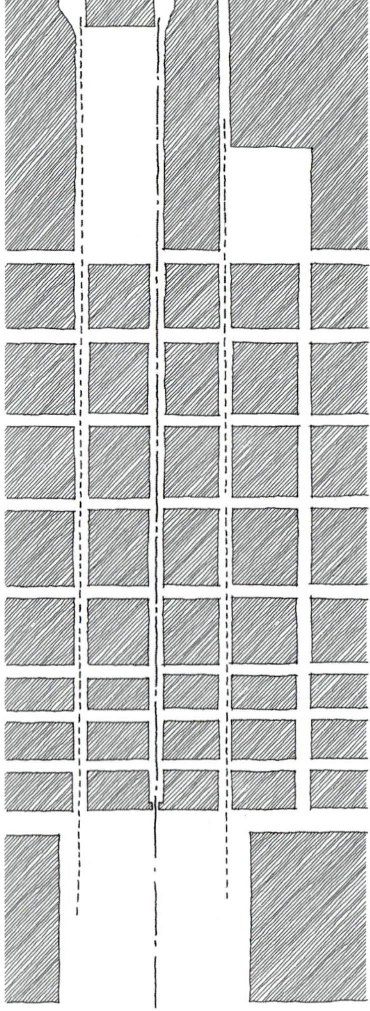

The Baxia with its lateral, then axial streets

Praça do Comércio

London

42

Belgrave Square and Wilton Crescent

London's West End reflects eighteenth and nineteenth century English social and political structure in which development favored small, exclusive developments around an identifiable square. As Londoners will point out, London is not so much one large city but more of an amalgamation of small villages or estates. Over the centuries these individual villages and estates grew together yet maintained much of their unique identities. This individual identity of smaller groups is part of a larger English cultural trend that leads to small, distinct groups with a predilection for private, interior oriented spaces (Pritchett 1962: 23). This is expressed in English towns and, as in Cambridge or Oxford, colleges with private quads exclusive to their members.

Correspondingly, speculative land development was piecemeal as estates grew into autonomous residential neighborhoods with well-manicured neighborhood squares at their centers. Shown here is Wilton Crescent, developed by Thomas Cubitt and designed by George Basevi between 1825 and 1860 (Besant 1909: 225). These squares were distinctly private, fenced-in amenities accessible only to the development's residents. While this has changed somewhat today, many squares remain exclusive.

To illustrate this same point, architect Steen Eiler Rasmussen compares London's public squares with those of Paris in his book *Towns and Buildings* (1969). He notes that unlike English cities, French cities grew within the fortifications and, when overcrowded, extended by decree all at once. Because of this growth by decree, squares and streets were often comprehensive designs, monumental in scale and lined with uniform façades (Rasmussen 1969: 103). This growth, density and social condition are reflected in the Parisian housing types that are predominately apartment blocks rather than individual terraced houses or row houses. Historian Roy Porter further underscores this in his book *London: A Social History* (1995), in which he notes that London did not have the "aesthetics of absolutism" in which scale "bespoke of power unopposed" (Porter 1995: 96). London, especially the West End,

> was not imposed from on high as an ensemble, it grew through piece meal development of self-contained aristocratic estates, forming individual building blocks. The coherence of the mosaic was due not to dictated vision but to shared values, strengthened by matrimonial alliances.
>
> (Porter 1995: 96)

A lesson of London is that urban form is highly dependent on social structure. An Italian piazza or a French *place royale* would be out of place in London. Not only would they not be generated, but also the housing needed to form them would not be used and the authority needed to make such grand moves would be difficult to secure. As such, London internal squares were individual cells without formal interstitial fabric. The result is that English economic and political power manifests its social and political structure – a structure that extended to English colonial towns such as Savannah, Philadelphia and New Haven (Olsen 1964: 4–7).

Wilton Crescent

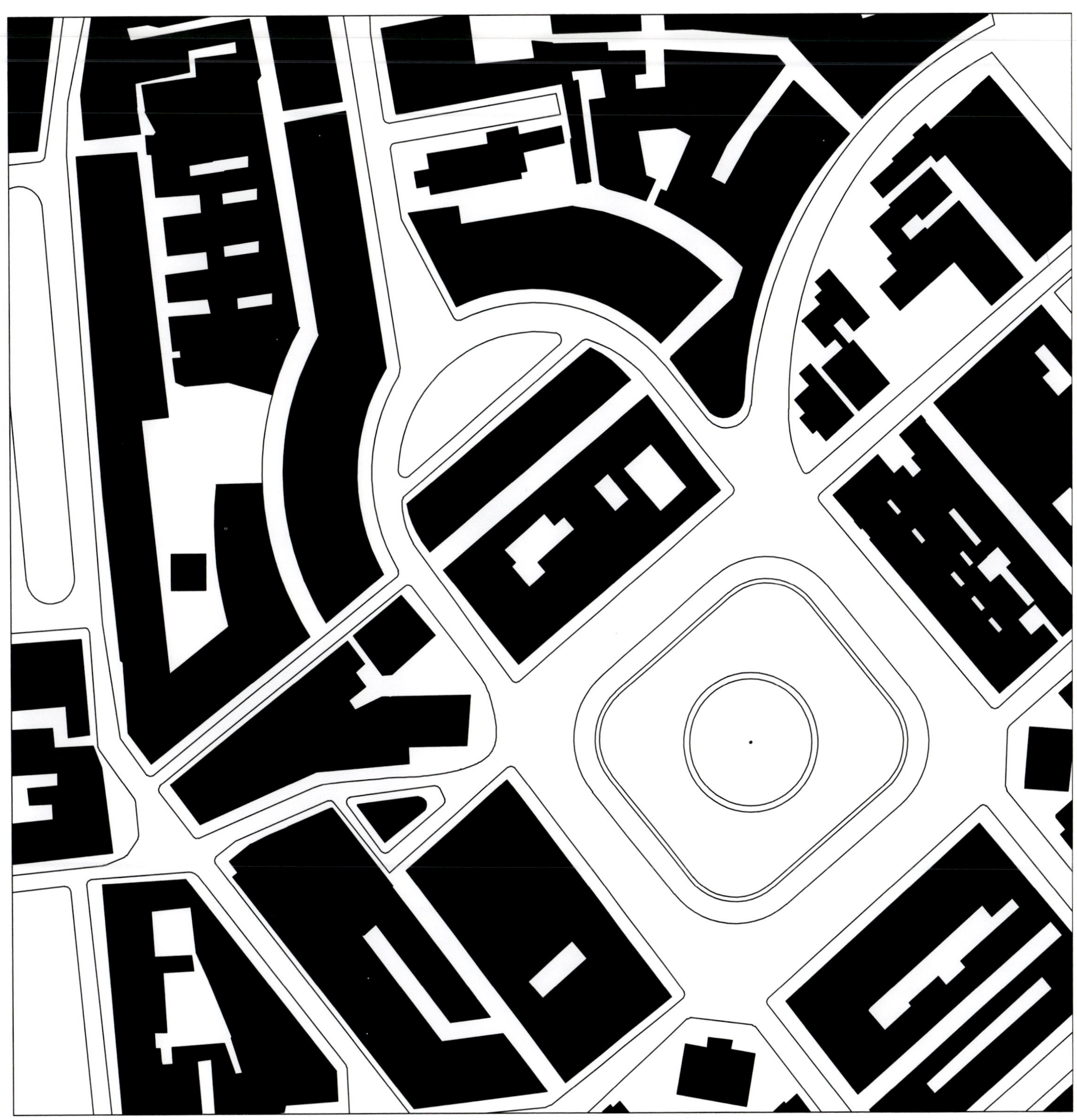

Belgrave Square and Wilton Crescent

London

43

Cavendish Square and Hanover Square

Like many successful developers today, London's seventeenth-, eighteenth- and nineteenth-century real estate speculators recognized that quality, status and amenities sell. Likewise, as the city grew westward and royal estates developed into residential enclaves, developers and designers used discrete residential squares as a primary selling feature (Rasmussen 1967: 177). As enclaves continued to expand across London, the demand for larger, more exclusive and distinct squares increased. This is clear in the early squares, such as Hanover Square (1714) and Cavendish Square (1717), compared to squares formed later, such as Park Crescent (1815) or Belgrave Square (1825) (Besant 1909: 219–226).

Individual terraced houses or row houses by and large surrounded the squares themselves. Though these were uniform and relatively homogenous, they remain small-scale, individual row houses with separate porches, doors and house numbers (Rasmussen 1967: 186–187). This is (as mentioned in Chapter 42), different from Parisian squares or even those in Bath in which the individual residences are subsumed into a uniform façade. In Bath, the most common residential housing type remained the individual party-wall houses, but in Paris, the type is apartment buildings sharing a central stairwell.

London's residential squares have become increasingly public and less residential as the cost of buildings surrounding them have become exorbitant. Squares are often home to larger institutions or prosperous organizations such as publishing houses, hotels, boutiques and embassies. Residential housing remains in the area, but has shifted to the squares' alter ego, the mews streets just behind terraced houses.

A lesson of London's residential square is that urban amenities ultimately raises land values and thus profits. Developments without amenities, although more efficient in land use, ultimately are less successful. This is true in other developments that deliberately insert amenity to increase value. An extreme example was New York's Rockefeller Center. Its developers could have increased rentable floor space and built to the site's maximum. They chose instead to insert a square and decrease the distance from elevator core to windows for better office space. As such, the building has remained one of the most sought-after pieces of real estate in Manhattan.

Cavendish Square

Cavendish Square

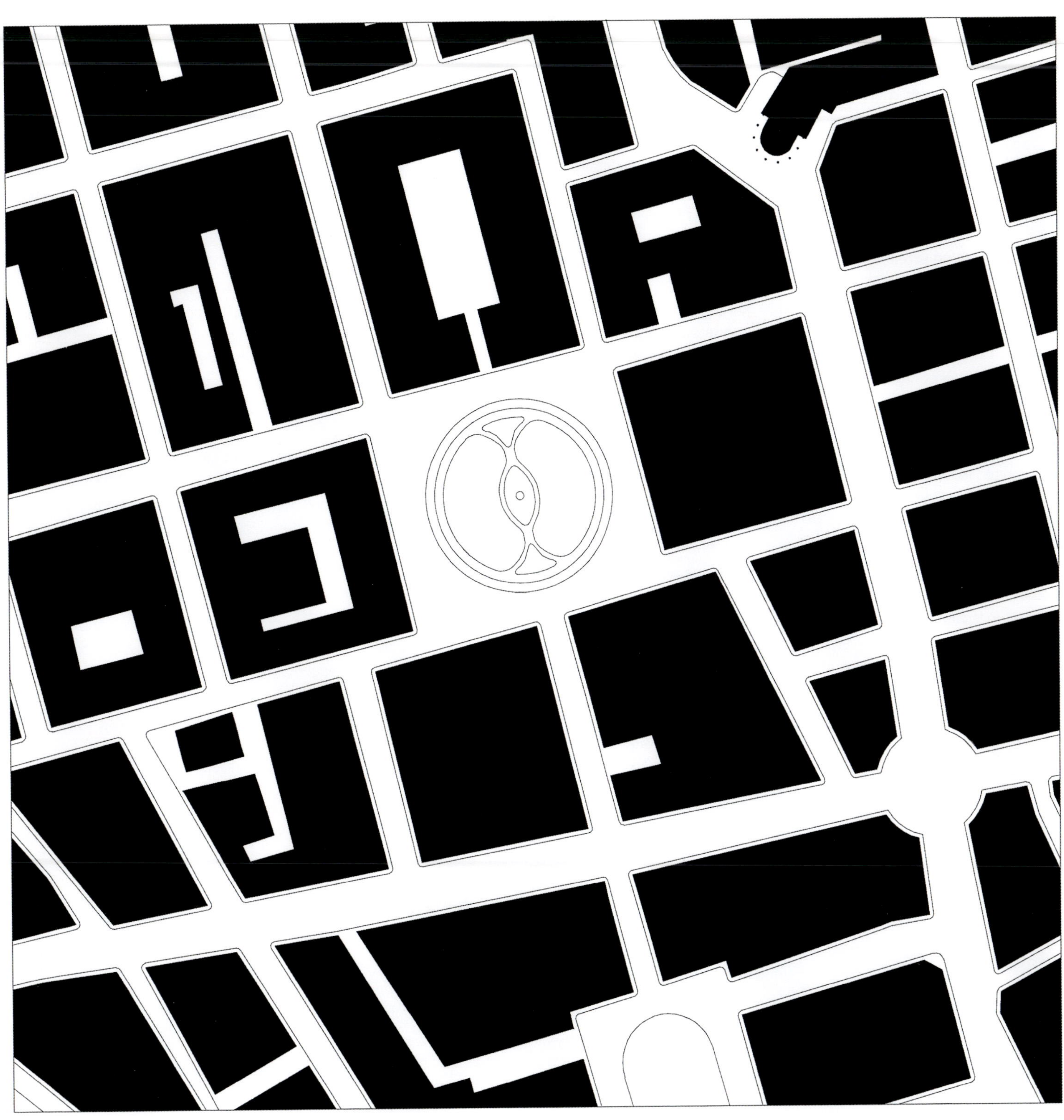

Cavendish Square and Hanover Square

London

Park Crescent and Park Square

44

The interrelated parks in London are thresholds between city and landscape. As such, they provide a gentle movement between park and urban fabric. The culmination of Regent Street, Park Crescent and Park Square are urban design moves that negotiate and build upon the city's existing urban fabric.

The source of Park Crescent and Park Square is Regent Street, a sinuous, two-kilometer-long street that connects Westminster to the south with Regent's Park to the north. When originally conceived by the Prince Regent and designed by John Nash in 1811, no single or elegant street passed through London's independently planned residential developments. Nash proposed a grand royal boulevard that would cut straight through central London's dense fabric and connect the Prince Regent's city residence nearby in Westminster to his new residence near Regent's Park (Rasmussen 1967: 271–272).

To gather public and parliamentary approval, supporters described the street as an improvement of London's hygiene and relief for the side streets by providing an expedient main north–south artery through the city. In the end, the project moved forward but adapted to a series of recalcitrant landowners and existing circumstances. Though it remains a clear and distinct street, it bends, jogs and otherwise negotiates through the city. As Edmund Bacon notes, Nash adjusted the street "rather than imposing a preconceived architectural form on the fabric of the city. Where he met an obstacle, he moved around it. Where necessary, he invented architectural forms to meet the requirements of his design structure" (Bacon 1967: 195).

Near its northern end and on vacant, uncontested land, Nash designed the semicircular Park Crescent and Park Square. These spaces, when approaching from the south, act as an anteroom to the park and a transitional space in the opposite direction. Rather than simply continue the main north–south thoroughfare into the park, the two spaces act as a link between the city and the open park. The crescent was initially a closed circus, much like the Circus in Bath, and matched with a larger, landscaped circus in Regent's Park's center. Due to financial difficulties, however, only the southern half was built. The crescent is lined with Nash's subdued four-story terraced houses with a uniform base of low columns.

Despite its royal sponsor and ostensible goals of a more hygienic city and populace, Regent Street would never be a Parisian boulevard. It is this final, sinuous path that reveals the political and economic differences between Paris and London. Unlike Napoleon I's Rue de Rivoli or Napoleon III's boulevards, both of which are autocratically uniform, Regent Street cooperates (Rasmussen 1967: 274). It is relatively polite, if still autocratic, and moves through the city and reflects or at least foreshadows the challenge of urban revitalization in the twentieth and twenty-first centuries. As Rasmussen notes, the street "was merely a succession of dexterous solutions of difficult problems" which is something that urban designers must face today (Rasmussen 1967: 282).

Houses along Park Crescent

Park Crescent and Regent's Park beyond

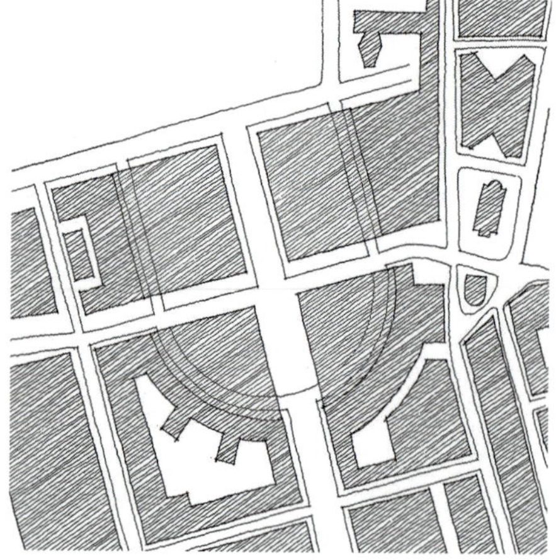

Without Park Crescent and Park Square, Regent Street would end abruptly in Regent's Park

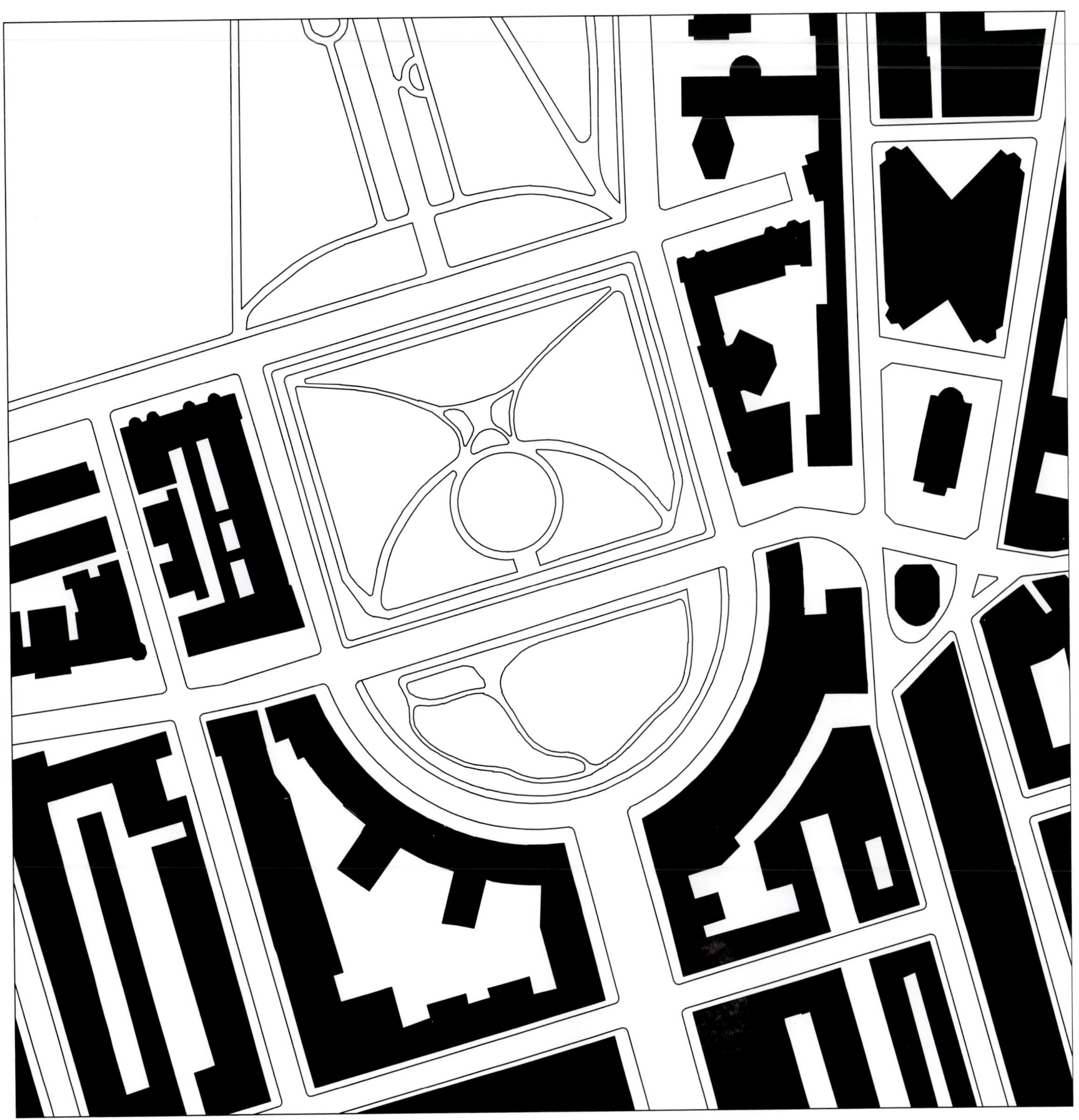

Park Crescent and Park Square

London

Trafalgar Square

45

Trafalgar Square in many ways symbolizes much of England's history from the late eighteenth century to today: with its monument to naval hero Lord Nelson and the Admiralty that reflect its sea power and the former colonial offices from around the world, it has been and remains a center of political, social and labor protest and celebration in central London.

As in London's residential squares, there is little tradition of an outdoor public space other than a public garden or street. Critic V.S. Pritchett notes in *London Perceived* (1962) that Trafalgar Square is London's

> characteristic alternative to the grande place or piazza. There are no central places, foreigners complain, where "Londoners meet" or stroll along together to pass the time of day. The answer to that is, first, that Londoners do not meet, do not gather, and reject the peculiar notion that people "like running across each other" in public spaces. They emphatically do not. We are full of clubs, pubs, cliques, coteries, sets, although the influences of mass life are changing us, so that even the London public house is becoming public.
>
> (Pritchett 1962: 12)

Moreover, he argues that the combination of merchant-dominated real estate and the parliamentary political system have thwarted extensive urban plans like those by Christopher Wren and notes that "dictators can be splendid, democracies can swagger, but parliaments cannot bear expense" (Pritchett 1962: 5).

Trafalgar Square from the southwest

View of the connection between the National Gallery and the square

Designed by Charles Barry in 1829, the square helped reconcile the intersections of several streets and set the location for a monument to the naval hero, Admiral Lord Nelson. Dominating the space is the large Corinthian column atop which is the statue of Lord Nelson, yet its most notable features are the terraces that lead from the northern side in front of the National Gallery to a lower level that spreads out to the city to the south. It is surrounded by nineteenth century neo-classical buildings of an imperial scale, yet, unlike Paris, these do not make a continuous edge to the space. On the north is the National Gallery. From the center on the south side arc and running along its west side are predominantly government buildings. Between these buildings is the Admiralty Arch that leads to Whitehall and the government district. From the center of the arc along the east are commercial buildings culminating with James Gibbs' St Martin-in-the-Fields at the upper east corner. As a gathering point of many avenues and its proximity to national political power, the square has been a place of political activity. In the late nineteenth century, sizeable demonstrations led to deadly confrontations. In response, Parliament attempted to discourage mass assembly by enacting laws and adding fountains in 1894 and, in 1916, proposed building over the entire square with temporary huts (Mace 1976: 200–211).

Trafalgar Square is an active square that resolves many forces dominated by encircling traffic with the exception of the pedestrian-only street in front of the National Gallery. Although the buildings surrounding it are somewhat similar, there is not enough vertical surface to clearly define the space like a Parisian square. One addition that helped "seal" the square's edges is the 1991 Venturi Scott-Brown and Associates' addition to the National Gallery, with its playful wall along the street edge.

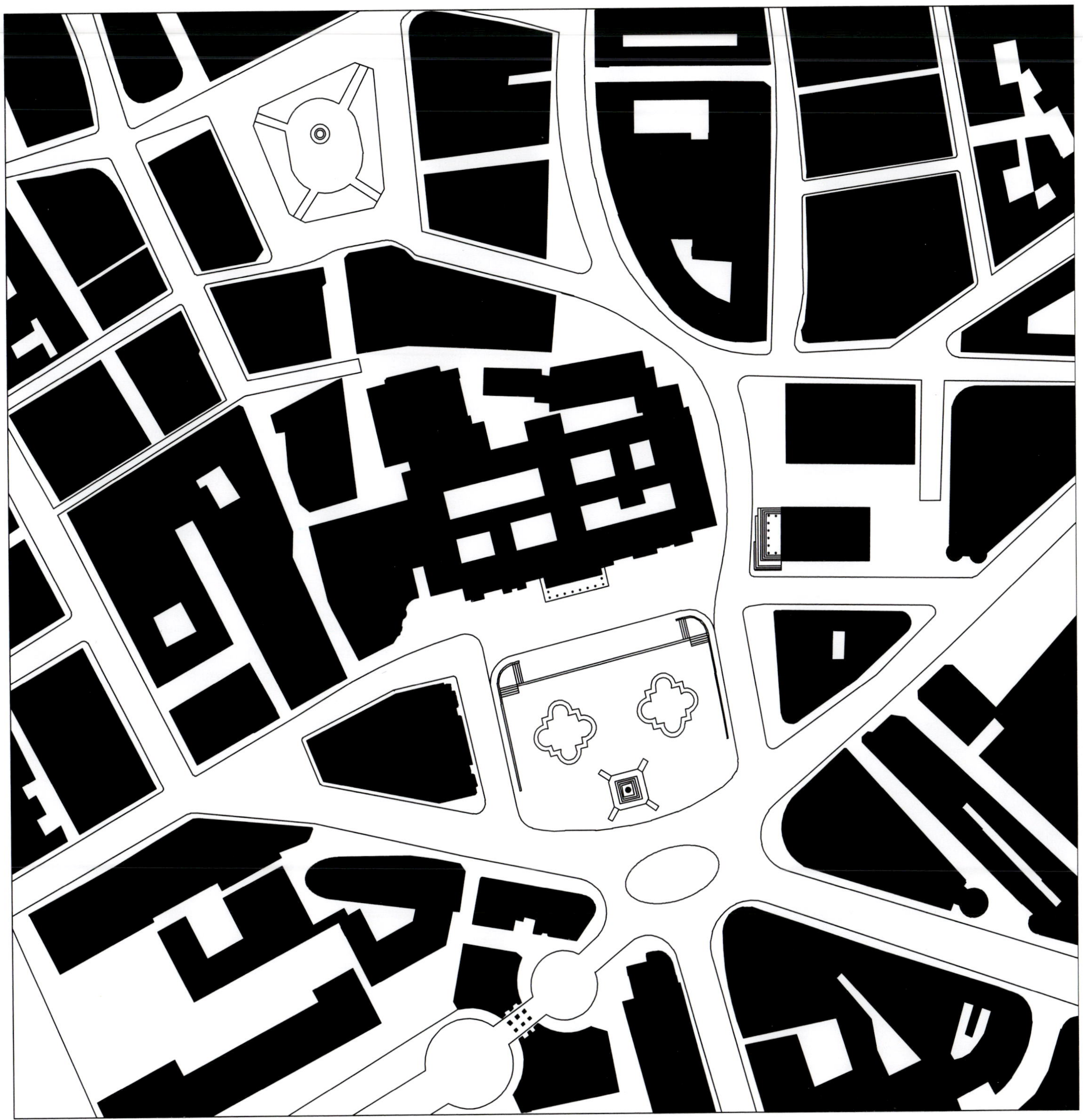

Trafalgar Square

Los Angeles

46

Pershing Square

Pershing Square, located at the eastern edge of the Los Angeles Financial District, has undergone successive renovations over the past two centuries in an attempt to accommodate changes in society and its downtown. Like Union Square in San Francisco and Copley Square in Boston, it has evolved from a simple park design to a multifaceted, often complicated plaza in an attempt to solve all problems through multiple mechanisms.

Initially designed as the plaza of an eighteenth century Spanish pueblo, it was designated La Plaza Abaja in 1866 (Reps 1965: 51). In 1877, it was landscaped and designated Los Angeles Park. In 1911, it was laid out as a more formal park and renamed Central Park though seven years later it was changed to Pershing Square in honor of World War I's General George Pershing. For more than thirty years it remained relatively untouched. In 1950, however, the city excavated the entire square and built an underground garage. Ramps leading into the garage effectively removed nearly 25 percent of the park, raised it above and away from the street edge, isolating it from the surrounding sidewalk and pedestrian activity. Between the mid-1950s and 1980s, downtown Los Angeles went into a steady decline from which it has barely recovered. Two attempts were made to resurrect the square. First, it was rehabilitated in conjunction with the 1984 Olympics and, two years later, James Wines won a design competition to fully renovate the square, though it was never implemented. In 1994, Mexican architect Ricardo Legoretta and landscape architect Laurie Olin with Barbara McCarren were selected to remake the square.

View of Pershing Square from the south

The Legoretta–Olin–McCarren design is quite aggressive and is part of a trend to redesign urban spaces with multiple functions, levels and idiosyncratic rooms. Rather than simply adding plantings and plazas, Legoretta divided it into three areas: a central space with a bell tower for general assembly and fairs, a grassy amphitheatre for concerts and other amusements and a center café with smaller garden segments. Despite attempts to improve the space, the context remains something beyond the architects' control. The surrounding fabric remains incomplete with parking lots abutting the square and the downtown remains troubled economically.

For better or worse, Pershing Square has undergone and may continue to undergo cyclical transformations as the city attempts to solve its urban problems and accommodate varied socio-economic groups. As mentioned with Cincinnati's Fountain Square, American urban plazas seem to be on a regular renovation cycle with each successive design attempting to ameliorate additional problems that it may have no power to affect.

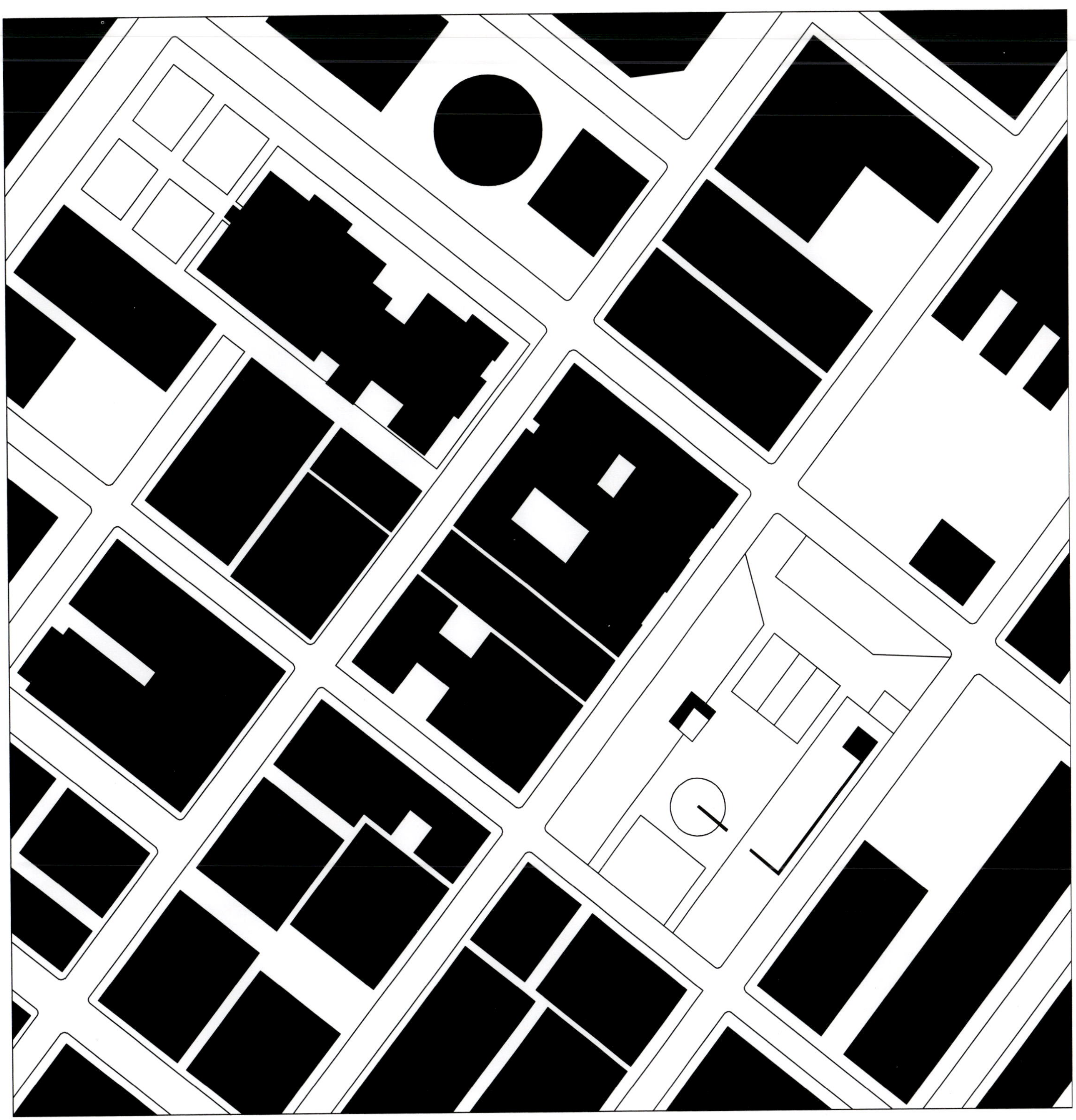

Pershing Square

Lucca

47

Piazza dell' Anfiteatro

Derived from the Roman town of Lucensis, present-day Lucca is a remnant of its ancient self with its grid and the Piazza dell' Anfiteatro as the most obvious trace. The piazza is one of those urban fossils, like Piazza Navona in Rome, that were neither erased by the urban fabric nor left as ruins in the city. Rather, the Piazza dell' Anfiteatro is a petrified, albeit strangely occupied, vestige of its Roman past.

Nearly the entire town of Lucca has maintained its original Roman form due mostly to the walls that still surround it today. Like other Roman settlements, Lucca was laid out in a gridiron pattern with two principal axes at right angles to one another at its center: the *decumanus maximus* and *kardo maximus*. This larger grid was further subdivided into a smaller street grid. At its center was the forum, now the Piazza San Michele with its San Michele in Foro, with the amphitheater at the town's periphery. Except for slight street modifications, such as the addition of the fourteenth century Palazzo Augusto just south of the main piazza and its growth outward to successive new fortifications, Lucca's plan has remained relatively undisturbed from its inception in the second century AD (Braunfels 1988: 58).

Piazza dell' Anfiteatro

Its amphitheater is a small example of this persistence with transformation. Though mined for its stone, it retained its fundamental geometry so that by the tenth century with the town's outward expansion, it became the foundation for houses and a center garden. In the mid-nineteenth century this center garden became a market that continued until the late 1930s when its stalls and other structures were removed and the space was transformed to its current appearance (Kato 1980: 50). The piazza is defined primarily by three- and four-story houses with some of the ground floor filled with cafés and shops. As Paul Zucker (1966: 152) notes, however, the Piazza dell' Anfiteatro is "simply a void" and courtyard for the houses rather than a living piazza. As such, Piazza dell' Anfiteatro is an example of how urban form is generated by the past yet often that past is no longer present or viable. At the same time, to avoid the spatial fossilization (perhaps even ossification), the space must be adapted to other uses to keep it alive. Perhaps the market that grew up there was appropriate and, once removed, kept the piazza somewhat fixed in time.

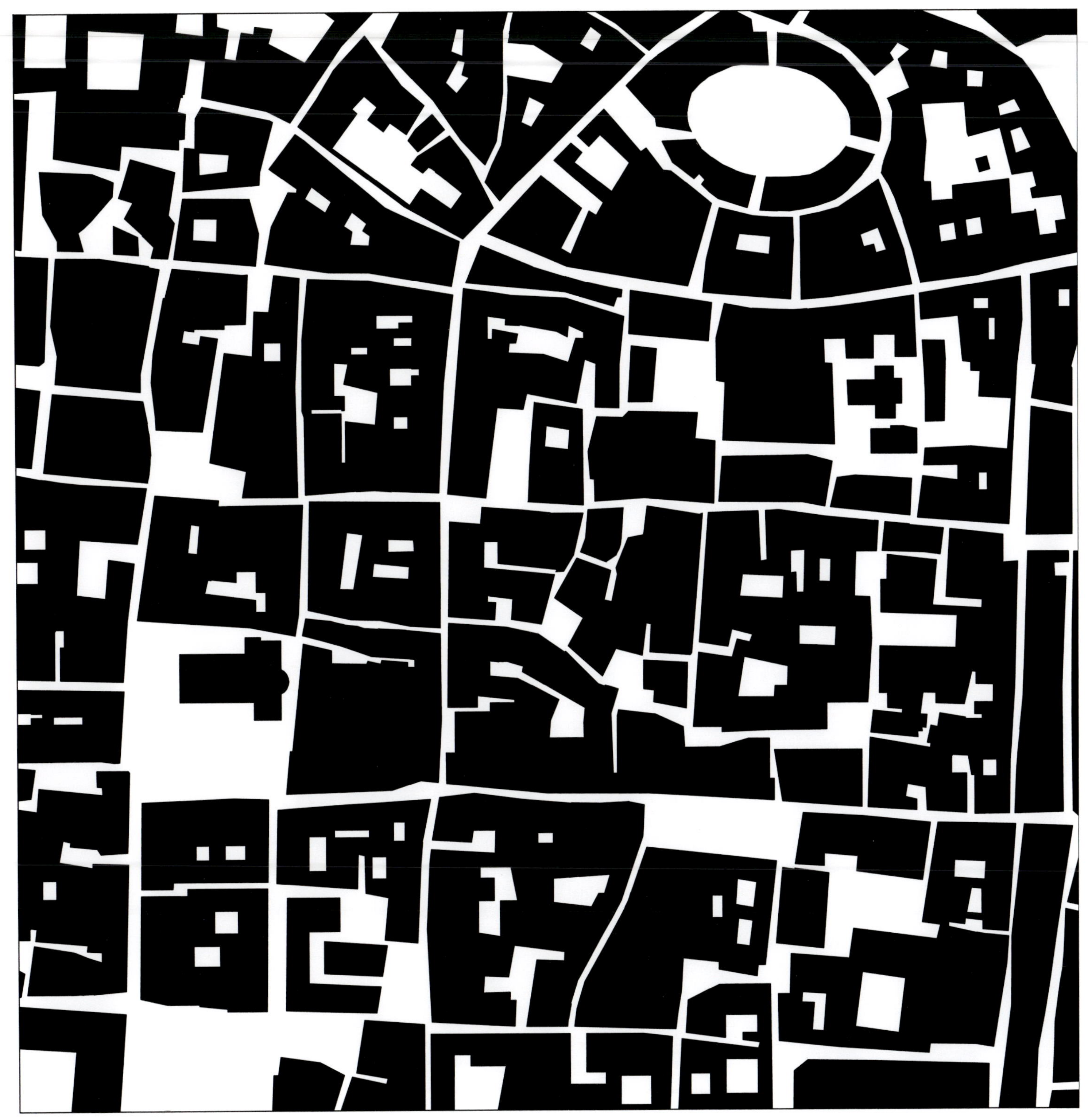

Piazza dell' Anfiteatro

Madrid

Plaza Mayor

48

In 1561, Spanish Habsburg Philip II declared Madrid, which was then a diminutive town, as Spain's new capital. Not long after, he sponsored construction of a new plaza that would not only accommodate courtly events but also symbolize the new imperial city. The result was the princely and uniform Plaza Mayor that reflected Philip's ambitions and the society's collective spirit.

The square's walls are four-story façades with a uniform colonnade along the ground level. The uniformity is only slightly punctuated by larger, one and a half-story archways that lead to side streets, and by four identical towers on the square's north and south sides. In contrast to the contemporary architecture of the late Renaissance and early Baroque, Plaza Mayor's façades are relatively subdued and unpretentious, which was common in the architecture sponsored by Philip II and reflected the King's experience in the rebuilding of the Monastery of San Lorenzo at El Escorial (Escobar 2004: 21–23). The plaza's main building, the Casa de la Panadería, which is along the square's northern edge, was a bread market with apartments above used as royal residences during court ceremonies.

The square seems to have been superimposed on the city with little regard for the existing street patterns. Despite the appearance, it was not superimposed but grew out of an existing square that became increasingly refined and regularized between the late sixteenth and early nineteenth centuries. Beginning in 1583, architects Juan Herrara and Juan de Valencia regularized the existing irregular square by unifying the façade and added the Panadería. In 1617, architect Juan Gomez de Mora continued to unify the square by rectifying its corners and establishing the link along the Calle Nueva. Following a 1672 fire, the square and the Panadería were reconstructed by Tomas Roman and later Teodoro Ardemas following de Mora's model (Escobar 2004: 253). After a 1790 fire that destroyed the square's western range, architect Juan de Villanueva even further unified the square by obscuring the once visible street entries with false archways (Escobar 2004: 257).

Like Place des Vosges or Salamanca's Plaza Mayor, Madrid's Plaza Mayor hosted court for ceremonies as well as civic and religious events in the city's center. Despite its similarities to its Salamancan and Parisian counterparts, it is even more ordered, uniform and differentiated from the existing fabric.

Plaza Mayor's uniform façade, plan and even its somewhat subdued articulation reveals a civil society that favored the group over the individual citizen. As historian Jesús Escobar reveals in his thorough studies, the process of building the Plaza "emulated the Spanish Hapsburg political structure and promoted the grand though often humbled building project which brought the modern capital city into being" (Escobar 2000: 97). Plaza Mayor, like other urban spaces throughout the world, reveals its distinct society: politics, economy and culture are embedded in its form and history.

Plaza Mayor

Plaza Mayor

Mexico City

Zócalo / Plaza de la Constitución

49

Mexico City and its main square, established on the ruins of a fourteenth century Aztec capital, represents the effect that Spanish colonial planning and politics had on urban form in the Americas. When originally founded in 1325, the pre-Columbian city of Mexico-Tenochtitlán was in an idyllic setting on an island in the middle of Lake Texcoco surrounded by mountains rich with vegetation and wildlife. The city, set out on a grid of streets and canals and dominated by a ceremonial precinct at its center, lasted only two hundred years when it was virtually destroyed following the Spanish incursion into the region. On Hernán Cortés' orders, the entire city was reconstructed using a "Law of the Indies" grid plan over the Aztec plan. By the middle of the sixteenth century, the Aztec central temple of Huitzilopochtli was razed and used to build a cathedral but this too was removed and a second cathedral built between 1667 and 1813. Remnants of the Tenochtitlán temple and the underlying urban plan are just northeast of the square.

Originally a Spanish colonial *plaza de armas*, the Zócalo has been the center of the city since the sixteenth century, yet has had different iterations and uses. Over the centuries it has been a market, parade ground and place of ceremonies. For most of this time, the square was planted with palm trees, but these were removed in 1956 to allow for large political rallies. Today, it is officially Constitution Square yet it is more commonly known as the Zócalo from the word "pedestal" in Spanish. This somewhat peculiar name was adopted as a jest on the large pedestal that once sat in the middle of the square. The pedestal sat empty awaiting a Monument of Independence from 1843 until it was finally removed in 1920. Since that time, towns throughout Mexico have adopted the name "Zócalo" for their own plazas.

Today, the Zócalo is, as writer Robert Payne describes, "agonizingly empty" (Payne 1968: 111). It is a vast square used primarily for public demonstrations and ceremonies with markets held on either side of the cathedral. The square is dominated by the National Palace to the east and the cathedral to the north while its remaining edges are commercial and apartment buildings.

Mexico City exemplifies how politics has and continues to play a role in urban design and form. From the conquistadors razing the city and replacing it with a Spanish city to the removal of trees to facilitate political demonstrations, the Zócalo has suffered under varied political powers. As geographer Joseph Scarpaci notes, Mexico City has been an "instrument of subjugation" that predates Spanish colonization: from its role as a place of sacrifice to contested elections, the square is activated more by extreme activities rather than day-to-day life (Scarpaci 2005: 235).

The Zócalo from the south

The Zócalo from the west

Zócalo / Plaza de la Constitución

Milan

50

Piazza del Duomo

Piazza del Duomo remains a perennially unsatisfactory square for many architects and urban designers and thus is constantly redesigned, with each new proposal suggesting an ultimate resolution ("La plaza interminabile" 1984: 14). The piazza that we see today is the result of several nineteenth and twentieth century attempts to regularize the parvis to match the imposing cathedral. The initial intention was to surround the piazza with uniform façades. This plan included the design of the Galleria Vittorio Emanuelle, by Guiseppe Mengoni, that would connect the Piazza del Duomo with the Piazza della Scala to the north. The entry to the Galleria is a monumental triumphal arch set within the massive four-story façade with ground level arcades. The Galleria and its connection to the north are important as the Galleria is a public street that is, in a way, an inverted duomo. It is a duomo of commerce. Its cruciform plan, glass ceiling and subdued façades act as a counterpoint to the white cathedral set in an open piazza. On the piazza's south and rarely photographed side are two buildings known as the Arengario built in 1939. These fascist buildings attempt to match, yet abstract, the northern arcades.

Dominating the piazza is Milan's Italian Gothic cathedral begun in 1387 and completed in the nineteenth century. Though no cathedral is easy to build, Milan's proved especially daunting as architects and consultants were frequently hired and dismissed from the project. Of those who worked on the cathedral, Leonardo da Vinci and Donato Bramante are the most notable.

Entrance to the Galleria

Piazza del Duomo remains difficult to resolve due in part to the nature of Milan as a large metropolitan city, the immense surrounding nineteenth century façades and the Piazza Reale, the trapezoidal space to the southeast that, for all intents and purposes, pulls energy away from the main square.

A main difficulty of the square is its recentness. The cathedral was completed only in the nineteenth century and the buildings around it finished in about the 1860s. In terms of other spaces in Italy, this is a brief history considering that Piazza Navona began as the Stadium of Domition in the first century AD and was not "completed" as a square until the seventeenth century. In other words, the resolution of the square and its final form may have to take several hundred more years to mature into the square that is deemed "finished" or "successful." Such is the issue of urban design which, in the United States at least, often requires a generation to complete.

Piazza del Duomo from the southeast

Piazza del Duomo

Montréal

51

Place d'Armes

Place d'Armes is one of several colonial era squares in downtown Montréal. A relatively small square in the middle of the city's oldest district, it was the center of Montréal's original French settlement, Ville-Marie, that was founded in 1642. Like any city, Montréal underwent significant social and political changes, especially in the eighteenth and twentieth centuries, echoed in the square's morphology.

As in other French colonial settlements, the square was a *place d'armes* – an open, unlandscaped area similar to public squares in France. Set aside primarily for military training, it was where city founder, Paul Chomedey de Maisonneuve, defeated the Iroquois tribe following years of heavy fighting between First Nation people and European settlers. Defining the square's south edge is the Notre-Dame Basilica initially founded in 1672 but rebuilt in 1829. The open area south of the square and next to the basilica is the courtyard to the Séminaire de Saint Suplice founded in the middle of the seventeenth century.

Place d'Armes

Architect Jean-Claude Marsan notes that the nature of the Place d'Armes reflects the changes from French to British domination after 1763 (Marsan 1990: 141–143). Under French dominion, it was very much a public open space but by the middle of the nineteenth century under British control, it became an increasingly insular, private realm planted with trees and demarcated with iron fencing like London's residential squares. A second transformation in the nineteenth century was the Basilica of Notre-Dame. Under the French, the church sat within the square with its main portico facing west on axis with Notre-Dame Street, the east–west street that currently runs along the square's south edge. As Marsan comments, "this manner of highlighting a monument by placing it at the far end of a visual perspective is more characteristic of the classical continental square than of the British" (Marsan 1990: 141). A similar condition occurs in the French colonial settlement of New Orleans in which the Cathedral of St. Louis is placed centrally on Jackson Square, formerly Place d'Armes, as a singular monument. When razed and rebuilt in the early nineteenth century, architects rotated the cathedral's axis clockwise and moved the cathedral to the south so that the front portico defined its southern edge while residences formed the square's remaining three sides. While the cathedral remained a monument on the square, it was less of one.

In the middle of the nineteenth century, the square began to attract financial institutions followed by commercial buildings of increasing height and mass. In 1887, the first skyscraper, the New York Life Insurance building, was built on the square and by the early twentieth century, buildings were reaching ten and twelve stories in height. In 1931, the Art Deco Aldred building rose on its east side and the Banque Canadienne Nationale building on its north. The square has remained somewhat similar except for the 1968 Le 500 Place d'Armes office building on the southwest side.

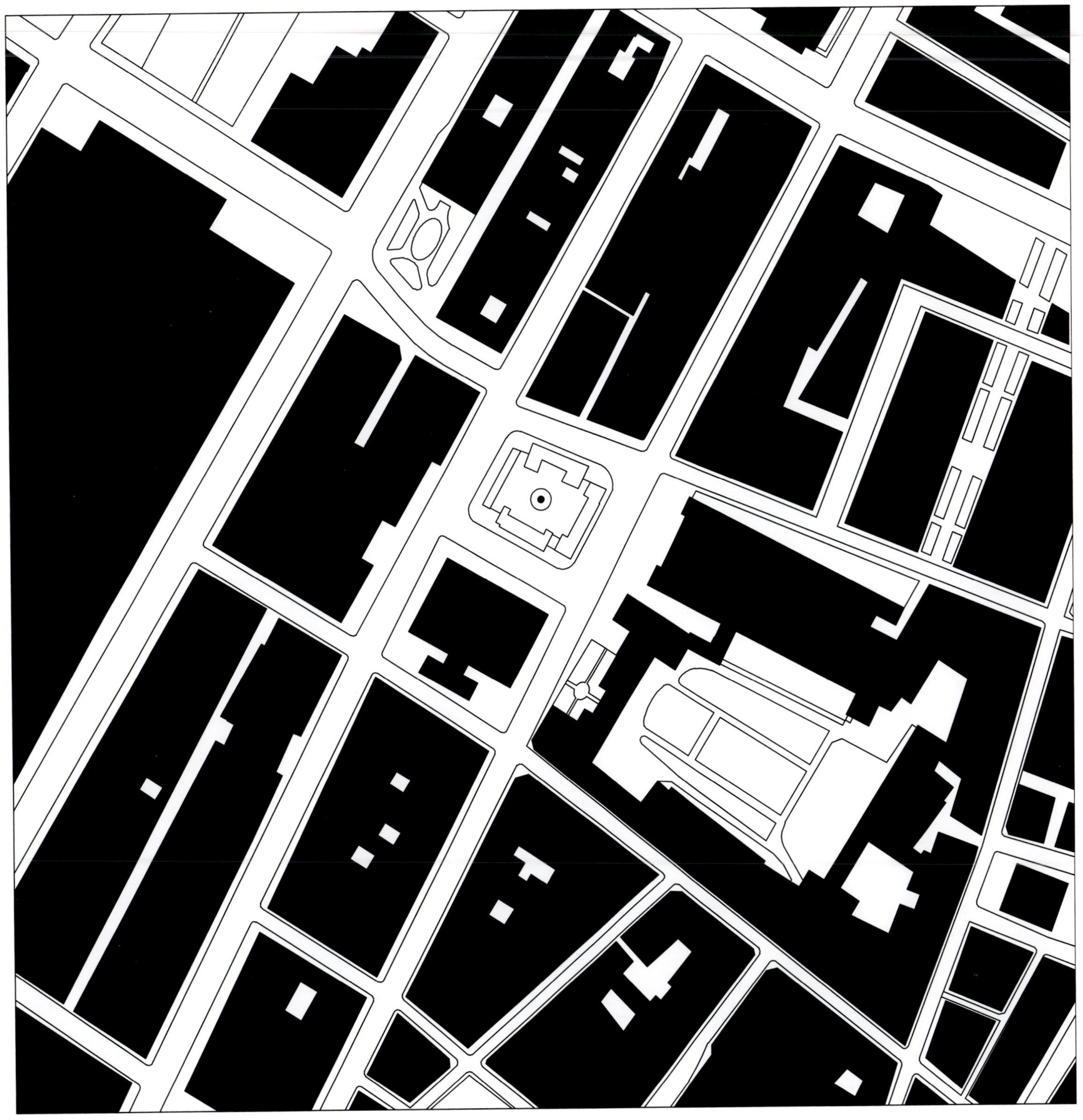

Place d'Armes

Moscow

52

Krasnaya Plóshchad

Krasnaya Plóshchad, or Red Square, is located in central Moscow and for many is and will always be associated with Soviet-era parades of choreographed, flag-waving citizens and soldiers marching alongside tanks and missile launchers. Though its name may seem derived from communist ideology, it actually predates the Soviet era and takes its name from the Russian word meaning "beautiful." Only its name and its configuration rooted in the traditional Russian market square were appropriated by successive leaders as a distinctly motherland square.

Several important Russian landmarks define the square. Along its western edge is the Kremlin, the center of Moscow since the twelfth century, with its somber red-brick walls; in front of this is Lenin's mausoleum from which Soviet leaders scrutinized parades. Opposite the Kremlin, to the east, is the GUM department store and to the north is the nineteenth century Historical Museum. To the south is the colorful, onion-domed St. Basil's cathedral.

Looking south

The square was initially Moscow's outdoor market built on state-owned land filled with stalls and assorted buildings and surrounded by walls. As a market it was at the intersection of several trade routes and the joint between the Kremlin palace complex and the residential neighborhood to the northeast. Between 1813 and 1818, following the city's near total destruction in the Napoleonic wars, architect Osip Ivanovich Beauvais redesigned much of Moscow, which included clearing Krasnaya Plóshchad of the market structures (Gutkind 1972b: 346–347).

Krasnaya Plóshchad looking north

The most noticeable aspect of Krasnaya Plóshchad is its size. Like most politically co-opted spaces, its enormity is impressive when filled with people and large military vehicles and equipment. Until the nineteenth century, Russians had little tradition of grand public squares. Like Saint Petersburg, Red Square did not become a formal space until after the Napoleonic wars coinciding with the Tsar's increased military and political power. As Erwin Gutkind notes in *Urban Development in Eastern Europe*, squares played a less important role in Russia and were usually limited to market or church squares (Gutkind 1972b: 257). Even these, he notes, were often undefined, irregular spaces with multiple floor levels open to the surrounding landscape. This lack of an overarching spatial unity did have the effect of creating a more picturesque square. Combined with Krasnaya Plóshchad's distinct Russian origins, its adjacency to the Kremlin and its linear organization, it became an ideal set piece for Soviet parades. Like other politically potent squares with overt symbolism, Krasnaya Plóshchad was for the Soviets a square of the Russian proletariat with links to Soviet ideals of workers.

Krasnaya Ploshchad

Nancy

53

Place Stanislas, Place de la Carrière and Place Général de Gaulle

Ordered yet dynamic, the spatial composition of Place Stanislas, Place de la Carrière and Place Général de Gaulle in Nancy is considered one of the more exquisite urban spaces in Europe. This high regard is due in part to the composition's intrinsic dualities: its scale is imperial, yet discreet and the spatial sequence is clear, yet provides a variegated flow. As such, it represents a high point in theatrical French Baroque urban design.

Conceived as a *place royale* in honor of Louis XV by the deposed Polish King Stanisław Leszczyński, Duke of the Lorraine region from 1736 to 1766, the ensemble would link two sections of the town and create a grand entry to the ducal palace and gardens on the city's edge. Designed by Emmanuel Héré de Corny between 1753 and 1760, the spaces are a series of volumetric rooms each with its own independent, sometimes opposing, form, orientation and scale. Though independent, each space plays a complementary and essential role in the overall composition and adds to a dynamic spatial sequence. It is essentially three primary spaces with two subsidiary links along a southwest–northeast axis. This axis begins at the Hôtel de Ville defining the southwest edge of Place Stanislas. The axis is actually perpendicular to Place Stanislas' long axis, formed by a northwest–southeast street which is the primary access into and out of Nancy. The composition's primary axis extends across the grain of the Place Stanislas and into a narrow street. This short street compresses the pedestrian and then an Arc de Triomphe at the end nearly completely encloses and further compresses the pedestrian; the arch leads to the linear Place de la Carrière. The Carrière is lined by three-story buildings and with an inner liner of trees. Through the Place de la Carrière, the pedestrian again moves through a slight threshold as the end of the Carrière is articulated and brought inward. Through this threshold is the cross-axial Place Général de Gaulle with hemicycles at both its ends. The palace ends the axis and forms the long side of the Place Général de Gaulle. Beyond the palace and the southern hemicycle are formal gardens.

An important lesson for urban designers is that the project is not a complete invention, superimposed on the city or landscape, but actually builds upon and incorporates the existing fabric and buildings into a cohesive whole. Existing conditions included the northwest–southeast road and moat that ran between Nancy's medieval and Renaissance districts. Perpendicular to this road and waterway was a relatively undefined tournament area known as the Place de la Carrière. At the southwest corner of the Carrière was the recently built Hôtel de Beauvau-Craon (1715). The Hôtel and Carrière became the primary source of the project. Héré de Corny duplicated the Hôtel's rhythm, massing, articulation and extended it along both sides of the Carrière. The Place Stanislas was then placed at the intersection of the Carrière's axis and the existing north–south road. The new town hall was placed on the Carrière axis and then complimented at the far end by the palace. In the end, the designer examined and embraced the site's conditions to initiate and sustain a viable design.

Place Stanislas

Place de la Carrière

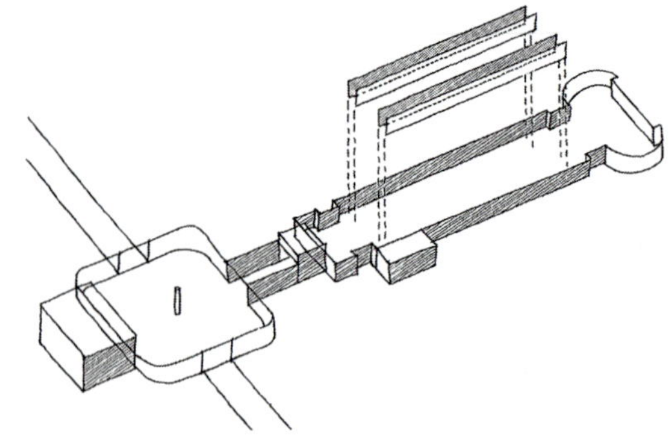
Spatial sequence and the role of the allée of trees in forming the space

Place Stanislas, Place de la Carrière and Place Général de Gaulle

New Haven

54

The Green

Colonial New Haven's plan is often positioned alongside William Penn's plan for Philadelphia (1683) as idealized colonial English urban plans in America. Visionary in its physical form and underlying ideals, like Philadelphia it continued to inform American urban planning as the nation extended west.

Established in 1683 as a fur-trading commercial venture and Puritan utopia, New Haven's plan was a large nine-square grid while a tenth, oblong block extended eccentrically from the lower corner toward the harbor. The founders reserved the entire center square of the nine-square plan, nearly 10 percent, for the town's Green. Like other New England greens, it was set aside for public buildings, markets and other civic activities. As John Reps notes in *The Making of Urban America* (1965), New Haven was unparalled in the amount of space dedicated to public use (Reps 1965: 130). Until the late eighteenth century the area was known as the Market Place, but with subsequent improvements, it was renamed the Green and planted with elm trees and well-tended lawns. By the early nineteenth century, New Haven had become known as the "City of Elms", maturing into the distinct early American idea of urban life merged with a sylvan landscape.

In the early nineteenth century, the town set aside three lots for churches on the Green. The decision to build three churches and perhaps more on a public space reveals the character of early American towns in which faith played a critical part in establishing a civic life and space.

The Green's original shape remains evident, yet, as with New Haven's original nine blocks, it was subdivided into smaller sections. Today, the square is divided into unequal halves by Temple Street. The larger, northwestern section with its three churches is a heavily treed area. The southeastern side is open and used for public festivals and other events. The northwest edge of the Green is Yale University, which is easily identified by its academic quads. Its southwest edge is Chapel Street, which is now New Haven's main commercial thoroughfare. Along its southeast edge is Church Street lined with New Haven's city hall, financial institutions, courthouse and federal buildings. Elm Street on the northeast edge is lined with several Yale University buildings, the public library and State Superior Court.

The Green's consistent charm, which has held for over two centuries, is due in part to a five-member committee of proprietors established in 1805. This non-governmental body, similar to non-profit organizations that manage contemporary squares in other US cities, oversees maintenance and landscaping decisions and has the final say on its use. Additionally, historian Elizabeth Mills Brown notes, the city's

> urbanist discipline created an architectural fabric around the perimeter that for many years was directed toward increasing the definition and enclosure of the space, dramatizing the concept of centrality. It is these two remarkable balancing acts – a balance of social functions, a balance of architectural scale and rhythms – that have hitherto given the Green its special visual quality.
> (Brown 1976: 103)

Original town plan and relationship to the harbor

Aerial view from the southwest

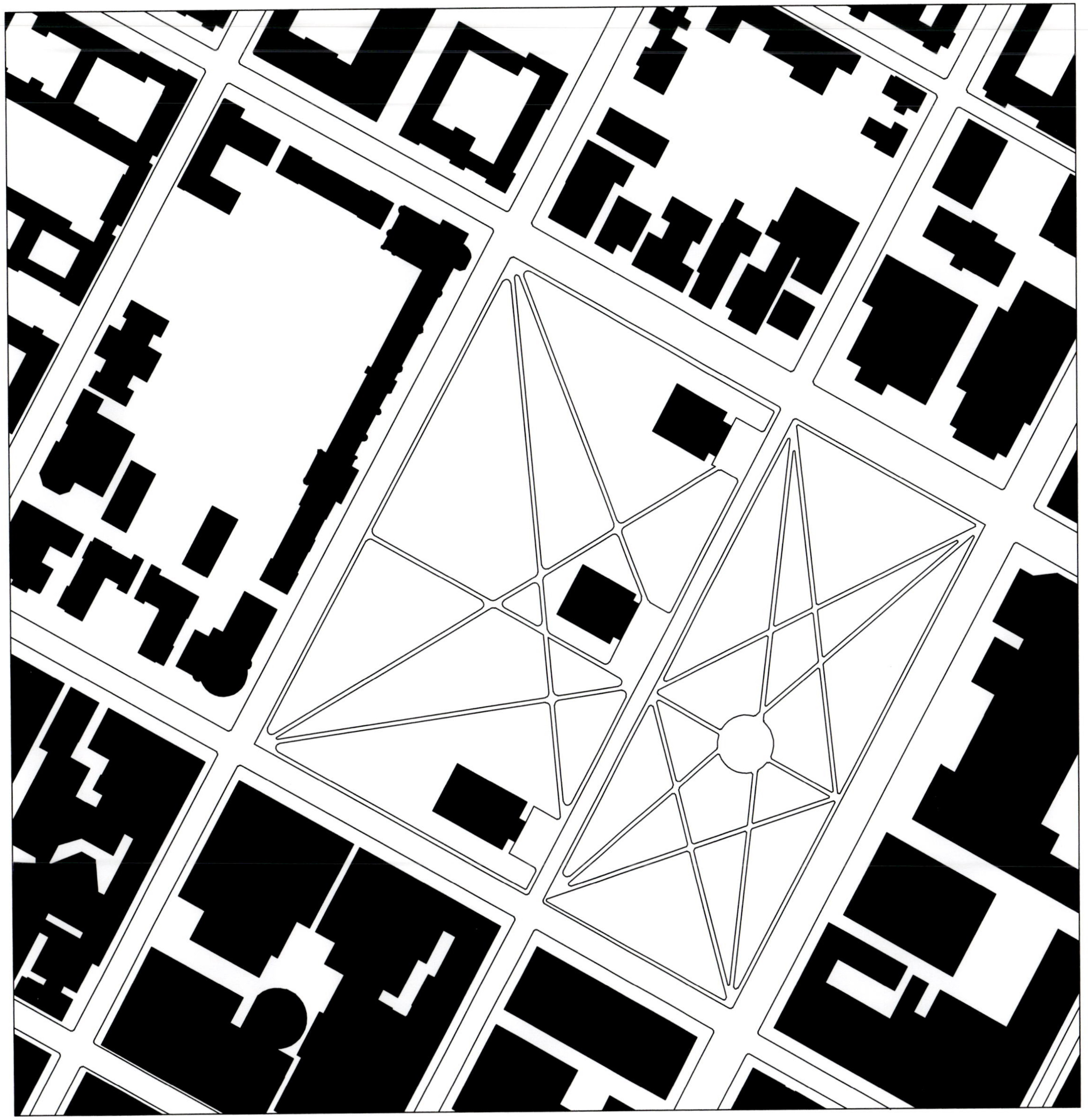

The Green

New Orleans

55

Jackson Square

At the center of New Orleans' Vieux Carré, or French Quarter, is Jackson Square, an open landscaped park that acts as a spatial release from the city's often enclosed streets and covered sidewalks. The square is a lively space due to its well-defined edges, the dominance of the cathedral and its park-like atmosphere opening onto the Mississippi River. As author August Heckscher comments in his book *Open Spaces: The Life of American Cities* (1977), the square

> stands today unsurpassed among effective open places in the nation. It has managed with grace and transition from one of the oldest of city squares to one that satisfies the contemporary need for a civic gathering place of young and old.
>
> (Heckscher 1977: 148–149)

Established by Jean-Baptiste de Bienville in 1718, New Orleans' gridiron plan was identical to other eighteenth century French colonial towns in North America such as St. Louis, Missouri and Mobile, Alabama. Likewise, New Orleans' main public square at its center, eccentrically disposed toward the water's edge, was initially a place d'armes used primarily as a parade ground for the militia (Reps 1965: 78–81). It remained open and unplanted until the 1850s when it was transformed into a landscaped park with a statue of Andrew Jackson at its center.

The square is defined by buildings on three sides yet is open to the south. At the square's northern side is the St. Louis cathedral which is flanked by the arcaded Cabildo and the Presbytère. On the east and west are nearly identical apartment buildings with light, cast-iron colonnades along their base. The southern edge faces Washington Artillery Park, the levee and a rail bed; however, it originally opened directly onto the Mississippi River.

The main north–south street through the Quarter is the Rue d'Orleans. This street, which bisects the original city blocks, extends the church's axis north into the city. A small park on the cathedral's rear side ends the street so that the view south along Rue d'Orleans toward the cathedral is terminated by this green park and the church's apse. Movement from the street toward the church leads to sidewalks aligned with the small park's edges that allow movement around the church to Jackson Square (Heckscher 1977: 151).

An important aspect of the square is that which was never built: an elevated highway between the river and the square. Like other cities set along rivers or waterways, its waterfront was viewed less as a recreational or cultural amenity but rather as an opportunity for highways and other services. Fortunately, New Orleans' citizens helped avert in their own city what happened along New York's East River, Philadelphia's Delaware and Skuykill rivers and, unfortunately, along Istanbul's Golden Horn.

Jackson Square

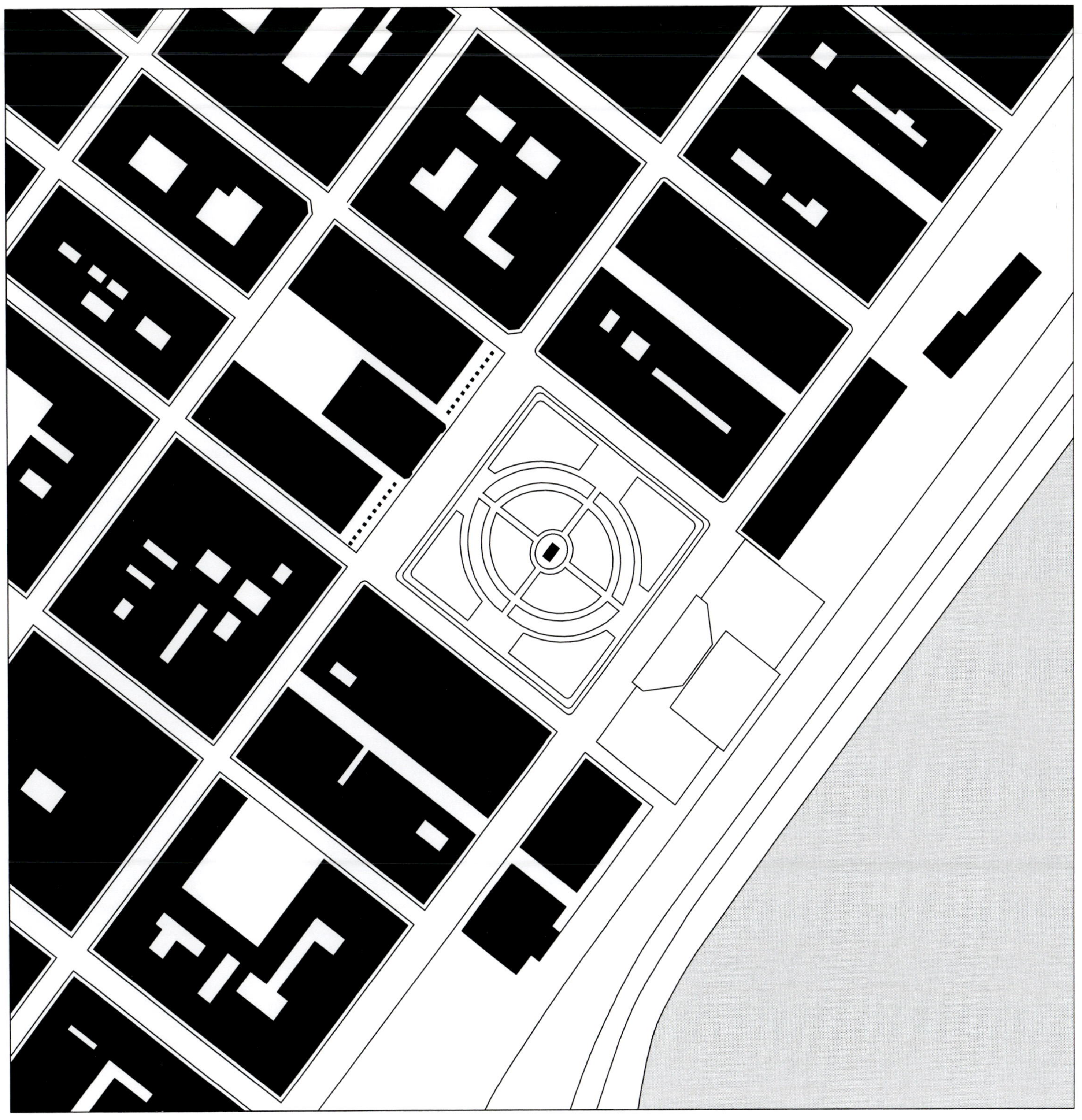

Jackson Square

New York

56

Bryant Park

Bryant Park represents the best of urban parks that were redeveloped and redesigned by public–private agreements managed by non-profit organizations in the late twentieth century. This agreement builds upon the tradition of Bryant Park as a public space for over three hundred years and celebrates the simplicity and clarity of its landscape design.

Located in midtown Manhattan, the park is situated between 40th and 42nd Street and by Sixth Avenue (Avenue of the Americas) to the west. To the east is the New York Public Library's rear façade. Though in the midst of dense urban development today, the area was, until a little more than two hundred years ago, in a relatively rural area of Manhattan Island.

The immediate area in and around the park has been public land since the seventeenth century but in the mid-nineteenth century became a public park called Reservoir Square adjacent to the city's former Croton reservoir on the site now occupied by the New York Public Library. This park was the site of the 1853 Exhibition of the Industry of All Nations with the Crystal Palace Exhibition pavilion, where Elisha Otis demonstrated his safety elevator that would change the New York and Chicago skyline. In 1884 the park was renamed Bryant Park in honor of poet and editor William Cullen Bryant, editor of the *New York Evening Post*. Though defined by the library in 1909 and the subsequent development on the north and south sides of the park, from 1878 until 1938 the park was dominated by the Sixth Avenue elevated rail line on its western edge. As such, the park was not an idyllic setting. After the removal of the elevated track bed, however, the park was redesigned into a slightly elevated formal garden surrounded by a balustrade (Diamonstein 1993: 546).

Unfortunately, the park suffered, like many other urban parks, with a general urban decline in post-World War II America. As New York declined into the late 1960s and 1970s, and with the help of the isolated raised ground and the balustrade that obscured activities, the park became a refuge for drug solicitation. In the 1980s, the park was reclaimed through an initiative of several agencies forming the non-profit Bryant Park Restoration Corporation. This group hired landscape architects Hanna/Olin to redesign the park by increasing visibility from the sidewalks and otherwise recapture the 1930s design. The corporation also added security and litter patrols, increased maintenance, and implemented marketing strategies that promoted the park and its programmed events. In 1992, the park opened cafés and concession stands and has, since that time, become a heavily trafficked garden in mid-town Manhattan. The park is an uncommonly simple formal park in the midst of the city.

Its success is due no doubt to the Bryant Park Restoration Corporation's initiative and continued management. Unfortunately, there is a significant trade-off as this public park was handed over to a private, albeit non-profit corporation that controls many aspects of its day-to-day use. The "public park" is now a privatized enclave and policed by private security who kindly request agreeable behavior of its visitors (Kent 2004: 162). Moreover, to maintain the park's viability, the corporation frequently leases the square for private events that restrict the park to only a specific clientele. The argument that if it were not for the corporation, the park would still be in the hands of drug dealers and petty criminals may be true; however, on recent visits, there has been a distinct feeling that there is a screening for appropriate behavior of visitors and the visitors themselves.

Bryant Park

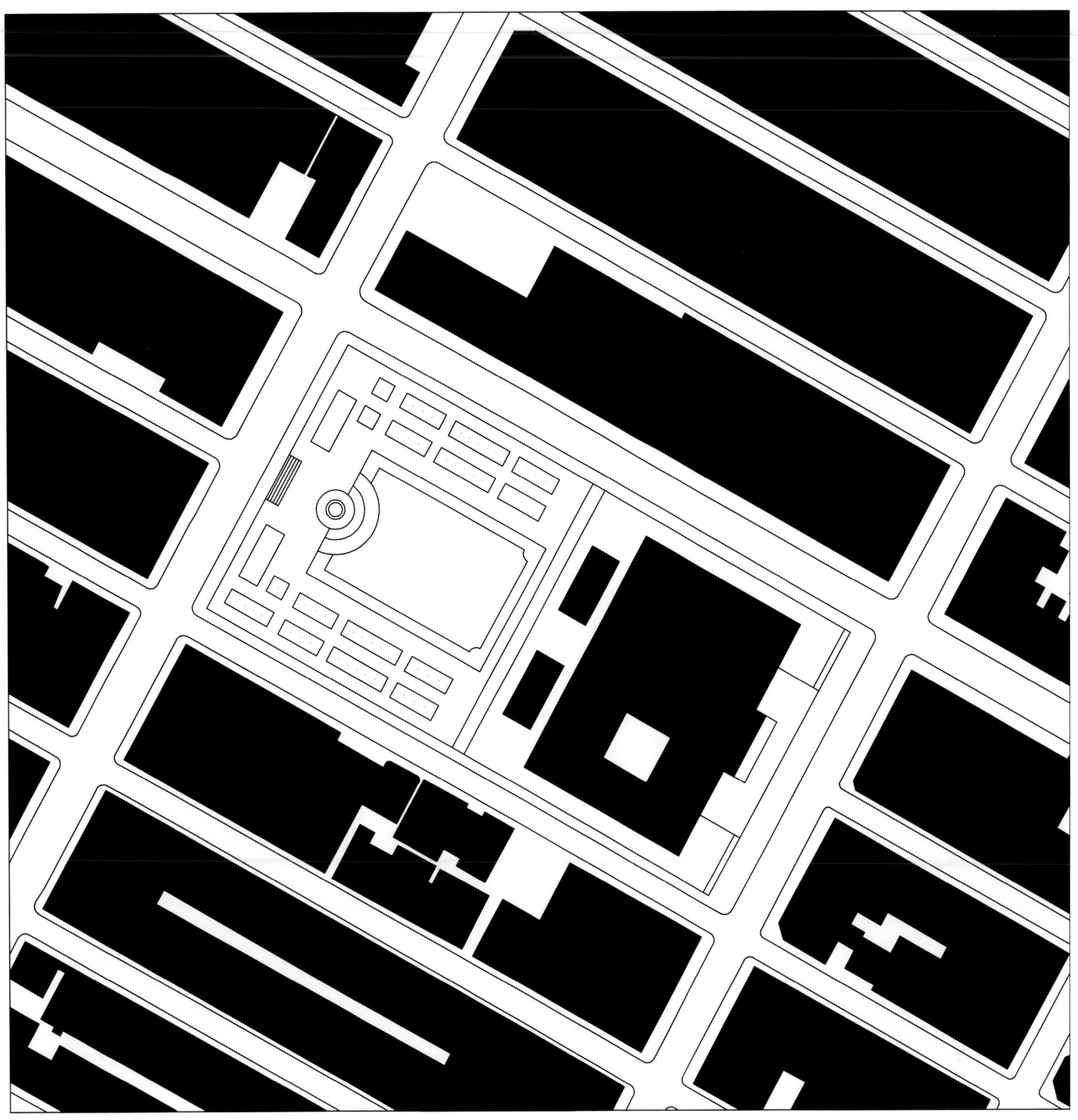

Bryant Park

New York

57

Rockefeller Center

Rockefeller Center, occupying nearly three full blocks between 48th and 51st Streets and from Fifth Avenue to Sixth Avenue (Avenue of the Americas) in midtown Manhattan, is a unique grouping of seventeen buildings accommodating a range of uses including retail, offices, production facilities and theaters. At its center is Rockefeller Plaza at the base of the seventy-story, Art Deco RCA (now GE) building. Though officially attributed to Associated Architects, a team of design firms comprised of Corbett, Harrison & MacMurray; Hood & Fouilhoux; and Reinhard & Hofmeister, the building's design was more than likely steered by architect Raymond Hood (Jordy 1976: 59).

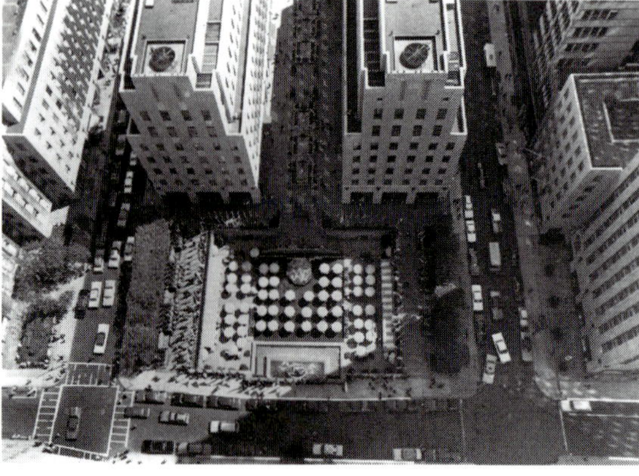

View from atop the RCA building, circa 1971

A most intriguing aspect of Rockefeller Center is that its owners and planners discovered a clever and imaginative way to use New York's zoning to optimize building mass, floor layout and thus increase the potential income of the investment. This required not a breaking of the zoning code, but understanding the rules well enough to work around it.

The New York zoning code delineates a building's mass based on the ground floor area and its relationship to the street. The ordinance's most notable rule is the "Sky Exposure Plane." This plane is an angle, originating from the street's center, that a building's mass could not penetrate. The only exception to this rule was that the building base could rise up from the property line without stepping back to maintain the street wall, but only until a specific height. Beyond that level, the building would have to step back to maintain the "Sky Exposure Plane" with only a slender tower able to penetrate it. The towers were to be relatively slender and, therefore, no more than 25 percent of the entire property (Jordy 1976: 40). Essentially, to achieve a viable tower, one with enough elevators, stairs and services as well as leasable space, required a large parcel of land. A large base allows for a large occupancy and, therefore, a more profitable tower. Within this code, strictly speaking, each parcel of land within the Rockefeller development could have been built out to a larger extent with its own tower much like "wedding cake" tiers.

Planners Andrew Reinhard and Henry Hofmeister examined the zoning carefully and, within the rules, created a project with a central amenity to attract tenants. By inserting a mid-block public square and private cross streets, its central building would be able to rise directly and dramatically from the ground without the obligatory stepping. The buildings near the perimeter step as needed; however, the seventy-story GE building rises nearly straight up from the sidewalk without substantial step backs. Additionally, the GE building's floor plate is, in comparison to other buildings, relatively narrow so that the office workers closest to the central core would receive natural light and ventilation (Jordy 1976: 45).

Rockefeller Center represents early twentieth-century concepts of civic space in conjunction with real estate investment and, acclaimed by Manfredo Tafuri in his essay "The Disenchanted Tower: The Skyscraper and the City," as the first example of skyscrapers grouped together consciously to make an urban space. (Ciucci et al. XXXX: 467) Consequently, it is the ultimate success story, financially, urbanistically and architecturally in challenging the architects and designers to examine the rules and ask questions in an innovative way.

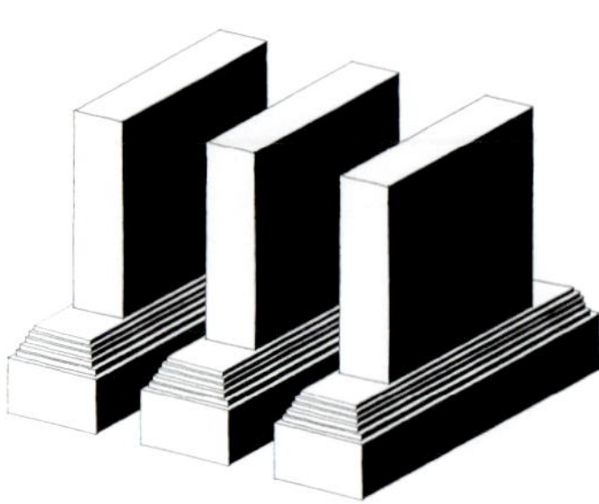

Massing of the site maximizing the site based on the zoning rules only

Massing of the site, as built, after introducing the central tower and plaza

Rockefeller Center

New York

58

Stuyvesant Square

Stuyvesant Square, a residential square in the heart of the Stuyvesant neighborhood approximately three blocks east of Union Square in Manhattan, reveals the connection of New York's design and citizenry to their European roots. Though founded by descendants of the Dutch colonists of New Amsterdam, it also shows the connection to the English concept of residential squares in London.

Located between East 15th and East 17th Streets and bisected by Second Avenue in Manhattan – an area that originally bordered directly onto the East River – it was laid out in 1836 and named for Petrus Stuyvesant, the last Director-General of the Dutch colony of New Netherlands. In 1789, Stuyvesant's great-grandson Petrus S. Stuyvesant named the area "Petersfield" and subdivided the land into housing lots with a street grid in a true north–south direction but was eventually absorbed into the 1811 Commissioners' Plan grid.

Initially the park was to be fenced and planted like Union Square and Washington Square. Also, similar to London's residential squares, it was the centerpiece of Stuyvesant's development and open only for the use of those who resided on its borders. Eventually, it was deeded to the city in 1836 but it was only in 1851 after years of legal battles between the family that the city took possession of the park.

By the late nineteenth century, Stuyvesant Square and "upper" Second Avenue became one of the fashionable neighborhoods of New York. Today, the park remains vibrant due mostly to the mix of residential, religious and institutional buildings such as the Beth Israel Medical Center and St. George's Church. Since the mid-1970s, the square and surrounding neighborhood are part of the Stuyvesant Square historic district and monitored by the Stuyvesant Park Neighborhood Association.

The square's most obvious characteristic is its partitioning by Second Avenue into two detached green spaces. Though this creates two separate spaces, it does allow Second Avenue traffic to move quickly through the square, while the side streets, Rutherford Place to the west and Perlman Place to the east, remain less active service streets. This can be contrasted with Gramercy Park four blocks to the northwest. Like Savannah's squares, Gramercy Park is not divided but vehicles on southbound Lexington Avenue must go around the square or, better yet, avoid it all together and use either north or southbound Third Avenue or Park Avenue to the west or east.

Stuyvesant Square

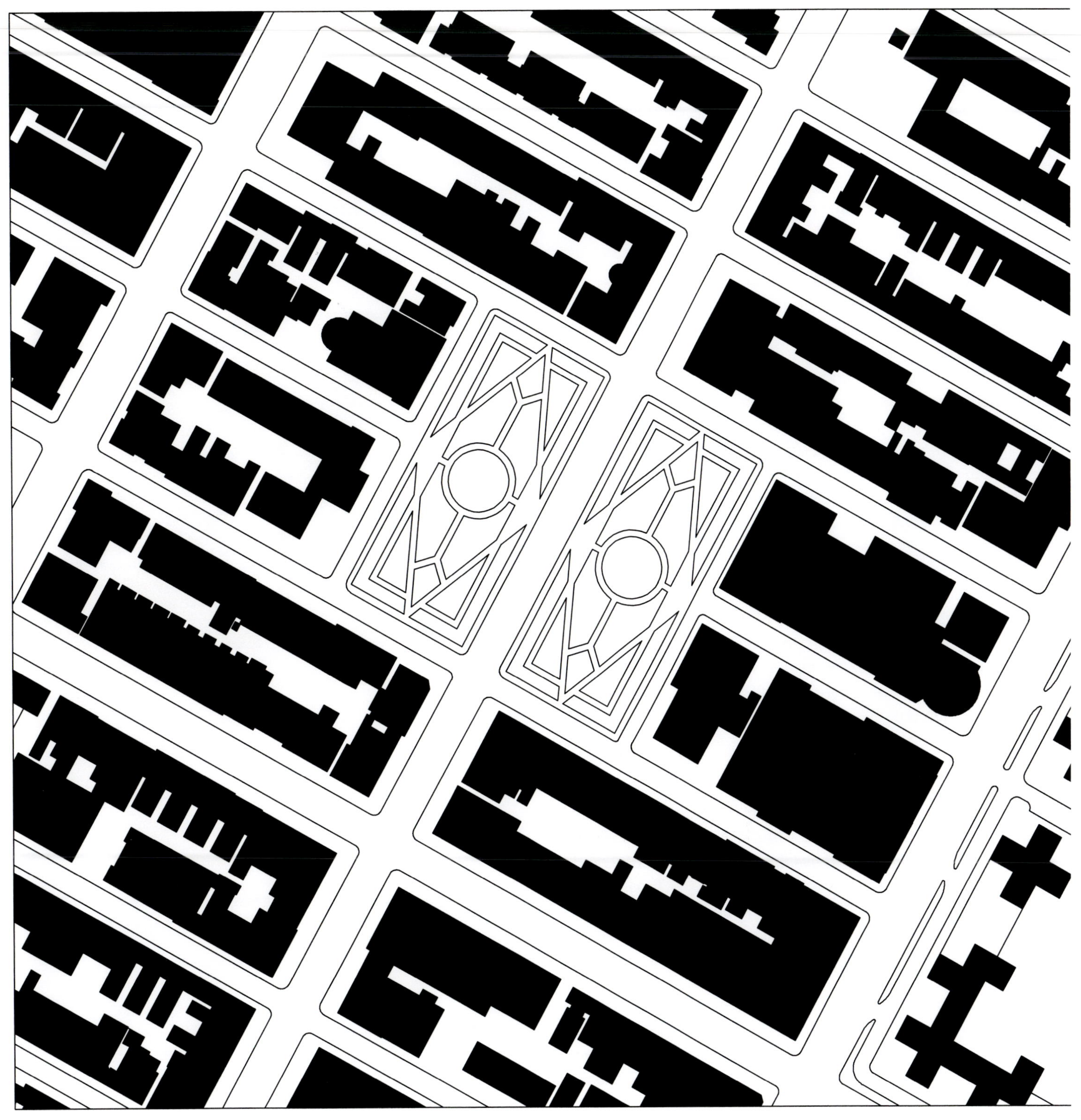

Stuyvesant Square

New York

59

Times Square

Times Square in midtown Manhattan is probably one of the most internationally renowned spaces in the world yet, like Tokyo's Hachiko Square, it is less of a square and more of an intersection dominated by billboards, theater signage and immense video screens.

Located between 42nd and 46th Streets where Broadway and Seventh Avenue cross, the area was known as Longacre Square until 1904 when, following the construction of the New York Times building, was renamed Times Square. The area has been associated with theaters since the late nineteenth century and, owing to the number of illuminated electric signs, the area has been known as the "Great White Way" since the early twentieth century. Two peninsula-like islands in the center of Times Square are the only relatively open areas within the square. To the north is Father Duffy Square, named after the former Army chaplain and priest who ministered in the Times Square area, and to the south is the Armed Forces recruiting station that has been there since World War II and probably will not want to give up the space any time soon.

By the late 1960s, however, evidence of the area's steady decline was evident as many theaters began featuring adult burlesque shows and films. In the mid-1970s, the square was plagued by crime and soon had the highest rate in the city, including drug dealing, armed robbery and prostitution.

In the late 1970s, the then Mayor Ed Koch with a cadre of real estate investors developed a series of proposals to revitalize the area that would eventually extend into the turn of the twenty-first century. As James Traub notes in his book, *The Devil's Playground* (2004) and Lynne Sagalyn in her book, *Times Square Roulette: Remaking the City Icon* (2001), the ultimate accomplishment of the Times Square revitalization was unique public–private agreements and economic incentives mixed with an interest in the square's pop imagery blended with corporate marketing. Today, the revitalized Times Square evokes in many, especially New Yorkers, ambiguous nostalgia. As is typical with nostalgia, there is a longing for a past that never existed. While no one misses the crime and grime, there is a real sense that those same characteristics were part of what made it authentic, chaotic and unusual. Today, legislated signage and artificially complex billboards create a comfortable simulacra: it resembles old Times Square, but not too much.

Besides this important lesson that successful urban design meshes real estate investment, zoning, economics, politics, personalities and any number of other factors, another lesson of Times Square is that it is a successful urban place which does not necessarily have to be a clearly contained urban room. An urban space can be a locus of economic activity involving spectacle and energized at its changeable, permeable and fluctuating edges.

Times Square from above

Times Square

Times Square

New York

60

Union Square

Union Square is unique in that it is an oval park set within New York's street grid. The resulting residual space between the curvilinear and orthogonal perimeter remained unclear until the 1970s when transformed into the square's daily Greenmarket. Because of this, Union Square is an example of how public spaces slowly but continually adapt over the centuries based on community need rather than sometimes artificial event programming.

A common misconception is that Union Square takes its name either from Civil War era confidence in the Union or from its use as a place for union marches. Its origin, however, is less lofty. Located between 14th and 17th Streets just north of Greenwich Village, its shape and name come from the awkward meeting of the diagonal Broadway and Bowery, now Fourth Avenue and the 1811 Commissioners' Plan's grid. Initially named Union Place, it was opened as a formally planned park in 1839; its natural slope toward the north was further augmented by the underlying subway tracks in the late nineteenth century.

In the early nineteenth century the area surrounding the park was inhabited by wealthy New Yorkers, but by mid-century it became increasingly commercialized and the home of theaters. These theaters would eventually move farther north to the Times Square district in the late nineteenth century. By the early twentieth century the square had became associated with labor and civil liberty demonstrations due, in part, to its proximity to the manufacturing districts in Lower Manhattan and the nearby union headquarters.

Like many other urban parks in Manhattan, Union Square went into a slow decline after World War II but was revitalized in the 1970s with the introduction of the Union Square Greenmarket. Initiated by the Union Square Partnership Local Development Corporation, a coalition that included the Council on the Environment and New York's Department of Planning and Department of Parks and Recreation, the daily, open air market allows farmers from the surrounding region to sell fresh produce directly to the public. A second public–private entity, the Union Square Partnership Business Improvement District, helps maintain the park and surrounding neighborhood. Today, the square's continued success is tied to the surrounding context that includes a variety of high-rise commercial, office and residential buildings with retail and restaurants on the ground floor.

Union Square

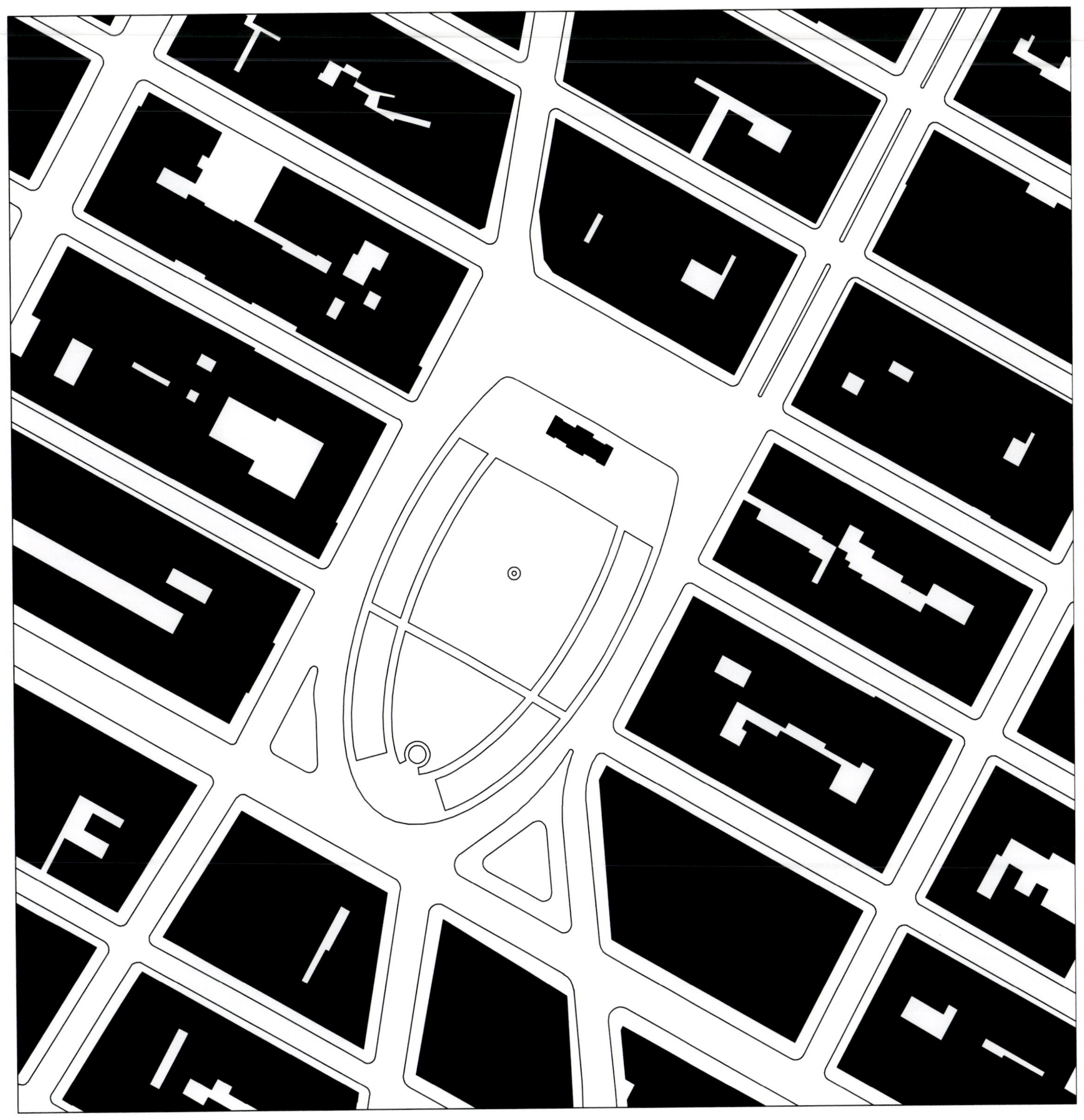

Union Square

New York

Washington Square

61

Originally a common burial ground or Potters Field, the area now occupied by Washington Square was a militia training ground and encampment through the eighteenth century. Reclaimed in 1797 to promote development in what was then the northern suburbs of Manhattan, it was designated a park in 1827 and quickly became and remains an integral component of surrounding Greenwich Village neighborhood.

Though parts of Manhattan Island north of Washington Square were settled by the early nineteenth century, in 1806, New York State began an extensive design for Manhattan Island. The result five years later was a uniform grid of twelve north–south avenues and one hundred and fifty five east–west streets beginning just north of Washington Square (Reps 1965: 296). Known as the 1811 Commissioners' Plan, it is apparent in this plan that Fifth Avenue, which aligns with the triumphal arch commemorating the centennial of George Washington's inauguration, designed by Stanford White, is slightly askew of the park's rectilinear geometry.

The park was redesigned in 1870 by M.A. Kellog and Ignaz Pilat, disciples of Frederick Law Olmstead, with curvilinear walkways, a central fountain and a sinuous, three-prong forked road connecting Fifth Avenue to Sullivan Street, Thompson Street and LaGuardia Street to the south. Washington Square has a history as a center of intellectuals including Henry James, Dos Passos and Edith Wharton throughout the nineteenth century. Much of this may have to do with the location of New York University, founded in 1831, which occupies nearly 75 percent of the square's surrounding buildings.

Washington Square, as the virtual heart of Greenwich Village, was nearly annihilated by New York planner Robert Moses who, in the late 1950s, proposed a depressed highway through the area like those he supervised in Harlem and other parts of Manhattan. As the center of grassroots activism and bohemian lifestyle that epitomized Greenwich Village culture, a resulting outcry from local activists seeking to preserve Washington Square ultimately thwarted these plans. With the Moses plan abandoned, a confederacy of well-meaning Village residents redesigned the square in 1970; this, unfortunately, illustrates the weakness of design by a committee intent on pleasing all members of the community. As architectural critic Paul Goldberger notes, "Nothing in New York stands as better proof of the old adage about committees – Washington Square Park is a camel" (Goldberger 1979: 74). Though a camel, the design did remove the through-street vehicular traffic but, overall, balkanized the park into a series of disparate elements such as the large sunken asphalt court around the fountain, concrete retaining walls and planters, mini-plazas including a "Teen Plaza" and children's play mounds (Ulam 2006: 106).

In 2006, the park was redesigned to unify the spaces, repair the infrastructure and, overall, restore the park closer to the original Olmstead-inspired plan (Ulam 2006: 110). This led, of course, to vociferous objections and even formation of coalitions to save specific elements in the park. Though everyone agrees that restoration is needed, all decisions are steeped in controversy. Like a leaking boat, everyone knows that it would be a good idea to bail and patch the holes, but how to actually do it is up for constant debate.

The issues magnified by Washington Square are its function as a public park. That said, any redesign, either simple or complicated, must cater to a myriad of forces in the Greenwich Village community. As Emily Kies Folpe notes in *It Happened on Washington Square*, the square is a "magnet" that allows people

> to linger, to play, to declaim; to celebrate, demonstrate, and mourn . . . It functions as a campus green, a crossroads, and a top sport for people-watching. Washington Square is a place not to escape from city life but to enter into it.
>
> (Folpe 2002: 2)

Of course, like other squares in the late twentieth century and early twenty-first century, Washington Square may have an opportunity to understand that a simple design, like Bryant Park, can allow for a myriad of interpretations rather than literal manifestation in which each person in the park has a specific design for their specific need.

Washington Square

Washington Square arch and its alignment with Fifth Avenue

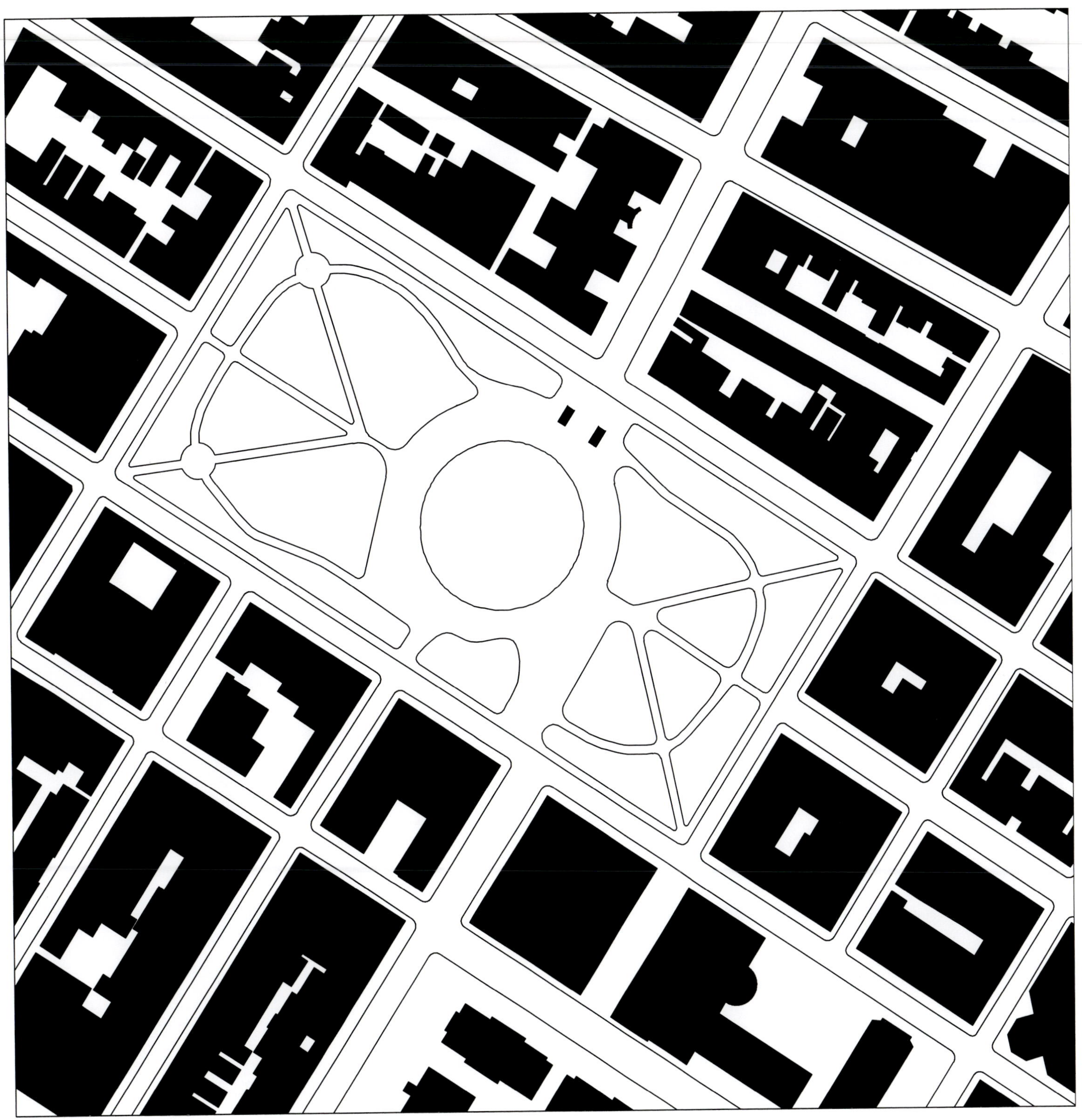

Washington Square

Oslo

62

Rådhus Plassen, Kronprincess Märthas Plassen and Eidsvolls Plass

Founded in 1624 as Christiana and renamed Oslo in 1924, the city's gridiron plan is set within a gently sloping basin where Loevla River disgorges into the head of the fjord to the southwest. The city was initially established north of a fourteenth century Akershus fortress, which is just off the edge of this plan to the south, and grew slowly to the northwest beginning in the eighteenth century. This street grid is now lined by four- and five-story nineteenth century office and apartment buildings with retail at the ground floor.

The new Rådhus or city hall, designed by Arnstein Arneberg and Magnus Poulsson in 1930 and completed in 1950, is part of the redevelopment of downtown Oslo in the early twentieth century that ordered the growing town and reconnected it to the waterfront. The city hall is a nearly symmetrical building that has a dual role of affronting the city while marking the waterfront and the city's connection with the fjord along its northeast–southwest axis. While it has an entry facing the harbor, its main entry affronts the semicircular Fridtjof Nansen Square to the northeast which aligns with Roald Amundsens Street, which becomes University Street. These streets lead to Oslo University and the National Gallery to the northeast. Bisecting these districts is the linear Student Square dominated by the Palace, just off the plan to the northwest, and Eidsvolls Squares terminated by Stortinget, the Parliament Building, to the southeast.

To the southwest, the city hall links the city across Town Hall Street to the Honnørbrygga or harbor and visually ends at the Vika bay and the Oslo fjord beyond. On the northwest side of the city hall is the small, trapezoidal Kronprincess Märthas Plassen or Crown Princess Martha's Square. Unfortunately, Crown Princess Martha's Square does not help the Rådhus Plassen. Unlike the city hall's southeastern side that is framed by building mass, the Crown Princess Martha's Square is a void that does not maintain the city's edge. Additionally, the link to the city remains somewhat visual but is undermined by the nearly one hundred meter wide expanse between the face of the city hall, across Rådhus Street to the water's edge.

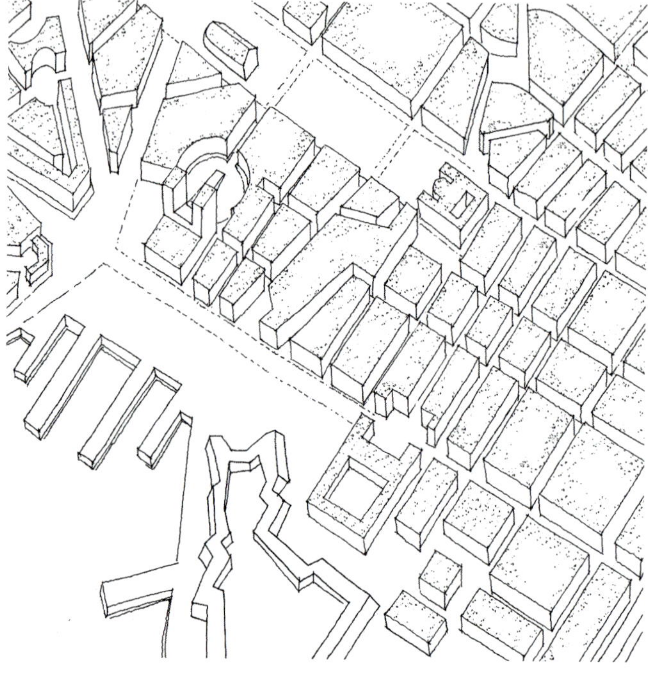

The Oslo waterfront

Oslo city hall from the waterfront

Oslo city hall from the north

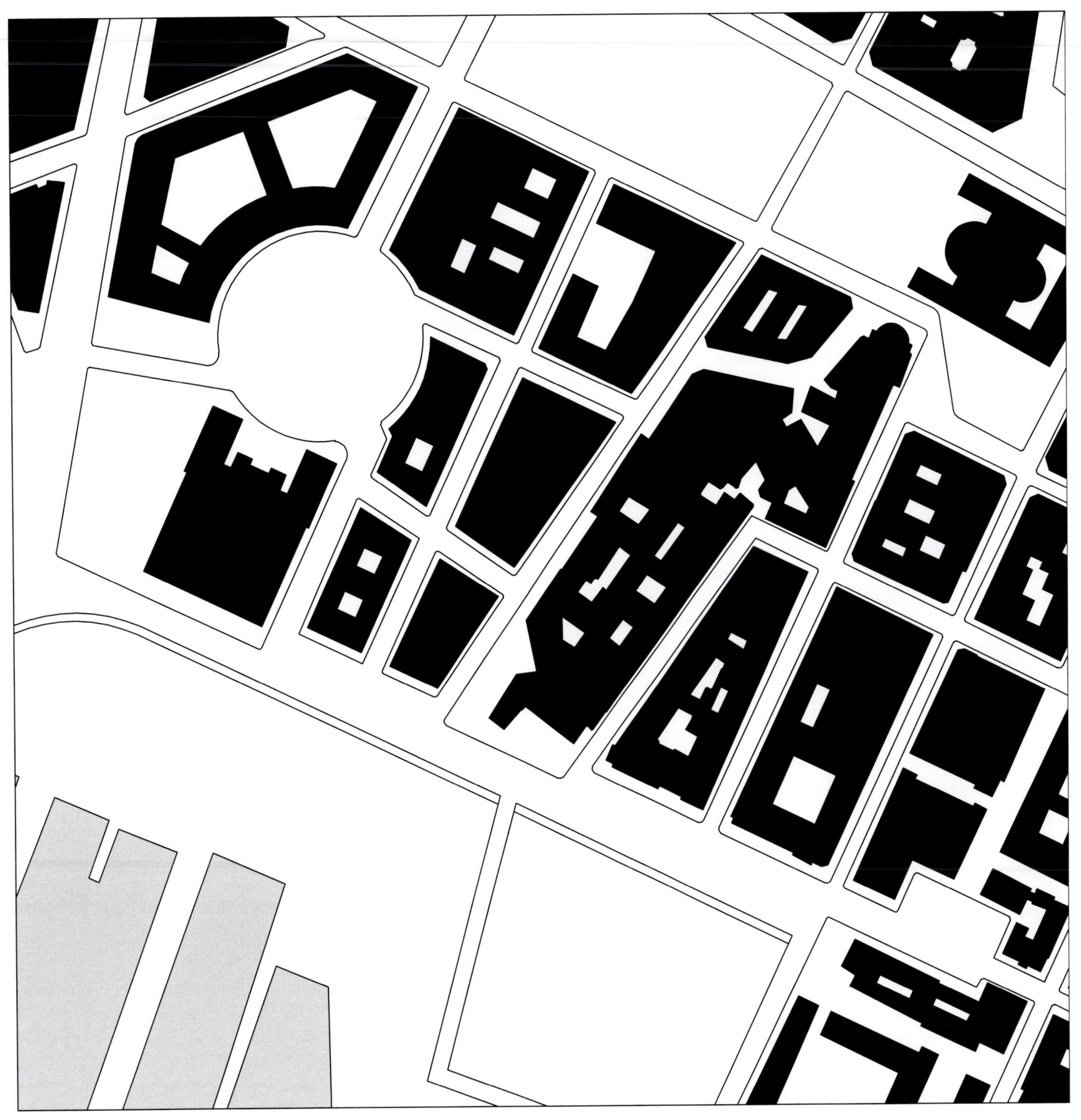

Rådhus Plassen, Kronprincess Märthas Plassen and Eidsvolls Plass

Paris

63

Palais Royal

Palais Royal, formerly Palais Cardinale, is a formal enclosed garden just north of the Louvre in central Paris. Designed originally as a palace for Cardinal Richelieu by architect Jacques Lemercier in 1635, it was transformed into a public space in the late eighteenth century. Part of this transformation was the introduction of a thin layer of colonnaded buildings on the inside edge of the gardens that would regulate and give order to the space. Though in the late eighteenth and into the nineteenth century it was associated with the tawdry side of life, today the gardens are a quiet repose in central Paris. As Colin Rowe and Fred Koetter remark in *Collage City*, the garden is an "instrument of field recognition, an identifiable stabilizer and a means of collective orientation" in Paris (Rowe and Koetter 1978: 82–83).

Palais Royal façade

Though its original design was a garden, it was less defined and essentially the informal side of Richelieu's palace. It continued as a palace following the Cardinal's death in 1642 until 1780 when architect Victor Louis under the direction of Philippe d'Orléans inserted what amounts to a liner of three-story buildings on the inner side of the existing palace to create a uniform internal façade to the garden. The ground level is colonnaded on all four sides, giving protection from the elements. A secondary liner to the colonnades are the four allées of well-trimmed trees. These trees help create additional zones in the space so that the colonnades, the trees and the central garden are a rich fabric in their entirety.

An interesting transformation of the colonnade is at the southern end. Here the colonnade is relieved of its upper stories and, as it moves across to form the short end of the space, it is doubled into two colonnades delimiting a small, lateral space – a move that helps mediate both the formal and spatial transition from the open Palais to the Louvre. First, the colonnades as curtain-like, interstitial screen helps in an orchestration of movement from open space to enclosed space. Second, and of more interest, is that it helps mediate the misaligned axes of the Palais and of the Louvre's Passage Richelieu.

Palais Royal

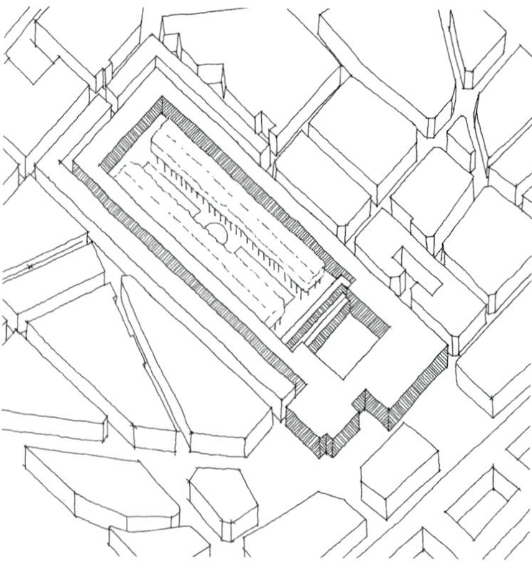

Insertion of the liner in the eighteenth century

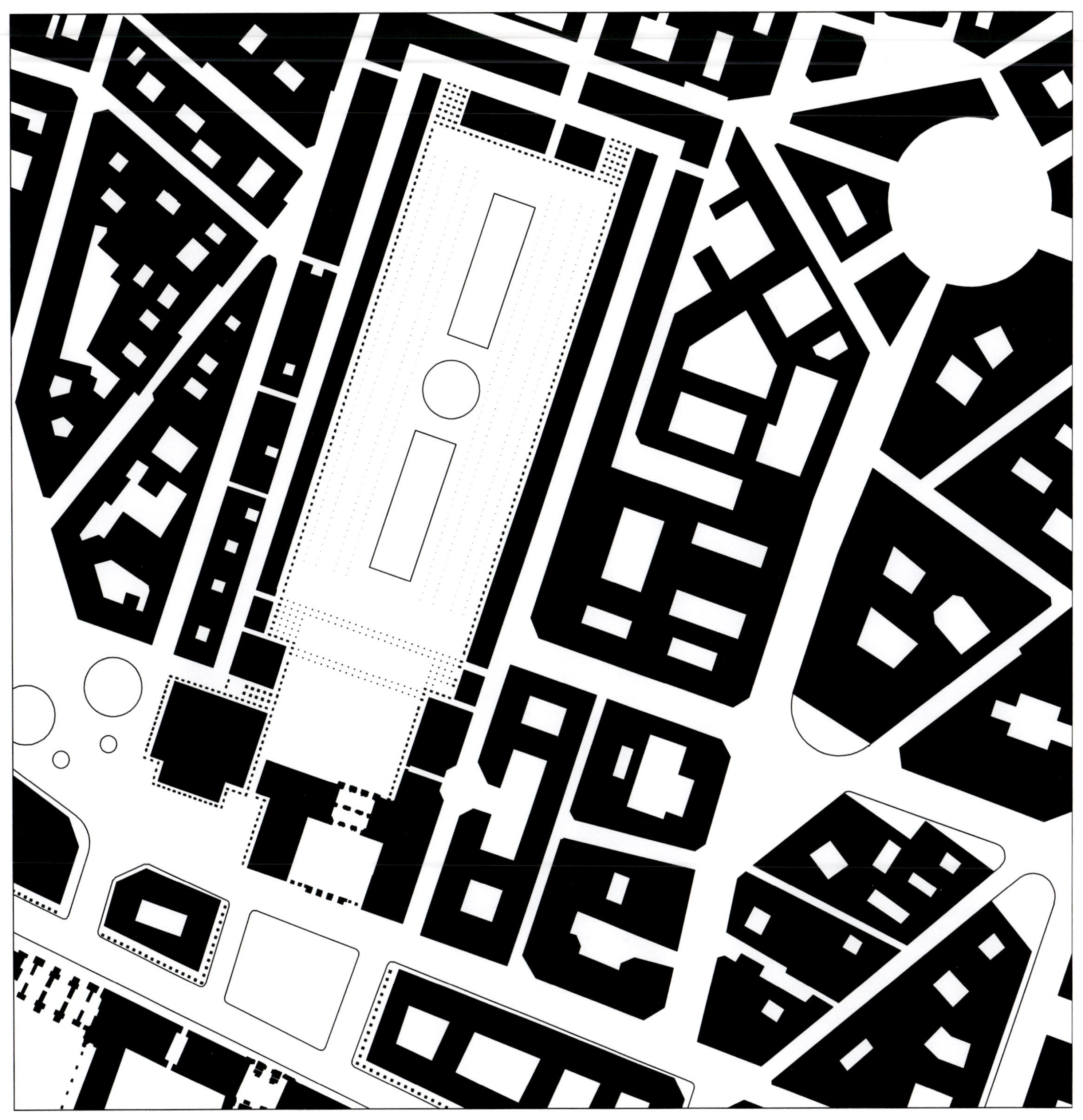

Palais Royal

Paris

64

Place Charles-de-Gaulle/Place de l'Etoile

Place Charles-de-Gaulle, more commonly known among Parisians by its original name of Place de l'Etoile, with the Arc de Triomphe at its center, is more of an immense traffic circle rather than a public gathering space. Every day it collects and redistributes several thousand automobiles, buses and trucks to and from twelve major avenues and all the while symbolizes Paris' urban form and reinforces the city's international image.

The space has held its fundamental configuration and location on the elevated Butte de Chaillot for several centuries. It was originally a *rond-point* in the rural outskirts of Paris. Like those found at Versailles, a star-shaped (*étoile*) *rond-point* is a circular clearing with radiating avenues once used in royal hunts. Participants in the royal hunt would stand in the circle while attendants drove game from the wooded areas into and across the broad avenues. As the game emerged, the royal hunting party had ample opportunity to dispatch their prey. By the late eighteenth century, it had become part of a royal garden and effectively marked Paris' pre-Revolutionary limits. The Arc de Triomphe was conceived as a city gate by Napoleon I in 1806 and was completed in 1836.

The Place is associated with Napoleon III's Second Empire urban development program under the guidance of Georges Haussmann. Between 1851 and 1871, Haussmann directed the reconstruction of Paris's medieval urban fabric and extended new streets and spaces into the yet undeveloped suburbs. Haussmann's venture doubled the number of streets and instituted a new civic governmental structure with added civic spaces and buildings that included new schools, parks and prisons and modernized the city's water and sewer systems. A common misconception is that Haussmann's avenues, streets and *rond-points* were designed for expedient troop movement to contain civic insurrection. Though not the sole reason, even Haussmann believed it could be a side benefit (Olsen 1986: 44). In Paris, Haussmann's refined existing *grande boulevards* and ordered façades such as the Rue de Rivoli and the *rond-points*, such as the Place de l'Etoile, outside the city's core.

Today, Place Charles-de-Gaulle is deep within Paris's urban fabric and marks the western end of Avenue des Champs-Elysées and the midpoint of the grand axis between the Louvre and La Défense. The Place continues to be a relatively successful traffic circle considering the number and speed of vehicular traffic that it accommodates. Its success, which might be measured by the traffic's effect on surrounding buildings and its ability to keep traffic moving relatively smoothly, is due in part to its size and to its inversion of the typical traffic circle type. Unlike more common traffic circles, such as Dupont Circle in Washington, DC, in which traffic moves between the buildings and around the green area, the Place Charles-de-Gaulle's eleven or more lanes are near its center while several rings of trees, planted at the same depth as the traffic lanes, act as an insulation to the buildings. A second, outer ring of the street allows local traffic to service the buildings on the circle.

Place Charles-de-Gaulle

Place Charles-de-Gaulle/Place de l'Etoile

Paris

65

Place des Vosges

Like many skillfully designed objects or spaces, Place des Vosges is a cohesive square which appears straightforward, yet is refined through its subtleties. Its mix of uses at different scales has allowed the square to be occupied by a range of people at different times of the day and illustrates how streets and spaces need a mix of incomes, activities and uses to keep the space vibrant and successful.

Envisioned as part of Paris's overall urban development in the sixteenth century, Place des Vosges is a distinct Parisian square initiated as a real estate investment to combine royal residences with commercial activity and public space. Sponsored by King Henry IV as the Place Royale, this cohesive square is attributed to Jacques II Androuet Ducerceau, Louis Métezeau and Salomon de Brosse (Ballon 1991: 57).

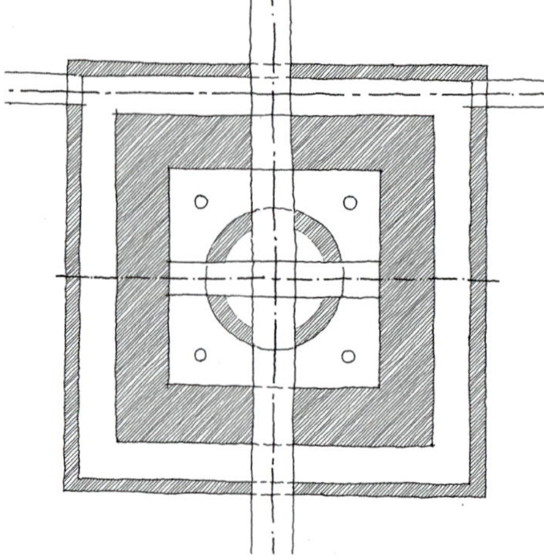

The layers of space within the square, the lateral streets and axial composition

To ensure uniformity and grandness of the square, each owner of the three-bay-wide segment of the square, to whom the land was gifted, was required to build façades as established by royal architects and reserve the ground floor for commercial use. The spaces above this level and behind the façades, however, could be whatever each owner required. This set a number of precedents in Paris including the Place Vendôme and Rue de Rivoli. The space itself was initially designed as a public place in the city yet, due to its noble clientele, became increasingly dominated by royal ceremonies and jousting tournaments. By the late eighteenth century, the grounds were limited to the nobility in the surrounding homes but this soon changed following the Revolution. Since the nineteenth century, the center has become the garden it resembles today. It did suffer neglect for many years, but now is a vital center for the surrounding community for recreation and passage to different parts of the city. As such, it is one of those "magically useless" spaces in the urban fabric (Rowe and Koetter 1978: 156).

Though a closed and well-defined square, it is a vibrant area because of subtle moves. While the edges are relatively uniform with a continuous arcade at ground level, the façade is punctuated by regular-hipped roof pavilions. Center pavilions on the south and north range, the King's and Queen's Pavilions respectively, rise above the other buildings with higher cornices and a larger hipped roof pavilion marks the two formal entrances. Though there are distinct center entries, a lateral street Rue du Pas de la Mule on the northern edge activates the square with some visual access and some spatial experience of the square without actually going through the heart of it. Especially noteworthy are the layers of Place des Vosges that help define the square. The arcade, street, walkway and trees produce a kind of series of layers from building to center thus making the square a complex weave of spaces for different uses without disrupting the overall idea of the square.

Place des Vosges looking north

Looking toward the southeast

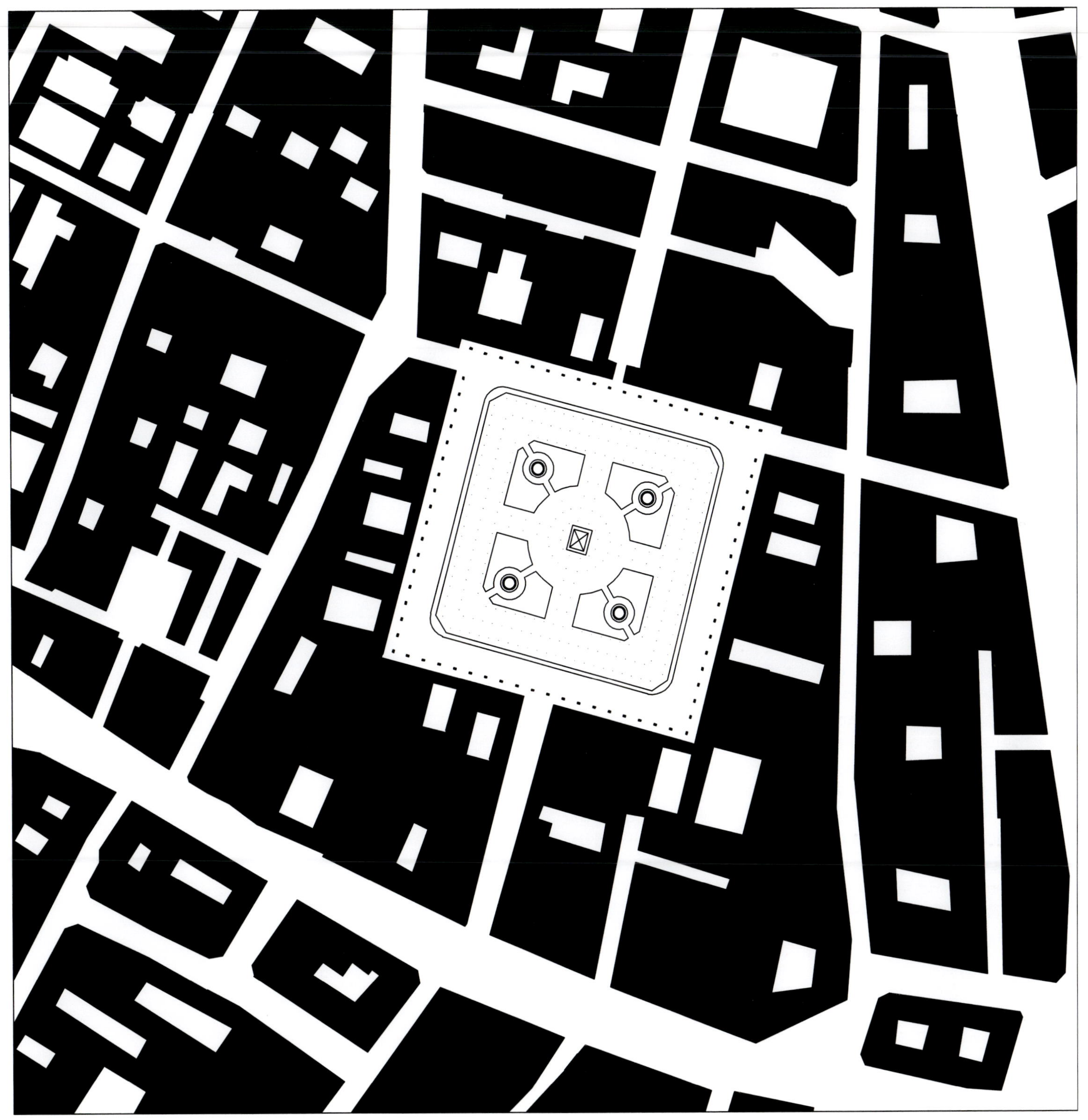

Place des Vosges

Paris

66

Musée du Louvre

The Palais du Louvre, now known as the Musée du Louvre, began as a twelfth century fortress one-fourth the size of the large square courtyard segment at the Louvre's east end. In the fourteenth century, the Louvre became the royal residence and inaugurated its extended seven-century transformation. Through each successive renovation, addition or removal, the common goal was strengthening the link between the palace on the east with the Tuileries Gardens to the west (Ballon 1991: 59). This problem was more difficult due in part to the two independent axes and great distance.

This westward drive manifests itself quite clearly in the Louvre's configuration today. The enclosed courtyard to the east, part of which was shaped by the original fortress' geometry, leads to the partially enclosed rectilinear court now containing I.M. Pei's pyramid. This open-ended court extends to the Place de Carrousel, which is framed by the tendril-like wings that seem to reach toward the Tuileries Gardens. This westward expansion continued into the nineteenth and twentieth centuries with the Louvre's axis extended along the Champs-Elysées, through the Arc de Triomphe and, eventually, to La Défense's Grande Arche.

This axial extension, however, was not always as extended. Though walls and galleries extended toward the gardens along the Seine, in the mid-sixteenth century Catherine de' Medici subsidized construction of the Tuileries Palace. This wall-like palace, constructed perpendicular to the Louvre's east–west axis, delimited the Tuileries' eastern edge and effectively severed the Louvre's connection to the gardens. From that time forward, successive kings and emperors extended the Louvre's wings toward the Medici palace and, by 1805, enclosed the Place du Carrousel between the original Louvre and Tuileries Palace. This enclosure did not last long. Following a fire in the late nineteenth century, Tuileries Palace was razed which opened the inner courtyard edged by the thin palace wings toward the gardens and the west.

Principally a museum since the early nineteenth century, no one anticipated the many thousands of visitors the Louvre would need to accommodate in the late twentieth century. By the late 1970s, the museum, which was already difficult to navigate, could hardly accommodate its visitors. I.M. Pei's project, of which the pyramid is, to a certain extent, the tip of the project's iceberg, was the total reorganization of the museum's circulation and collection. As a grand project, it is part of the long tradition of government sponsored visionary urban projects in Paris. From Place des Vosges to the Palais Royale and from Haussmann's boulevards to François Mitterand's *grand projets*, the French government has played an active role in revitalizing entire districts and, to a greater extent, establishing Paris as one of the great cities of the world.

Musée du Louvre

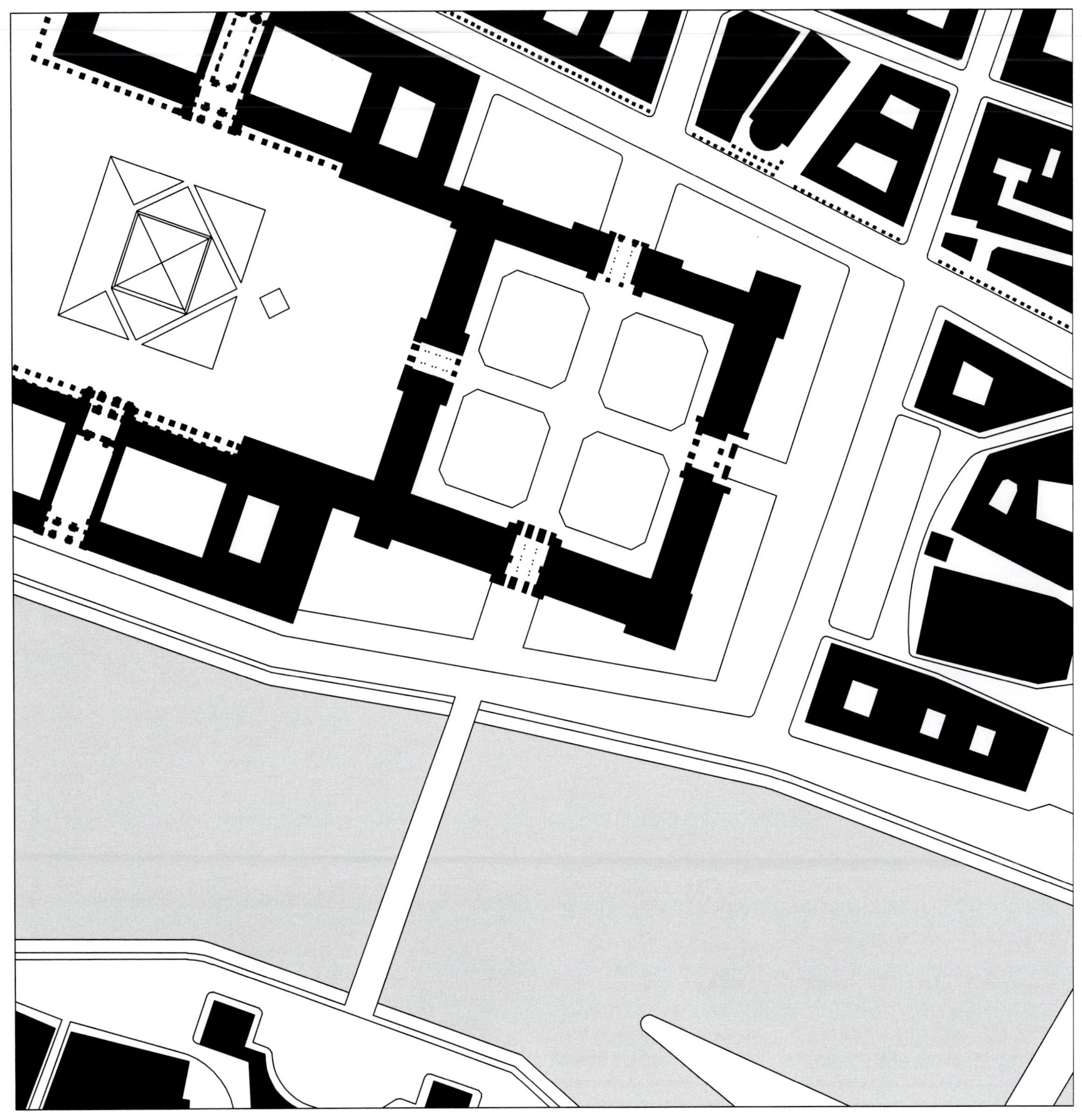

Musée du Louvre

Paris

67

Place Vendôme

Place Vendôme, with its extended octagonal geometry and axial order, is considered a quintessential French Baroque urban space and "represents the epitome of the closed square and, moreover, generally the most conscious space creation of the French classicist baroque" (Zucker 1966: 176). Following in the same tradition of Parisian urban spaces, Place Vendôme was part of a larger investment in the urban fabric sponsored in cooperation between the crown and private investors. As such, it was a distinctly Parisian approach in which the individual acceded to civic space.

Centered on the estate of the Duc de Vendôme just north of the Tuileries Gardens, this real estate project hoped to capitalize on the likely development of Paris north of the Louvre. The project, attributed to the Marquis de Louvois, began in 1685 as a U-shaped space, designated Place de Nos Conquêtes and later Place Louis-le-Grand, would have been part of a ceremonial entry toward the Louvre and incorporate several government ministries and residences (Ziskin 1999: 5; Cleary 1998: 48). Unfortunately, in the tradition of real estate investments, the project suffered from doubtful investors, unfavorable location and wavering financial markets, which stopped the project for over ten years. Finally, in 1699, the king removed his support and handed the project over to the city. A new group of investors razed parts already constructed and began once more with a new design by Jules Hardouin-Mansart. The new, uniform three-story façades were started in 1701 with most of the buildings behind finished by 1718 (Cleary 1998: 50).

The Place's center was initially occupied by an equestrian statue of Louis XIV but was replaced in 1805 with a monumental column capped by a statue of Napoleon Bonaparte. The forty-meter high column, similar to Trajan's Column in Rome and later Nelson's Column in London, is nearly three times the height of the surrounding buildings. To many critics, the column is out of proportion and diminishes the original proportions of the square.

Though the square has many similarities to Place des Vosges, it has some distinctive differences. The rectangle space with chamfered corners is slightly longer and bisected by Rue de la Paix on its north–south axis. Projecting bays and pediments, however, mark its cross axis. Vendôme's façades were built and only then sold to individual investors – in five-bay minimums – who then built behind what they pleased. These nearly uniform, non-hierarchical façades give no indication of the individual uses. This idea continued in Paris, for example the Rue de Rivoli, and influenced other developers outside France such as in Bath, England.

Probably the greatest difference between Place Vendôme and Place des Vosges is the street access. Unlike Vosges with its minor axis and lateral street that allows movement through without disrupting the space, Vendôme is effectively bisected by the Rue de la Paix forming two zones similar to New York's Stuyvesant Square. This bisection was further aggravated in the nineteenth century when the avenue extended beyond a single block as it was initially designed. This extension opened the space visually and increased traffic through the middle of the square thus making it a less intimate space. As a result, it is more path than destination. The square has always been considered a less effective urban space first due to isolation from the center of Paris but now due to isolation of the bisecting street and its completely paved floor. Home to elite shops and hotels, only a very small portion of society of a certain economic status tends to use this place as a destination.

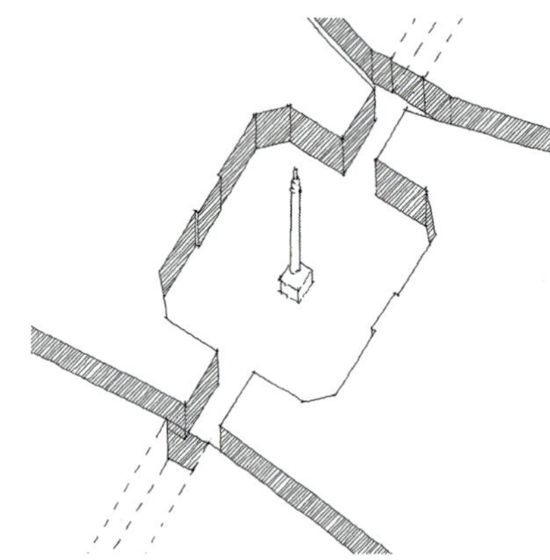

The Place Vendôme before the streets were opened to the north and south

Place Vendôme

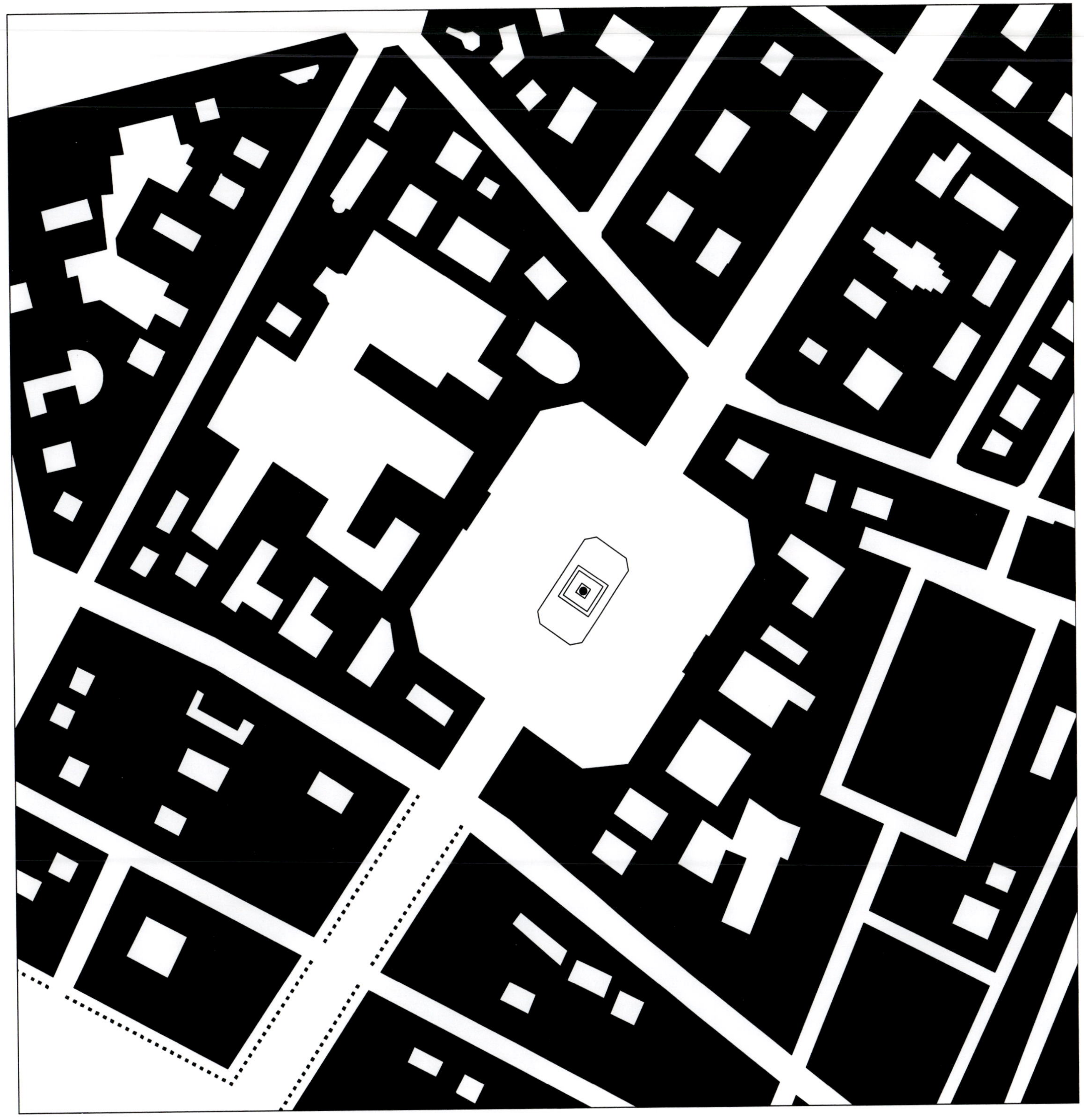

Place Vendôme

Paris

Voison Plan

68

> The Voison scheme does not claim to have found a final solution to the problem of the centre of Paris; but it may serve to raise the discussion to a level keeping with the spirit of our age, and to provide us with reasonable standards by which to judge the problem. It sets up principles as against the medley of silly little reforms with which we are constantly deceiving ourselves.
>
> (Le Corbusier, *The City of To-Morrow and its Planning*, 1929)

The Voison Plan, proposed by Le Corbusier and first exhibited in the Pavilion of the Esprit Nouveau of the International Exhibition of Decorative Arts in 1925, was purposefully devised to arouse debate. That, of course, is what it did and continues to do. The debate stems not only from its dimensions but also because it asks, as we continue to do, how a city might adequately and appropriately reflect contemporary economic, technological and social systems.

Named after the French automobile manufacturer that funded the research and design studies – Le Corbusier also approached but was turned away by Citroën and Peugot – the "Voison" scheme is a vertical city made possible by new building technologies that help ameliorate what the architect saw as "unhealthy" streets inherited by pre-industrial society. It was, as he describes in *The City of To-Morrow and its Planning*, a "frontal attack on the most diseased quarters of the city" (Le Corbusier 1929: 280). Ideas explored in this project also appeared in other projects including the *Contemporary City for 3 Million* in 1922 and the *Ville Radieuse* in 1933. None of these, however, used an existing city as its setting.

The project was extensive: Le Corbusier proposed razing 250 hectares of central Paris in an L-shaped tract north of the Rue de Rivoli. The L's long arm extended east–west from just above the Arc de Triomphe to the Place de la République while its short arm extended north to Gare l'Est.

He arranged twenty-eight, 180-meter-high, glass, cruciform skyscrapers and low-scale residential bar buildings within a green landscape traversed by high-speed roads of varying dimensions. The plan was a formal gridiron system that, as he notes, is "based on axes, as is every true architectural creation" and is seen thirty years later in Chandigarh (Le Corbusier 1929: 282).

A reading of this project today gives a superficial impression of folly and irony. In fact, the project was a serious attempt to raise questions and, as Le Corbusier states, save the city that he admired. This saving would occur through surgically removing unhealthy districts so that the more pleasant areas would survive as traffic and businesses were moved away from monuments and pedestrian streets into a new city. He writes that through this project "the historical past, our common inheritance, is respected. More than that, it is rescued" (Le Corbusier 1929: 287). While whole districts would be demolished, several churches and historical artifacts would be preserved, but as he notes, mostly because they worked with the scheme's composition. Le Corbusier was well aware of the project's dimensions and scope and saw only that the scale was a way to illicit discussion. He was well aware that skyscrapers set in an immense garden was "beyond the powers of imagination" (Le Corbusier 1929: 281).

The scheme was and still is misinterpreted. For example, the city was divided into a residential district and a business district. The skyscrapers depicted in this plan were only for businesses while meandering, low-scale residential buildings, with small-scale courtyards, were residential.

It is easy to criticize this project from an early twenty-first century point of view. After seeing what the vision wrought, one can be astounded and even infer irony or humor from the design. Yet, the importance of this project is that it initiated debate. Today, as we face new urban designs that revert to nostalgic architectural and urban forms reminiscent of pre-modern social and technological systems, we have to ask ourselves if there is another way. Le Corbusier's proposal, when manifested, was not acceptable but neither are nostalgic urban and architectural forms that act as a panacea to the real issues of the twenty-first century.

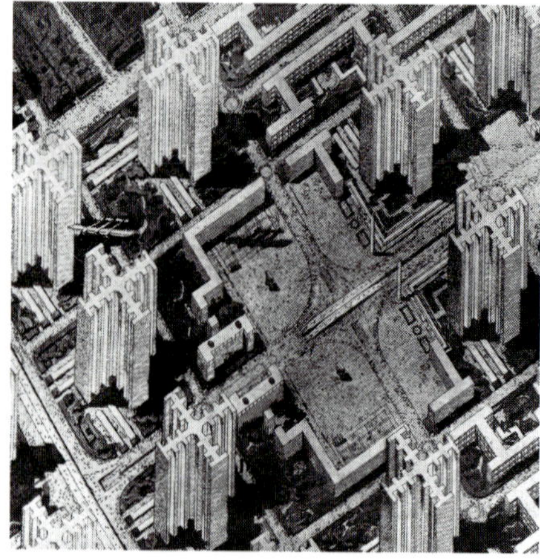

Axonometric of the Voison Plan

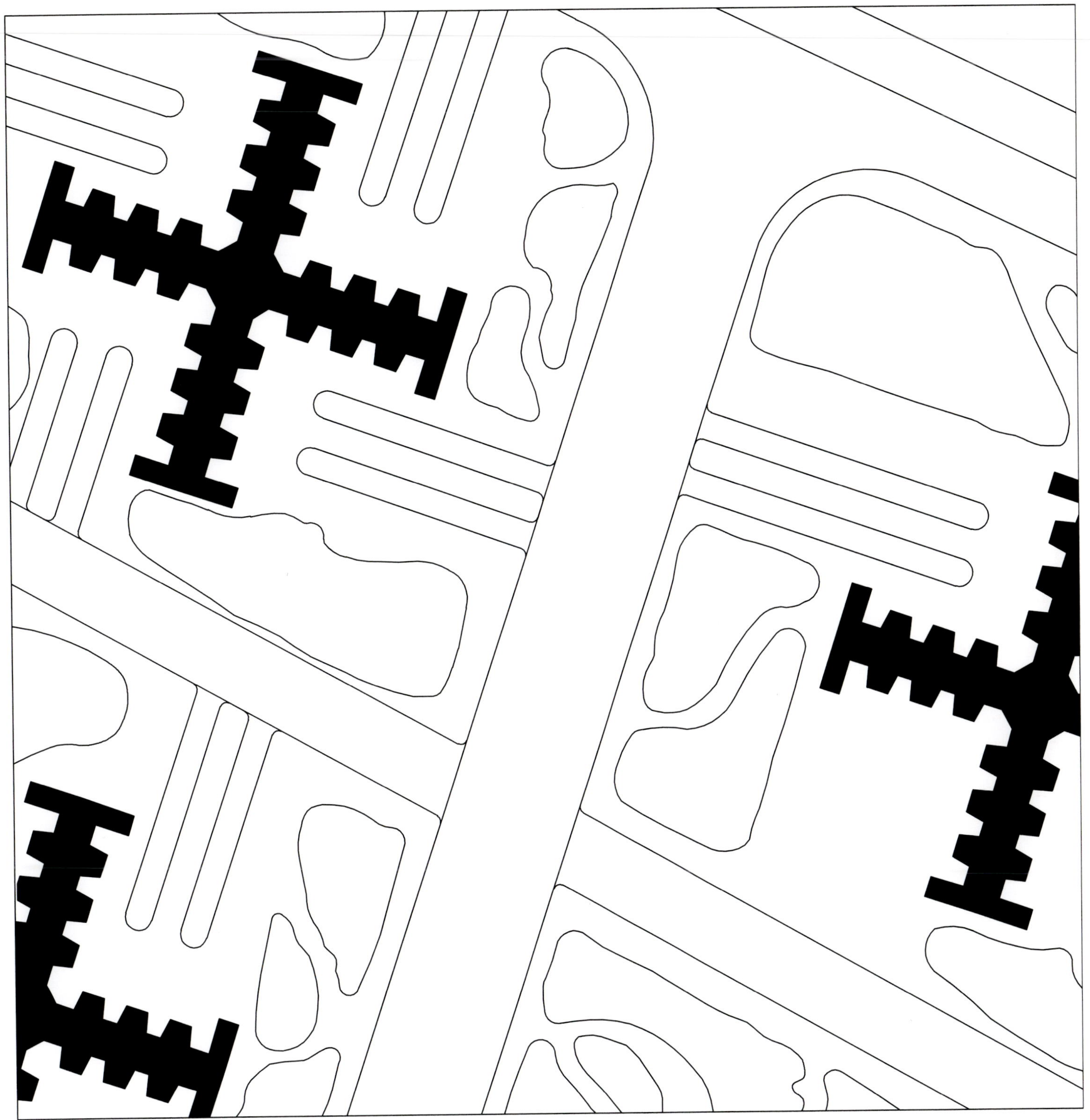

Voison Plan

Philadelphia

69

Rittenhouse Square

One of the original five spaces reserved for public use in William Penn's 1681 plan of Philadelphia, Rittenhouse Square is active throughout the day and night owing to the varied uses in the surrounding buildings. As such, Penn's idea of a "green country town" with squares for recreation seems to hold true and remains the epicenter of the surrounding Rittenhouse neighborhood (Reps 1965: 314). Much of the square remains as it was in the early 1960s when Jane Jacobs wrote in *The Death and Life of Great American Cities* (1993) that the square

> possesses a diverse rim and diverse neighborhood hinterland . . . This mixture of uses of buildings directly produces for the park a mixture of users who enter and leave the park at different times . . . The park thus possesses an intricate sequence of uses and users.
>
> (J. Jacobs 1993: 124–126)

Located on the southwestern quadrant of central Philadelphia, Rittenhouse Square, named after astronomer David Rittenhouse, was redesigned by Paul Cret in 1913. The diverse businesses and residences in the surrounding neighborhood include the Curtis Institute of Music, the Church of the Holy Trinity, several hotels, cafés and condominiums. The presence of condominiums, which have increased substantially since the mid-1990s, more than likely contribute the greatest activity to the square. Unlike civic squares in central business districts such as downtown Washington, DC, Rittenhouse Square remains active into the evenings and on the weekends. Both allowing and reinforcing these activities are zoning rules that allow for outdoor cafés and restaurants on and near the park (Huffman 2006: 108–109). Moreover, just as immediate surroundings are important, so too are the more distant surroundings. People walk from neighborhoods southwest through Rittenhouse Square toward City Hall, the Penn Center and the business district along Market Street.

Rittenhouse Square

While the other four public reserves of Penn's plan remain in some form or another, only Washington Square in Philadelphia is somewhat comparable and, as such, offers a contrasting case in how a similar plan can have very different results depending on context and participation of its citizens. Though the scale of and use of buildings surrounding Washington Square is somewhat different, probably the most important difference between Rittenhouse and Washington is that Washington Square is not singular or hierarchical in the immediate urban fabric. It is directly adjacent to Independence Park, which makes it less of a neighborhood square but more tourist oriented. Moreover, it is less unique because it must compete with a neighboring park.

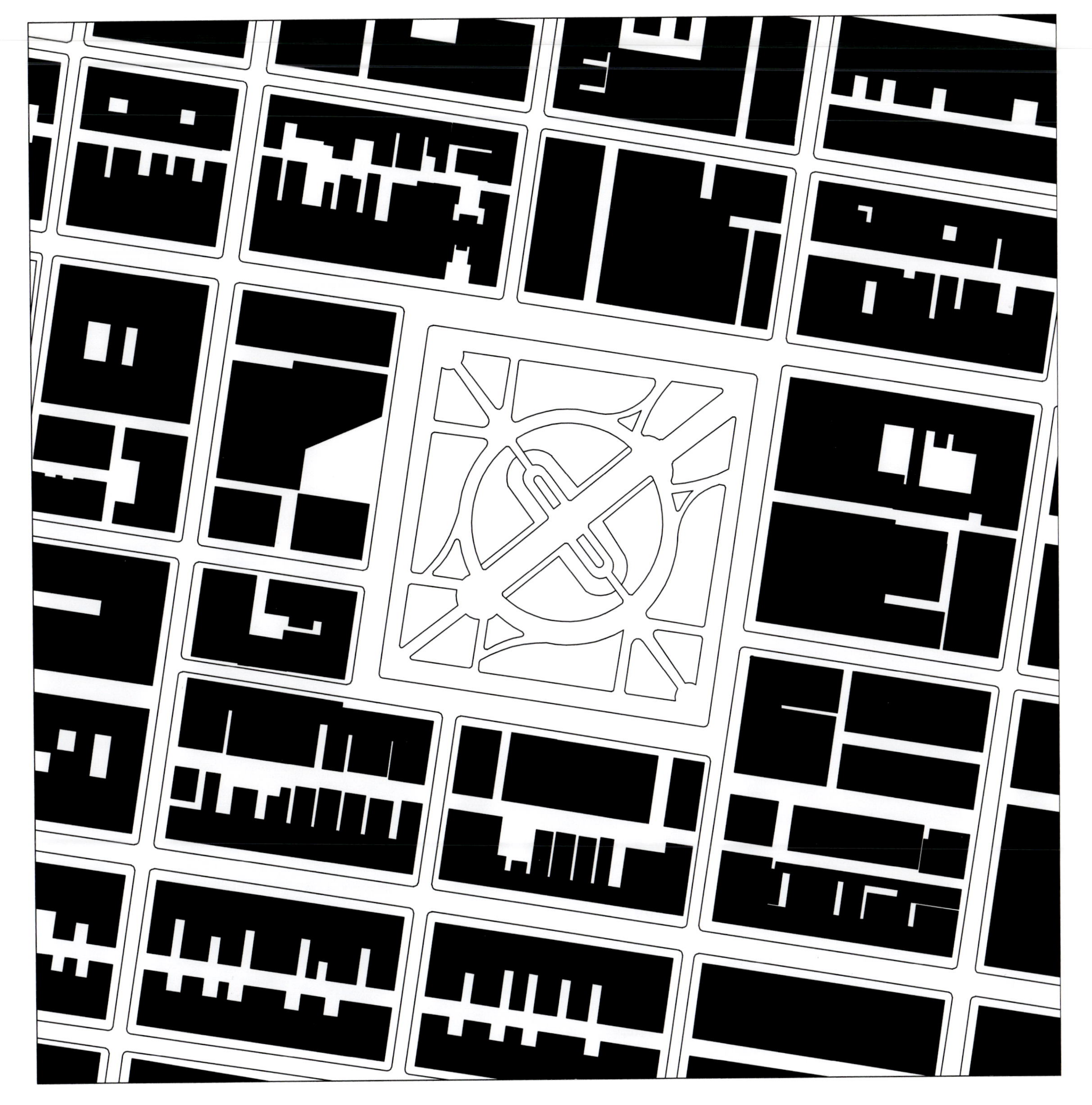

Rittenhouse Square

Portland

70

Pioneer Courthouse Square

Designed by Willard Martin and J. Douglas Macy, Portland's Pioneer Courthouse Square has been a key component in revitalizing Portland's downtown and a part of the city's overall progressive urban design and transportation initiatives. Today, the square and the city have become role models for financially viable, yet environmental and socially progressive initiatives that promote urban infrastructure, environmental awareness, mass transportation and urban living while controlling sprawl.

The square is a product of over three decades of work by Portland's citizens, planner and politicians. Once the site of the Portland Hotel, razed in 1951 and replaced with a parking garage, the city designated the parcel as a future park in 1972 and purchased it in 1979. A competition for the park was held in 1980 but the plans proceeded slowly. A citizen group called the Friends of Pioneer Square began a grassroots effort to move the project forward by selling parts of the park, such as pavers, fixtures and street furniture, to individual and corporate sponsors. With both public support and funding, the square was built and officially opened in 1984.

The design, like other American civic squares, is more of a mixture of individual architectural and spatial elements centered on a main terraced space. In this case, the predominant element is an amphitheater with a small fountain and surrounded by a freestanding row of columns, café pavilions and smaller sitting areas. Though the designers described the design as a series of "architectural episodes" facilitating varied activities, the square seems over eager (Leccese 1989: 61). In addition to trees, vending kiosks and information center, it is densely populated by bronze chess boards, an echo chamber, a series of bronze historic tiles depicting Portland's history, a mile-post sign indicating distances to Portland's sister cities, the former Portland Hotel gateway, a waterfall fountain, a public lectern, a weather machine, and, of course, a Seward Johnson life-sized, realistic bronze statue.

Organizing the day-to-day activities is, like New York's Bryant Park, a non-profit organization that oversees maintenance, fundraising, scheduling of events and policing. This system, of course, raises the question of whether the design is truly successful and viable if it is dependent upon management. As the Project for Public Spaces remarks,

> Pioneer Courthouse Square is one of the first in a new generation of public squares. No longer just passive green spaces, these squares are designed to be programmed and used by the public. In fact, the infrastructure for such uses is built-in, and the spaces have management entities in charge of them to assure their ongoing effective use.
>
> (www.pps.org)

While there is no doubt that American civic spaces need management and Portland's public–private financial infrastructure is quite successful, assuring use through programming by "management entities" is somewhat worrisome as many American civic spaces become increasingly privatized.

Amphitheater

Pioneer Courthouse Square from above

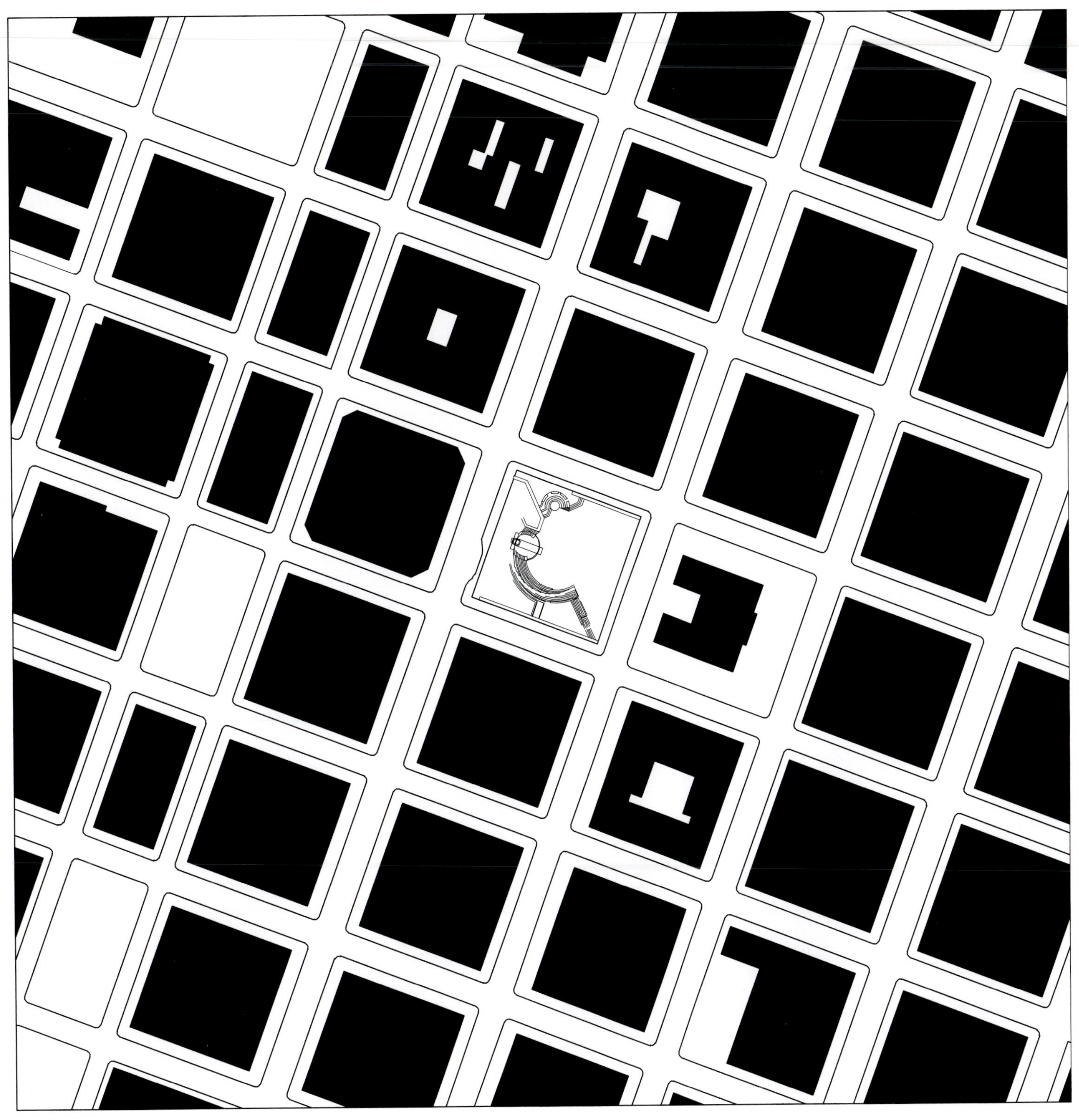

Pioneer Courthouse Square

Prague

Staroměstské Náměstí

At its heart, Prague's Staroměstské Náměstí or Old Town Square is a medieval square formed at a trading route's crossroads. While it has changed little for several centuries, in the nineteenth and twentieth centuries it underwent several dramatic alterations. From 1893 to 1896, the city revitalized the northern Jewish quarter of the old city and cuts through the wide Parizska Street from the Vltava river to the square. Until that time, all streets leading into the square were similar to those on the other three sides. The mid-twentieth century saw the destruction of the Town Hall's north wing which defined the square's western edge (Stankova et al. 1992: 42). Today, the square is defined by a variety of buildings including Gothic, Renaissance and Baroque houses and is dominated by the Gothic Church of Our Lady Before Tyn to the east, the Town Hall (Staroměstská Radnice) to the west and the Baroque St. Nicholas Church to the northwest.

The square from the Town Hall tower

A distinctive element in the square is absence rather than presence. This absence is the vacant land on the square's west side, once the site of the Town Hall's north and west wings. Destroyed by the Nazis in retribution for the May 1945 Prague Uprising, this void remains an unresolved cavity both physically and culturally for Czechs. While two bays of the razed building remain as a monument to the Uprising, the rest of the site quickly became and continues to be the focus of debate. Essentially, this debate centers on how a new building can reconcile both the square's re-completion and address contemporary Czech cultural, architectural and urban issues and concerns (Janak 1947: 51–54).

The void in the square

The square from the west

The fundamental argument is between those who favor a design that replicates the original Gothic façade and form versus those that prefer a contemporary building with contemporary material, form and spatial organization that might possibly reshape the square. Fortunately, the post-war redevelopment was less of an "old" versus "new", rather it was a possible dialectic of "both" as any new building could represent unique Czech identity within a tradition that has prided itself on embracing modernity, social reform and democracy with a representative architecture and urban design. Regrettably, this internal debate quickly transformed following the 1989 Velvet Revolution and the subsequent influx of the tourism industry. Gradually shifting from more philosophical issues, the debate has been influenced by more economic and perhaps superficial factors: What impact will a new building have on a burgeoning tourist trade that is more comfortable with traditional imagery and possibly ersatz architecture?

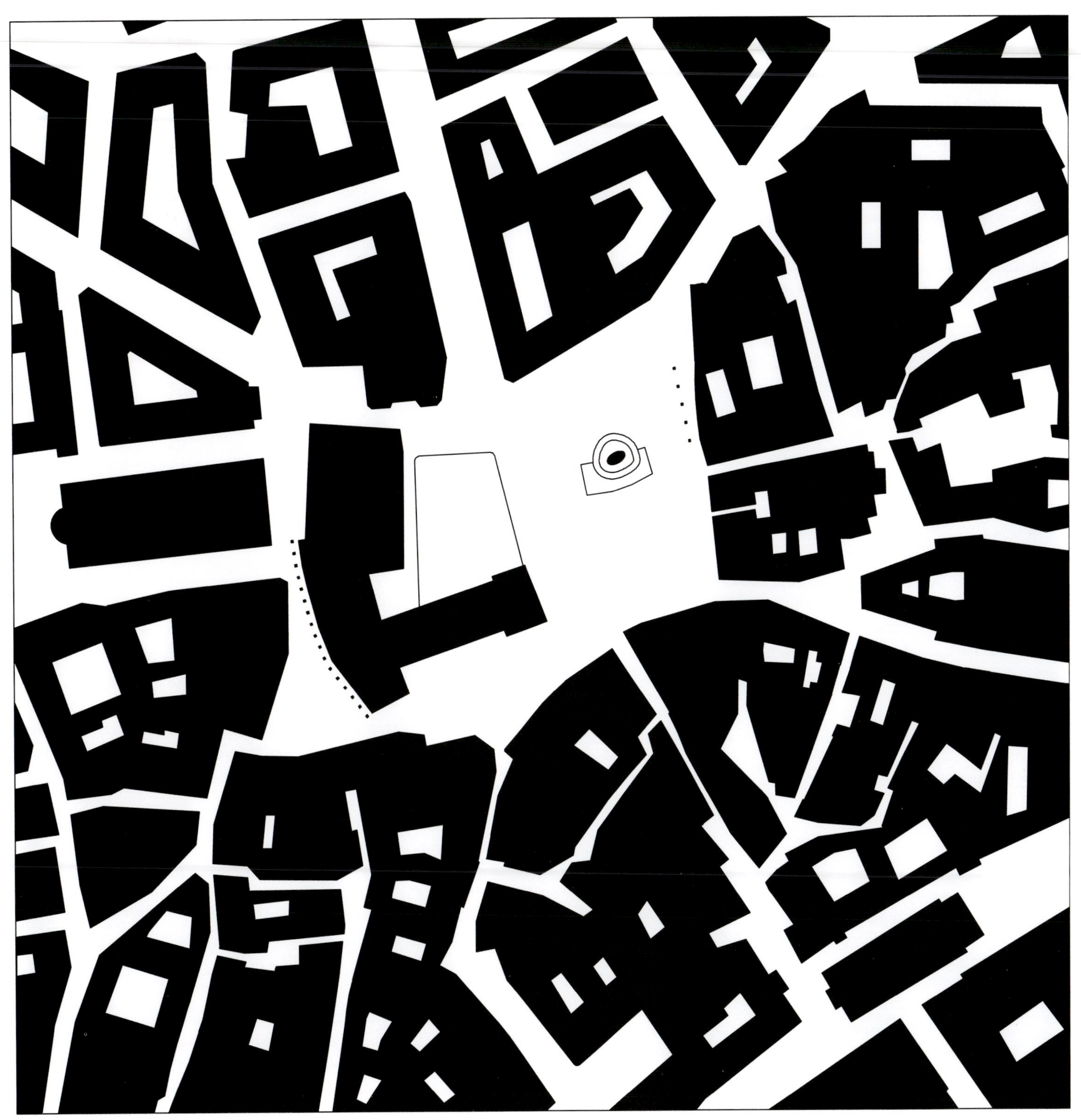

Staroměstské Náměstí

Rome

Piazza del Campidoglio

72

The Piazza del Campidoglio was commissioned by Pope Paul III in 1536 and was, essentially, a Renaissance urban redevelopment project. Though it had been the center of Rome's civic administration since antiquity, by the sixteenth century it had fallen into decay. Paul III requested that Michelangelo remake the Capitoline Hill into a new civic center to symbolize the renaissance of Rome.

At the time, the Capitoline was an irregular open area bordered on adjacent sides by two decrepit buildings, the Palazzo del Senatore to the southeast and the Palazzo dei Conservatori to the southwest. Michelangelo reoriented and clarified this otherwise irregular space by first establishing an organizing center axis from the Palazzo del Senatore's center toward the northwest and Renaissance Rome. About this axis he set, at an equal and opposite angle to the Palazzo dei Conservatori, the location for a new complementary building.

The result is a coherent, trapezoidal space occupied by a paved, slightly mounded oval upon which sits the equestrian statue of Marcus Aurelius. The slightly splayed walls of the old and new palazzi manipulate perspective to frame the Palazzo del Senatore's main façade. Toward the northwest end of the Piazza del Campidoglio is a grand sloping road, known as the Cordonata, which leads down to what was then Renaissance Rome.

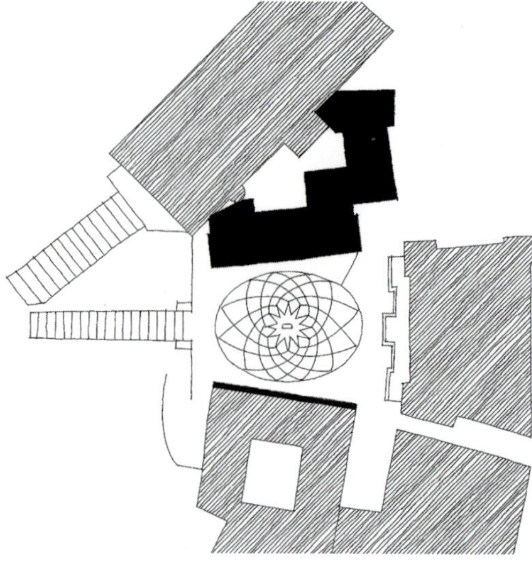

The inserted Palazzo Nuovo defines the space

In addition to its plan and massing, Michelangelo called for nearly identical façades to unify the buildings and thus the entire piazza. The façade of the new complementary palazzo, aptly named the Palazzo Nuovo, and the refaced Palazzo dei Conservatori have two, distinctly scaled orders. The first is the colossal Corinthian pilasters that are scaled to the piazza and tie together the buildings' two stories. Interposed within the colossal order is the smaller Ionic order on each side of the loggia openings and second story windows.

The overall design is, in many respects, an elegantly simple solution because it embraced existing conditions. Instead of razing the existing buildings, Michelangelo used them to create a dynamic, yet unified, space. In *The Design of Cities* (1967), Edmund Bacon observes that Michelangelo's clever reworking proved "that humility and power can coexist" and that "it is possible to create a great work without destroying what is already there" (Bacon 1967: 102).

The Campidoglio continues to be Rome's civic center. The Palazzo del Senatore, the façade of which is attributed to Girolamo and Carlo Rainaldi and Giacomo della Porta, houses the city's administrative offices. The Palazzo dei Conservatori now houses a museum with a collection mainly consisting of sculpture and paintings. The Palazzo Nuovo is home to the Capitoline Museum, which is known both for its wealth of material and for the fact that it is the oldest museum collection in the world.

Piazza del Campidoglio

Piazza del Campidoglio

Rome

73

Campo dei Fiori

The Campo dei Fiori is unique because it has maintained its medieval organic form and use rather than being overly refined into a precious gem. It continues to function primarily as a daily market square for the city's residents. Though other squares in Rome continue as functioning spaces for Rome's inhabitants, many of the squares, such as Piazza Navona or the Piazza del Rotunda, are inundated with tourists. As such, they are not so much local squares but international squares. By its use, size, surrounding buildings and those that use it, Campo dei Fiori remains a comfortable, unselfconscious space in the city.

Its name and origins are open to debate. Literally translated as a "field of flowers", its name has been attributed to flowers that were sold there or to the flowers that grew there when it was an abandoned and weed-strewn open area through the Middle Ages. It was not until the fifteenth century that the space became a paved public space. By the seventeenth century the area was used for all manner of public activities including markets, tournaments, executions, and reading of edicts. The streets leading from the square lead to various spaces and important rooms in the city. To the south Via d'Corda leads to Michelangelo's Piazza Farnese. To the north, Via Paradiso aligns with Baldassare Peruzzi's Palazzo Massimo.

The space is also unique in that it is surrounded by a hodge-podge of buildings that seem appropriately haphazard for the reality of the market's grittiness and authenticity. The base of the buildings are mostly cafés, shops and restaurants while the upper levels are residential including pensiones, hotels and apartments many of which house American architecture students studying in Rome.

Today, the square is a vibrant vegetable and flower market with a life that runs continuously twenty-four hours a day. Well before sunrise, the market begins with the arrival of vendors who begin setting up their stalls. By seven o'clock, the market is humming with people buying fresh vegetables and flowers. Each day around one o'clock the clang of the fishmonger's stand marks the unofficial beginning of the end for the market day. By four o'clock in the afternoon, the stalls are nearly gone as city workers move in to sweep and collect piles of garbage. In the early evening, the cafés start to emerge. By mid-evening, the surrounding restaurants slowly fill and stay that way well into the early hours of the morning. The square seems as if it is going to sleep, but there are bars along its edge that never allow it to completely rest. Soon, the vendors reappear to begin the cycle again.

Campo dei Fiori

The campo emphasizes the necessity for background spaces that can continue to take on the fundamental needs of the citizens. There is a real risk that many cities, especially cities in Italy, are becoming denuded of their citizens and replaced by tourists and those catering to tourists. To ensure that the cities remain livable and truly vibrant places, squares and services like Campo dei Fiori, efforts must be taken to allow these spaces and the citizens to actually live in these cities. The square is not precious and should not be. It is a real and likewise sometimes not pretty site, but that is part of what makes it successful.

Campo dei Fiori

Rome

Piazza Navona

74

Located in central Rome just west of the Pantheon and north of the Corso Vittorio Emanuele II, Piazza Navona is unique among Italian piazzas. Unlike more centralized spaces that evolved from gaps in the city fabric like the Campo dei Fiori or more deliberately and idealized Renaissance and Baroque spaces such as Piazza San Pietro, Navona is the remnant of a first century Roman circus just as Lucca's Piazza dell' Anfiteatro owes its shape to a Roman amphitheater. In Navona, the circus' long, slender form, even with the apsoidal end (and perhaps owing to its origins as a stadium) remains conducive to promenade.

Nearly all of the piazza's walls are comprised of background buildings with no overall or uniform design. The only exceptions to this are two churches. The first, on the east side, is the fifteenth century San Gicaomo degli Spagnuoli and the other, on its west side, the seventeenth century façade of Sant' Agnese by Francesco Borromini. It is the façade of Sant' Agnese that both solves a problem with the site and augments the piazza's walls in a unique way. The church's site was, first of all, problematic. It was an extremely shallow, one building thick site with a street just beyond the west side of the piazza. Moreover, the piazza itself allowed mostly oblique views so that any dramatic articulation would be lost to those inside the piazza. Borromini essentially created an optical illusion by compressing or flattening the building's façade, cupola and enclosing side towers to make the façade deeper than it appears. This compression allows the church to remain a landmark in the piazza yet does not violate the piazza's volume.

Architects, urban designers and historians have noted that Piazza Navona is a successful square despite flying in the face of systematized rules of successful squares. Urban historians Paul Zucker and Cliff Moughtin note that the elements contributing to the space's success are actually Navona's three fountains (Zucker 1966: 153; Moughtin 1999: 108). The most prominent is the central Fountain of the Four Rivers designed by Gian Lorenzo Bernini in 1650 in front of Sant' Agnese. The second fountain, at the north end of the square, is the Fountain of Neptune based on Bernini's design. The third, at the south end, near the Church of San Giacomo degli Spagnuoli, is the Fountain of the Moor. Beyond their sculptural gracefulness or as sources for cooling water and sound, the fountains actually orchestrate movement through the square. The three fountains, all placed on the square's central, longitudinal axis, partition the long square into several zones so that the square seems smaller and more intimate than in reality. More interesting, however, is that though they are placed on the square's central axis, both the Fountain of Rivers and the Fountain of the Moor are off axis with the adjacent churches. This shift allows the axis of the church to slide by the fountain and relieve the tightness or crowdedness that might occur. Moreover, it allows a kind of spatial flow around the square. If they were aligned, the relationship would be overly formal and static and thus be less helpful in making movement in the space (Zucker 1966: 153). Instead of arranging the squares formally, they were, like the sculptures in Florence's Piazza della Signoria, sited strategically.

Piazza Navona

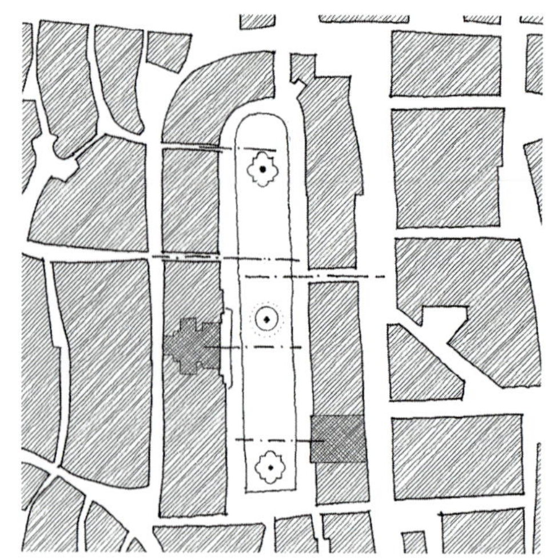

The relationship of the fountains and church entries

Piazza Navona

Rome

75

Piazza San Pietro in Vaticano

Probably one of the best known squares in this collection, Piazza San Pietro in Vaticano is an immense square that holds special meaning for nearly one billion Catholics through the world. Appropriately, its symbolic enfolding arms must contain the thousands of worshipers and other visitors during weekly Papal audiences, on special occasions such as Easter and Christmas and as a place of vigil during Papal elections. Besides its size and symbolism, the square is technically not in Italy but in the Vatican See, a separate nation city-state established with the Lateran Treaty of 1929. Though important in the past, it has not been an issue: the only way to know you have entered a separate nation is a white line painted on the pavement along its perimeter.

From the Via della Conciliazione

Gian Lorenzo Bernini's design for the piazza, as initially conceived in 1656, is a synthesis of three separate, yet interdependent spatial components along the basilica's central axis. The first component, closest to the basilica, is the *piazza retta*. This area is dominated by a vast, flowing stairway and a series of sloped surfaces that flow outward into the piazza and is used primarily as an altar for outdoor masses. Its walls are oblique to the basilica's façade and provide, like Michelangelo's Campidoglio, the appearance that the façade is narrower than it is in reality.

The second component, and the most identifiable, is the colonnaded ellipsoidal *piazza obliqua*. Rather than elongating this space, Bernini created a cross axis between two enfolding colonnades. This cross axis creates, as Paul Zucker notes, "spatial tension so desirable from the viewpoint of the late baroque" (Zucker 1966: 151). The third space was to have been the *piazza rusticucci* near the eastern end of where Piazza Pio XII is today. This space is effectively close to what Bernini had in mind: a forecourt to the *piazza obliqua*.

A subtle spatial experience of these three spaces is where these squares touch, Bernini created a kind of ephemeral plane which defines increasing degrees of sacredness. There is a sense of moving into an increasingly sacred realm that culminates at the doors of the basilica. This planar is subtly contrasted by the colonnade which has an explicit yet permeable edge or columnar screen that acts much like a filter allowing movement from the profane into a sacred realm.

Besides what was built, there is what was removed between 1936 and 1950. Beginning in the early 1930s, Mussolini's architects, Piacentini and Spaccarelli designed the axial Via della Conciliazione or "Way of Reconciliation" to celebrate the treaty between Italy and the Vatican, just east of the piazza toward the center of Rome. Before that time, this area was an enclosed, dense urban fabric that afforded a spatial surprise or relief of moving from this dense area to the openness of the piazza contributed to the power of the spatial experience. Today, San Pietro and the piazza can be seen nearly one and a half kilometers down the Tiber, which generally diminishes any spatial surprise.

Piazza San Pietro

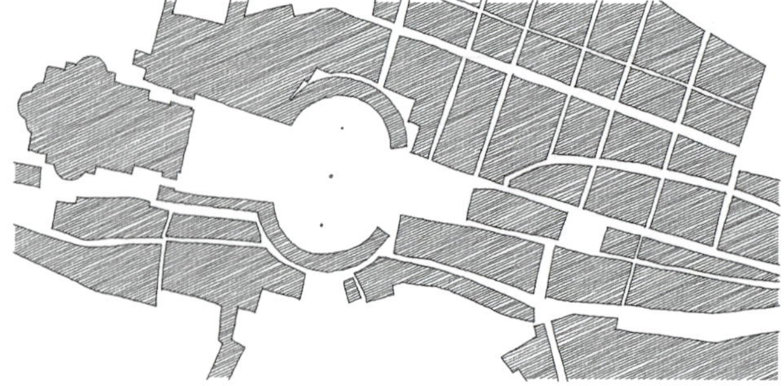

The pre-1936 plan

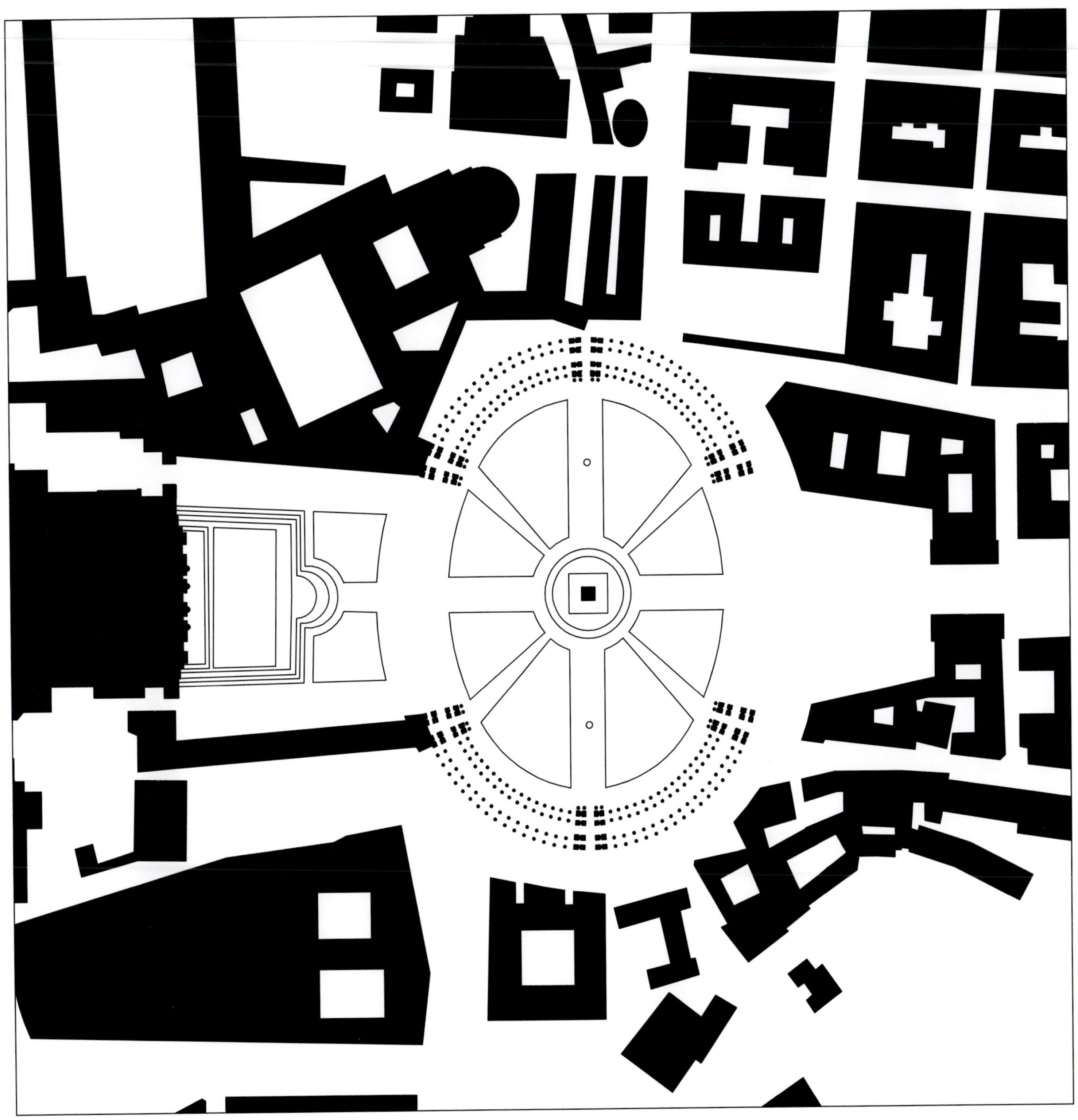

Piazza San Pietro in Vaticano

Saint Petersburg

76

Dvortsóvaya Plóshchad

Palace Square, designed and built in the early nineteenth century, is formed by the concave General Staff building and the rectilinear Winter Palace to the northwest. The General Staff building, like the other government buildings in the area, accommodated the new military and ministerial bureaucracy needed to run the new superpower (Egorov 1969: 85). Moreover, the square and other squares were distinctly imperial symbols of the tsar's military power following the Napoleonic Wars. In the tradition of military showplaces, it was designed for grand ceremonies and exercises to show the Russian people and visiting dignitaries Russia's new military might. Appropriately grand and opulent, the space is one of the largest enclosed and completely uniform urban spaces in the world.

Palace Square

Palace Square, formerly known as Dvortsóvaya Square, is the spatial culmination of a series of large squares to the southwest including Admiralty Square (Admiralteiskaia), Peter's Square (Petrofskaia) and St. Isaac's Square (Isakievskaia). These are all part of an entire, waterfront imperial district of Saint Petersburg comprised of the imperial government buildings, the Admiralty, Winter Palace, Theater, Hermitage, Marble Palace and Summer Garden. The General Staff building, designed by Karlo Rossi in 1819, is divided in half by a street with a triumphal arch threshold that aligns with the Alexander column and the center of the Winter Palace. As historian Iurii Egorov notes in *The Architectural Planning of St. Petersburg* (1969), Rossi carefully studied the column's location along the axis between the triumphal arch and the Winter Palace (Egorov 1969: 149). Egorov's analysis shows that while the column remained on the main axis, its location along the axis had an important impact on the square's spatial layout. Like the placement of fountains in Piazza Navona in Rome and sculpture in Piazza della Signoria in Florence, the column is placed strategically rather than formally.

A second compositional move is that the General Staff building is not a half circle but a splayed half circle. Unlike a half circle, the sinuous curve is more dynamic as it allows the space to flow in and flow out. Analogous spaces are the Piazza San Pietro in Vaticano, whose sides are segments of an arc, and the Royal Crescent in Bath that is, in contrast, a pinched segment of an arc.

An important lesson of Palace Square is how Rossi responded to existing conditions to shape the square and building. When commissioned, Rossi found an awkward, segmented building on the southwest and an assortment of buildings to the northeast (Egorov 1969: 138). Rossi's resolution was quite simple and clever. He used the existing arced segment and mirrored it to the northeast. At the intersection of the two curves he inserted the triumphal arch. Architecturally, Rossi played off the Winter Palace with the new, curvilinear building not by replicating the architectural language, but abstracting it (Egorov 1969: 142). Though he used lines and rhythms, the General Staff building's simple, plastic surface acts as a foil to the frame to the Winter Palace's complex, baroque and articulated façade. As in the Piazza del Campidoglio in Rome or Place Stanislas in Nancy, much of urban design involves examining existing patterns and augmenting those patterns. Augmentation does not always mean slavish duplication, but thoughtful response.

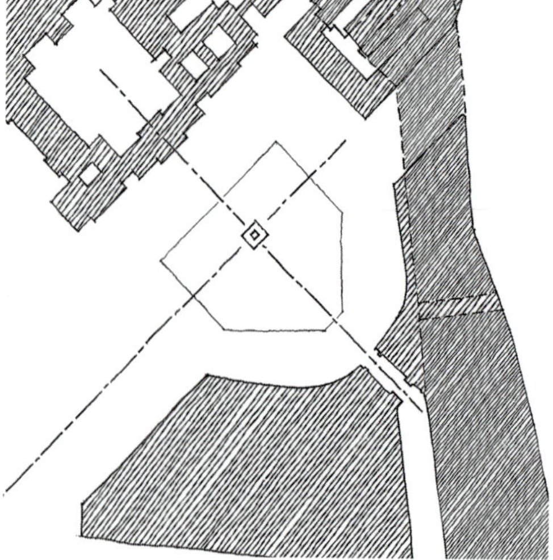

Rossi's new building overlaid on the existing situation

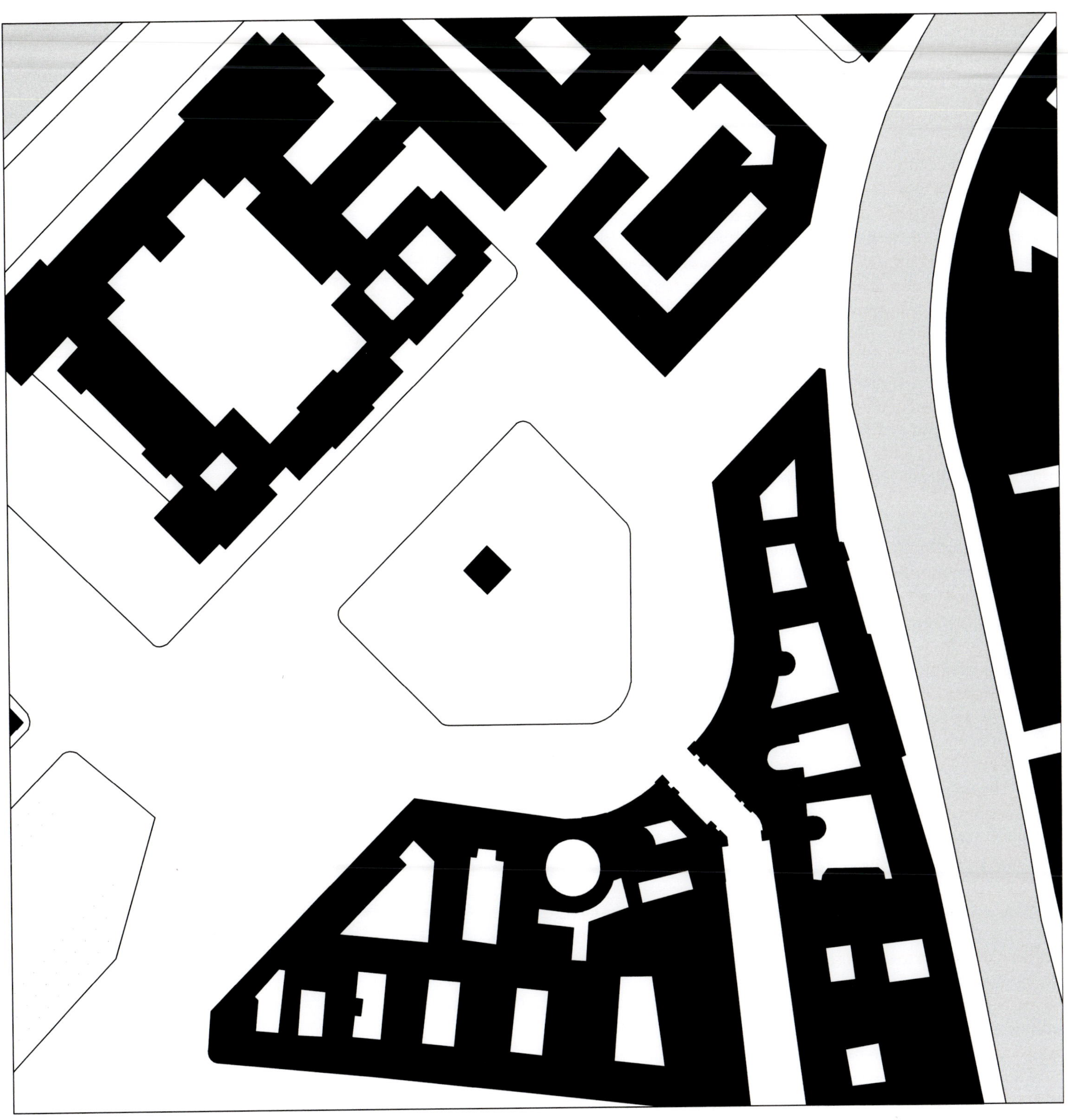

Dvortsóvaya Plóshchad

Salamanca

77

Plaza Mayor

Considered one of the more beautiful squares in Spain with exquisite proportions in its balance of horizontal to vertical lines of the façades, Salamanca's Baroque Plaza Mayor is described by Erwin Gutkind simultaneously as "nothing unusual" and "the climax of civic design and achievement" (Gutkind 1967: 275). This is interesting in that to make a space unsurpassable it does not take acrobatics but simplicity and complexity. This is echoed in other unsurpassable spaces such as the Piazza del Campidoglio in Rome or the Plaza Reial in Barcelona.

Designed by Andreas Garcia de Quinones, J. Garcia de Quinones, Jose de Lara and Nicolas Churriguera and built between 1720 and1755, it is square in plan and formed on all sides by uniform four-story residences with the town hall on the northern range. The ground floor is occupied by shops, restaurants and cafés that expand into the square.

This unvaried envelope is accentuated only by selected entry points and the town hall. While there are more than seven streets leading into the square, all but three are subsumed behind the arcade like Madrid's Plaza Mayor. The remaining three are marked by two-story arches set within the arcade's rhyme. The second modulation is the town hall's façade that projects from the plaza's interior surface and extends above its north range. Only the town hall's arches are slightly larger than the surrounding arcades.

Plaza Mayor

Like Madrid's Plaza Mayor, Salamanca's Plaza Mayor is lined with a tracery of balconies projecting from the façade. Unlike Madrid, however, these balconies are continuous and thus create a strong horizontal banding along the entire façade and are reminiscent of spectator galleries in Spanish bull rings.

The plaza seems to be a natural extension of Salamanca's urban fabric and renown as a university town. To the south is the Cathedral of San Martin and next to a smaller forecourt a plaza, the market to the east.

Plaza Mayor

As Paul Zucker notes, Salamanca's Plaza Mayor "owes its monumental splendor to the strict discipline of surrounding structures" (Zucker 1966: 229). As such, the discipline or rigor of Salamanca results in its ability to establish order but break that order to emphasize important moments. Of course, the test of this in Salamanca is the removal of either the underlying order or of the break in that order. When the order is removed, the accents become independent elements with no connection. When the disorder is removed, the space becomes banal.

Plaza Mayor

Salzburg

78

Domplatz, Residenzplatz and Kapitalplatz

Encircling Salzburg's cathedral is a series of distinct grouped squares. These semi-autonomous yet interdependent public rooms each play a particular, often complementary role in the civic life of the city. The cathedral, initially designed by Scamozzi but completed by Santino Solari, defines Salzburg's square ensemble. Placing the cathedral at the center of a large space effectively created three distinct squares each representing and fulfilling the three aspects of civic life: religious, governmental and commercial. The most formal of the three is the Domplatz or Cathedral Square. This geometrically pure and closed square is essentially a parvis or church forecourt often used for religious ceremonies. Demarcated by the cathedral's façade and by the Residenz and the Abbey of St. Peter on the three remaining sides, its central axis leads from the cathedral's main entry toward the smaller church of St. Peter. Despite its clear axial organization and tight enclosure, two colonnades on either side of the cathedral's façade offer a glimpse to spaces skirting either side of the cathedral. The colonnades continue the enclosure, like Piazza San Pietro in Vaticano, creates a permeable edge through which a pedestrian connects to spaces beyond. These colonnades also help emphasize the transition from the formal parvis by offering a spatial compression that then open into the Residenzplatz to the north and to the Kapitalplatz to the south.

The Residenzplatz serves as the government square for the city. This square is less formal than the Domplatz with a rectilinear form dominated by the Residenz's central tower yet with entries at the corners. The corner opposite the Domplatz colonnade leads to Mozartplatz, which might be thought of as a fourth square in the ensemble. On the opposite of the cathedral is the Kapitalplatz, used primarily for commercial activity. Of the three spaces, Kapitalplatz is the least clearly defined and is almost a residual space within the city. Despite its shape, it remains an identifiable space due in part to its role as a market place and its identity as part of an ensemble of spaces that are varied in scale and formality. In a sense, each square is complementary and thus contributes to a spatially active area around the cathedral.

The cathedral from the south

Domplatz, Residenzplatz and Kapitalplatz

San Francisco

79

Union Square

Located in San Francisco's commercial district, Union Square like other urban squares in the United States has undergone numerous changes as architects and landscape architects try to accommodate the varied social and economic changes in American cities. These changes have pushed landscape architects toward more complex spaces often with undulating surfaces, pavilions and other planned or programmed events. As suggested in the comments on Cincinnati's Fountain Square, Los Angeles' Pershing Square and Portland's Pioneer Courthouse Square, it seems that at some point American public squares seem overburdened with institutional programming and spatial articulation. There is a concern that a resulting over-articulation will become so specific that the spaces will be used by only a few and only at specific times.

San Francisco's Union Square has been a public reserve since the 1851 planned expansion following the 1849 gold rush. In the early twentieth century the surrounding neighborhood became known as a shopping and theater district and in 1942, a four-level underground parking garage was added beneath its surface. Today, the square remains associated with shopping and theaters as well as several hotels and office buildings.

In 1997, the San Francisco Planning and Urban Research Association sponsored a design competition for the square's rejuvenation, which received 320 submissions. The winning design by landscape architects Phillips + Fotheringham Partnership transformed the square into a social "stage" upon which a range of informal and formal social and cultural events might occur ("Phillips + Fotheringham Partnership: Redesign of Union Square" 2002: 3–4). The design features a center court bounded on four sides with the long side dominated by rows of trees alongside parking garage ramps. At its short ends are cafés and ticket pavilions. A stage on the square's main cross axis aligns with the monumental column erected in 1903 to honor Admiral Dewey and his accomplishments during the Spanish-American war. Along the southern edge of this hardscape space is a series of slender objects including a mist fountain, a memorial and light sculpture. The park caters to a variety of groups with different needs. During the weekday, it is filled with office workers eating lunch or sunbathing. In the evenings and weekends it is available for public gatherings and performances.

An important aspect of this space is using public squares and streets as underground parking. While this has been done since the 1940s, Union Square is one of the earliest examples. Many of these were not successful because of the space consumed by protruding vehicular ramps and the lack of soil above the garage for substantial planting. As a result, parks such as Los Angeles' Pershing Square were somewhat isolated and without sufficient trees to make it feel like a park. In essence, they feel like they are atop a parking garage. A success story, not included in this book however, is Boston's Post Office Square, with a seven-level parking garage which maintains the existing grade and incorporates ramps and other access points into park pavilions.

Union Square

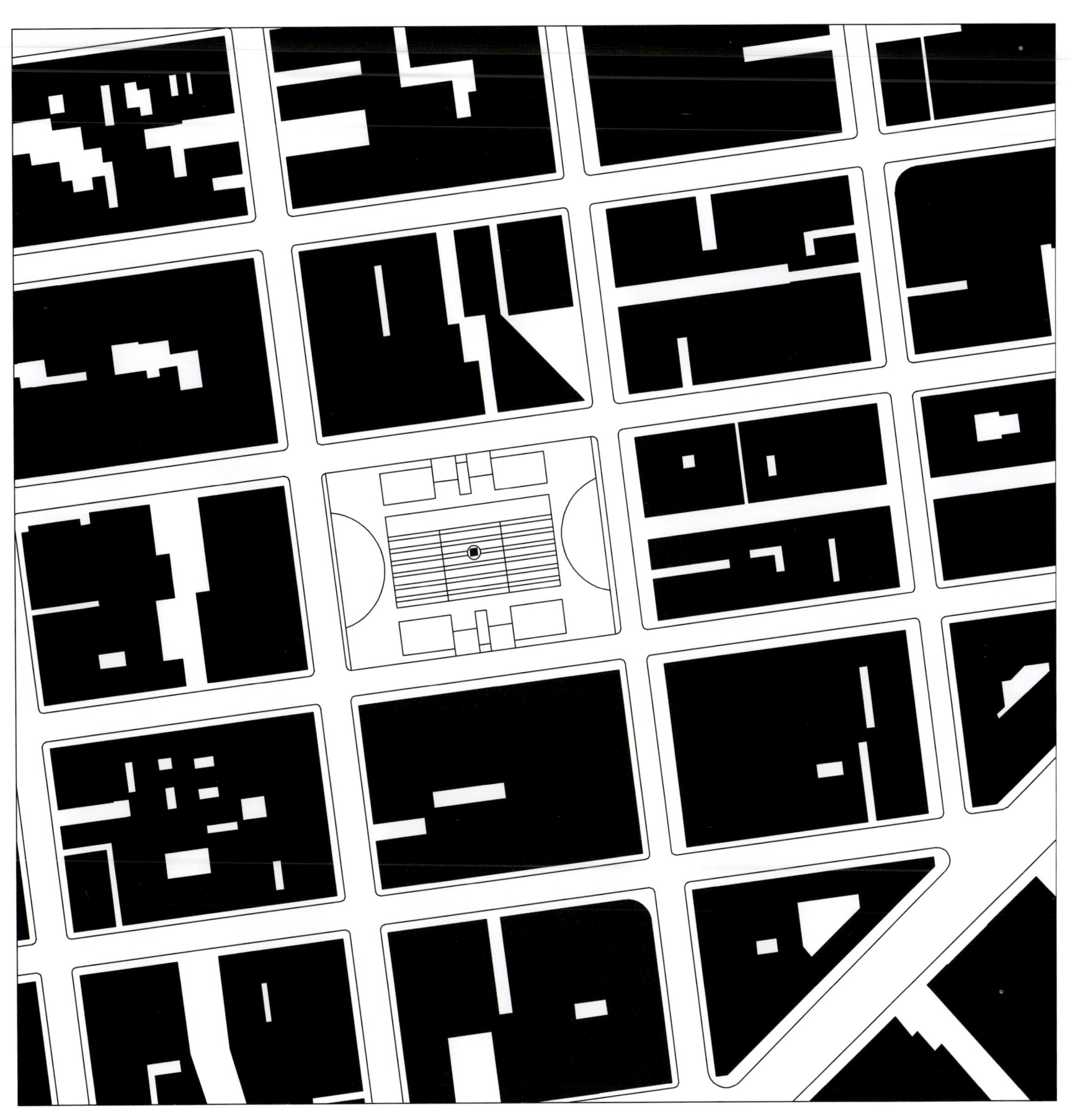

Union Square

Santiago

80

Plaza de Armas

Of the Spanish colonial *plazes de armas* or military parade grounds included in this collection, Santiago's Plaza de Armas is the most park-like and remains an integral component in the public life of the city. While Mexico City's Zócalo is an open, hardscaped plaza and Buenos Aires Plaza de Mayo is landscaped, both remain more political squares rather involved in the day to day life of the city.

Santiago was founded in 1541 by Pedro de Valdivia at the foot of the Andes Mountains along the Mapocho River approximately one hundred kilometers from the Pacific Ocean. Like other Spanish colonial towns, Santiago was laid out following the Royal stipulations that predated but were consistent with the Laws of the Indies. As such, the plaza is a regular rectangle surrounded by the cathedral, administrative buildings and former court building, the Real Audiencia, which is now the Museo Nacional Historico. Santiago is also known for its other plazas. In addition to the Plaza de Armas, in 1575 and then again in 1703, the city established additional market and neighborhood plazas. Today, the area immediately adjacent to the plaza is a pedestrian only zone and the plaza is home to a variety of everyday activities of a range of Santiagans. The city remains the political and cultural, and commercial center of Chile.

As discussed in the Buenos Aires' commentary in this collection, the Laws of the Indies allowed for expedient colonization and demarcation of property, towns and buildings in newly colonized areas. Stemming from practical demands and a need for ideological contrivances, the Spanish Laws of the Indies were comprehensive guidelines influenced by Roman and Islamic tradition. The result was, according to D.P Crouch, D.J. Garr and A.L. Mundigo, that the Spanish founded over three hundred and fifty towns in the Americas between 1493 to 1781. (Crouch et al. 1982, 27). Though laws were used since the late fifteenth century, Philip X codified them in 1573 into one hundred and forty eight articles that delineated colonial establishment from the town's layout to political, social and religious structures. While there were similarities in the laws that produced uniform plans, there were variations. For example, the articles usually contained stipulations that would adapt to local climatic variations, seaside or inland locations. In addition to the physical and economic structure, the laws deliberately outlined how the indigenous populations should be respected yet converted into Christians.

The most fundamental, if least poignant aspect of the Laws, was the uniform gridiron that proved so successful in quickly and rationally demarcating land that a similar demarcation helped lay out most of the United States in the eighteenth and nineteenth centuries. The grid continues to play a role in urban design to this day as it is easier to demarcate for land subdivisions and quickly establish towns.

View to the west

View to the northwest

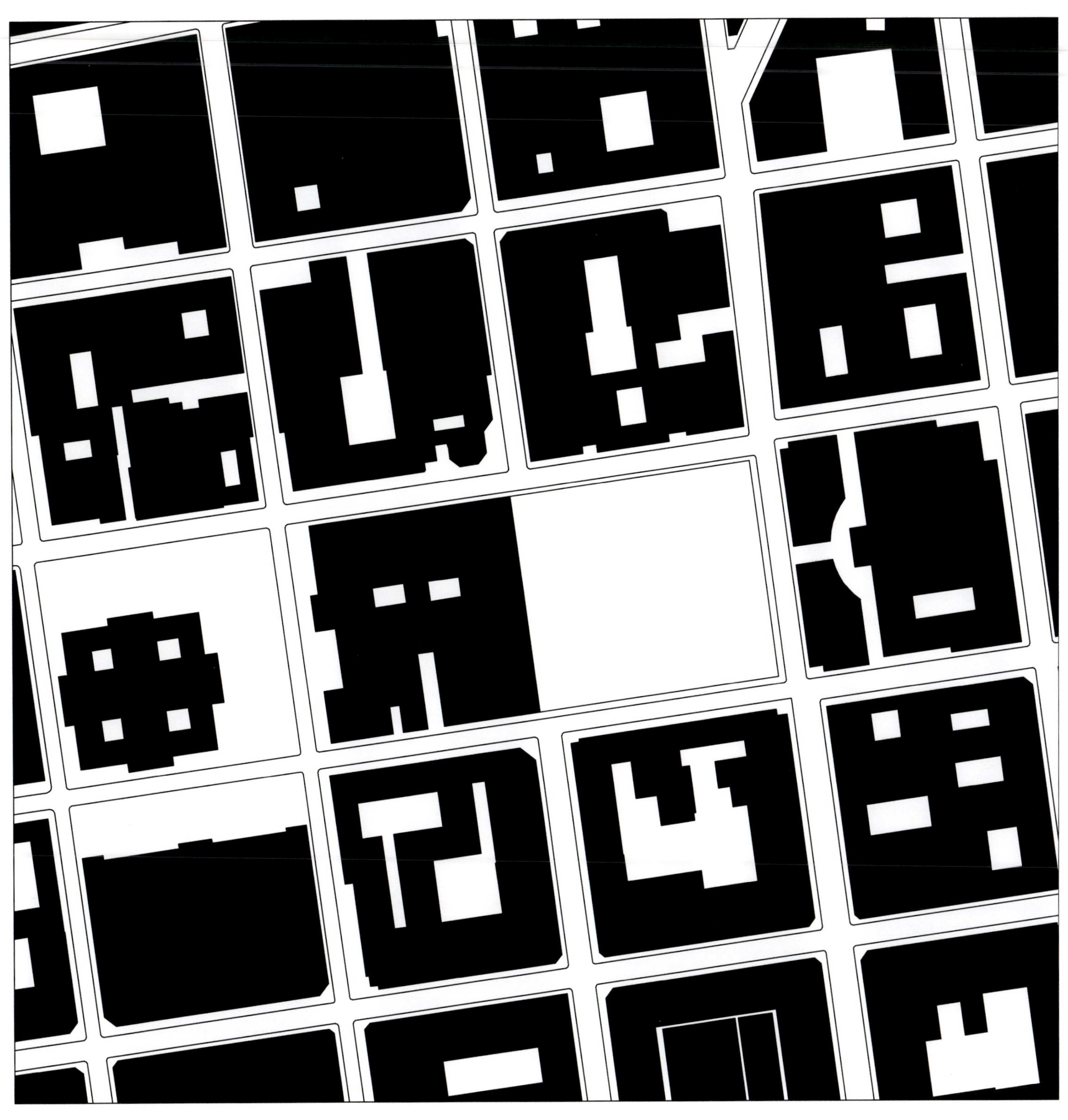

Plaza de Armas

Savannah

81

Historic District

Savannah's 1733 plan is a unique and sophisticated allotment of streets and parks. The plan is a complex, hierarchical grid much like a Scottish tartan based upon one fundamental element: a rectilinear cellular unit called a ward with a public square at its center. Each ward is nearly identical and comprised of one primary north–south street on axis with the square while two east–west streets run laterally along the north and south edge of the square. Three additional east–west tertiary streets bisect the blocks resulting in a woven pattern of twelve parcels with room for forty houses. The ward unit was then duplicated and set alongside adjacent units. Where the two units met became a continuous street through the city. Today, each square has evolved into its own character including residential, commercial and governmental. The squares shown here are, clockwise from upper left, Johnson Square, Warren Square, Oglethorpe, Wright Square and St. James Square.

Attributed to Savannah's founder, James Oglethorpe, a Member of Parliament and social reformer who was more than likely influenced by, as Turpin Bannister (1961) argues, Renaissance ideal plans such as those included in Pietro di Giacomo Cataneo's *L'Architettura* (1554) or Vincenzo Scamozzi's plan for Palma Nova (1593) (Bannister 1961: 56–57). Another, more immediate source put forth by Stanford Anderson (1993) is Richard Newcourt's proposed 1666 plan for rebuilding London (Anderson 1993: 126). In each of these plans, however, only Savannah is distinctly non-hierarchical in the overall plan of the town. Even if the specific source is unknown, the idea of a residential square was relatively common in England and Ireland and the idea that houses would surround a common green was seen as a civilizing amenity to the residences surrounding it.

One lesson of Savannah's plan, as Spiro Kostof points out, is that it proves "that grids can be much more than dull blueprints of land division" (Kostof 1987: 154). Unfortunately, the Savannah grid was never duplicated as the United States expanded westward. The reasons for this are unclear; however, it may have to do with a plan that appears more complicated than a standard grid and therefore may have seemed a daunting task to plot and divide for speculation. The uniformly endless grids seen in Chicago, Phoenix, Salt Lake City and other American towns are astoundingly easy to establish, sell and erect with little "wasted" land dedicated to public parks.

Another important lesson is the spatial sequence of Savannah. Though a grid, each street offers different spatial sequences for pedestrian and vehicular traffic. For the pedestrian moving north–south, the sequence is a rhythm of square-street-square as the sidewalks align with the paths through the square. Alternatively, the east–west experience alternates between buildings and laterally along the squares' edges. For vehicular traffic, the plan accommodates both local traffic that must move around the squares and through-traffic on the streets that separates each ward. Moreover, commercial vehicles can move on the outer edge of the ward without circumnavigating each square. Because it is a series of units, the feeling of moving through Savannah is that you are part of a conglomeration of parks within a city rather than a city with parks. Overall, Savannah can inspire refined urban patterns that can be straightforward and clean yet complex.

Savannah from above

Complex woven patterns within Savannah's plan

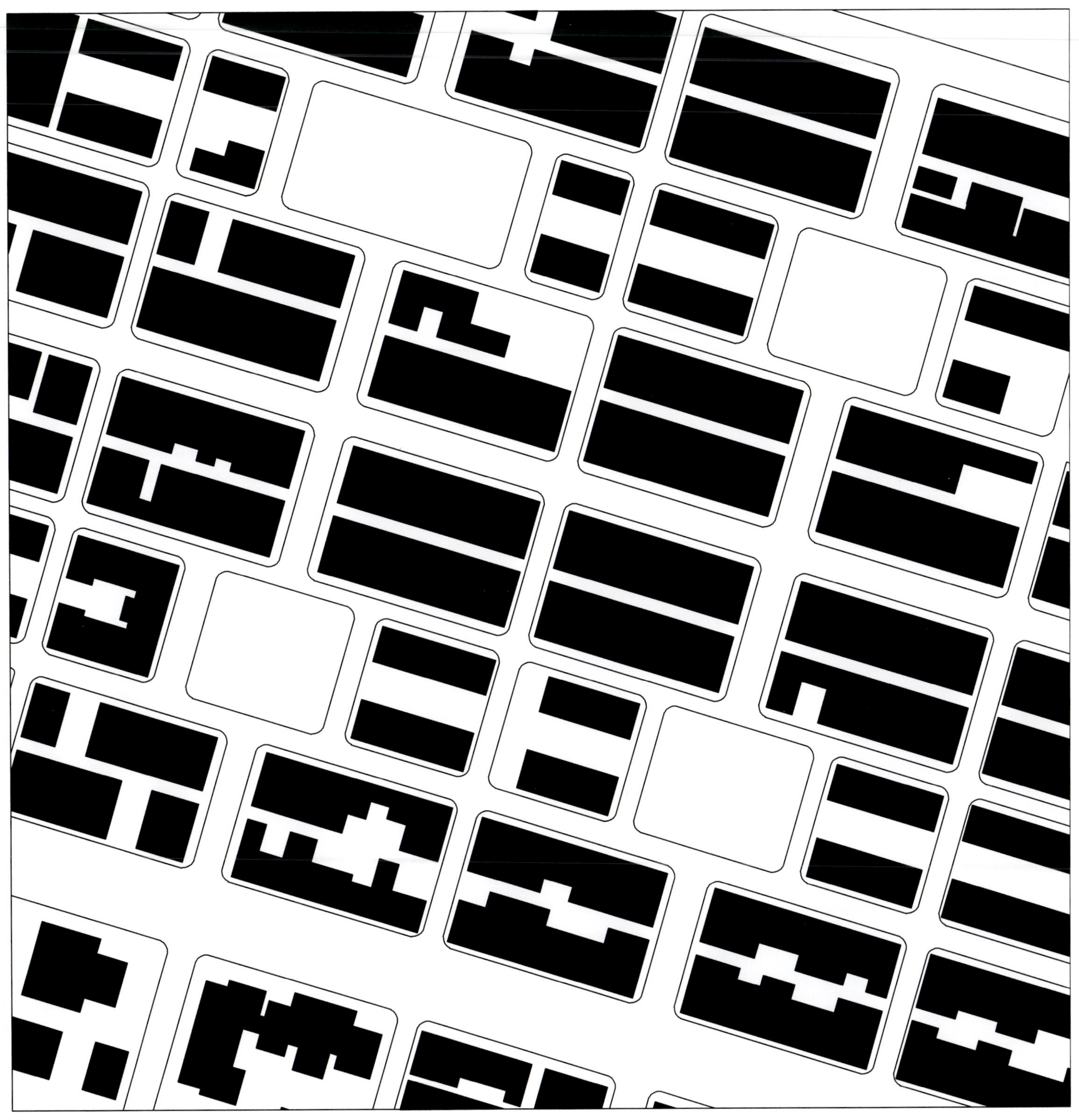

Historic District

Seattle

Pioneer Square

82

Pioneer Square is not actually a "square" but a district within Seattle with two primary urban spaces: the triangular Pioneer Place Park and Occidental Park. As its name implies, it is the area settled by pioneers in the mid-nineteenth century and established as the new city's industrial and shipping base. A young city compared to many of the cities illustrated in this collection, Seattle was founded in 1852 on relatively level waterfront land and quickly became a center of trade and finances in America's northwest. In 1889, the area was devastated by a fire but rebuilt with brick commercial buildings. The area's zenith was at the beginning of the twentieth century following the Alaskan gold rush, which resulted in an influx of people and money that inaugurated a commercial building boom, docks, warehouses and two rail stations: the King Street station built in 1906 and Union Station built in 1911 (Miles 1989: 8).

In the 1920s, the area began a steady decline as Seattle grew to the north and soon the area was better known for its saloons, missions and skid row. In the late twentieth century, however, the area began a slow but steady revitalization. Though slated for comprehensive urban renewal in the 1960s, both independent commercial interest and the efforts of Seattle's citizens prevented this sweeping move. Through their efforts, it was designated a Historic District in 1970 with additional parcels added into the 1980s (Miles 1989: 8). Today, the area is now a successful neighborhood of art galleries, bookstores and other businesses. Moreover, the city's mandated mixed use development incorporates housing to help keep the area active throughout the day and week. The area even manages to survive despite the elevated highway blocking access to the waterfront.

The brick-paved Pioneer Place Park, defined by the Pioneer Building and lined with trees, is a shaded break in the city. The square is part of a north–south pedestrian access along First Avenue South from downtown Seattle into the area and to the city's Seahawks football stadium and the Mariners' baseball park five blocks to the south. Occidental Square, one block east of First Avenue, is the pedestrianized segment of Occidental Avenue South. Paved with brick and substantial shade trees, Occidental Square is strangely vacant in contrast to the Pioneer Square district as a whole.

Seattle's urban designers shared a common misconception among many American urban designers in the 1970s. Hoping to manufacture public space and bring people into the city, many cities pedestrianized their street by removing all vehicular traffic. The idea was that a pedestrianized street would attract people simply because it was limited to pedestrians. Unfortunately, since the newly created spaces were not part of an existing or new pedestrian pattern and with the traffic and related bustle removed these pedestrian-only zones became vacuous tracts with little activity. By the 1980s, cities realized that automobile traffic actually enlivens streets and that automobiles could be integrated without endangering pedestrians or threatening the street's beauty.

Despite its rather pleasing physical form, Occidental Park suffers from continued pedestrianization. One possible direction to its revitalization is the reintroduction of vehicular traffic as in Barcelona's Ramblas that actually has two lanes of vehicular traffic but is one of the best known strolling streets in Europe. Moreover, the Ramblas offers the inspiration of other formerly pedestrianized streets that have been re-vehicularized and, as a result, the life of these streets has returned. This idea, regrettably, was not part of a 2006 revitalization plan. Rather, like the solution to other faltering American spaces, the plan simply calls for events such as films and concerts to enliven the space.

Pioneer Square from the south

This shows how Occidental Square is off the main, north–south pedestrian paths

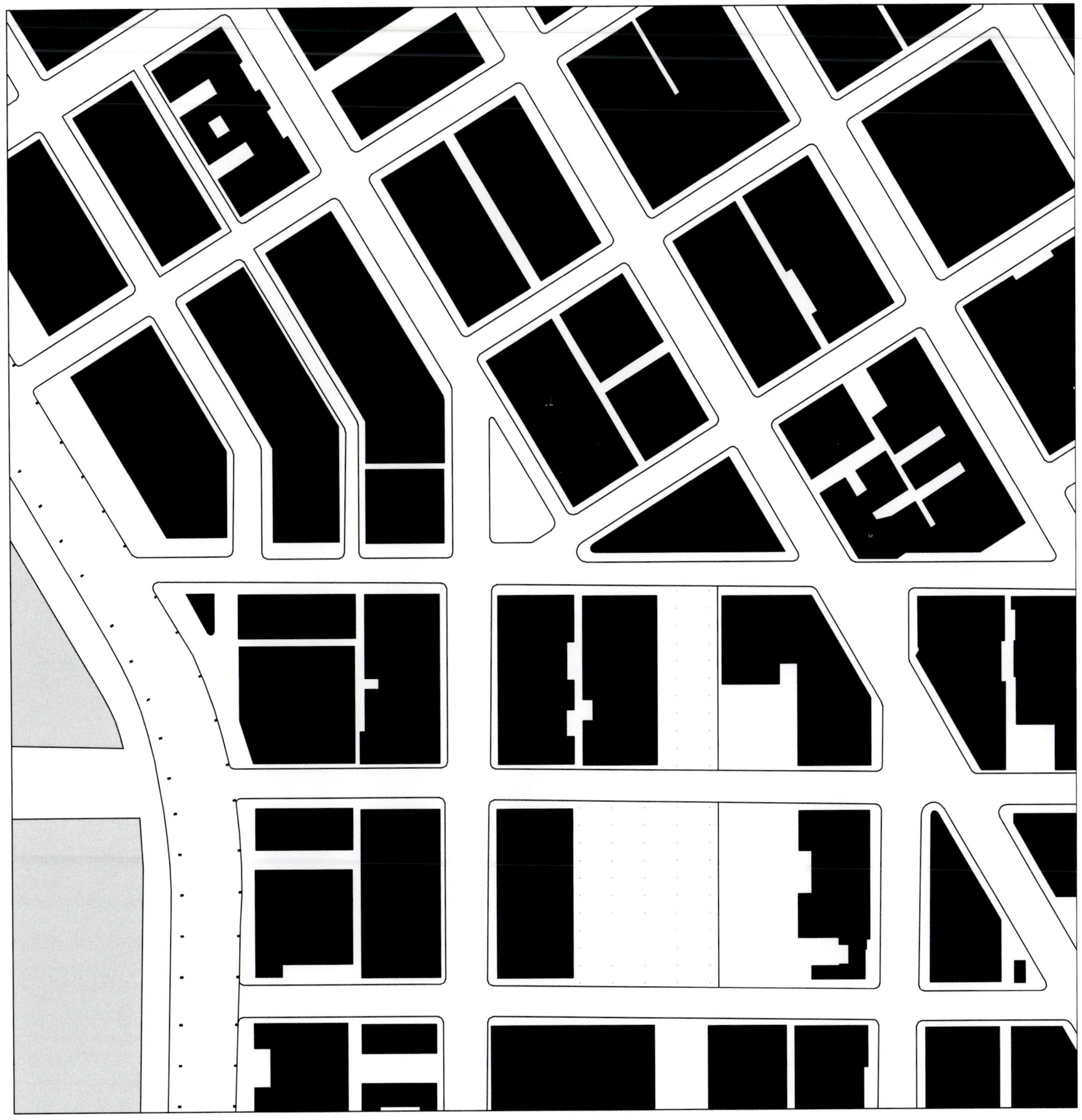

Pioneer Square

Seville

Plaza del Triunfo, Patio de los Naranjos and Real Alcázar

Seville reflects the climate in which it is built with its shaded streets, plazas, gardens and patios that give refuge from the heat and bright sun. The three squares illustrated here, the Plaza del Triunfo, the Patio de los Naranjos and the Alcázar gardens located in Seville's Santa Cruz Quarter, represent that character as a series of individual spaces that emerged from the natural climate and the intermingling of cultures over the centuries.

View into Plaza del Triunfo

Though Seville dates to pre-Roman times, it became important as a Roman colony with the nearby Trajana the birthplace of Roman Emperors Hadrian and Trajan. From the eighth to the thirteenth centuries, Seville was dominated by the Moors, vestiges of which remain present in its urban form and architecture. This is especially true in the sense of the small courtyards endemic of Islamic cities. Like Jerusalem and Tunis, the city is, at its core, an Islamic city, albeit transformed over generations by the Spaniards into a series of tight, familial scale courtyards interwoven with narrow streets. Seville can be hot with narrow streets often covered in tarps while patios and tree-covered plazas shade pedestrians from the sun, making the city bearable at its hottest. Though the city grew in wealth with the opening of the New World that had, by royal decree, sole rights to trade with New Spain, the city remained a relatively small city in scope and feel. It is distinguished by a series of intimate squares that are connected by narrow streets, most of which are now covered with fabric and awnings to protect pedestrians from the sun.

Patio de los Naranjos from above

As a small, pedestrian scale city, Seville, as Erwin Gutkind remarks, "radiates an atmosphere of the utmost intensity, beauty and variety" (Gutkind 1967: 502). This is no clearer than in the Santa Cruz Quarter. The narrow streets, alleys, courtyards and plaza of this former ghetto offer protection from hot sun. The heart of this district is the Plaza del Triunfo, an L-shaped plaza formed by the Alcázar palace to the south, the Exchange building and a corner of the cathedral. The cathedral, like the entire city, grew from Islamic origins. The most apparent indication of its origins are the belfry which was the former minaret, or La Giralda, and the Patio de los Naranjos, the rectilinear courtyard next to the church, planted with a grid of orange trees, that was once the mosque's forecourt (Laffón 1966: 21–22). To the south of the Real Alcázar, a former fortress, there is a series of gardens that, like the rest of Seville, again reveals the intermingling of Moorish and Spanish Renaissance design.

Plaza del Triunfo

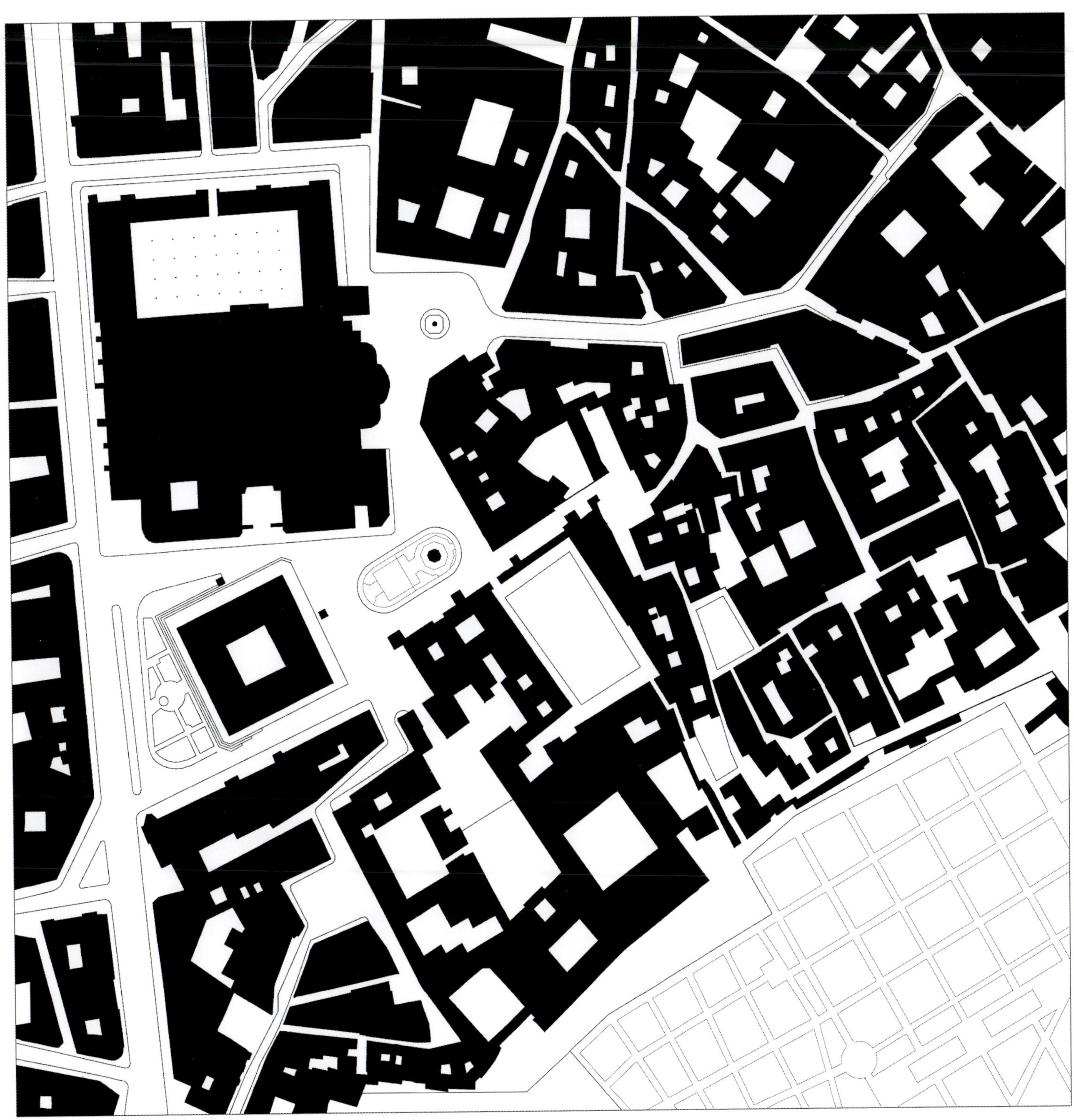

Plaza del Triunfo, Patio de los Naranjos and Real Alcázar

Siena

84

Piazza del Campo

The Piazza del Campo is a quintessential medieval Italian public space which is more popularly known for the Palio, the annual horse race between *contrade* or districts within the city. As the primary civic space in Siena it is now populated mostly by tourists yet remains a Sienese meeting place.

Taking its form from the underlying topography of the hillside, the piazza is a shell-shaped space both in plan and section. Its floor gently slopes down from the curved sides towards the center. The slope's focus along the flat side of the square is the Palazzo Pubblico or town hall with the tower, the Torre del Mangia and the Cappella di Piazza. While the town hall belonged to the citizens, the surrounding buildings of curved walls of the piazza belonged to merchants and nobility. The piazza's floor pattern, which helps water drain from the upper level to the lowest level and toward the Fonte Gaia (Fountain of Joy), is divided into nine segments representing the fourteenth century government called "The Nine."

Entering the piazza

Siena's town hall

Seldom discussed in architectural and urban texts are the sloped floors of many Italian piazzas. Either accommodating a specific topography or used to focus on a particular aspect of the square, the floor actually plays an important role in forming the outdoor room. For example, the floor of the Piazza del Campidoglio in Rome is a slight mound that emphasizes the equestrian statue and creates a nearly unconscious dynamic between the two opposing palazzos.

The piazza from above

A second lesson is that Siena represents a medieval square that grew more or less organically. Organic planning, as Lewis Mumford notes in *The City in History* (1961), is growth "from need to need, from opportunity to opportunity, in a series of adaptations that themselves become increasingly coherent and purposeful, so that they generate a complex, final design, hardly less unified than pre-formed geometric pattern" (Mumford 1961: 302). As such, the slowly evolving urban form occurs within accepted, if uncodified, rules. These underlying rules or agreement lead to a very clear hierarchy of forms so, for example, that background buildings do not dominate the city hall. Though it did grow more or less organically, Siena is one of the earliest examples of codified building ordinances. Beginning in the early thirteenth century, the city residents recognized the importance of the civic space and required that buildings surrounding the piazza have windows shaped like those in the Palazzo Pubblico. For Siena, the organic growth embraced the topography and what otherwise may be a design problem turns out to be a design highlight.

Piazza del Campo

Stockholm

85

Slottsbacken and Stortorget

The Slottsbacken (Palace Slope) and Stortorget (Big Square) are a series of spaces in the center of Stockholm that link the harbor to the city's Old Town. The arrangement of Stockholm's royal palace and other buildings were not designed in isolation, but developed by accretion to integrate into an overall urban scheme. As such, as buildings appeared and as the city grew, the city matured into a unified whole. Buildings become less of objects and more of participants by often deferring to the greater role of making space in the city.

Looking southwest up the Slottsbacken

Stockholm's Old Town was founded in the mid-thirteenth century on Stadsholmen Island set in the east–west channel between Lake Mälaren and Saltsjön, a tributary of the Baltic and along the north–south land trading route (Åström 1967: 14). The city's success was due in no small part to its control of these important crossroads reinforced by the fortified Borgen on the northeast corner of the island, now the site of the royal palace.

The island's original contours and remnants of jetty extensions into the harbor remain evident in the Old Town's plan. On its edges, narrow streets lead from the center toward the quay while inner roads curve slightly to reveal the original contours. Later additions outside of this area show the impact of the Renaissance with its street grid and palaces (Andersson 1998: 36–37).

Based on shipping and on steel and copper production, Stockholm grew steadily and, with the Peace of Westphalia, had become a leading power in the Baltic. By the seventeenth century, the town grew to the mainland to the Norrmalm to the north and Södermalm to the south. In an effort to unify the island with the city's northern district and rebuild the city after the devastating 1697 fire, the city and crown commissioned architect Nicodemus Tessin the Younger to design a new royal palace. Sweden's decline following its defeat by Russia in 1709, and later the treaty in 1721, delayed Stockholm's urban development. By 1727, however, construction of the palace resumed under the supervision of architect Carl Hårleman (Åström 1967: 24–25).

Aerial view of Stockholm

Linking the Old Town with the northern Renaissance city are a series of bridges and streets between civic buildings including the Supreme Court and across the small island of Helgeandsholmen with the Parliament building Riksdag. Linking the northeastern quay to the old town is the Slottsbacken, a slightly tapered and inclined square defined by the Royal Palace to the north and the edge of the Old Town to the south. Framed at the top of this incline is the Storkyrkan church. This leads to the Stortorget square in the middle of the Old Town now dominated by the stock exchange.

Slottsbacken and Stortorget

Tallinn

Raekoja Plats

86

Tallinn is one of the few cities that, like Bruges, has maintained a medieval urban fabric. The winding streets that lead from the harbor to the town square and the castle beyond disclose the city's mercantile tradition and its roots as an important trading center in medieval Eastern Europe. As the capital of Estonia, Tallinn is located on a small bay on the eastern edge of the Baltic Sea that has served, since the eleventh century, as a trading port between Russia and Europe. Additionally, the town was along several land routes which converged on the town's main square.

Tallinn is divided into two parts – the Upper Town, or Toompea, and the Lower Town, or All-inn. The Toompea is predominantly the fortified area of the city (H. Miller 1998: 3–4). This area was populated by German traders who were, as in Bergen, members of the Hanseatic League. The All-inn is the town proper with the market place, guild halls, town hall, church and, in general, the day-to-day life of the city. Though considered the "lower town" it is still above the harbor and reached through a series of sloped streets that lead from the harbor into the town's center, the heart of which is the Raekoja Plats or Town Hall Square.

This square is a traditional medieval square that began as a market place surrounded by guild houses. Streets off the square are named after the crafts that lined them including Shoemaker Street and Goldsmith Street (H. Miller 1998: 21). The square is formed by four-story stucco, neo-classical buildings but is dominated by the fifteenth century Raekoda or town hall. Today, the Plats is lined with cafés, shops and restaurants on the ground floor while the square itself is used predominantly for festivals, concerts and folk market.

Tallinn is important because it represents how many medieval towns, especially those in the Hanseatic League, were not isolated and inverted villages, but integral elements in trading networks that often extended across Europe (Zucker 1966: 71). As such, the organization of these towns was built upon commerce with streets, squares and buildings becoming a tool of trade. As in Arras, Bern or Bruges, the towns developed a sophisticated social and mercantile order that would remain until the rise of international ocean-based trade in the fifteenth and sixteenth centuries.

Town Hall

Town Hall from side street

Raekoja Plats

Telč

87

Náměstí Zachariáše z Hradce

Of the three towns from the Czech Republic included in this collection, two of them – České Budějovice and Telč – were selected for their archetypal public squares. The first type epitomized by České Budějovice, as well as Kroměříž, Kolín and Nový Jičín, is a typical planned colonial town with a regular, enclosed central square distributed throughout the Bohemian and Moravian kingdoms. The second type epitomized by Telč, like Chleb and Olomouc, is planned but with an elongated, slightly triangular, closed square formed more by topography and existing trade routes. These two representative squares illustrate that Bohemian and Moravian towns followed similar patterns that have remained astonishingly unchanged over the past several centuries. Moreover, despite the differences between centralized or elongated, each town's square remains successful.

Set in southern Moravia approximately 75 kilometers from České Budějovice and 125 kilometers from Prague, Telč is considered one of the Czech Republic's most picturesque towns. Established in the fourteenth century, the town was a major junction and stronghold along the trade routes that interconnected Bohemia, Moravia and Austria.

Telč's design exploited a naturally occurring moat so that the town, set on an elongated point of land, would be surrounded on the north and south by small lakes while a fourth edge could be protected by a single wall that ran from northeast to southwest (Morris 1994: 101). The moat was also used as a fishery and, like other Czech towns, used both as a source of income and food for the town's residents. Anchoring the town's northern end is the fourteenth century palace that was substantially rebuilt during the Renaissance and Baroque periods.

View from the north

View from the south

Telč's most distinguishing architectural feature is the gabled, arcaded *mazhaus* or brewhouse type dwellings with long corridors extending away from the square (Jaroslav Wagner, in Novotny 1975: 347). These houses are known for their Renaissance and Baroque façades, many of which were, at one time, decorated with graffiti. The balance of the uniform type with gable, details and paint color variations produces an elegant urban space.

Fortunately, Telč remained relatively unscathed from the Baroque period through today as industrial development and housing were shifted to the town's suburbs. Most of the area adjoining the two lakes is now reserved for parkland and, in a way, intensifies the town's detachment from time.

Telč's square, while beautiful, does have some awkward spatial conditions. This is especially true at the southern end, which is isolated and not part of the square's path. This main thoroughfare does not lead from that portion, but diverts toward the south and out of the town. A second spatial awkwardness is more than likely due to its shape. As an elongated square, it lacks a center or focus making it difficult to find a place to stop and rest despite its slight slope from the northwest and southeast toward its center. Even the small monuments and fountains on the south end are isolated median strips rather than an area of repose.

Náměstí Zachariáše z Hradce

Tokyo

88

Asakusa Nakamise Dori

Located in Tokyo's Asakusa district, Nakamise is a popular destination for tourists and Tokyo residents alike. The narrow, open-air pedestrian street is a series of attenuated, single-story kiosks offering a wide variety of items for sale such as inexpensive souvenirs, trinkets and clothing. To the urban designer and architect, it represents a distinctly Japanese concept of public open space centered on a temple precinct and the public street.

Nakamise is essentially a shopping street. First built in the late seventeenth century and rebuilt twice in the twentieth century, it is essentially the main axial passageway of the Sensoji temple. The 275-meter long street links the large Kaminarimon Gate and forecourt on the south end to and through the Hozomon Gate at the temple proper to the north. Asakusa itself is a relatively unique part of Tokyo with a tight grid of streets with two- and three-story small-scale buildings predominantly commercial retail on the ground floor with commercial and residential on the upper levels. The brightly painted, somewhat flimsy pergola-like kiosks act as a datum to the district that is bisected north and south by Asakusa Shin-Nakamise covered shopping arcade.

As literary critic Roland Barthes notes in *Empire of Signs* (1982), Tokyo "can be known only by an activity of an ethnographic kind: you must orient yourself in it not by book, by address, but by walking, by sight, by habit, by experience" (Barthes 1982: 36). Unlike the western tradition of a public, often secular, hardscaped square, the Japanese, like other Asian and Middle Eastern cultures, have a tradition of public space associated, generally, with religious centers and with street life. This stems from the Japanese social tradition in which private life outside of the day-to-day, non-religious activities is focused on the home or other similar private domains rather than in public open settings. For those times when there is social interaction among strangers, the Japanese have public spaces that are not fixed, hierarchical and designated space but are what architect Jinnai Hidenobu describes in *Tokyo: A Spatial Anthropology* as ludic space (Hidenobu 1995: 91). Ludic space, originally associated with theater districts, are less physical spaces, but temporary, animated situations. These situations, either deliberately or accidentally fabricated by ephemeral occurrences, become the public sphere. While they are no less solid or real than public squares in Europe, they simply appear and disappear depending on the day, the time or event. Architect Shun Kanda explains that the Japanese word *hiroba*, which literally translates as "open, or wide space or ground," aligns with identifying a place of human activity hinged more to time rather than fixed space (Kanda 1974: 85–86).

View from the south

View from the north

Carrying a shrine through the streets

Though Asakusa, owing to its history as the entertainment district with its somewhat shoddy pavilions, is quintessential *hiroba*, this can also be seen in other parts of Tokyo such as Hachiko Square in the Shibuya district and even in those public spaces akin to western spaces. Though non-Japanese or *gaijin* spaces can be found, they were established following the post-1854 opening of Japan to the west and, most often, after World War II. Notwithstanding Tokyo's Ueno Park or plazas at the base of corporate buildings, purely public squares, and even public benches, remain uncommon in Japan.

Carrying a shrine through the streets

Asakusa Nakamise Dori

Tokyo

Hachiko Square

89

Hachiko Square, located in Tokyo's Shibuya district, is a vibrant intersection surrounded by multi-storied office buildings, department stores, hotels, apartment buildings and mixed use complexes and illuminated with competing animated billboards and large screen televisions. Like other Japanese public spaces, it is not a traditional "square" as much as it is a center of activity. Hachiko Square is more spectacle than space – a spectacle best observed in an American coffee shop's upper level that seems to have been designed for this purpose. From this vantage point, it is easy to appreciate what is called a "Barnes Dance" crossing. In this crossing, made famous by Henry Barnes, a former traffic commissioner who did not invent but used this system in Denver, traffic signals stop vehicular traffic in all directions simultaneously. Within seconds, the entire intersection is filled with a moving crowd. Within a few minutes, however, the crowd dissipates and the vehicles once again move through the square.

As mentioned in the discussion of Tokyo's Asakusa Nakamise, Japanese public space is generally limited to temple precincts and streets. Exceptions to this are post-1854 parks and corporate sponsored plazas and also include "terminal plazas" that are centered around rail, tram or subway stations. Hachiko Square is essentially a vast terminal plaza with the above and below ground Shibuya Station that services six rail lines including the Ginza line and the JNR line. Additionally, it is the intersection of four major streets and several minor service streets. Because of its multiple levels above the ground plane, a figure-ground drawing that is more endemic to western spaces does the area little justice.

Like other "ludic" spaces described by Jinnai Hidenobu in *Tokyo: A Spatial Anthropology* (1995), Hachiko Square appears and disappears at different times of the day, hour and even minute (Hidenobu 1995: 91). The often frenetic and multifaceted spaces are quintessentially Japanese and may offer a glimpse of twenty-first and twenty-second century urban spaces throughout the world. Like Los Angeles as depicted in Ridley Scott's *Blade Runner* (1982) or even Las Vegas today, the city's public life is not limited to the ground plane but involves the vertical, the overhead and the below.

Just as the Japanese concept of public space does not adhere to static and hierarchical organizations in the ground plane, it does not adhere to the vertical hierarchy predominant in western cities. Unlike western cities that have increasingly private spaces with each floor above grade, in Japan it is common to find retail and restaurants on upper levels reached by a warren of stairs, elevators and escalators. While this form is also driven by real estate necessity, it has also been embraced by the Japanese as part of urban life, which proves there are no boiler-plate solutions for good urban space design or real estate development but that good design requires close examination of the forces on the site and the cultural context in the design process. This vertical, non-hierarchical examination of architecture no doubt foreshadows future urban spaces shaped by economic and environmental forces so that cities may become further vertically differentiated to accommodate varied uses. Cities can survive with upper level retail and alleyway restaurants. Though Japanese concepts of public spaces are distinctly different from western societies, all successful spaces depend on highly adjacent activities such as subway stations, high-density housing and mixed uses.

Before the lights change

After the lights change

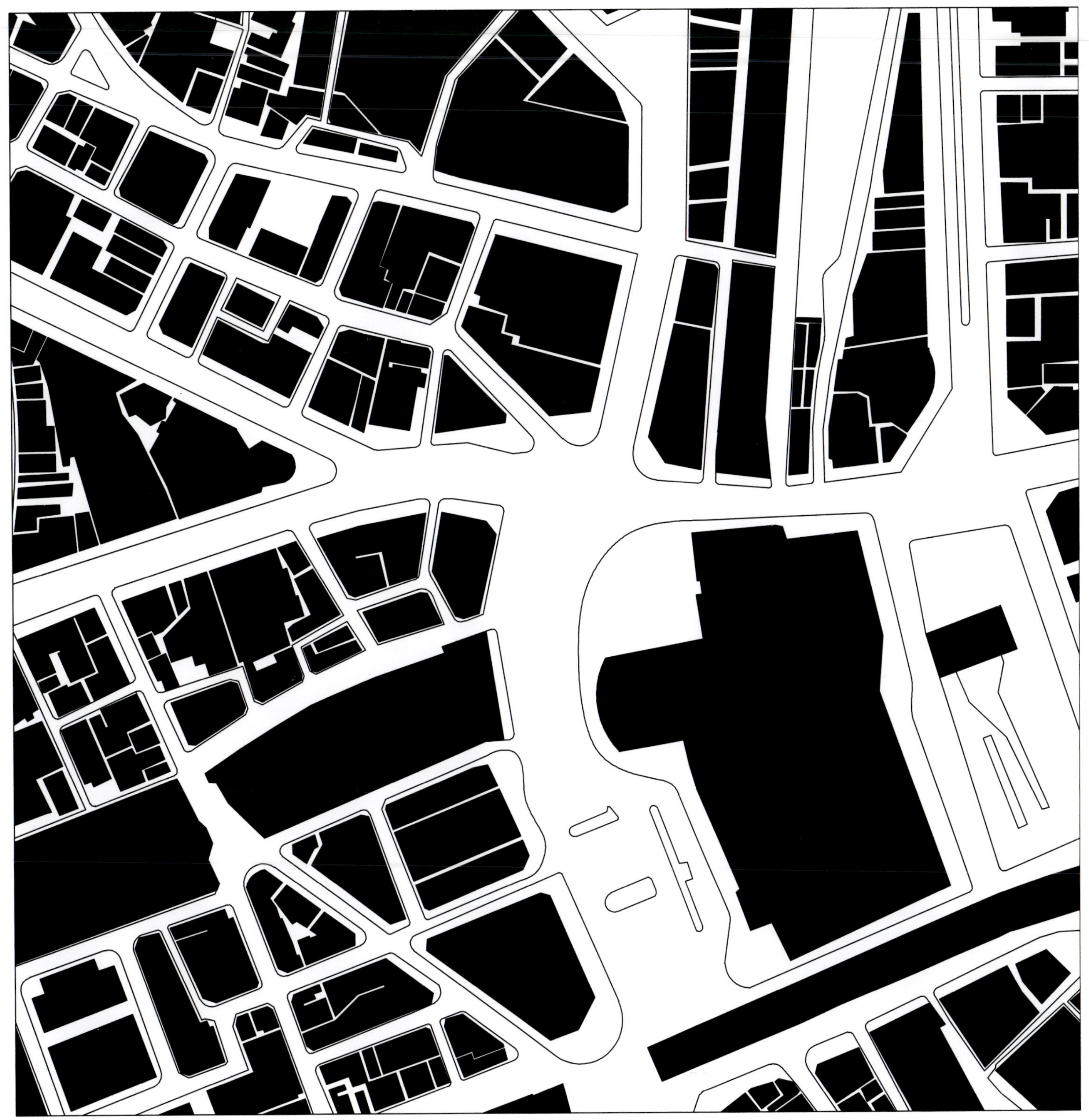

Hachiko Square

Torino

90

Piazza San Carlo

Commissioned by Duke Carlo Emanuelle I, Piazza San Carlo in Torino, originally the Piazza Reale, was to symbolize his power, his benevolence and ability of his government to develop Torino into a sixteenth and seventeenth century capital city. This princely square, with arcades on all sides, was more than likely influenced by Henry IV's Place Royale (Place des Vosges) in Paris especially considering Henry IV's daughter, Cristina, married Carlo Emanuelle I's son, Vittorio Amedeo.

Attributed to Ascanio Vittozzi and implemented by Carlo di Castellamonte in 1637, the design and construction extended over thirty years. The piazza was part of an overall redevelopment of Torino from the city center to the new ceremonial gate at the city's southern edge. At the center of a twelve-block, grid redevelopment was the grand street *contrada nuova* that connected the palace with the southern gate. The square became a center of civic activity as a market and parade ground. Today, the square remains more of a traffic thoroughfare; beneath its arcades are a mixture of financial offices, cafés and clothing stores.

The square is a rectilinear volume bisected by the north–south street Via Roma that begins at the Piazza Castello three blocks to the north and continues three blocks south to the Piazza Carlo Felice and the Porta Nueva train station, formerly the southern gate of the city. Uniform, three-story façades with a consistent cornice line define the square as well as the streets leading into and out of it. Bounding the south end of the square and on either side of Via Roma are the twin Baroque churches of San Cristina, to the west, and San Carlo to the east. While twin churches on a piazza is similar to the Piazza del Popolo, the organization here is unusual in that unlike many enclosed squares that have primary street entry at the edge, Piazza San Carlo has a primary entrance in its center. Moreover, unlike the Piazza del Popolo's twin churches that project into the space making them somewhat more theatrical Baroque objects, in Torino, the twin churches become almost a backdrop to the action within the square.

Two significant changes were made to the square since its inception that altered the square's image and effectiveness as a stately plaza. The first alteration was in the eighteenth century when the space between the doubled columns was filled to make a solid pier. This eliminated the arcade's delicacy and isolated those beneath the arcade from the square with a more opaque partition. A second, albeit external, transformation was the increased speed of vehicles through the space. The common impression of the square today is out of the window of an automobile that is certainly different than when viewed on horseback or by carriage. This obvious difference, one suffered by

View toward the south

many squares since the beginning of the twentieth century, also further subdivides the piazza into a widened street rather than a break in the pedestrian movement.

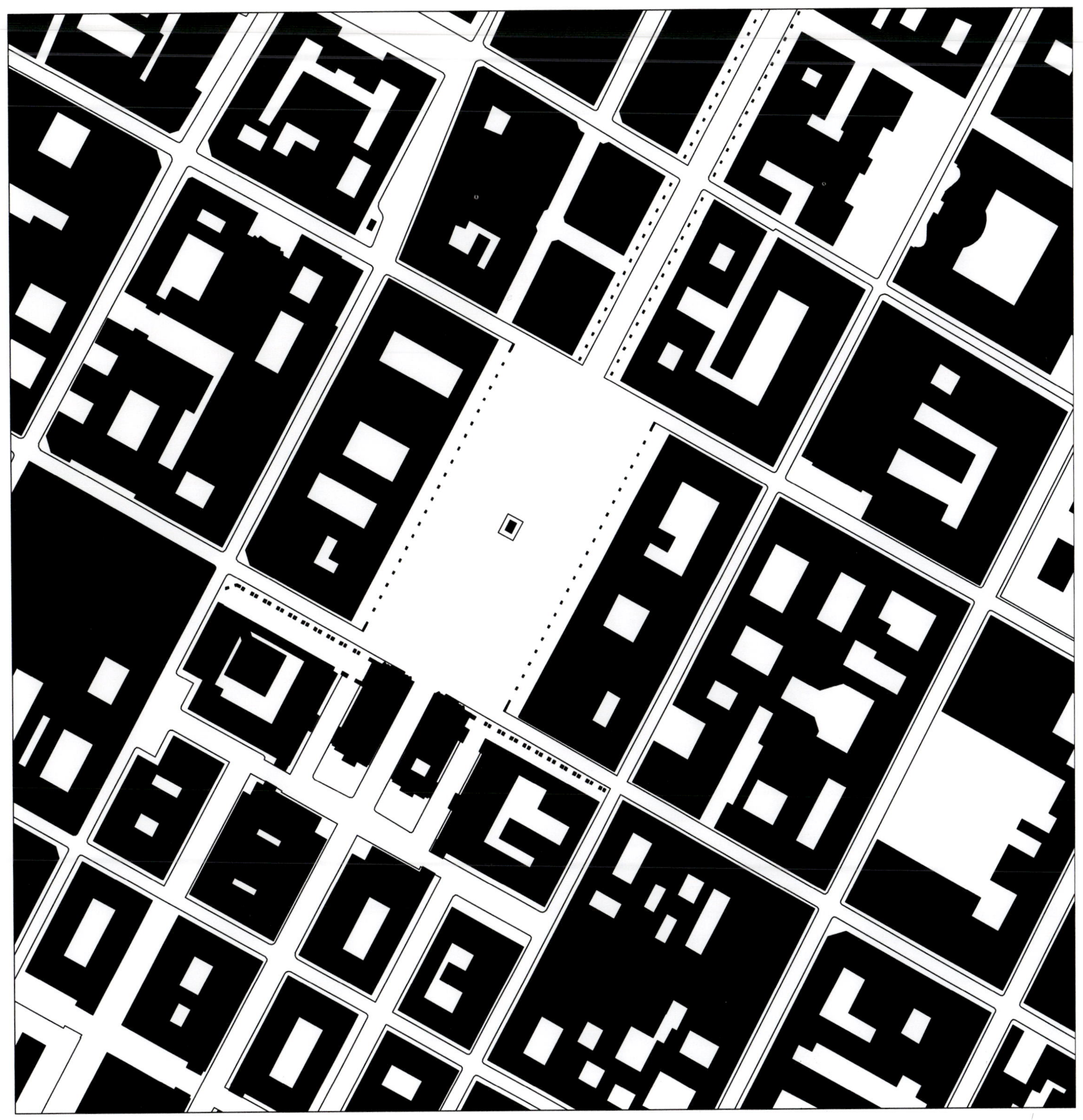

Piazza San Carlo

Trieste

91

Canal Grande

Trieste's Canal Grande is emblematic of its city in that, as Jan Morris (2001: 153) notes in *Trieste and the Meaning of Nowhere*, it "is not exactly Germanesque, it is not precisely Italian." While the canal resembles a Venetian canal, it is really an artificial inlet and its Italianate tempietto is offset by almost severe Germanic buildings. It is the hybrid nature that contributes to Trieste's urban form.

The Canal Grande

Connected to Italy only by a narrow appendage at the northern end of the Adriatic and only five miles from the Slovenian border, it is a blend of Germanic, Slavic and Italian cultures. Under Austrian rule from the fourteenth century until the twentieth century, it was Central Europe's access to the Mediterranean and a thriving merchant and banking center.

Austria's interest in Trieste during the early eighteenth century helped initiate a series of urban projects. The earliest of these is the area around the Canal Grande known as the Borgo Teresiano. Designed in the middle of the eighteenth century by Venetian architects Matteo Pirona and Rodolfo Deretti, the gridiron, fifty-block plan was a real estate development project built over a former salt works (Fabiani 2003: 10). The architects created the Canal Grande by enlarging the salt work's canal between 1754 and 1756 so that small merchant ships could unload directly into the surrounding warehouses (Fabiani 2003: 41). The eighteenth and nineteenth century neo-classical buildings along its edges are distinctly Austro-Hungarian and recall Budapest and Vienna in that, like those cities, Trieste has a sense of lost power and faded grandiosity. Terminating the canal on the east is the Church of Sant' Antonio Taumaturgo, first built in 1768 and then rebuilt in the mid-nineteenth century; it is a domed tempietto that once abutted directly on the canal, which was, however, filled in in 1934. The districts around it lead to several smaller civic and market squares. Midway along the canal is the Piazza del Ponterosso used as a market. This square is bisected by the Via Roma, which connects to a smaller square to the north and eventually to the city's southern quarter.

Following World War I, the city was consigned to Italy. However, with Genoa, Naples and Venice closer to the main body of the country, Italy had no need for Trieste's isolated port. Though held briefly by the Germans again during World War II, Yugoslavia took an interest in the city, but was contested by the United States and Britain, who were concerned that it could become a warm water port for the Soviet bloc countries.

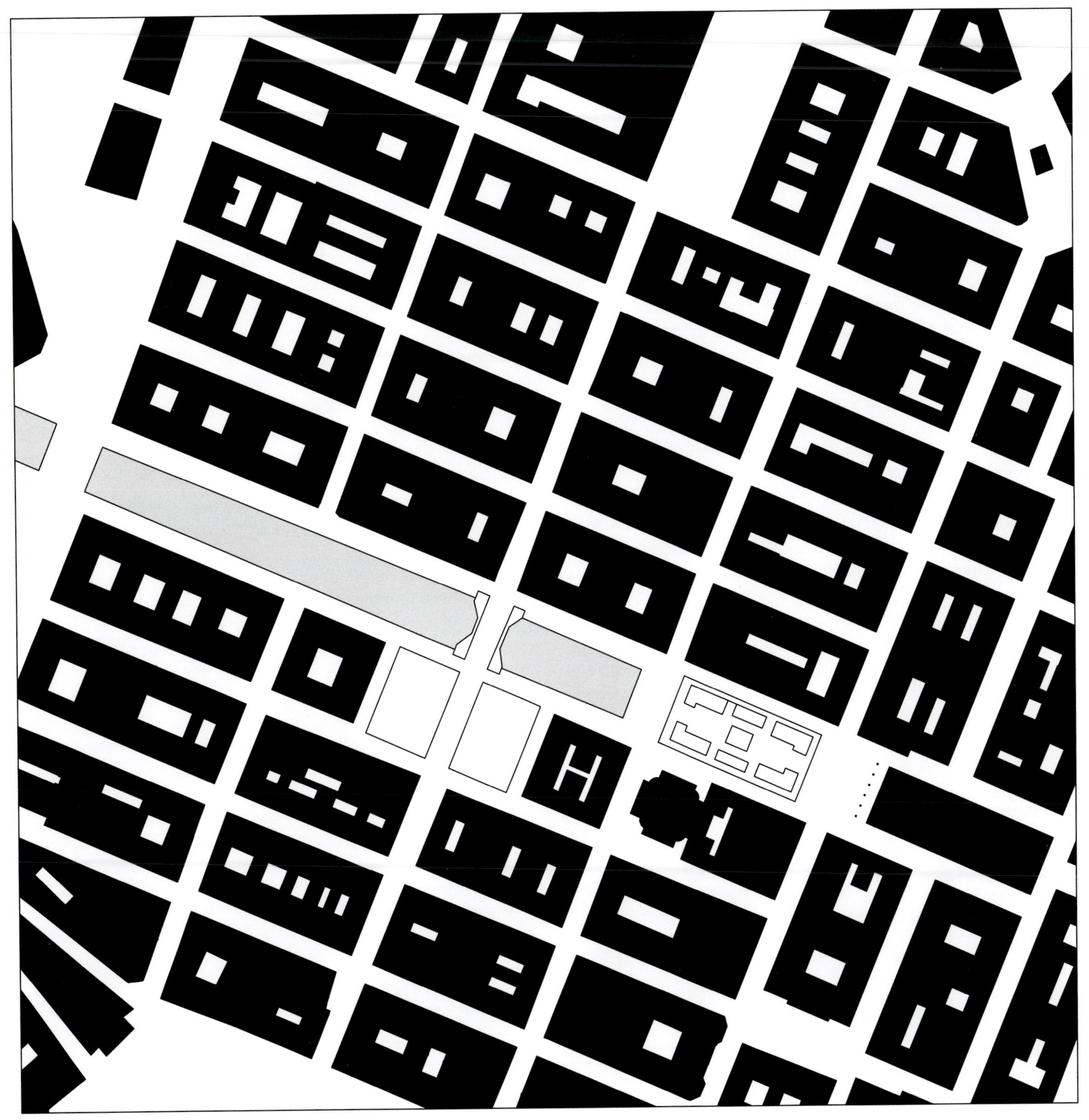

Canal Grande

Tunis

Medina

92

Tunis' Medina urban design exemplifies the North African and Middle Eastern settlement patterns influenced by Islamic tradition. While there are regional variations and, especially in the twentieth century, the rise of secular institutions and patterns, the universality of the Prophet Muhammad's teachings guided personal and public life as well as regularized urban patterns. At first, these Arab-Islamic urban patterns appear random or informal. However, it belies a highly regimented social system and manifests what is in fact highly differentiated.

Cities and towns are, like any culture, based upon the traditions of private and public life. For a Muslim, one who submits to Allah, this tradition is based upon the tenets of Islam transmuted from Allah to the Prophet and described in the Quran. These tenets were further codified in the Sunna, a behavior code that, among others, delineated specific spatial settlement and even individual building patterns. In general, this codification reinforced privacy, width of streets, right to noise protection, waste drainage, water access and other by-right amenities.

Muslim life is based on the family and is considered sacred. Likewise, the home and immediate surroundings are considered sacred and autonomous. As such, housing is organized into internally oriented, familial clusters that delimit private spheres. Culs-de-sac that limit access to a select group of people connect these private areas and contribute to layers of privacy. Conversely, public streets contract to minimum essentials and function primarily, except when they are *suqs* or markets, as passageways through the city.

Medina Street

Muslims accept Allah's omnipresence and, therefore, understand that all places can be the province of worship. Rather than explicit secular and sacrosanct spaces and buildings, the Arab-Islamic urban fabric is far less spatially hierarchical and the mosque is fused within that fabric. Just as they are integrated, the mosque took on responsibility more commonly associated with civic institutions. Therefore, traditionally, there was no need for civic institutions, since, as Stefano Bianca notes in *Urban Form in the Arab World* (2000), the Muslim's "ritualized living patterns dispensed with the need for many formal institutions" (Bianca 2000: 30). Correspondingly, artificial institutional structures might interfere with Allah's natural order and obstruct the link to Allah. As such, large-scale urban public works projects or city planning remained relatively absent or at the periphery. Instead, cities expanded as needed and by individual cellular units. When there was a need for large public spaces, such as markets, these were more temporary and generally located at the city's perimeter.

The result is a somewhat homogenous city with internally oriented archetypal subsystems. There is little concept of a public square. There are exceptions such as welfare compounds or paradise gardens like those at Isfahan. Simply put, there is no social or cultural need for squares and, therefore, no interest in making generalized public spaces.

Arab-Islamic urban patterning illustrates how urban design or any design can develop on individual rules yet still provide viable living conditions. This is important today because a city, neighborhood or home can be ordered yet this order is apparent and useful only to those who dwell in it. In a sense, the way to make cities is not limited to particular formal patterns but to the underlying social, cultural and religious systems of those that live in the city.

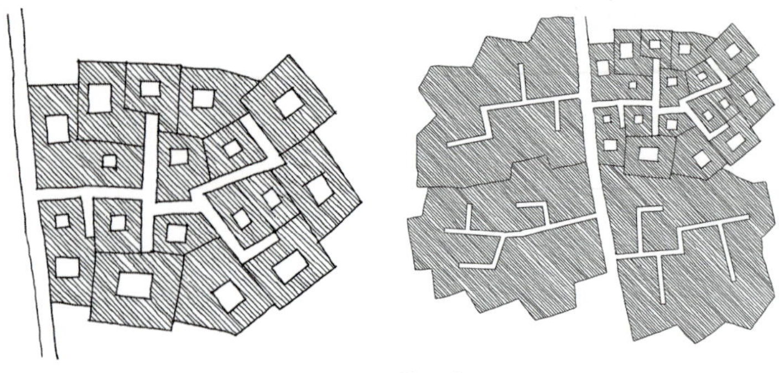

Local housing cluster

Conglomeration of housing clusters

Medina

Vancouver

93

Robson Square

Though a relatively young city, Vancouver has undergone a series of rapid transformations since its founding in the latter half of the nineteenth century. Like other North American cities it rose quickly yet, like many North American cities, suffered from post-war decline. Since the early 1980s, however, Vancouver has rebounded with a progressive campaign of urban housing and waterfront development often cited as a model for many cities.

Founded as Granville in 1870 on a small peninsula surrounded by False Creek, English Bay and the Burrard Inlet and dominated by picturesque mountains, Vancouver is considered one of the most livable cities in North America. Much of its success is a distinctive culture that promotes social consciousness and a long-term economic view that has brought about, among other things, well-maintained public amenities such as parks, beaches, markets and waterfront promenades within blocks of downtown.

Robson Square proper was originally a single block bordered by Robson, Georgia, Hornby and Howe Streets with the 1912 neo-classical Provincial Courthouse at its center. Following extensive downtown revitalization in the 1970s, the courts relocated to Canadian architect Arthur Erikson's new complex across Robson Street and the Vancouver Art Gallery occupied the old building. Today, "Robson Square" is essentially a three-block long area extending from Georgia Street to Smithe Street and is surrounded by a variety of uses including retail, a university, conference center, hotels, housing and office buildings. Erikson's new courthouse, one that challenged the traditional organization of a court building, introduces distinctly informal terraced gardens into the more formal grid of the city (Iglauer 1981: 110–111).

Robson Square seems to defy conventional principles of what is considered "good" urban space. The informal gardens with often-ambiguous delineation, the lack of clearer edges and traffic moving through and around it could make it a likely candidate for failure or at least significant revitalization common to many contemporary spaces in the United States. Despite this, it is a hub of activity. It is bustling with local residents and tourists alike. Young artists display their work in front of the art museum's unused staircase. The subterranean gathering area is less successful but recent attempts to bring the University of British Columbia to the area may help to enliven it. Much of the activity may have less to do with its shape than with the lack of a definitively public room in downtown. Also, the square's health may be attributable to the rebirth of Vancouver not only as a tourist destination due in part to the cruise ship port but also with the increased high-density housing introduced since the early 1990s. Moreover, Vancouver residents tend to use the city as a place of activity and the spaces have a distinctly European feel. What is interesting about this is that rather than following prescriptive rules about architecture and urban space, the culture and context of the city must be taken into consideration.

Robson Square from the north

Robson Square with below grade plaza, conference center and dance floor

Art Gallery steps that do not lead to the entrance but are used for people watching and by amateur artists displaying and selling their work

Robson Square

Venice

94

Piazza San Marco and Piazzetta di San Marco

Piazza San Marco balances disciplined uniformity with subtle, often intangible, nuances. The space is at once comprehensible and straightforward, yet it conceals the moves that transform it from a simple enclosed, regularized space. Much of its success can be attributed to the continuous façade with arcades at the ground floor. Like Piazza San Pietro in Vaticano or Piazza Ducale in Vigévano, the arcades are permeable surfaces that offer a transition from tight urban fabric to the piazza itself. Though this perimeter is quite uniform, it is not as uniform as it appears. The most obvious distortion is its trapezoidal plan in which walls diverge toward the basilica that shifts perspective and challenges expectations of scale and distance. A more subtle variation is on the piazza's north side that has more petite columns and a face that bows slightly giving the square a subtle plasticity.

The piazza did not appear all at once but over several centuries. As Lewis Mumford (1961) points out, the beginning of San Marco as a public space was in the late tenth century but its enclosure formed slowly. The south side of Sansovino's Library was added only in 1520 and the western end opposite the San Marco cathedral was completed only in 1805. Mumford notes that "both the form and contents of the Piazza were, in brief, the products of cumulative urban purposes, modified by circumstance, function and time: organic products that no single human genius could produce in a few months" (Mumford 1961: 322). Piazza San Marco is not a fixed instant project but one adapted to changes in Venetian culture and society. Unfortunately, it has, especially since the 1950s, become less of an active part of Venetian culture but more ossified tourist destination.

The lessons of Piazza San Marco are manifold. Worth noting here, however, are the contrasts between Venetian streets and the piazza and subtle composition of its surface and objects that contribute to a dynamic spatial experience.

The piazza owes much to Venice's surrounding urban fabric. In contrast to the piazza, the fabric is predominantly a warren of streets interweaving a series of small squares and canal crossings. This fabric, alternating between open and closed, helps build a kind of spatial tension and anticipation. Then, after moving beneath a covered collonade, the warren gives way to the piazza that is, except for the Grand Canal, a singular spatial release in the city.

Piazza San Marco itself has its own compelling moves. The first is its diverging walls that, in addition to the perspectival shift, appear only to meet at two points while all other corners remain hidden. For example, the walls do not touch the basilica but slide past it so that the basilica seems to float within the square. This is similar to Vigevano where the piazza and church façades do not touch but are "joined" with a reveal. A second move is the campanile that is disengaged from the piazza walls. The campanile itself acts as a pivot point for the space. As a fulcrum, it emphasizes the joint between the main piazza and piazzetta and allows for a dynamic shift from large to smaller space. These and other moves are actually most noticeable or significant when they are removed or regularized. If, for example, the walls met neatly at corners, the surfaces parallel and the campanile engaged the square's wall or, for that matter, was completely removed, the space would be completely altered and more than likely result in a banal square.

Piazza San Marco looking east

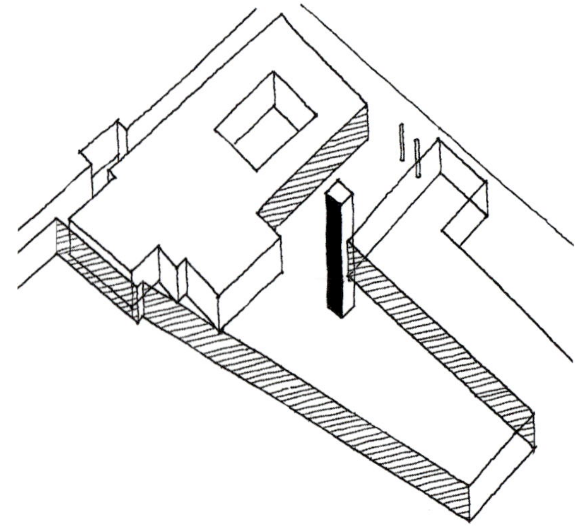

This shows planar slippage and undefined intersections

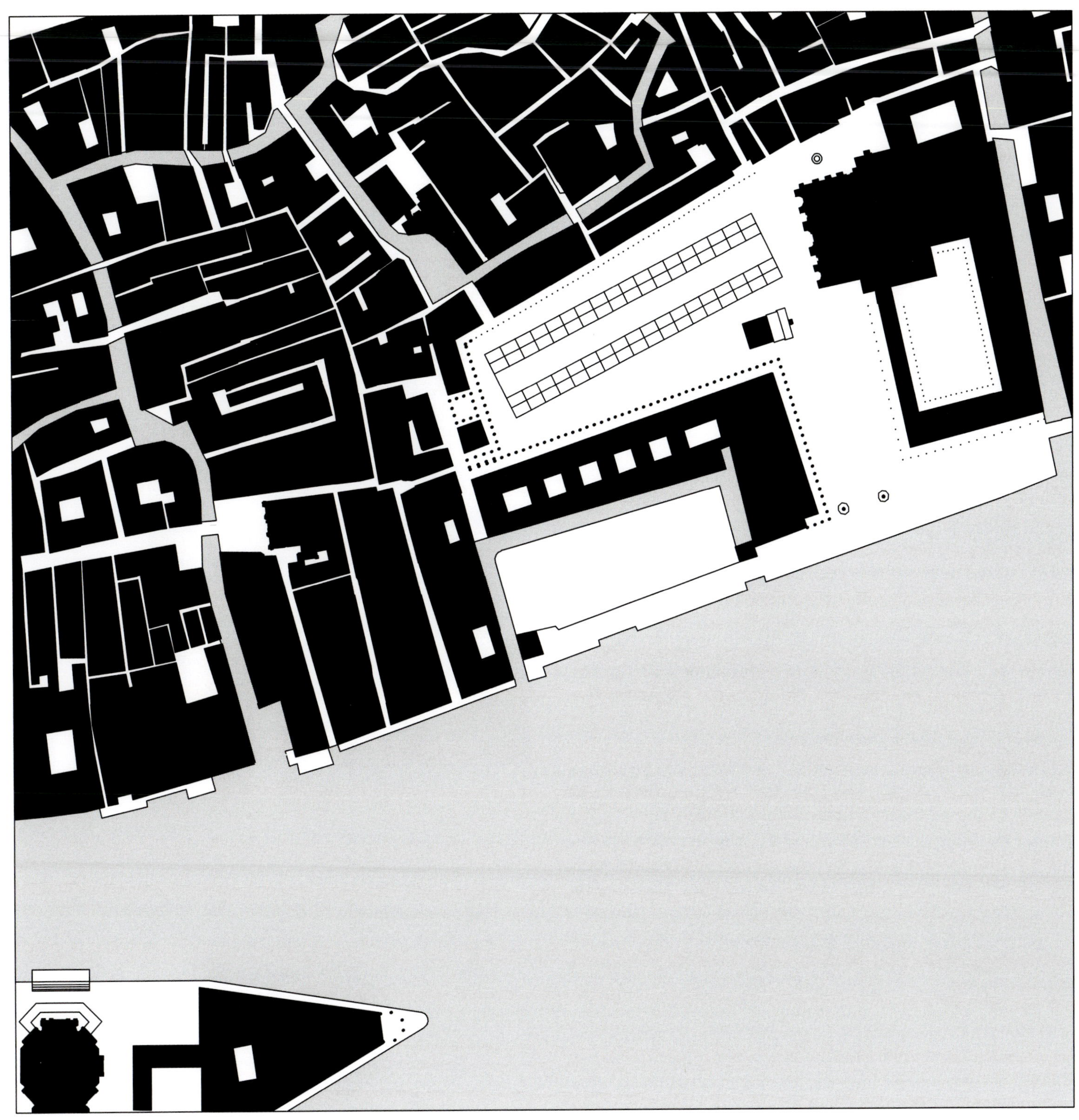

Piazza San Marco and Piazzetta di San Marco

Verona

95

Piazza delle Erbe and Piazza dei Signori

These two medieval squares, like those in Arras and Salzburg, are grouped squares each playing its particular role in the city – Piazza delle Erbe for commerce and Piazza dei Signori for governing – each with its own individual identity, form and atmosphere. Each space is at once unique but complementary. Moreover, the architectural language and elements of the square participate in defining the space. Rather than an arbitrary architecture, the urban and architectural composition seems befitting to their use. Like Florence's Piazza della Signoria, the freestanding elements and towers play an important role in the spatial experience (Zucker 1966: 88). The clear two-dimensional plan is only as successful as the three-dimensional articulation.

Piazza delle Erbe from above

Like many other towns in Italy, Verona began as a Roman colonial town. The grid remains apparent as does its public spaces. Piazza delle Erbe occupies roughly the same area as the original Roman forum. Today, with the exception of the town hall and Baroque Palazzo Maffei, the square's edges are modest three- and four-story buildings with shops and cafés on the ground floor. It is the main market square of Verona and, like Campo dei Fiori in Rome, the stalls are set up and then removed each day. Fixed along its spine are four freestanding elements including the colonna del Mercato, the fontana di Madonna Verona, the colonna di San Marco and a small *baldacchino*-like gazebo. These elements act as a datum to the space that bulges slightly at its center.

Additionally, two towers, the central Palazzo del Comune's Tower Lamberti at the northeast edge of the piazza and a smaller Torre del Gardello to the northwest provide a visual balance to the space. Without the town hall tower, the square would appear more of a wide street yet this anchors the center while the Torre del Gardello marks the square's extent and gives a differentiation to the square's ends. Both vertical elements help anchor the space and give a sense of arrival. The result is a dynamic market space, fed by both ends and by secondary streets near its center, that is both part of pathway and a destination.

Contrasting this active market is the more reserved Piazza dei Signori. Separated from the Piazza delle Erbe and the rest of the town through a series of narrow streets marked with archways and surrounded by the town hall, courts and other administrative buildings there is a distinct impression that the space is more of a large courtyard rather than a public square. Compounding this courtyard sense are several loggias that unify the façades.

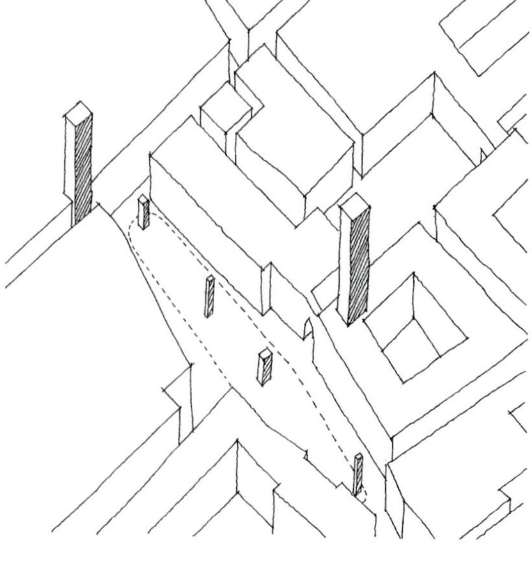

This shows the relationship of towers in the squares

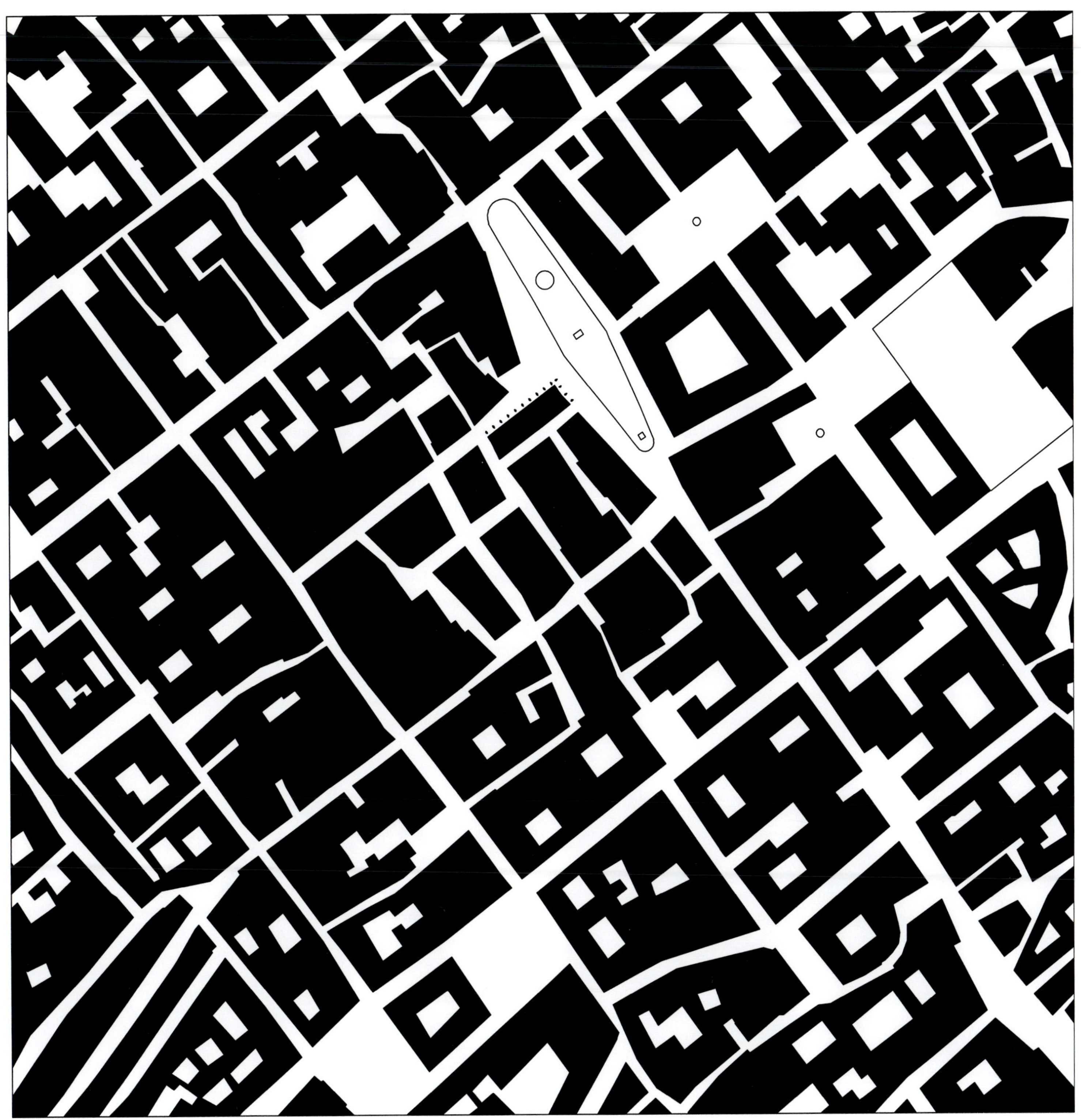

Piazza delle Erbe and Piazza dei Signori

Vienna

96

Ringstrasse

Facing possible and sometimes real attacks by the Ottoman Turks, the city of Vienna, on the eastern edge of Europe, was surrounded by a series of fortifications for several centuries and would remain in place until the middle of the nineteenth century. Growth beyond the city walls and moats was limited and the inner *altstadt* remained relatively unchanged since medieval times. By 1857, when Emperor Franz Josef I decreed that the bastions be removed, the entire defensible zone encircling the city was over 400 meters wide and capable of significant urban revitalization and space for the royal city. The emperor's decree outlined the construction of an opera house, museums, library, archives and other government office buildings. This area, now known as the Ringstrasse, allowed for late nineteenth century institutions with ceremonial functions to be condensed into a single distinct area.

The Ringstrasse follows the approximate outline of the segmented bastions and is comprised of two parallel streets creating two parallel zones for civic buildings and spaces. The primary street, the wider Ringstrasse itself, runs between the two zones while a narrower service street rings the outer perimeter. Rather than the continuous vistas of contemporaneous Haussmann Paris, the Ringstrasse is comprised of two parallel streets that move around the city in a segmented arc. Each segment is a distinct zone with little interconnection. The zones were divided into more specific zones, one for the middle class with the stock exchange and banking union buildings, a government zone around the Rathausplatz with the parliament, university buildings, opera house and museums facing the Hofburg Imperial Palace. The plan here shows one of the primary segments: the Rathausplatz across from the Burgtheater. The overall design of the Ringstrasse follows straightforward patterns. Public ceremonial buildings such as the opera house, theater and church are freestanding. Other buildings in the ensemble such as the museums, courthouse, university and the town hall are background buildings that line the public spaces.

A situation in which a large infrastructure that became obsolete or disruptive to a city's growth continues to be an important issue to this day. In the eighteenth and nineteenth centuries, bastions were quite common in European cities such as Prague and Kraków and each city developed its own version of contemporary urban design and offered opportunities for urban design solutions outside or often within a dense urban fabric. This situation is comparable to twenty-first century opportunities resulting from nineteenth and twentieth century impositions on American cities such as federal housing projects, factories or highways. For example, Boston's formerly raised Central Artery that cut through downtown until it was entombed in the late 1990s has resulted in an opportunity for both commercial and civic buildings within a ribbon park through the city.

Rathaus

The Ringstrasse in relation to the old city

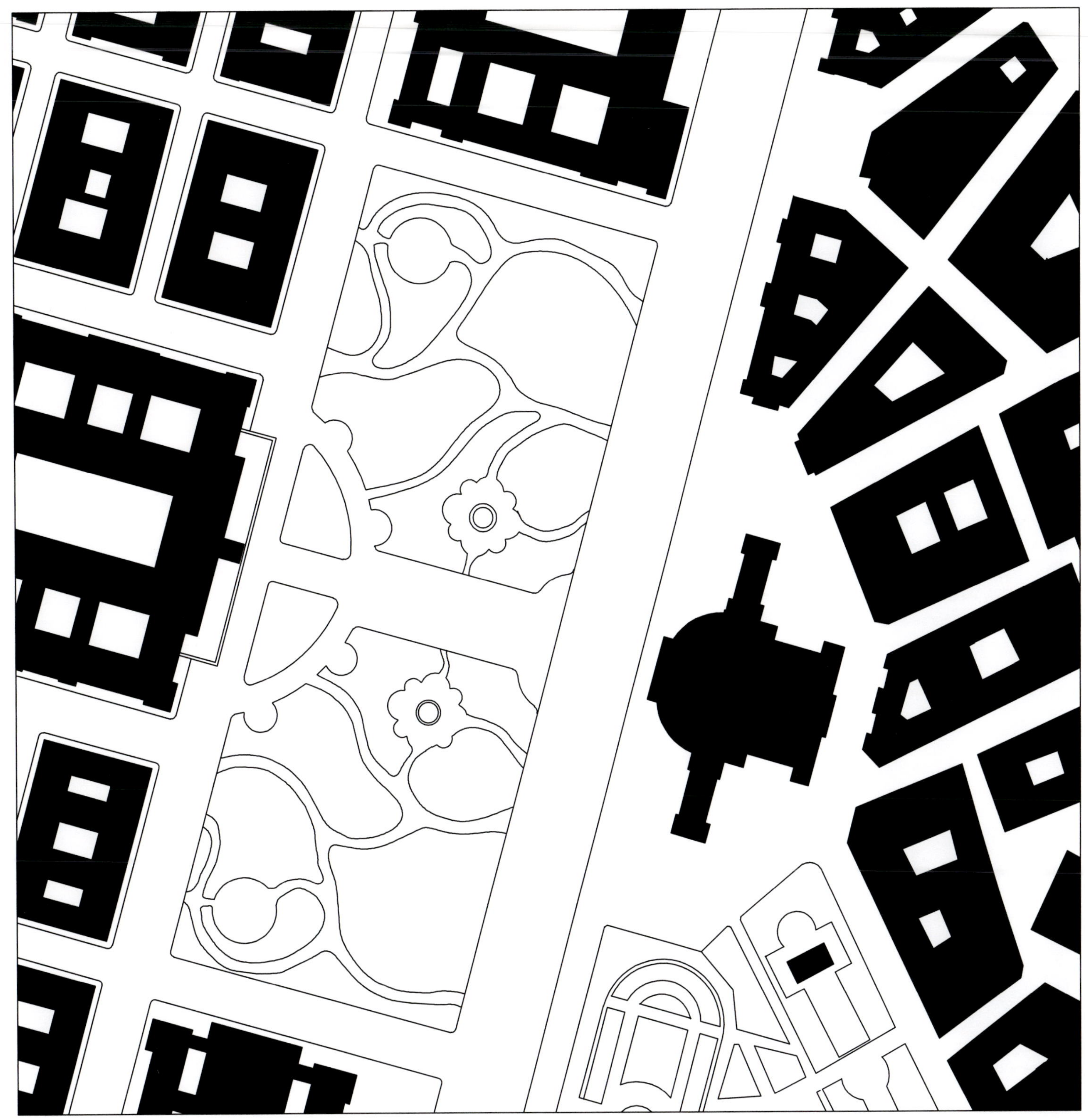

Ringstrasse

Vigévano

Piazza Ducale

Piazza Ducale is considered one of the earliest examples of a fully realized Renaissance square. Attributed to Donato Bramante and Leonardo da Vinci, though this has never been fully confirmed, it represents the late fifteenth century influence of classical ideals outlined by Vitruvius and further codified by Averlino Filerete and Leone Battista Alberti. Regularity and order dominate. The space, its order and form, are primary with the background buildings – those forming the context – taking a secondary role resulting in a well-proportioned space carved out of a medieval fabric.

To attain the order, three of its sides are lined with unified regular arcades to conceal the irregular medieval buildings beyond. The fourth edge is the more recent seventeenth century façade of San Ambrogio that dominates the square in elevation and plan. It is twice the height of the arcaded walls with a slightly rounded pediment. This face is also concave and receives, if you will, the force of the longitudinal axis. Moreover, the curved surface helps conceal an interesting secret. Though the façade is centered on the piazza's longitudinal axis, the church's axis is actually shifted approximately fifteen degrees to the north. The curved surface allows an easy shift from the piazza's geometry to that of the nave's axis. To further resolve this shift, the façade continues beyond its interior so that the church's fourth door is actually a side street.

Though it is a nearly idealized plan, scholars have discovered that Piazza Ducale was not always as pure and as uniform as it appears today. At one time it was an L-shaped piazza to connect to the palace to the south and its colonnade was superimposed with triumphal arches to emphasize its long and cross axes (Schofield 1992–1993: 161–162).

View down the Piazza Ducale's axis from the west

Like Venice, the most predominant entry points are from medieval streets through the colonnade that create a dynamic spatial experience from closed street to open square. An exception to this is the street that runs along the front of San Ambrogio's façade. The lateral street allows passage through the square without actually entering into it. This gap between the arcade and the church acts also as a kind of reveal so that the joint between the two is resolved by not joining. This resolution of a spatial gasket is seen at other church façade–piazza wall resolutions including Piazza San Marco in Venice and to a lesser extent in Piazza San Pietro in Vaticano.

The Piazza Ducale and its underlying ideals continue to influence spaces in Europe and the Americas. Squares such as Piazza San Carlo in Torino, Place des Vosges in Paris, Jackson Square in New Orleans and Thomas Jefferson's University of Virginia are quite clearly derived from the ideals executed in Vigévano (Kultermann 1982: 115).

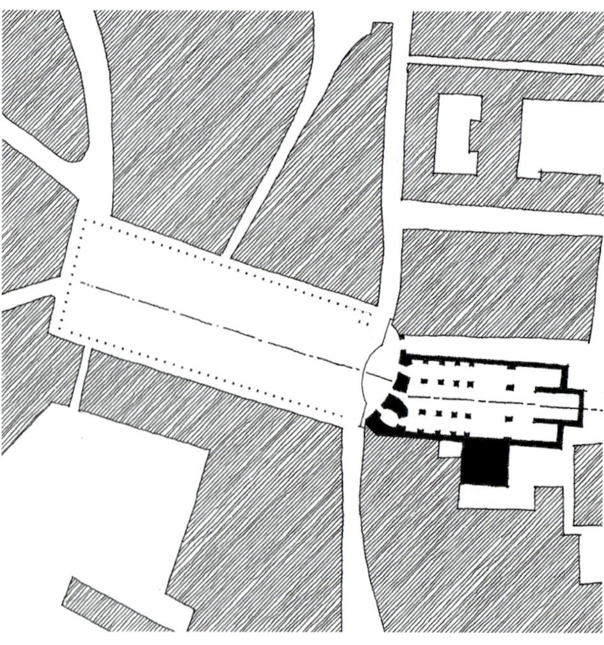

The relationship of the piazza's axis and shift in the Church of San Ambrogio

Piazza Ducale

Washington, DC

98

Dupont Circle

Dupont Circle, the center of a vibrant and fashionable area of Washington, DC since the nineteenth century, is north of the city's monumental core and an important node and threshold between the commercial and residential areas. Set along the Connecticut Avenue corridor extending eight blocks northwest from the White House, it is at the intersection of the diagonal of New Hampshire Avenue and Massachusetts Avenue and the orthogonal P Street and 19th Street. Though its immediate edge is three lanes of traffic, the surrounding buildings are a mix of eight- and ten-story office buildings with several three-story commercial buildings. The surrounding neighborhood includes commercial buildings to the south and east and retail and residential predominantly to the north and west. The circle acts as a vinculum gathering multiple modes of transportation. Besides the five streets above, beneath the circle are three levels of transportation including four lanes of Connecticut Avenue, the Metro and a little-known abandoned, semicircular streetcar terminal.

The circle itself has three concentric zones. The outermost zone is a pathway with inward facing benches and, on the east side, chess tables. The next zone is a grass lawn used by office workers, local residents and others for napping and picnicking. The innermost zone is a hardscaped circular space dominated by a nineteenth century marble fountain and enclosed with a one-meter high neatly trimmed hedge. This area, which is small enough to identify those who enter it, is a place of both accidental and prearranged encounters.

Dupont Circle illustrates how "type" can manifest into extremely different outcomes. As a type, it is a fairly typical Washington, DC traffic circle sharing dimension within over two meters and relatively commensurate position in the city's geography of the corollary Washington Circle and Logan Circle. Compared to these two circles, however, Dupont is unsurpassed in its vibrancy that may be attributed to three factors: street, topography and context.

While streets intersect each circle, only Dupont Circle has more than two diagonal avenues. This would usually decrease the circle's enclosure; it does increase the traffic and activity around it. Dupont Circle's topography differs from Washington Circle and Logan Circle in that it is on a slight plateau so that walking up from the downtown to Dupont Circle, there is a welcome rest and destination. Though these factors have their role, the most important factor contributing to its success is context. Unlike Logan and Washington Circles, Dupont Circle is surrounded by variety: housing, commercial and institutional building types and a Metro stop. Moreover, the housing

Dupont Circle's outer edge

is a mix of low, medium and high density housing. The amount and variety of people enlivens the space throughout the day and night that contributes to a self-perpetuating use cycle. Throughout the day, the mix of residential, office and commercial activities enliven the space. This, in turn, keeps the place vibrant, well used, safe and interesting. This, of course, makes the entire area desirable to live, work and relax in. Dupont Circle is a simple space without artificial articulation, enlivened by the surrounding density and mixed use areas.

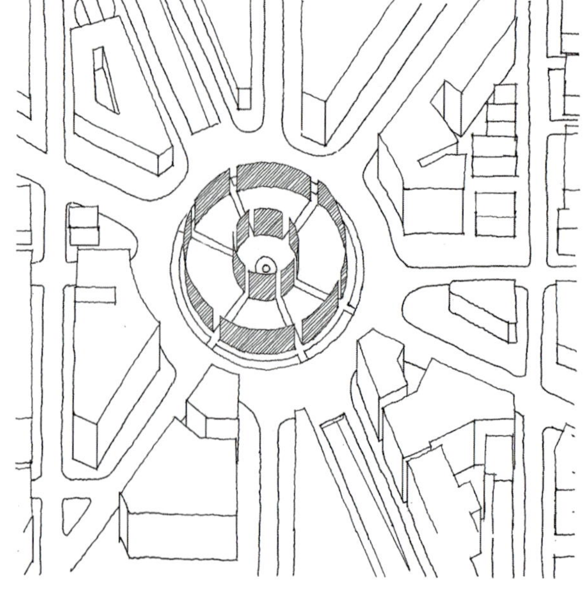

The zones within the circle

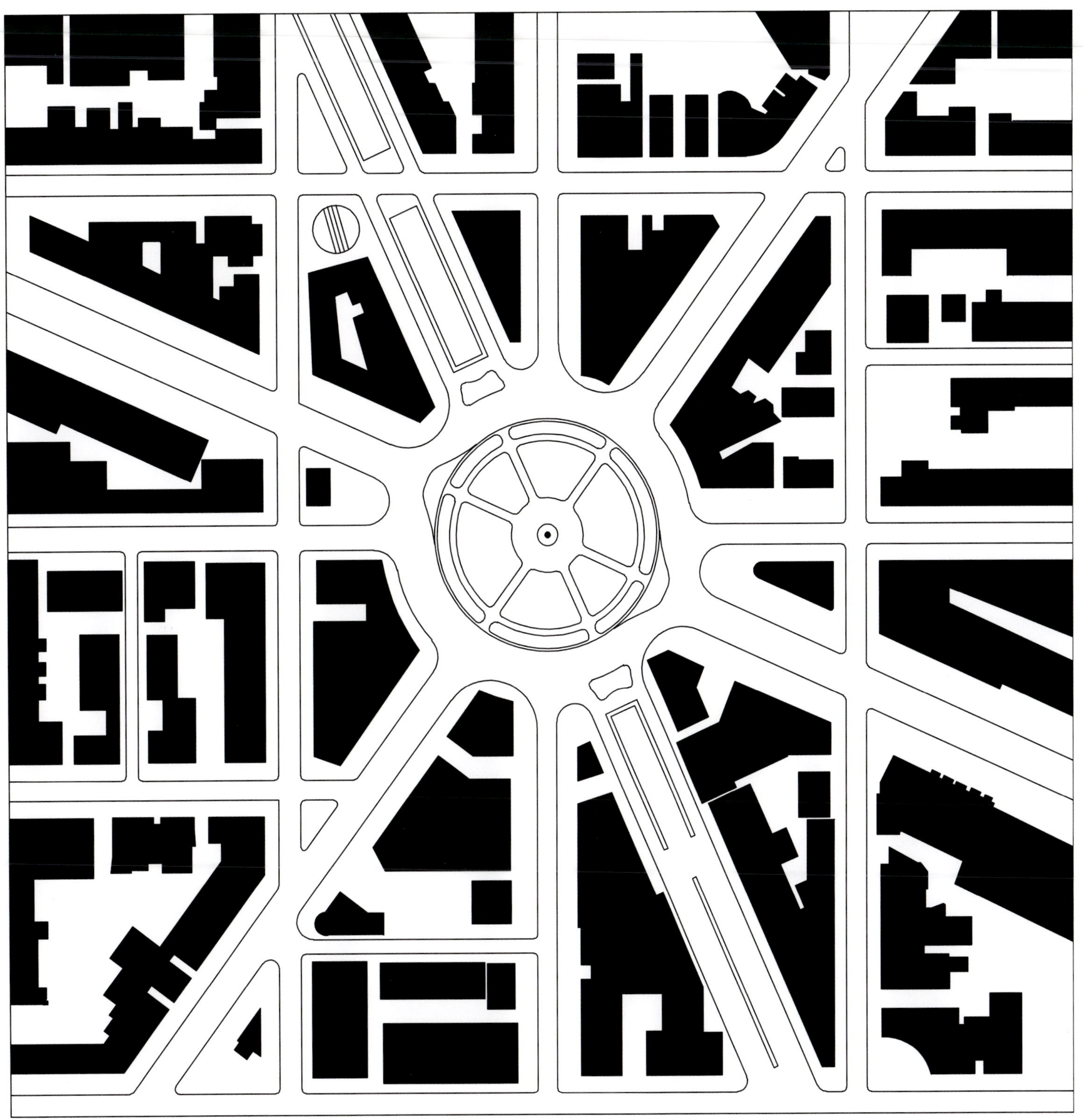

Dupont Circle

Washington, DC

Grand Plaza, Woodrow Wilson Plaza and Daniel Patrick Moynihan Place

The Grand Plaza was conceived as the centerpiece of Washington, DC's immense Federal Triangle governmental complex and represents the American approach to making symbolic democratic spaces. From Washington, DC's city plan to its streets, avenues, public buildings and monuments, the city's built form exemplifies and embodies the open democratic state and its high ideals. Correspondingly, with increased security risks and concerns, many of Washington's public spaces have become closed or limited to a select few. Just as grand spaces represent optimistic ideals, concrete barriers, closed streets and electronic monitoring proclaim our fear and anxiety.

Grand Plaza is an exterior circular, albeit fragmented, room bisected by north-south 12th Street with neo-Romanesque and Beaux-Arts buildings on either side. The Grand Plaza's east half was never finished due to delays in razing the rectilinear Romanesque Old Post Office building (1892–1899) to the northeast. The Depression and World War II continued delays and ultimately allowed for preservation to save the Victorian building.

Buildings shaping the space are, to the west, the semicircular Ariel Rios Federal Building, also known as the United States Post Office building. To the southeast is the segmented Internal Revenue Service. The buildings, designed by Delano & Aldrich between 1931 and 1935, have arcades on the ground level that lead to an east–west pedestrian-only cross axis. A large portico marks this axis while the embellished towers on either side of 12th Street mark the Plaza's thresholds (Scott and Lee 1993: 173–174).

The Federal Triangle's completion finally occurred in the 1990s. The Ariel Rios building, which forms the Grand Plaza's western half, includes a second, smaller, inverse hemicycle along the east–west pedestrian axis. For seventy years, this smaller hemicycle faced one of the largest parking lots in downtown Washington. This edge and the linked spaces were completed with construction of Pei and Freed's Ronald Reagan Building and International Trade Center with the Woodrow Wilson Plaza and Daniel Patrick Moynihan Place. Wilson Plaza extends the Grand Plaza's cross axis toward the Reagan Building's entrance while overlapping with Moynihan Place that extends the 13th Street axis from the north and connects to the American History Museum across Constitution Avenue to the south.

From the Old Post Office's tower

View from 12th Street

Despite security concerns following the 1995 Oklahoma City bombing and September 11, 2001 terrorist attacks, these three plazas and the interstitial arcades and passages remain open to the public. Though monitored, it is with some surprise and satisfaction that they remain open. It is an optimistic decision that should be applauded. It provides some hope that one day other public squares and streets in Washington that were closed after each attack will reopen and again be representative democratic spaces.

Federal Triangle from above

View of Woodrow Wilson Plaza and Daniel Patrick Moynihan Place aligning with 13th Street to the north

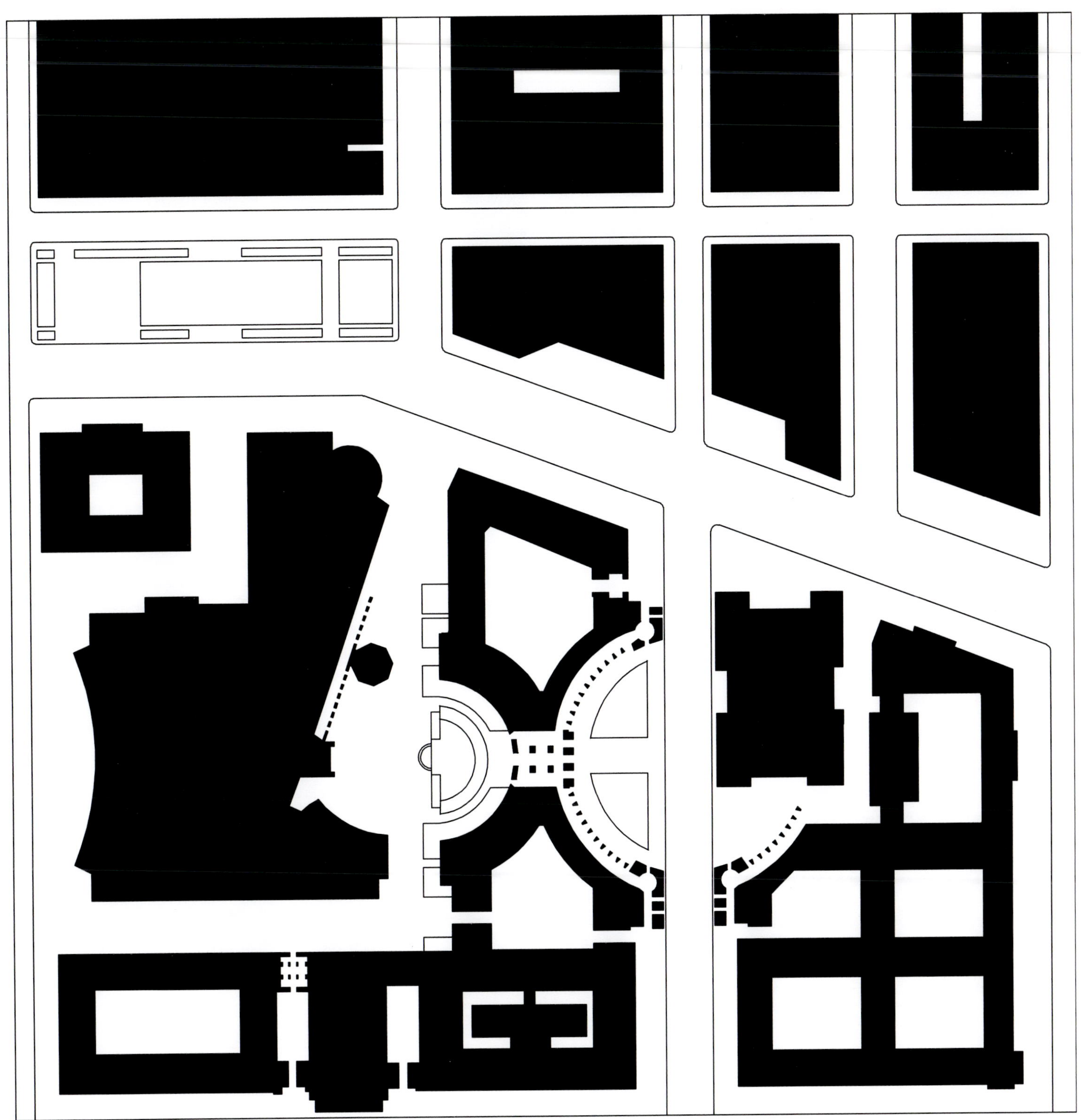

Grand Plaza, Woodrow Wilson Plaza and Daniel Patrick Moynihan Place

Washington, DC

Judiciary Square

100

Judiciary Square is best known as the setting for the National Law Enforcement Officers Memorial and forecourt of the National Building Museum, formerly the United States Pension Building. The square itself is part of a larger tract in the District of Columbia, designated "Judiciary Square" by George Washington and Thomas Jefferson, and reserved for the Supreme Court of the United States in Pierre L'Enfant's 1791 plan of Washington, DC. This area, defined by G Street to the north, Indiana Avenue to the south, and 4th and 5th Streets to the east and west respectively, is one of the original seventeen reservations set aside for specific public use in the national capital. Though it never housed the Supreme Court, it has, since the early nineteenth century, been the center of the District of Columbia's local court, federal district court and home to local government agencies and, at one time, the district's city hall (Stanley 1968: 21).

Today, the heart of Judiciary Square is the tree-lined National Law Enforcement Officers Memorial inserted between two court office buildings between E Street and F Street. The main element in the memorial is an oval space defined by two one-meter-high granite walls engraved with the names of fallen officers. Parallel to the walls are two rows of neatly trimmed deciduous trees. This liner creates a series of layered spaces for varied uses while offering pedestrians three paths through the site. Pedestrians have the option of moving quickly along the central axis and through a ceremonial space, along the inside edge of the stone wall to view the carved names or along the outside edge between the trees and the buildings.

Though the site is a memorial with a center space used for ceremonies, it is used primarily as a place to relax during the day or as a path to and from work. As a path and forecourt for the National Building Museum to the north, it remains disconnected from the court buildings to the south. Separated by higher speed through traffic on E Street, the court building's forecourt or rear court is used as a parking area with no direct access to the court building. Fortunately, this may change with a new entry and forecourt of the court building's north side that is, as of this writing, in the planning stages.

In much the same way as the rectilinear *allée* of neatly trimmed trees like those in Nancy's Place de la Carrière or the Palais Royal in Paris, it is an example of how vegetation can define a space and create a secondary liner to the space that is just as vital in forming the space as the surrounding buildings. Another important aspect of the memorial, especially for Washington, DC planners and residents, is that it is an example of how a memorial can be built within the city. In 1994,

Judiciary Square from the National Building Museum

View from the south

Congress passed a law prohibiting new memorials from being built on the increasingly crowded National Mall. The law was a response to overcrowding and the city planners' vision to take visitors into surrounding neighborhood. The National Law Enforcement Officers Memorial, designed by Davis Buckley Architects and Planners in 1991, is appropriately sited since Judiciary Square has been home to law courts and law enforcement since the city's founding. The memorial is now part of the daily life of citizens, giving them a fine civic place and sense of security. It is interesting that it memorializes those who provide that service in our daily lives. As an active memorial off the National Mall it is successful in not being isolated, but celebrated as part of everyday life.

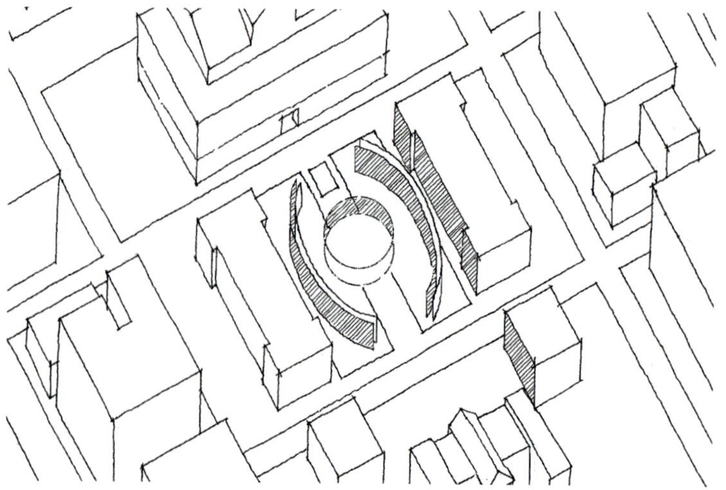

The liners that define the rooms within the square

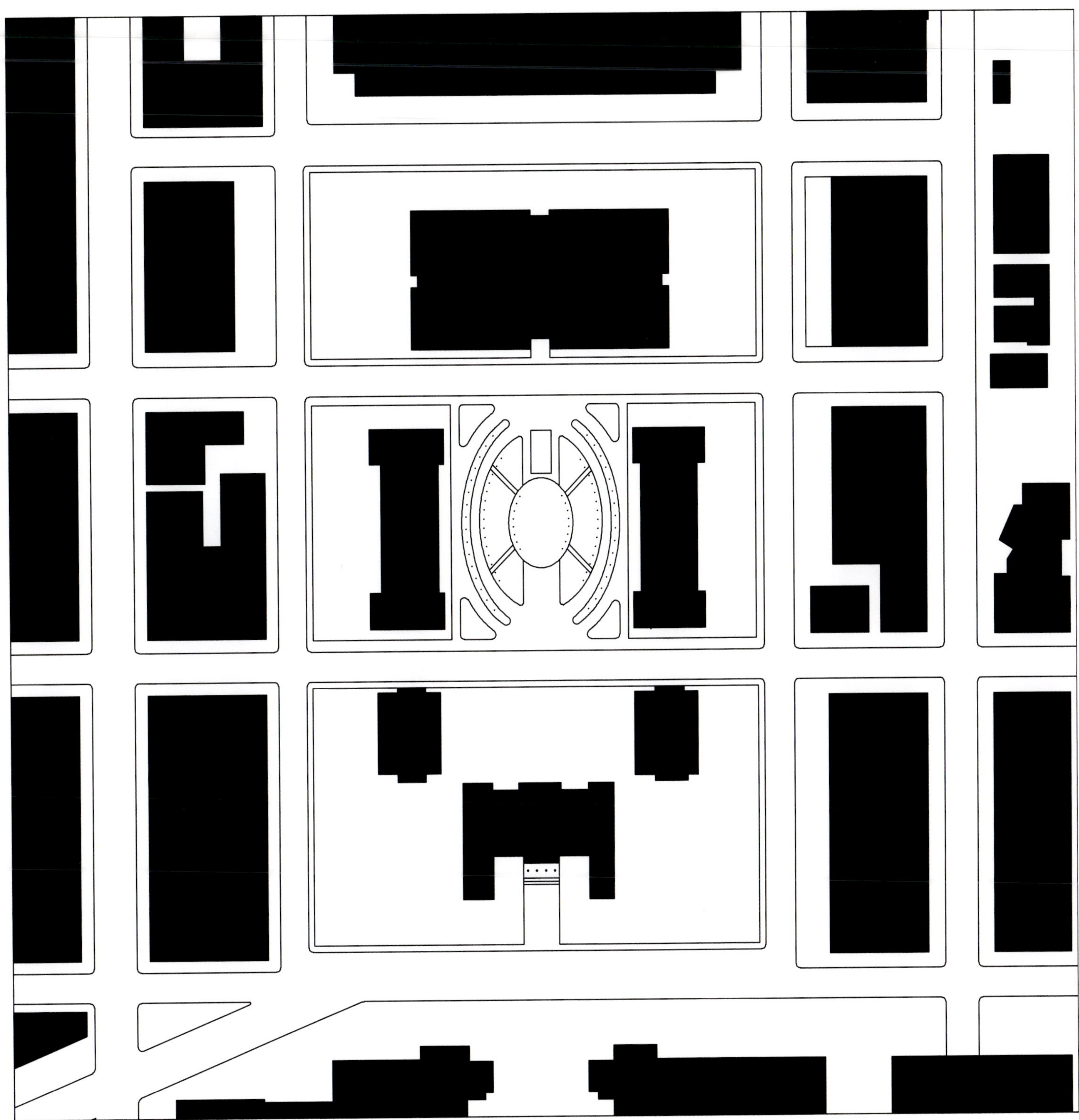

Judiciary Square

Plan sources

Amsterdam

Amsterdam Dienst der Publieke Werken (1976) *Kaart van Amsterdam*, Amsterdam: Dienst der Publieke Werken.

Atlas Amsterdam Stadsplattegrond, http://adres.asp4all.nl/asp/get.asp?zoom=2500&xdl=Stadsplattegrond

Arras

Arras Ministère de l'équipement et du logement (1969) *Arras (Pas-de-Calais)*, Cartographie issue d'orthophotoplan hypsometrique type 1969. Etabli sous la direction de la Division des travaux topographiques.

Auzelle, R. (1947) *Encyclopédie de l'urbanisme*, Paris: Vincent, Fréal.

Athens

Hyperesia Oikismou (1960) *Lekanopedion-Athenon 1:5000*, Hypourgeion Synkoin. & Dem. Ergon, Hyperesia Oikismou.

Baltimore

City of Baltimore, Department of Public Works, *Planimetric Base Map*, April 2000.

Barcelona

Servico Topografio del Ayuntamiento (1930) *Plano de Barcelona*, Barcelona.

Barcelona, Servicio del Plano de la Ciudad (1949) *Plano de Barcelona en nueve hojas; hoja especial del casco antiguo*, Barcelona.

Editorial Pamias (1971) *Barcelona plano guía urbana*, Barcelona.

Comisión de Urbanismo y Servicios Comunes de Barcelona y Otros Municipios (1970) *Plano topográfico del área metropolitana de Barcelona*, Barcelona.

Bath

Great Britain Ordnance Survey (1989) *Georgian Bath, Historical Map and Guide*, Southampton: Ordnance Survey.

Great Britain Ordnance Survey (1982) *Bath City Map*, Southampton: Ordnance Survey.

Auzelle, R. (1947) *Encyclopédie de l'urbanisme*, Paris: Vincent, Fréal.

Beijing

United States Central Intelligence Agency (1988) *Beijing*, Washington, DC: Central Intelligence Agency.

Di tu chu ban she (1957) *Beijing you lan tu*, Beijing.

Bergen

Bergen Kommune, *Kommunedelplan Store Lungegårdsvann* http://www.bergen.kommune.no/planavdelingen_/ekstern/

Bergen Kommune, KDP Sentrum – Arealdelen, *Arealbruk*, http://www.bergen.kommune.no/planavdelingen_/ekstern/

Berlin

Karte von Berlin 1:4000, Senator fur Bua-und Wohnungswesen, 1985.

Great Britain Directorate of Military Survey (1982) *Germany City*

Maps: West Berlin, produced under the direction of the Director of Military Survey, Ministry of Defence, United Kingdom, Ed.-GSGs, London: HMSO.

Germany (East), Verwaltung Vermessungs- und Kartenwesen (1960) *Topographische Karte 1:2000*, DDR Berlin: Ministerium des Innern, Verwaltung Vermessungs- und Kartenwesen.

Stimmann, H. (2000) *Berlino, 1940, 1953, 1989, 2000, 2010: fisionomia di una grande città = Berlin: Physiognomy of a Metropolis*, Milan: Skira.

Bern

Bern Vermessungsamt (1953) *Bern 1:2000*, Bern.

Stadt Bern, *City Map of Bern*, http://www.stadtplan.bern.ch/default.asp

Bologna

Favole, P. (1971) *Piazze d'Italia: Architettura e urbanistica della piazza in Italia*, Milan: Bramante.

Bocchi, F. (1995) *Bologna*, Bologna: Grafis.

Auzelle, R. (1947) *Encyclopédie de l'urbanisme*, Paris: Vincent, Fréal.

Gottarelli, E. (1978) *Urbanistica e Architettura a Bologna Agli esordi dell'unità d'Italia*, Bologna: Cappelli.

Gresleri, G. and Massaretti, P.G. (2001) *Norma e arbitrio: architetti e ingegneri a Bologna 1850–1950*, Venice: Marsilio.

Commune di Bologna: *Carta Tecnica Comunale*

http://sit.comune.bologna.it/sit/doc_scaricabili/panoramica_ct_web.pdf

Commune di Bologna: *Carta Tecnica Comunale*

http://sit.comune.bologna.it/sit/ctweb.htm?name=tecnica&ch=1&nu=0&t=936570&l=677231&b=921434&r=693529&d=0&mm=i&i=21&cr34=1&cr36=1&Navigatore=netscape&Version=4.5#

Bordeaux

Auzelle, R. (1947) *Encyclopédie de l'urbanisme*, Paris: Vincent, Fréal.

France Ministère de la Culture, Secteur Sauvegardé de Saint Emilion, http://www.culture.gouv.fr/culture/sites-sdaps/sdap33/protec/ss/bdx_psmv.htm

Atlas de la communauté urbaine de Bordeaux, Talence, France: Centre d'études des espaces urbains, Maison des sciences l'homme d'Aquitaine, 1983.

Boston

Boston Redevelopment Authority (BRA), *The Boston Atlas*, http://www.mapjunction.com/places/Boston_BRA/main.pl?ht=864

Brasília

Companhia do Desenvolvimento do Planalto Central (1991) *Plantas urbanas do Distrito Federal*, Brasília: CODEPLAN.

Distrito Federal (Brazil), Departamento de Estradas de Rodagem (1984) *Distrito Federal*, mapa rodoviário-84, Brasília, Brazil: DER DF.

Bruges

Belgium, Service de topographie et de photogrammétrie, Brugge, Brussel: Ministerie van Openbare Werken, Dienst voor Topografie en Fotogrammetrie, 1961.

Vereeniging van Officieel Gidiplomeerde Gidsen, Brugge centrum, Eeklo, Belgium: Druk. Pauwels 1978.

Buenos Aires

Gobierno de la Ciudad de Buenos Aires, *Mapa Interactive*, http://usig.buenosaires.gov.ar/

Buenos Aires Departamento Geotopográfico División Fotogrametría, *Buenos Aires, Partido de General Juan Madariaga zona urbana y alrededores*, Departamento Geotopográfico, División Fotogrametría y División Cartografía, Buenos Aires, Provincia de Buenos Aires, MOP, Dirección de Geodesia, 1976.

Buenos Aires (Argentina: Province), Departamento Fotocartográfico, División Fotogrametría, *Partido de General Alvear, General Alvear, zona urbana y alrededores / Departamento Fotocartográfico, División Fotogrametría [y] División Cartografía*, República Argentina, Provincia de Buenos Aires, MOP, Dirección de Geodesia, 1977.

Cairo

Quality Standards Information Technology, *egymaps.com*, copyright © 2004 EgyMaps.

Amin, N.Y. (1987) *Downtown Cairo and Garden City Map Guide*, Cairo: N.Y. Amin.

České Budějovice

Paměť měst: mestské památkové rezervace v Ceských zemích, Prague: Odeon, 1975.

České Budějovice, Planning and Architecture Department, *Mapa města*, http://www.c-budejovice.cz/EN/01/

Nakladatelství Olympus, *České Budějovice plán mesta*, České Budějovice: Nakl. Olympus, 1991.

Chandigarh

Le Corbusier (1966) *Œuvre complète 1952–1957*, publiée par W. Boesiger, 4th edn, Zurich: Les Editions d'Architecture, Artémis.

Chandigarh Administration, Department of Urban Planning Town Planning Unit, http://sampark.chd.nic.in/pls/esampark_web/city_map

Chicago

Blaser, W. (2004) *Mies van der Rohe, Federal Center, Chicago*, Basel: Birkhäuser.

Chicago Department of Development and Planning (1974) *Chicago Land Use Atlas, 1970*, Chicago, IL: Department of Development and Planning.

Chicago Bureau of Maps and Plats (1980–1981) *Atlas of City of Chicago*, Bureau of Maps and Plats.

City of Chicago, Zoning Department, *Interactive Map*, http://w28.cityofchicago.org/website/zoning/

Cincinnati

City of Cincinnati, Cincinnati Area Geographic Information Systems, Cincinnati and Hamilton County Interactive Map, http://cagis.hamilton-co.org/map/cagis.htm

Ohio Department of Transportation (1991) *Downtown Cincinnati*, Columbus, OH: Ohio Department of Transportation.

Cleveland

Ohio Department of Transportation (1991) *Downtown Cleveland*, Columbus, OH: Ohio Department of Transportation.

City of Cleveland City Planning Commission, *Basemap*, http://planning.city.cleveland.oh.us/gis/cpc/basemap.jsp

Copenhagen

Auzelle, R. (1947) *Encyclopédie de l'urbanisme*, Paris: Vincent, Fréal.

Bollmann Bildkarten Verlag (1978) *København*, Bollmann-Bildkarten-Verlag KG, Braunschweig, Arhus, Denmark: Skandinaviske billedkort I/S.

Rasmussen, S.E. (1969) *Towns and Buildings*, Cambridge, MA: MIT Press.

Cuzco

Instituto Geográfico Militar Peru (IGM) (1969) *Cuzco: Ciudad del Cuzco / pictomapa preparado por el IGM en colaboración con el I.A.G.S. con fotografías aéreas tomadas en 1962 elaborado a base de fotomosaico no controlado*, Lima, Peru: IGM.

Will, W. (1989) *Atlas Urbano de la Ciudad del Cusco*, Cusco, Peru: Centro de Estudios Rurales Andinos, Bartolomé de las Casas.

Denver

Barkema, K. (1987) *Denver Central Business District*, Denver, CO: Denver Metro Building Owners and Managers Association.

Vantage Advertising, Inc. (1982) *Zoning Map of Downtown Denver*, Denver, CO: Denver Equities.

Detroit

Detroit 300, *Campus Martius Park*, http://www.campusmartiuspark.org/park_siteplan.htm

City of Detroit, Planning and Development Department, Planning Division, *Advanced Planning and Mapping*, http://www.ci.detroit.mi.us/plandevl/advplanning/cinfo/adv/default.htm

Dresden

Landkartenverlag (1970) *Stadtplan Dresden*, Berlin: VEB Landkartenverlag.

Landeshauptstadt Dresden, Department for City Development, City Surveyor´s Office, *Thematic Map*, http://www.dresden.de/index.html?node=6947

Dublin

Dublin City Council, Dublin City Development Plan, 2005–2011 from the Ordnance Survey of Ireland, 2005.

Dubrovnik

Grad Dubrovnik, http://www.dubrovnik.hr/
The Institute for the Restoration of Dubrovnik, http://orlando.laus.hr/~zzod_web/
Futagawa, Y. (1974) *Adoriakai No Mura to Machi*, Tokyo: A.D.A. EDITA.
Kartográfiai Vállalat (1988) *Dubrovnik*, Kartográfiai Vállalat, 6. jav. kiad., Budapest: Kartográfiai Vállalat.

Edinburgh

Great Britain Ordnance Survey (1895) *Edinburgh and its Environs*, Southampton: Ordnance Survey.
Ordnance Survey National Grid maps, 1944–1991, http://geo.nls.uk/indexes/default.html
Craig, J. (1965) *Plan of the New Streets and Squares Intended for the City of Edinburgh*, Ithaca, NY: Historic Urban Plans.

Florence

Bacon, E. (1967) *The Design of Cities*, New York: Viking Press.
Italy Istituto Geografico Militare (IGM) (1952) *Florence*, Florence: IGM.
Atlante di Firenze: La Forma del Centro Storico in Scala 1:1000 nel Fotopiano e nella Carta Numerica / Compagnia Generale Ripresaeree, Selca, Venice: Marsilio; Florence: Assessorato all'urbanistica ed edlizia privata del Comune di Firenze, 1993.
Fanelli, G. (1982) *Città antica in Toscana*, Florence: Sansoni.

Genoa

Mazzino, E. (1969) *Il centro storico di Genova*, Genoa: Stringa Editore.
Provincia di Genova, *Cartografia Tematica On-Line*, http://cartogis.provincia.genova.it/cartogis/pdb/
Provincia di Genova, http://cartogis.provincia.genova.it/cartogis/pdb/ambito14/ambito14/13_fasce_centro.htm
Poleggi, E. (2005) *De Ferrari: La Piazza dei Genovesi*, Genoa: De Ferrari.

Indianapolis

City of Indianapolis, Department of Metropolitan Development, Division of Planning, *Zoning Base Map*, http://imaps.indygov.org/prod/GeneralViewer/viewer.htm
Indianapolis City Plan Commission (1922) *Indianapolis Zoning Ordinance Map*, Indianapolis, IN.

Isfahan

Herdeg, K. (1991) *Formal Structure in Islamic Architecture of Iran and Turkistan*, New York: Rizzoli.

Istanbul

Ístanbul Beledívesi, Ímar Planlama Müdürlügü EskÍ Eseler Bürosunda, 1965 Subat Taríhlerí Arasinda.
Fincancilar Yokusu Haliç Sahili Arasi, 19° Asir Sonu Itibari Ile, 1/500, DGSA YMB, Rölöve Kürsüsü, 6/3/79.
Ístanbul Büyükşehir Belediyesi Kent Harita, http://kentrehberi.ibb.gov.tr/
Sumner-Boyd, H. and Freely, J. (1987) *Strolling through Istanbul: A Guide to the City*, London: KPI.

Jerusalem

Israel, Maḥleḳet ha-medidot (1972) *Jerusalem: The Old City*. Tel-Aviv: Survey of Israel.
Israel, Agaf ha-medidot (1976) *Jerusalem: The Old City*, Tel-Aviv: Survey of Israel.

Kraków

Państwowe Przedsiebiorstwo Wydawnictw Kartograficznych (1973) *Kraków*, Warsaw: Redaktor Teresa Zakrzewska.
Wydawnictwo Kartograficzne Witański (1992) *Kraków, Stare Miasto, mapa*, Katowice, Poland: Wydawn. Kartograficzne Witański.

Lisbon

Auzelle, R. (1947) *Encyclopédie de l'urbanisme*, Paris: Vincent, Fréal.
Portugal Servicos Geológicos (1935) *Carta geológica dos arredores de Lisboa*, Lisboa.

London

Great Britain Ordnance Survey (1935) *London*, Southampton: Ordance Survey.
John Bartholomew and Son (1972) *Central London*, Edinburgh: John Bartholomew and Son.
Ed. J. Burrow & Co. (1940) *Street Plan of Holborn*, designed, Ed. J. Burrow & Co. Ltd. and Holborn Borough Council, 2nd edn, Cheltenham: Burrow, 195–.

Auzelle, R. (1947) *Encyclopédie de l'urbanisme*, Paris: Vincent, Fréal.
Moos, S. (1999) *Venturi, Scott Brown & Associates: Buildings and Projects, 1986–1998*, New York: Monacelli Press.
City of London, Planning and Development, http://planning.london.gov.uk/LDD/LDD/PublicMapInvoke.do?querytype=london
City of London, PublicAccess Home – Mapping, http://www.planning.cityoflondon.gov.uk/mapping/map/map_detailview.aspx

Los Angeles

City of Los Angeles iMapLA Interactive Mapping, MapLA, http://imapla.lacity.org/Viewer/GIS/Viewer.asp
McCann, W. (1968) *Downtown Los Angeles*, Los Angeles, CA: Geotronics.
Western Economic Research Co. (1990) *Downtown Los Angeles*, Panorama City, CA: Western Economic Research Co.

Lucca

Commune di Lucca (2004) *Perimetrazione delle Zone Omogene e Destinazioni d'Uso*, Settore Planificazione Urbanistica e Tutel Ambientale. http://www.comune.lucca.it/l/3B5FCBC9.htm
Fanelli, G. (1982) *Città antica in Toscana*, Florence: Sansoni.

Madrid

Cátedra de Dibujo Técnico, curso 77/78, Escuela T.S. de Arquitectura de Madrid, *La Expresión arquitectónica de la Plaza Mayor de Madrid a través del lenguaje gráfico*, Madrid: Colegio Oficial de Arquitectos, 1979.
Comisión de Planeamiento y Coordinación del Area Metropolitana de Madrid (Spain) (1967) *City Planning Map of Madrid*, Madrid: Ministerio de la Vivienda, COPLACO.
Editorial Almax (1969) *Plano de Madrid*, 5th edn, Madrid: Editorial Almax.
Ayuntamiento de Madrid, Nueva Guía Urbana http://www.munimadrid.es/SicWeb/Result?TIPO_BUSQ=0&BNOMBRE=map&IDIOMA=2

Mexico City

Gobierno del Distrito Federal, Secretaría de Desarrolo Urbano y Vivienda, Sistema de Información Geográfica, City http://201.134.137.2/sigseduvi97/web/cuenta.htm

Milan

Geist, J.F. (1983) *Arcades: The History of a Building Type*, Cambridge, MA: MIT Press.

Montréal

Ville de Montréal, *The Urban Navigator*, http://www.navurb.com/nu_inter/
Communauté urbaine de Montréal, Planning Department (1986) *Montréal, Access to the Cit*, Planning Department of the Montréal Urban Community, Québec: Tourisme Québec.

Moscow

Geist, J.F. (1983) *Arcades: The History of a Building Type*, Cambridge, MA: MIT Press.
Felber, J.E. (1963) *The Kremlin*, Newark, NJ: Printing Consultants.
Ingit, Moscow, CD-ROM atlas detailed maps of Moscow city and Moscow Oblast, Tacoma, WA: AO Ingit, Hamilton Global Management, 2000.
Plan Moskvy, Kartoskhemy, Ukazatel i Sprvochnye Svedeniia, Moskva, 1968.

Nancy

Plan de ville de Nancy, Nancy, 1972.
Société d'éditions cartographiques (1985) *Plan guide cités 2000*, Cannes, France: Société d'éditions cartographiques Bleu.
Auzelle, R. (1947) *Encyclopédie de l'urbanisme*, Paris: Vincent, Fréal.
France Ministère de l'équipement et du logement (1967) *Nancy, Meurthe-et-Moselle. Plan topographique. Cartographie établie sous la direction de la Division des travaux topographiques*, Paris.
Pumain, D. (1989) *Atlas des villes de France*, Denise Pumain et Thérèse Saint-Julien avec la collaboration de Michèle Béguin, Montpellier, France: RECLUS / Paris: Documentation française.

New Haven

City of New Haven, City Plan Department, Neighborhood Planning Maps, *Downtown*, http://www.cityofnewhaven.com/CityPlan/pdfs/Maps/NeighborhoodPlanningMaps/Downtown.pdf

New Orleans

Wilson, S. (ed.) (1968) *The Vieux Carré, New Orleans: Its Plan, its Growth, its Architecture*, New Orleans, LA: City of New Orleans.

Lafaye, S.P. (1920) *Commercial District of New Orleans, La.*, New Orleans, LA: S.P. Lafaye.

New Orleans Central District & Vieux Carré, New Orleans, 1977.

New Orleans Map Co. (1977) *Map of New Orleans East*, New Orleans, LA: New Orleans Map Co.

National Geographic Society (2002) *Louisiana: Seamless USGS Topographic Maps on CD-ROM*, Ed: Version 2.7.5, San Francisco, CA: National Geographic Holdings.

New York

Sagalyn, L.B. (2001) *Times Square Roulette: Remaking the City Icon*, Cambridge, MA: MIT Press.

New York City, Department of Planning, *Zoning Map*, http://www.nyc.gov/html/dcp/html/zone/mn_zonedex.shtml

New York City, City Planning Commission (1945) *Sectional Map of the City of New York*, New York: City Planning Commission.

Oslo

Oslo (Norway), Plan- og bygningsetaten (1998) *Kjørekart, 1998, for sentrale byområder: gratis: [Oslo, Norge] / kartet er utarbeidet av Plan- og bygningsetaten*, Oslo: Oslo kommune, Plan- og bygningsetaten.

Oslo oppmålingsvesen (1989) *Kjørekart: slik kan du kjøre i Oslos sentrale byområder / kartet er utarbeidet av Oslo oppmålingsvesen i samarbeid med Oslo veivesen og informasjonskontoret*, Oslo: Oslo kommune informerer.

Paris

Seine, Prefecture (1938) *Plan of Paris 1:2500*, Paris: Service Technique du Plan Paris.

Seine, Prefecture (1939) *Plan of Paris*, Paris.

Auzelle, R. (1947) *Encyclopédie de l'urbanisme*, Paris: Vincent, Fréal.

Le Corbusier (1929) *The City of To-Morrow and its Planning*, trans. from the 8th French edn by F. Etchells, London: J. Rodker.

Dennis, M. (1986) *Court and Garden: From the French Hôtel to the City of Modern Architecture*, Cambridge, MA: MIT Press.

Philadelphia

City of Philadelphia, GIS Services Group, City Planning Commission, http://citymaps.phila.gov/citymaps/cmAddressRequest.aspx?URL=cmZoningMap.aspx

Smith, E.V. (1921) *Atlas of the 6th, 9th and 10th Wards of the City of Philadelphia*, Philadelphia, PA: Smith.

Bromley, G.W. (1922) *Atlas of the City of Philadelphia*, George W. and Walter S. Bromley, Philadelphia, PA: G.W. Bromley.

Portland

City of Portland, Bureau of Planning, Corporate GIS, http://www.portlandmaps.com/detail.cfm?&action=Explorer

Prague

Praha Kartografie (1980) *Plan Práhy z roku 1791*, Plan der K.K. Haupstadt Prag im Königr, Böheim.

Melantrich (1948) *Praha*, Prague.

Kartografie (1970) *Praha*, Prague: Kartografické nakl.

Rome

Novelli, I. (1991) *Atlante di Roma: la forma del centro storico in scala 1:1000 nel fotopiano e nella carta numerica*, 2nd edn, Venice: Marsilio.

Centro studi di storia urbanistica (1963) *Studi per una operante storia urbana di Roma di Saverio Muratori*, Rome: Consiglio nazionale delle ricerche.

Visceglia, E. (1955) *Pianta de Roma e suburbio*, scala 1: 3000, Rome: Istituto cartografico Visceglia.

Saint Petersburg

Leningrad Geografo-ekonomicheskii nauchno-issledovatelskii institut (1967) *Atlas Leningradskoi oblasti*, Moskva, Glav. upravlenie geodezii i kartografii.

Ducamp, E. (1995) *The Winter Palace, Saint Petersburg*, Paris: Alain de Gourcuff / Saint Petersburg: State Hermitage Museum.

United States Central Intelligence Agency (1971) *Central Leningrad*, Washington, DC: CIA.

Egorov, U.A. (1969) *The Architectural Planning of St. Petersburg*, trans. E. Dluhosch, Athens, OH: Ohio University Press.

Salamanca

Auzelle, R. (1947) *Encyclopédie de l'urbanisme*, Paris: Vincent, Fréal.
Salamanca, plano ciudad y nomenclator de calles, 1973.
Ayuntamiento de Salamanca, *Plan General de Ordenación Urbana del Municipio de Salamanca*, http://www.aytosalamanca.es/pgou/

Salzburg

Salzburg Feuerwehr (1943) *Salzburg*, Salzburg, Austria.
Salzburg Stadtbauamt (1946) *Stadt Salzburg*, Salzburg.
Cartographia Kft. (2001) *Salzburg, Budapest*, Cartographia Kft.
Austria Bundesamt für Eich- und Vermessungswesen (1952) *Town Plan, Salzburg*, Vienna.

San Francisco

Reineck & Reineck (1992) *San Francisco: Downtown Commercial Real Estate Map*, San Francisco, CA: Reineck & Reineck.
San Francisco, Bureau of Engineering (1982) *Map of the City and County of San Francisco*, San Francisco, CA: Department of Public Works, Bureau of Engineering.
City & County of San Francisco, San Francisco Enterprise Geographic Information Systems (GIS), http://www.sfgov.org/site/gis_index.asp?id=371
City & County of San Francisco, San Francisco's Enterprise Geographic Information Systems (GIS), http://gispubweb.sfgov.org/website/sfviewer/INDEX.htm
"Philips + Fotheringham Partnership: Redesign of Union Square, San Francisco, California," *Architecture and Urbanism*, January 2002, 376: 3–4.

Santiago

Plano (1950–1957) *Santiago oriente Cinco sectores planos*, Santiago, Chile.
Comuna de Providencia (1975) *Plano oficial de urbanización 1974*, escala 1:5000, Santiago, Chile.
Municipalidad de Santiago, *Plano Regulador*, http://planoregulador.munistgo.cl
Colom, J.M, Vergara, A.N. and Vicuña, P.B. (1983) *Las Plazas de Santiago*, Santiago, Chile: Ediciones Universidad Católica de Chile.

Savannah

City of Savannah, Metropolitan Planning Commission, and Chatham County, http://www.sagis.org

Seattle

Kroll Map Company (1980) *Kroll's Map of Seattle Central Business District*, Seattle, WA: Kroll Map Co.
City of Seattle, Department of Planning and Development City Maps, *Seattle GIS*, http://www.seattle.gov/dpd/planning/

Seville

Plano de Sevilla, Excmo Ayuntamiento de Sevilla, Seville, Spain: Ayuntamiento, 1960.
Núñez Castain, J. (1992) *Sivilia Forma Urbis: la forma del centro storico in scala 1:1000 nel fotopiano e nella carta*, Venice: Marsilio editori.
Cadastral Map of Seville, Seville, Spain, 1969

Siena

Favole, P. (1971) *Piazze d'Italia: Architettura e urbanistica della piazza in Italia*, Milan: Bramante.
Auzelle, R. (1947) *Encyclopédie de l'urbanisme*, Paris: Vincent, Fréal.
Franchina, L., Forlani Conti, M., Morandi, U. and Bartolomei, S. (1983) *Piazza del Campo: Evoluzione di Una Immagine, Documenti, Vicende, Ricostruzioni*, Siena, Italy: Ministero per i beni culturali e ambientali, Archivio di stato di Siena, Soprintendenza per i beni ambientali e architettonici per le province di Siena e Grosseto.
Siena, Pianta della Città, Florence: Litografia artistica cartografica, 1985.
Guidoni, E. and Maccari, P. (2000) *Siena e i centri senesi sulla via Francigena*, Florence: Giunta regionale toscana / Rome: Bonsignori.
Fanelli, G. (1982) *Città antica in Toscana*, Florence: Sansoni.
Commune di Siena, Cartografia Tematica, *Piano Regolatore Generale*, http://mapserver3.ldpassociati.it/siena/PRG/home/fr_int.cfm

Stockholm

Esselte kartor (1984) *Gamla Stan Map and Guide, Stockholm: 1:2 500: the Old Town, map, history, sights = Karta, historik, sevardheter*, Esselte kartor, Generalstabens litografiska anstalt, Stockholm: Esselte kartor.
Stockholm, Sweden (1993) *Stadsbyggnadskontoret.Kommunkarta*

Stockholm / kommunkarta uppra_ttad av Stockholms stadsbyggnadskontor, Stockholm: Stockholms stadsbyggnadskontor.

Tallinn

Tallinn City Council Department of Planning and Zoning Map http://www.tallinn.ee/est/g2810/maps?pre_set_grupp=14&lang=0

Tallinn, linnaplaan 1:2 000, Tallinn, 193?

A/S Optiset (1993) *Tallinn, kesklinn, Pirita*, Tallinn: AS Optiset.

Telč

Pamet mest: mestské památkové rezervace v Ceských zemích, Prague: Odeon, 1975.

Mapové projekty http://www.telc-etc.cz/telc/

Tokyo

Shobunsha (1991) *Tokyo Metropolitan Atlas: All 23 Wards Plus Greater Tokyo and Vicinity*, Tokyo, Japan: Shobunsha.

Zenrin, Kabushiki Kaisha (1999) *Tokyo-to 1, Chiyoda-ku*, Kitakyushu-shi, Japan: Kabushiki Kaisha Zenrin.

Zenrin, Kabushiki Kaisha (1999) *Tokyo-to 2, Chiyoda-ku*, Kitakyushu-shi, Japan: Kabushiki Kaisha Zenrin.

Torino

Cittí di Torino, *Mappa proposta dalla Città di Torino*, http://www.comune.torino.it/canaleturismo/it/mappa.htm

Dal Bianco, M.P. and Marenco di Santarosa, C. (eds) (2001) *Piazza San Carlo a Torino*, Milan: Lybra Immagine.

Trieste

Regione Autonoma Friuli-Venezia Giulia, Commune di Trieste (2005) *Area Pianificazione Territoriale Servizio Pianificazione Urban*, Tavola 1–10.

Territorio comunale percorso dal fuoco http://www.retecivica.trieste.it/edilizia/prg/incendi/qu_incendi.html

Sistema Informativo Territoriale della pianificazione urbana, http://www.retecivica.trieste.it/new/default.asp?pagina=-&ids=18&id_sx=57&tipo=monoblocchi&tabella_padre=dx&id_padre=380

Tunis

Tunisia Secretariat d'état aux travaux publics et a l'habitat, Division topographique (1968) *Grand Tunis*, Tunis.

Saussois, A. (1971) *Découvrez la Médina de Tunis*, Tunis.

Tunisis Service topographique (1960) *Plan de Tunis*, Tunis.

Vancouver

Vancouver, British Columbia, Department of Planning and Civic Development (1982) *Downtown Peninsula: Plan no. 4593 G-1*, Vancouver.

City of Vancouver, *The VanMap Interface*, http://vancouver.ca/vanmap/interface/index.htm

Naim, J. (1980) "Vancouver's Grand New Government Center," *Architectural Record*, 168, 8: 65–75.

Venice

Salzano, E. (1991) *Atlante di Venezia : la forma della città in scala 1:1000 nel fotopiano e nella carta numerica*, 4th edn, Venezia: Comune di Venezia / Marsilio.

Salzano, E. (1985) *Venezia forma urbis: il fotopiano a colori del centro storico in scala 1:500 = Color Photomap of the Historic City, Scale 1:500*, Venice: Marsilio Editori.

Futagawa, Y. (1974) *Adoriakai No Mura to Machi*, Tokyo: A.D.A. EDITA.

Auzelle, R. (1947) *Encyclopédie de l'urbanisme*, Paris: Vincent, Fréal.

Verona

Mappa di Verona, http://www.verona.com/cgi-bin/mapserv.exe?mapOverX=266&mapOverY=265&zoomdir=1&mode=browse&box=true&drag=false&imgbox=231+231+266+265&zoomsize=2&imgxy=231+231&imgext=1645091.959629+5022985.283014+1668022.502802+5045915.826187&map=d%3A%5Chtml%5Cgis%5Cgis_verona.map&savequery=true&mapext=shapes&page=gis

Auzelle, R. (1947) *Encyclopédie de l'Urbanisme*, Paris: Vincent, Fréal.

Fanelli, G. (1982) *Città antica in Toscana*, Florence: Sansoni.

Vienna

Vienna, Stadtbuaamt (1943) *General-Stadt-Plan: 1:2500*, Wein und Umgeburg, Vienna.

Feuerwehr der Stadt Wien (1926) *Wien und umgebung*, Vienna.

Vigévano

Cítta di Vigévano, Nuovo Piano Regolatore Generale, Ottobre 2003, http://www.comune.vigevano.pv.it/prg/CS.htm

Cítta di Vigévano, http://www.comune.vigevano.pv.it/prg/S3.jpg

Washington, DC

District of Columbia, Department of Planning and Zoning (1999) *Zoning Map*, Washington, DC.

District of Columbia, Geographic Information System, http://dcgis.dc.gov/dcgis/site/default.asp

Bibliography

Abu-Lughod, J.L. (1971) *Cairo: 1001 Years of the City Victorious*, Princeton, NJ: Princeton University Press.

Adler, L. (2003) *Savannah Renaissance*, Charleston, SC: Wyrick & Co.

Anderson, S. (1993) "Savannah and the Issue of Precedent: City Plan as Resource," in R. Bennett (ed.) *Settlements in the Americas: Cross-Cultural Perspectives*, Newark, DE: University of Delaware Press.

Andersson, M. (1998) *Stockholm's Annual Rings: A Glimpse into the Development of the City*, trans. W.M. Pardon, Stockholm: Stockholmia Förlag.

Appelo, T. (1985) "Rescue In Seattle: Pike Place Market and Pioneer Square," *Historic Preservation*, 37, 5: 34–39.

Artigas, J.B. (1990) *Centros Historicos America Latina*, Bogotá: Escala.

Åström, K. (1967) *City Planning In Sweden*, Stockholm: Svenska Institutet.

Auzelle, R. (1947) *Encyclopédie de l'urbanisme*, vols. I, II and III, Paris: Vincent, Fréal.

Bacon, E. (1967) *The Design of Cities*, New York: Viking Press.

Ballon, H. (1991) *Paris of Henri IV: Architecture and Urbanism*, Cambridge, MA: MIT Press.

Balus, W. (2001) "Cracow," *Centropa*, 1, 1: 24–29.

Bannister, T.C. (1961) "Oglethorpe's Sources for the Savannah Plan," *Journal of the Society of Architectural Historians*, 20: 47–62.

Barnett, J. (1986) *The Elusive City*, New York: Harper & Row.

Barthes, R. (1982) *Empire of Signs*, trans. R. Howard, New York: Hill & Wang.

Bastéa, E. (1994) "Athens: Etching Images on the Street," in Z. Çelik, D. Favro and R. Ingersoll (eds) *Streets: Critical Perspectives on Public Space*, Berkeley, CA: University of California Press.

Beattie, A. (2005) *Cairo: A Cultural History*, Oxford: Oxford University Press.

Beltrán, M. (1970) *Cuzco: Window on Peru*, 2nd edn, New York: Knopf.

Benevolo, L. (1980) *The History of the City*, trans. G. Culverwell, Cambridge, MA: MIT Press.

Bennett, D. (1991) *Encyclopaedia of Dublin*, Dublin: Gill & Macmillan.

Bennett, P. (2003) "Cairo, Once the Paris of the Nile, Tries to Regain Design Stature," *Architectural Record*, 191, 4: 79–80.

Besant, W. (1903) *London in the Time of the Stuarts*, London: A. & C. Black.

Besant, W. (1909) *London in the Nineteenth Century*, London: A. & C. Black.

Besant, W. (1912) *London, South of the Thames*, London: A. & C. Black.

Bianca, S. (2000) *Urban Form in the Arab World: Past and Present*, New York: Thames & Hudson.

Blaser, W. (ed.) (1983) *Drawings of Great Buildings*, Basel: Birkhäuser.

Blaser, W. (2004) *Mies van der Rohe, Federal Center, Chicago*, Basel: Birkhäuser.

Bluestone, D. (1988) "Detroit's City Beautiful and the Problem of Commerce," *Journal of the Society of Architectural Historians*, 47, 3: 245–262.

Blunt, W. (1966) *Isfahan: Pearl of Asia*, New York: Stein & Day.

Bosselmann, P. (1988) *Representation of Places: Reality and Realism in City Design*, Berkeley, CA: University of California Press.

Boyer, M.C. (1994) *City of Collective Memory: Its Historical Imagery and Architectural Entertainments*, Cambridge, MA: MIT Press.

Brace, R.M. (1968) *Bordeaux and the Gironde 1789–94*, New York: Russell & Russell.

Branch, M.C. (1997) *Comparative Urban Design: Rare Engravings, 1830–1843*, New York: Princeton Architectural Press.

Braunfels, W. (1988) *Urban Design in Western Europe*, trans. K.J. Northcott, Chicago, IL: University of Chicago Press.

Broadbent, G. (1990) *Emerging Concepts in Urban Space Design*, London: Van Nostrand Reinhold.

Brown, E.M. (1976) *New Haven: A Guide to Architecture and Urban Design*, New Haven, CT: Yale University Press.

Brückelmann, L. (1996) "An Involuntary Lesson – The Baxia Pombalina In Lisbon," *Daidolos*, 59: 32–45.

Burg, A. (1999) *Bau und Raum Annual*, Berlin: Hatje Cantz Verlag.

Cantaucuzino, S. and Browne, K. (1976) 'Isfahan', *The Architectural Review*, 159, 951 (entire issue).

Carmona, M., Heath, T., Oc, T. and Tiesdell, S. (2002) *Public Places – Urban Spaces: The Dimensions of Urban Design*, Boston, MA: Architectural Press.

Carr, S. (1992) *Public Space*, Cambridge: Cambridge University Press.

Çelik, Z. (1986) *Remaking of Istanbul: Portrait of an Ottoman City in the Nineteenth Century*, Seattle, WA: University of Washington Press.

Çelik, Z., Favro, D. and Ingersoll, R. (eds) (1994) *Streets: Critical Perspectives on Public Space*, Berkeley, CA: University of California Press.

Cerdá, I. (1999) *Cerdá: The Five Bases of the General Theory of Urbanization*, ed. A. Soria y Puig, trans. B. Miller and M. Fons i Fleming, Madrid: Electa.

Chabrier, Y.V. (1985) "The Greening of Copley Square," *Landscape Architecture*, 75, 6: 70–76.

Chamberlain, S. (1928) "Bruges," *American Architect*, 133, 2547: 813–818.

Chancellor, E.B. (1907) *The History of the Squares of London*, London: K. Paul, Trench, Trübner.

Childs, M.C. (2004) *Squares: A Public Place Design Guide for Urbanists*, Albuquerque, NM: University of New Mexico Press.

Ciucci, G., Dal Co, F., Manieri-Elia, M. and Tafuri, M. (1979) *The American City*, trans. B.L. La Penta, Cambridge, MA: MIT Press.

Cleary, R.L. (1998) *The Place Royale and Urban Design in the Ancient Regime*, New York: Cambridge University Press.

Cohn, R. (1989) "Square Deals: The Public Is Invited," *Landscape Architecture*, 79, 6: 54–61.

Colom, J.M., Vergara, A.N. and Vicuña, P.B. (1983) *Las Plazas de Santiago*, Santiago, Chile: Ediciones Universidad Católica de Chile.

Cooper-Hewitt Museum (1981) *Urban Open Spaces*, New York: Rizzoli.

Copper, W. (1967) "The Figure/Grounds," Master's Thesis, Department of Architecture, Cornell University, Ithaca, NY.

Copper, W. (1982) "The Figure/Grounds," *Cornell Journal of Architecture*, 2: 42–53.

Coradeschi, S. (1986) *Il Rilievo a Vista: La Piazza*, Milan: Di Baio.

Coubier, H. (1985) *Europeanische Stadt-Plätze*, Cologne: DuMont Buchverlag.

Crouch, D., Garr, D. and Mundigo, A. (1982) *Spanish City Planning in North America*, Cambridge, MA: MIT Press.

Cruft, K. and Andrew, F. (eds) (1995) *James Craig, 1744–1795*, Edinburgh: Mercat Press.

Czaplicka, J.J. and Ruble, B.A. (eds) (2003) *Composing Urban History and the Constitution of Civic Identities*, Washington, DC: Woodrow Wilson Center Press.

Dal Bianco, M.P. and Marenco di Santarosa, C. (eds) (2001) *Piazza San Carlo a Torino*, Milan: Lybra Immagine.

Dallett, F.J. (1968) *An Architectural View of Washington Square*, Frome, UK: Butler & Tanner.

Davidson-Powers, C. (1987) "Indianapolis: Parking Spaces, Bricks and Races," *Inland Architect*, 31, 4: 34–41.

Deegan, G.G. and Toman, J.A. (1999) *The Heart of Cleveland: Public Square in the 20th Century*, Cleveland, OH: Cleveland Landmarks Press.

Dennis, M. (1986) *Court and Garden: From the French Hôtel to the City of Modern Architecture*, Cambridge, MA: MIT Press.

Denver Foundation for Architecture (2001) *Guide to Denver Architecture with Regional Highlights*, Englewood, CO: Westcliffe.

Diamonstein, B. (1993) *The Landmarks of New York*, New York: H.N. Abrams.

Dixon, J.M. (ed.) (1999) *Urban Spaces*, New York: Visual Reference Publications.

Dorsey, R. and Roth, G.F. (eds) (1987) *Architecture and Construction in Cincinnati: A Guide to Buildings, Designers, and Builders.* Cincinnati, OH: Architectural Foundation of Cincinnati.

Dziewonski, K. (1943) "The Plan of Cracow: Its Origin, Design and Evolution," *Town Planning Review*, 19, 1: 29–37.

Easterling, K. (1993) *American Town Plans: A Comparative Time Line*, New York: Princeton Architectural Press.

Eckstut, S. (1994) "Tales of Trustees – Creating Great Urban Places: Lessons from Battery Park and Los Angeles' Union Station," *Blueprints*, 12, 2: 14–16.

Egorov, I.A. (1969) *The Architectural Planning of St. Petersburg*, trans. E. Dluhosch, Athens, OH: Ohio University Press.

Escobar, J. (2000) "Architects, Masons, and Bureaucrats in the Royal Works of Madrid," *Annali di Architettura*, 12: 91–98.

Escobar, J. (2004) *The Plaza Mayor and the Shaping of Baroque Madrid*, Cambridge: Cambridge University Press.

Evenson, N. (1966) *Chandigarh*, Berkeley, CA: University of California Press.

Fabiani, R. (2003) *Trieste*, trans. R. Sadleir, Milan: Electa.

Fanelli, G. (1982) *Città antica in Toscana*, Florence: Sansoni.

Favole, P. (1971) *Piazze d'Italia: Architettura e urbanistica della piazza in Italia*, Milan: Bramante.

Favole, P. (1995) *Piazze ell'architettura Contemporanea*, Milan: Federico Motta.

Fisher, D. with Maestro, R. and Sala, M. (1978) "Jerusalem: Il Muro Del Pianto (The Western Wall)," *L'architettura*, 2: 97–111.

Folpe, E.K. (2002) *It Happened on Washington Square*, Baltimore, MD: Johns Hopkins University Press.

Francesca Morrison, F. and Young, E. (1994) "Square Milieu," *Architectural Review*, 194, 1169: 68–73.

Frank, R. (1992) *Platz und Monument*, Berlin: Reimer.

French, J.S. (1978) *Urban Space: A Brief History of the City Square*, Dubuque, IA: Kendall/Hunt.

Futagawa, Y. (1975) *Villages and Towns*, Tokyo: A.D.A. EDITA.

Gaines, T.A. (1987) "Belgium's Choice Squares," *Places*, 4, 1: 60–67.

Gallion, A.B. and Eisner, S. (1963) *The Urban Pattern: City Planning and Design*, 2nd edn, Princeton, NJ: Van Nostrand.

Gardiner, S. (1989) "The Source Renewed," *Landscape Architecture*, 79, 6: 40–49.

Geist, J.F. (1983) *Arcades: The History of a Building Type*, Cambridge, MA: MIT Press.

Gerkan, A. (1922) *Der Nordmarkt und der Hafen an der Löwenbucht*, Berlin: Vereinigung wissenschaftlicher verleger.

Gibberd, F. (1967) *Town Design*, 5th edn, London: Architectural Press.

Glazer, N. and Lilla, M. (eds) (1987) *Public Face of Architecture: Civic Culture and Public Spaces*, New York: Free Press.

Godoli, E. (1984) *Trieste*, Rome: Laterza.

Goldberger, P. (1979) *The City Observed: A Guide to the Architecture of Manhattan*, New York: Random House.

Gottarelli, E. (1978) *Urbanistica e Architettura a Bologna Agli esordi dell'unità d'Italia*, Bologna: Cappelli.

Gournay, I. and Vanlaethem, F. (eds) (1998) *Montreal Metropolis, 1880–1930*, Toronto: Canadian Centre for Architecture.

Gutkind, E.A. (1964) *Urban Development in Central Europe*, vol. I, New York: Free Press.

Gutkind, E.A. (1965) *Urban Development in the Alpine and Scandinavian Countries*, vol. II, New York: Free Press.

Gutkind, E.A. (1967) *Urban Development in Southern Europe: Spain and Portugal*, vol. III, New York: Free Press.

Gutkind, E.A. (1969) *Urban Development in Southern Europe: Italy and Greece*, vol. IV, New York: Free Press.

Gutkind, E.A. (1970) *Urban Development in Western Europe: France and Belgium*, vol. V, New York: Free Press.

Gutkind, E.A. (1971) *Urban Development in Western Europe: The Netherlands and Great Britain*, vol. VI, New York: Free Press.

Gutkind, E.A. (1972a) *Urban Development in East-Central Europe: Poland, Czechoslovakia, and Hungary*, vol. VII, New York: Free Press.

Gutkind, E.A. (1972b) *Urban Development in Eastern Europe: Bulgaria, Romania, and the U.S.S.R.*, vol. VIII, New York: Free Press.

Hakim, B.S. (1986) *Arabic-Islamic Cities: Building and Planning Principles*, London: KPI.

Hall, T. (1997) *Planning Europe's Capital Cities: Aspects of Nineteenth-Century Urban Development*, London: E & FN Spon.

Hardoy, J. and Collins, G.R. (eds) (1968) *Urban Planning in Pre-Columbian America*, New York: George Brazilier.

Harris, W.D. and Rodriguez-Camilloni, H.L. (1971) *The Growth of Latin American Cities*, Athens, OH: Ohio University Press.

Heckscher, A. (1977) *Open Spaces: The Life of American Cities*, New York: Harper & Row.

Hedman, R. and Jaszewski, A. (1984) *Fundamentals of Urban Design*, Washington, DC: Planners Press.

Hegemann, W. and Peets, E. (1988) *The American Vitruvius: An Architects' Handbook of Civic Art*, New York: Princeton Architectural Press.

Herdeg, K. (1991) *Formal Structure in Islamic Architecture of Iran and Turkistan*, New York: Rizzoli.

Hidenobu, J. (1995) *Tokyo: A Spatial Anthropology*, trans. K. Nishimura, Berkeley, CA: University of California Press.

Historic Savannah Foundation (1968) *Historic Savannah*, Savannah, GA: Historic Savannah Foundation.

Hoag, J.D. (1975) *Islamic Architecture*, New York: H.N. Abrams.

Holston, J. (1989) *The Modernist City: An Anthropological Critique of Brasilia*, Chicago, IL: University of Chicago Press.

Howland, R.H. and Spencer, E.P. (1953) *Architecture of Baltimore*, Baltimore, MD: Johns Hopkins University Press.

Huffman, R. (2006) "The Value of Urban Space: Philadelphia's Rittenhouse Square," *Urban Land*, 65, 1: 108–111.

Hughes, R. (1992) *Barcelona*, New York: Knopf.

Iglauer, E. (1981) *Seven Stones: A Portrait of Arthur Erikson, Architect*, Seattle, WA: University of Washington Press.

Jacob, C. (2006) *The Sovereign Map: Theoretical Approaches in Cartography throughout History*, trans. T. Conley, Chicago, IL: University of Chicago Press.

Jacobs, A.B. (1993) *Great Streets*, Cambridge, MA: MIT Press.

Jacobs, J. (1993) *The Death and Life of Great American Cities*, New York: Random House.

Janak, P. (1947) "Staromestke Namesti a Radnice," *Architektura CSR* 1947.

Janson, A. and Bürklin, T. (2002) *Auftritte: Interaktionen mit dem architektonishen Raum: die Campi Venedigs/ Scenes: Interaction with Architectural Space: The Campi of Venice*, Basel: Birkhäuser.

Jordy, W.H. (1976) *American Buildings and their Architects*, New York: Anchor Press/Doubleday.

Jung-Beeman, M., Bowden, E.M., Haberman, J., Frymiare, J.L., Arambel-Liu, S., et al. (2004) "Neural Activity When People Solve Verbal Problems with Insight," *PLoS Biol*, 2, 4: e97. Online.

Jürgens, O. (1926) *Spanische Städte*, Hamburg: Kommissions-verlag L. Friederichsen.

Kalm, M. (2001) "Stalinism Meets Gothic: A Case Study of Some Post-World War II Architecture in the Old Town of Tallinn," *Centropa*, 1, 2: 117–124.

Kalve, T. and Smedsvig, A. (2002a) *Landscape Architecture in Scandinavia*, Munich: Callwey.

Kalve, T. and Smedsvig, A. (2002b) "Neue Stadmitte für Bergen, Norwegen" / "New Squares for Bergen, Norway," in *Landschaftsarchitektu in Skandinavien: Projekte aus Danemark, Schweden, Norwegen, Finnland and Island = Landscape architecture in Scandinavia: Projects from Denmark, Sweden, Norway, Finland and Iceland*, Munich: Callwey.

Kanda, S. (1974) "The 'Street' and 'Hiroba' of Japan," in D. Kennedy and M. Kennedy (eds) *The Inner City*, New York: Wiley.

Kato, A. (1980) "The Plaza in Italian Culture," *Process Architecture*, 16: 5–118.

Kent, E. (2004) "When Bad Things Happen to Good Parks: New York's Bryant Park, A Tremendous Comeback Story," *Landscape Architecture*, 94, 11: 162.

Kent, F. and Schwarz, A.G. (2001) "The Return of the Civic Square," *Places*, 14, 1: 66–67.

Kolson, K.L. (2001) *Big Plans: The Allure and Folly of Urban Design*, Baltimore, MD: Johns Hopkins University Press.

Kostof, S. (1987) *America by Design*, New York: Oxford University Press.

Kostof, S. (1991) *The City Shaped: Urban Patterns and Meanings through History*, Boston, MA: Little, Brown.

Kostof, S. (1992) *The City Assembled: The Elements of Urban Form through History*, Boston, MA: Little, Brown.

Kultermann, U. (1982) "The Piazza Ducale In Vigevano and the Typology of Post-Medieval Squares In Europe," *Architecture and Urbanism*, 7, 142: 109–116.

Laffón, R. (1966) *Seville*, trans. J. Forrester, 6th edn, Barcelona: Editorial Nogue.

Lakeman, S.D. (1994) *Natural Light and the Italian Piazza: Siena, as a Case Study*, 2nd edn, San Luis Obispo, CA: Natural Light Books.

Lane, M. (2001) *Savannah Revisited: History and Architecture*, 5th edn, Savannah, GA: Beehive Press.

Langdon, E.M. (1979) *Denver Landmarks*, Denver, CO: C.W. Cleworth.

"La plaza interminabile: Milan urban design three projects by E. Mari for the redesign of Piazza del Duomo," *Domus*, April 1984, 649: 14–19.

Lässig, K., Linke, R. and Rietdorf, W. (1967) *Strassen und Plätzen*, Berlin: VEG.

Leary, E. (1971) *Indianapolis: The Story of a City*, Indianapolis, IN: Bobbs-Merrill.

Leccese, M. (1989) "Portland's Pioneer Square," *Landscape Architecture*, 79, 6: 61.

Leccese, M. (1998) "The Death and Life of American Plazas," *Urban Land*, 57, 11: 78–85, 104.

Le Corbusier (1929) *The City of To-Morrow and its Planning*, trans. from the 8th French edn by F. Etchells, London: John Rodker.

Lehman, K. (1999) "Akropolis der Künste," in P. Deitze and B. Finke (eds) *Bau und Raum*, Ostfildern, Germany: Hatje Cantz Verlag.

Leonard, S.J. and Noel, T.J. (1990) *Denver: Mining Camp to Metropolis*, Niwot, CO: University Press of Colorado.

Lincoln, C. (1992) *Dublin as a Work of Art*, Dublin: O'Brien Press.

Lotz, W. (1977) *Studies in Italian Renaissance Architecture*, Cambridge, MA: MIT Press.

Lubell, H. and McCallum, D. (1978) *Bogota: Urban Development and Employment*, Geneva: International Labour Office.

Lynch, K. (1960) *The Image of the City*, Cambridge, MA: Technology Press.

Mcclendon, C.B. (1989) "The History of the Site of St. Peter's Basilica, Rome," *Perspecta*, 25: 32–65.

McDonagh, B. (1993) *Belgium and Luxembourg*, 8th edn, London: A. & C. Black.

Mace, R. (1976) *Trafalgar Square: Emblem of Empire*, London: Lawrence & Wishart.

Machado, R. (1988) "Public Places for American Cities: Three Projects," *Assemblage*, 6: 98–113.

Madanipour, A. (1996) *Design of Urban Space: An Inquiry into a Socio-Spatial Process*, New York: Wiley.

Madanipour, A. (2003) *Public and Private Spaces of the City*, New York: Routledge.

Mari, E. (1984) "La Plaza Interminabile," *Domus*, 649: 14–19.

Marpillero, S. (1990) "Arte Como Arquitectura Como Ciudad (Art-As-Architecture-As-Town)," *Arquitectura*, 72, 285: 126–137.

Marsan, J-C. (1990) *Montreal in Evolution*, Montreal: McGill-Queen's University Press.

Martin, W.K. (1985) "Rose City Agora: Portland's Pioneer Courthouse Square," *Progressive Architecture*, 66, 8: 93–98.

Matas, J. (1983) *Las plazas de Santiago*, Santiago, Chile: Ediciones Universidad Católica de Chile.

Miles, D.C. (1989) "Pioneer Square: A Case Study," *Preservation Forum*, 3, 1: 8–11.

Miller, H. (1998) *Tallinn*, Tallinn: Huma.

Miller, N. (1989) *Renaissance Bologna*, New York: P. Lang.

Miller, N. and Morgan, K. (1990) *Boston Architecture 1975–1990*, Munich: Prestel.

Möntmann, N. and Dziewior, Y. (2004) *Mapping a City*, Ostfildern, Germany: Hatje Cantz Verlag.

Morris, A.E.J. (1994) *History of Urban Form: Before the Industrial Revolutions*, London: Prentice Hall.

Morris, J. (2001) *Trieste and the Meaning of Nowhere*, New York: Simon & Schuster.

Moughtin, C. (1999) *Urban Design: Street and Square*, 2nd edn, Oxford: Architectural Press.

Mumford, E.P. (2000) *CIAM Discourse on Urbanism*, 1928–1960, Cambridge, MA: MIT Press.

Mumford, L. (1961) *The City in History: Its Origins, its Transformations, and its Prospects*, New York: Harcourt, Brace & World.

Murray, M. (2002) "City Profile: Denver," *Cities*, 19, 4: 283–294.

Naim, J. (1980) "Vancouver's Grand New Government Center," *Architectural Record*, 168, 8: 65–75.

Nicodemi, G. (1982) "Paradigma Della Città Borghese = Paradigm of the Bourgeois City," *Area*, 2, 4: 36–39.

Nordhagen, P.J. (1992) *Bergen: Guide and Handbook – Historical Monuments, Art and Architecture*, Urban Development, Bergen: Bergensiana-forlaget.

Nováková-Skalická, M. (1979) *Telč*, trans. J. Hepner, Brno, Czech Republic: Oblastnoi tsentr upravleniia po okhrane pamiatnikov stariny i prirody.

Novotny, V. (ed.) (1975) *Pamět' Měst*, Prague: Odeon.

Oechslin, W. (1996) "Römische Grösse: St. Peter In Rom, Inbegriff Und Paradigma = Roman Bigness: St. Peter's In Rome, Epitome and Paradigm," *Daidalos*, 61: 30–43.

Olesen, P. (1990) *Copenhagen Open Spaces*, trans. P. Shield, Copenhagen: Borgen.

Olsen, D.J. (1964) *Town Planning in London: The Eighteenth and Nineteenth Centuries*, New Haven, CT: Yale University Press.

Olsen, D.J. (1986) *The City as a Work of Art*, New Haven, CT: Yale University Press.

O'Regan, J. and Dearey, N. (1997) "Three Urban Spaces, Temple Bar, Dublin," *New Irish Architecture*, 12: 59–61.

Payne, R. (1968) *Mexico City*, New York: Harcourt, Brace and World.

Pearson, P. (2000) *The Heart of Dublin: Resurgence of an Historic City*, Dublin: O'Brien Press.

Perényi, I. (1973) *Town Centres: Planning and Renewal*, trans. K. Nagy, Budapest: Akadémiai Kiadó.

"Philips + Fotheringham Partnership: Redesign of Union Square, San Francisco, California," *Architecture and Urbanism*, January 2002, 376: 3–4.

"Plazas In Southern Europe," *Process Architecture*, 1985, 16: 85–113.

"Plazas: A Barcelona," *Abitare*, 1986, 246: 192–199.

Poleggi, E. (2005) *De Ferrari: La Piazza dei Genovesi*, Genoa: De Ferrari.

Porter, R. (1995) *London: A Social History*, Cambridge, MA: Harvard University Press.

Portes, A. and Walton, J. (1976) *Urban Latin America: The Political Condition from Above and Below*, Austin, TX: University of Texas Press.

Prakash, V. (2002) *Chandigarh's Le Corbusier: The Struggle for Modernity in Postcolonial India*, Seattle, WA: University of Washington Press.

Pritchett, V.S. (1962) *London Perceived*, New York: Harcourt, Brace & World.

Project for Public Spaces: http://www.pps.org/great_public_spaces/one?public_place_id=19

Protzen, J-P. and Rowe, J.H. (1994) "Cuzco: Hawkaypata the Terrace of Leisure," in Z. Çelik, D. Favro and R. Ingersoll (eds) *Streets: Critical Perspectives on Public Space*, Berkeley, CA: University of California Press.

Raafat, S. (1998) "Midan Al-Tahrir," *Cairo Times*, December 10.

Raikula, E. (1972) *Raekoja Plats*, Tallinn: Eesti Raamat.

Ramati, R. (1979) "The Plaza as an Amenity," *Urban Land*, 38, 2: 9–12.

Rasmussen, S.E. (1967) *London: The Unique City*, 3rd edn, Cambridge, MA: MIT Press.

Rasmussen, S.E. (1969) *Towns and Buildings*, Cambridge, MA: MIT Press.

Reps, J.W. (1965) *The Making of Urban America*, Princeton, NJ: Princeton University Press.

Rincon Garcia, W. (1999) *Plazas de Espana*, Madrid: Espasa.

Rörig, F. (1967) *The Medieval Town*, trans. D. Bryant, London: Batsford.

Rothstein, F. (1967) *Beautiful Squares*, trans. S. Furness and F.R. Stevenson, Leipzig: VEB.

Rowe, C. (1996) *As I Was Saying*, ed. A. Caragone, Cambridge, MA: MIT Press.

Rowe, C. and Koetter, F. (1978) *Collage City*, Cambridge, MA: MIT Press.

Rutteri, S. (1968) *Trieste: Spunti dal suo Passato*, Trieste, Italy: Eugenio Borsatti Editore.

Saalman, H. (1971) *Haussmann: Paris Transformed*, New York: G. Braziller.

Saarinen, E. (1965) *The City: Its Growth, its Decay, its Future*, Cambridge, MA: MIT Press.

Sagalyn, L.B. (2001) *Times Square Roulette: Remaking the City Icon*, Cambridge, MA: MIT Press.

Scarpaci, J.L. (2005) *Plazas and Barrios: Heritage Tourism and Globalization in the Latin American Centro Histórico*, Tucson, AZ: University of Arizona Press.

Schäfer, R. (2002) "European Cities' New Urban Spaces," *Architecture and Urbanism*, 12, 387: 6–9.

Schmertz, M.F. (1985) "Coping with Cairo: A Study In Urban Decline," *Architectural Record*, 173, 6: 91–93.

Schofield, R. (1992–1993) "Ludovico Il Moro's Piazzas: New Sources and Observations," *Annali di Architettura*, 4–5: 157–167.

Schumacher, T. (1971) "Contextualism: Urban Ideals and Deformations," *Casabella*, 359–360: 79–86.

Scott, P. and Lee, A.J. (1993) *Buildings of the District of Columbia*, New York: Oxford University Press.

Sears, A. (ed.) (2002) *Urban Places, Urban Pleasures: The Cultural Use of Civic Space*, Windsor, Ont.: Humanities Research Group, University of Windsor.

Shane, D.G. (2006) "A Bus System Transforms Bogotá's Prospects," *Architecture*, 7: 54.

Sherwood, R. (1978) *Modern Housing Prototypes*, Cambridge, MA: Harvard University Press.

Shorto, R. (2004) *The Island at the Center of the World*, New York: Doubleday.

Sitte, C. (1945) *The Art of Building Cities: City Building According to its Artistic Fundamentals*, trans. C.T. Stewart, New York: Reinhold.

Sorkin, M. (2001) "Deciphering Greater Cairo," *Architectural Record*, 4: 83–90.

Spreiregen, P.D. (1968) *On the Art of Designing Cities: Selected Essays of Elbert Peets*, Cambridge, MA: MIT Press.

Stamp, G. (1989) "History In the Making: Bruges," *Architects' Journal*, 190, 4: 32–47.

Stankova, J., Stursa, J. and Svatopluk, V. (1992) *Prague: Eleven Centuries of Architecture Historical Guide*, Prague: PAV.

Stanley, J.H. (1968) *Judiciary Square, Washington, D.C.: A Park History*, Washington, DC: Division of History, US Office of Archeology and Historic Preservation.

Stary, O. (1947) "Verejná Soutez Na Starometskou Radnici," *Architektura CSR*, 2: 37–54.

Strauss, B. and Strauss, F. (1974) *Barcelona Step by Step*, trans. A. Cirici, Barcelona: Teide.

Sumner-Boyd, H. and Freely, J. (1987) *Strolling through Istanbul: A Guide to the City*, London: KPI.

Tenuth, J. (2004) *Indianapolis: A Circle City History*, Charleston, SC: Arcadia.

Thiis-Evensen, T. (1999) *Archetypes of Urbanism: A Method for the Esthetic Design of Cities*, trans. S. Campbell, Oslo: Universitetsforlaget.

Thompson, J. and Schmertz, M. (2006) "A Marketplace of Ideas," *Boston Architecture*, 9, 4: 46–51.

Toledano, R. (1997) *Savannah*, New York: Preservation Press.

Torre, S. (1981) "American Square," *Precis*, 3: 31–34.

Trancik, R. (1986) *Finding Lost Space: Theories of Urban Design*, New York: Van Nostrand Reinhold.

Traub, J. (2004) *The Devil's Playground: A Century of Pleasure and Profit in Times Square*, New York: Random House.

Treib, M. (1992) "Arte Pubblica E Spazi Pubblici," *Casabella*, 56, 586–587: 94–99,124–125.

Tuttle, R.J. (1994) "Urban Design Strategies In Renaissance Bologna: Piazza Maggiore," *Annali di Architettura*, 6: 39–63.

Ulam, A. (2006) "Square Deal? Will Impending Changes to Washington Square Park Offer Needed Improvements or Impose a Bogus Take on History?," *Landscape Architecture*, 96, 3: 102–111.

Valena, T.F. (1980) *Prague: Urban Morphology*, Monticello, IL: Vance Bibliographies.

Vance, J.E. (1990) *The Continuing City: Urban Morphology in Western Civilization*, Baltimore, MD: Johns Hopkins University Press.

Vance, M. (1981) *Plazas: A Bibliography*, Monticello, IL: Vance Bibliographies.

Vianelli, A. (1979) *Le Piazze di Bologna*, Rome: Newton Compton.

Vogel, C. (1996) "Das Schloss? Project for the Site of the Former Castle," *The New City*, Fall: 142.

Voyce, A. (1954) *The Moscow Kremlin: Its History, Architecture, and Art Treasures*, Berkeley, CA: University of California Press.

Walter, R.J. (2005) *Politics and Urban Growth in Santiago, Chile, 1891–1941*, Stanford, CA: Stanford University Press.

Ward, P.M. (1997) *Mexico City*, 2nd edn, Chichester: Wiley.

Webb, M. (1990) *The City Square: A Historical Evolution*, New York: Whitney Library of Design.

Webb, M. (1994) "Criticism: Pershing Square: Creating Common Ground," *Architecture and Urbanism*, 10, 289: 6–73.

Weston, R. (2004) *Key Buildings of the Twentieth Century: Plans, Sections, and Elevations*, New York: Norton.

Whitehill, W.M. (1968) *Boston: A Topographical History*, 2nd edn, Cambridge, MA: Harvard University Press.

Whyte, W.H. (2002) "The Social Life of Small Urban Spaces," in A. LaFarge (ed.) *The Essential William H. Whyte*, New York: Fordham University Press.

Willensky, E. and White, N. (1988) *AIA Guide to New York*, 3rd edn, San Diego, CA: Harcourt Brace Jovanovich.

Wilson, S. (ed.) (1968) *The Vieux Carré, New Orleans: Its Plan, its Growth, its Architecture*, New Orleans, LA: City of New Orleans.

Wojciech, B. (2001) "Cracow," *Centropa*, 1, 1: 4–29.

Wu, H. (2005) *Remaking Beijing: Tiananmen Square and the Creation of a Political Space*, Chicago, IL: University of Chicago Press.

Wycherley, R.E. (1976) *How the Greeks Built Cities*, 2nd edn, New York: Norton.

Youngson, A.J. (1966) *The Making of Classical Edinburgh: 1750–1840*, Edinburgh: Edinburgh University Press.

Yücel, E. (1972) *Yeni Cami and its Sultan's Gallery*, Istanbul: Türkiye Turing ve Otomobil Kurumu.

Ziskin, R. (1999) *The Place Vendôme: Architecture and Social Mobility in Eighteenth-Century Paris*, Cambridge: Cambridge University Press.

Zucker, P. (1966) *Town and Square*, New York: Columbia University Press.

Index

agora 10
ambiguous and composite buildings 66
ambiguous enclosure 26, 50, 190
amenity, as open space 60, 70, 88, 90, 114, 166, 190; cultural 36, 114, 118; role of in real estate development 36, 88, 90, 114, 118
American cities, decline of 76, 116, 162, 168, 190, 196
American public space, in accommodating multiple uses 34, 144, 162; as democratic 202; in the nineteenth century 54, 60; reconsidered in the City Beautiful Movement 54, 60; redesign of 52, 96, 144, 162, 168; within gridiron plan 166; formed from pedestrianization 168, Amsterdam 6, 120; Dam Square 6
arcades, as ordering device 8, 28, 30, 78, 86, 114, 134, 158, 178, 184, 192, 198; role in delineating space 8, 20, 46, 158, 192, 202; role in pedestrian experience 20, 30, 46, 178, 180
Archer, Dennis 62
Arras 8, 40, 46, 176, 194; Grande Place 8; Place des Héros (Petite Place) 8
Asian civic space 20, 180, 182
Athens 10; Platia Syntagmatos 10
Aubert, Louis-Urbain 32

Bacon, Edmund 10, 38, 56, 92, 148
Baltimore 12, 36, 70; Mount Vernon Place 12
Bannister, Turpin 166
Barcelona 14, 16, 52, 158, 168; Barri Gòtic 14; Eixample 16; Plaça de la Catedral 14; Plaça Reial 14; Ramblas 14, 168
Barnes Dance 182
Barnes, Henry 182
baroque, buildings 24, 46, 58, 146, 178, 184, 194; spatial concepts of 64, 154, 184; urban space 32, 64, 100, 110, 138, 152, 154, 156, 158
Barthes, Roland 180
Bastéa, Eleni 10
Bates, Frederick 62
Bath 18, 70, 72, 90, 92, 138, 156; Circus 18, 62, 92; Queens Square 18; Royal Crescent 18, 156
Baxter, Hodell, and Donnelly & Preston 52
Beijing 20; Tiananmen Square 20
Bennett, Edward H. 60
Bergen 22, 46, 176; Fisketorget 22; Torgalmenningen 22
Berlin 20, 24, 26; Alexanderplatz 24; Bebelplatz 24; Brandenburg Gate 24; Friederichstadt 24; Leipziger Platz 26; Lustgarten 24; Museuminsel 24; Pariserplatz 24; Potsdamer Platz 26; Unter den Linden 24
Bern 28, 46, 176; Altstadt 28
Bernini, Gian Lorenzo 152, 154
Bianca, Stefano 188
Bienville, Jean-Baptiste de 114
Bohemian town planning 46, 178
Bologna 30, 72; Piazza Maggiore 30; Piazza del Nettuno 30; Via della Indipendenza 30; Via Rizzoli 30
Bonaparte, Napoleon 138
Bordeaux 32; Allées de Tourny 32; Place de la Comédie 32; Place de Louis XVI 32
Borromini, Francesco 152
Boston 12, 28, 34, 36, 52, 72, 96, 162, 196; Copley Square 34, 52, 96; Faneuil Hall 36; Back Bay 12, 34, 36; Boston Common 36; City Hall 36; Post Office Square 162
boulevards 10, 24, 32, 92
Bramante, Donato 198
Brasília 38, 48; Praça dos Três Poderes 38
Brazil 38
Breisach (Germany) 28
Brosse, Salomon de 134
Bruges 40, 176; Burg 40; Grand-Place 40; Markt Platz 40
Brunner, Arnold W. 60
Buenos Aires 42, 164; Plaza de Mayo (May Square) 42, 164; Recova 42
bulvirke 32
Burnham, Daniel 16, 54, 60

Cadillac, Antoine de la Mothe 62
Cairo 44; Midan al-Tahrir (Liberation Square) 44
Canberra (Australia) 38
capitals, national 10, 38, 76, 84, 100, 102, 148, 176, 204; state 48, 60, 76
Carr, D.J. 164
Castellamonte, Carlo di 184
Cerdà, Ildefons 16
České Budějovice 46, 178; Náměstí Přemysla Otakara II 46
Chandigarh 38, 48, 140; Capitol Complex 48
Chicago 50, 60, 116, 166; Federal Center 50
Chleb (Poland) 178
Churriguera, Nicolas 158
Cincinnati 34, 52, 96, 162; Fountain Square 52, 96, 162
City Beautiful Movement 16, 60
Clarke and Rapuano, Inc 34
Cleaveland, Moses 54
Cleveland 54, 60, 76; Public Square 54
Cleveland Group Plan 54
closed squares 8, 14, 80, 86, 130, 134, 138, 160, 178, 192
colonial town planning: Bohemian 46, 178; Dutch 120; English 48, 54, 88, 112; French 106, 114; Greek 10; Polish 84; Roman 18, 32, 170; 194; Spanish 42, 58, 102, 164
colonnade: as ordering device 42, 56, 100, 130; as spatial experience 154, 160, 192, 198
Commissioners' Plan 120, 124, 126

composition: role of in shaping urban space 38, 50, 78, 156, 192; problem arising from formal 54, 62; of spatial experience 10, 18, 70, 72, 110; role in modernist city planning 50, 140; of architectural elements 56, 118, 194
Congres Internationaux d'Architecture Moderne (CIAM) 38
contemporary urban space, design of 66, 190, 196; needs of 38, 114, 140, 146; management of 112,116, 124, 144
Contemporary City for 3 Million 140
context, role of in evaluating a space 50, 68, 182, 190; role of in success of a space 62, 88, 96, 124, 142, 198, 200
continuous space 38
Copenhagen 56; Amaliengade 56; Amalienborg Slotsplads 56; Frederiksstad 56
corporations, role of 112, 116, 124, 144
Correa, Federico 14
Costa, Lúcio 38
Craig's New Town 28, 70
criticism of urban spaces 26, 38
Crouch, D.P. 164
culture and society 68, 182; as a role in the use of urban spaces 22, 180, 182, 188, 190; as represented in urban design 10, 20, 24, 26, 30, 74, 80, 88, 100, 164; intermixing of 46, 84, 170, 186
Cuzco 58, 170; Plaza de Armas 58, 164

da Vinci, Leonardo 198
Davenport, John 112
Abbot, Dean 34
democratic space 20, 202
Denver 60, 182; Civic Center 60
Detroit 62, 76; Cadillac Square 62; Campus Martius 62
discipline in design 18, 28, 56, 112, 158, 192
d'Orléans, Philippe 130
Dresden 64; Zwinger and Theaterplatz 64
Drew, Jane 48
Dublin 66; Temple Bar 66
Dubrovnik 68; Placa 68
Ducerceau, Jacques II Androuet 134

E. Maxwell Fry 48
Eaton, Theophilus 112
economics and economy, role of in shaping urban spaces 38, 44, 66, 80, 92, 122, 146, 182, 190; role of in establishing new towns 46, 74, 84, 88, 140, 164; role of in urban decay 76, 96, 162
Edinburgh 28, 70; St Andrew Square 70
Egorov, Iurii 156
Eigtved, Nikolai 56
enclosure 34, 64, 92, 130, 154, 156, 178, 192, 198
English: colonial towns 54, 106, 112; social and cultural impact on urban space 88, 120; towns 88; urban spaces 88, 120
Erikson, Arthur 190
existing buildings, use of 110, 148, 156
existing thoroughfares and streets 110, 132, 178
existing urban fabric: use of 36, 44, 86, 92, 100; disregard of 140, 168

Filson, John 52
floor of squares 14, 86, 94, 138, 172, 200
Florence 72, 152, 156; Palazzo Uffizi 72; Piazza della Signoria 46, 72, 156, 194
Folpe, Emily Keis 126
Forbidden City (Beijing) 20
Fordham, Elias 76
French, baroque 32, 110, 138; colonies 62, 106, 114; squares 88, 106, 114, 136; urban design 88
frontier towns 46, 54, 62
Functionalist City 38

Garden City Movement 16
Gary, Indiana 62
Genoa 74, 186; Piazza de Ferrari 74
Goldberger, Paul 126
Gramercy Park 120
green belts 46, 84, 196
grid plans: hierarchical 16, 86, 98, 166; relationship with topography 10, 58; use in urban design 16, 48, 128, 164, 180, 184; use in colonial towns 42, 46, 98, 112, 120, 164; Bohemian colonial towns 46; English colonial towns 112, 166; French colonial towns 114; Greek colonial towns 10; Polish colonial towns 84; Spanish 98, 102; American frontier towns 54, 60, 62, 76, 112; juxtaposition of multiple 34, 62, 76, 124; potential for monotony 16, 42, 48, 60, 166; complexity of 16, 86, 98, 166; ease of 46, 98, 120, 164, 166
grouped squares 8, 40, 160, 194
Griffin, John 62
Gutkind, Erwin 22, 28, 30, 40, 46, 74, 108, 158, 170

Hanseatic League,22, 176
Hardouin-Mansart, Jules 138
Hårleman, Carl 174
Haussmann, Georges 16, 32, 44, 132
Heckscher, August 114
Herdeg, Klaus 78
Héré, Emmanuel 110
Hidenobu, Jinnai 180, 182
Hilmer, Heinz 26
hiroba 180
Hoffmann, Ludwig 24
Holston, James 38
Howard, Ebenezer 16
Howard, John Eager 12

Indianapolis 76; Monument Circle 76
Isfahan 78, 188; Maidan-i-Shah 78
Islam, impact of on urban settlement patterns 78, 80, 82, 164, 170, 188, 170, 188
Isozaki, Arata 26
Istanbul 80, 114, 170; Misir Çarsisi 80; Yeni Cami 80

Jacobs, Allan 14
Jacobs, Jane 142
Jahn, Helmut 26
Jeanneret, Pierre 48
Jefferson, Thomas 56, 62, 198, 204
Jerusalem 82, 170; Temple Mount 82; Western Wall Plaza 82

Kahn, Louis 48
Kalve, Terje 22
Kleanthes, Stamatios 10
Klenze, Leo von 10
Koetter, Fred 66, 130, 134
Kostof, Spiro 166
Kraków 46, 84, 196; Rynek Główny 84
Kromeriz (Czech Republic) 178
Kolin (Czech Republic) 178
külliye 80

L'Enfant, Pierre 62, 76, 204
La Compañia 58
lateral movement through squares 8, 72, 130, 134, 138, 146, 198
lauben 28
Law of the Indies *see* Leyes de Indias
Le Corbusier 48, 140
Legoretta, Ricardo 96
Lemercier, Jacques 130
Leszczyński, Stanisław 110
ley lines 58
Leyes de Indias (Law of the Indies) 42, 102, 164
Libeskind, Daniel 60
Lisbon 86; Praça do Comércio 86
loggias 72, 148, 194
London 12, 64, 74, 88, 90, 92, 94, 106, 120, 138, 166; Belgrave Square 88, 90; Cavendish Square 90; Hanover Square 90; Park Crescent 90, 92; Park Square 92; Trafalgar Square 12, 94; Wilton Crescent 88
Los Angeles 34, 52, 96, 162, 182; Pershing Square 34, 52, 96, 162
Louis, Victor 130

Lucca 98, 152; Piazza dell' Anfiteatro 98
ludic space 180
Ludlow, Israel 52
Lynch, Kevin 68

Macy, J. Douglas 144
Madrid 100, 158; Plaza Mayor 100, 158
Maidan-i-Shah 78
Maia, Manuel da 86
markets: buildings; 32, 36, 40, 42, 78, 84, 100; streets 28, 176, 188; squares 8, 30, 76, 84, 102, 112, 124, 150, 176, 194; as basis of design 28, 30, 34, 40, 42, 80, 98, 100, 108, 112, 176, 184, 194; use of spaces for 34, 52, 116, 124
Martin, Willard 144
McCarren, Barbara 96
McKim, George 60
medieval, origins 24, 28, 40, 70, 150; squares 30, 84, 146, 172, 194; urban fabric 32, 46, 84, 132, 176, 198
Messel, Alfred 24
Métézeau, Louis 134
Mexico City 102, 164, 170; Zócalo (Plaza de la Constitucíon) 102
Michelangelo 148
Milá, Alfonso 14
Milan 104; Piazza del Duomo 104
Mobile, Alabama 114
modern urban design 44, 66
modernist city planning 38, 48, 50, 64
modernization 44, 46, 132, 146
Moltkein, Adam 56
Moneo, José Rafael 26
Montréal 106; Place d'Armes 106
Morris, Jan 186
Moscow 108; Krasnaya Plóshchad 108
Moses, Robert 126
Moughtin, Cliff 152
Mumford, Lewis 18, 172, 192
Mundigo, A.L. 164

Nancy 72, 110, 156, 204; Place de la Carrière 110, 204; Place Général de Gaulle 110; Place Stanislas 110, 156
Nehru, Jawaharlal 48
New England town planning 112; impact of on frontier urban design 34, 54
New Haven 54, 88, 112; The Green 112
New Orleans 106, 114, 198; Jackson Square 86, 106, 114, 198
New York 12, 36, 90, 106, 114, 116, 118, 120, 122, 124, 126, 138, 144; Bryant Park 116, 126, 144; Father Duffy Square 122; Manhattan 90, 116, 118, 120, 122, 124, 126; Rockefeller Center 90, 118; Stuyvesant Square 120; Times Square 122, 124; Union Square 120, 124; Washington Square 126, 142
New Urbanism 66, 140
Niemeyer, Oscar 38
nineteenth century American city planning 54, 76, 112, 168, 200, 204; formalism 10, 94, 104; urban renewal 16, 32, 44, 84, 116, 136, 138, 146, 156, 196
non-profit development 34, 62, 116 *also see* corporations
non-profit public space management 26, 34, 116, 122, 124, 144; *also see* corporations
nostalgia 66, 122, 140
Novy Jicin (Czech Republic) 178

Old Town Square 146
Olin, Laurie 96
Olmstead, Frederick Law, Jr 60
Olmstead, Frederick Law, Sr. 126
Olomouc (Czech Republic) 178
order in design 30, 86, 100, 130, 132, 138, 158, 188, 198
Oslo 22, 128; Eidsvolls Plass 128; Kronprincess Märthas Plassen 128; Rådhus Plassen 128

Paris 32, 44, 64, 74, 80, 88, 90, 92, 94, 146, 196, 198; Louvre 130, 132, 136, 138; Musée du Louvre 136; Palais Royal 130, 136, 204; Place Charles-de-Gaulle 132; Place l'Etoil 132; Place des Vosges 100, 134, 136, 138, 184; Place Vendôme 18, 56, 134, 138; Rue de Rivoli 134, 140; Tuileries Gardens 136, 138; Tuileries Palace 136; Voison Plan 140
parking 4, 52, 54, 96, 144, 162, 202, 204
Parris, Alexander 36
Pasha Khedive Ismail 44
Pasha Mohammed Ali 44
paths, as spatial edges 8, 166, 200, 204; and spatial sequence 56, 68, 72, 92, 138, 166, 194, 204
pedestrianization 168
pedestrian-only streets and squares 22, 26, 48, 52, 118, 164, 168, 180, 202
Pei Cobb Freed and Partners 34, 202
Pei, I.M. 136
Penn, Williams 142
Philadelphia 88, 112, 114, 142; Rittenhouse Square 142
Phillips + Fotheringham Partnership 162
Piano, Renzo 26
Place Louis-le-Grand *see* Place Vendôme
Place Royale *see* Place des Vosges
political system: role of in shaping spaces 10, 32, 38, 42, 44, 74, 80, 84, 88, 92, 94, 164; and use in signification of urban space 20, 24, 30, 58, 82, 100, 102, 108
Pöppelman, Mathäus Daniel 64
Porter, Roy 88
Portland 144, 162; Pioneer Courthouse Square 144
Prague 46, 146, 178, 196; Staroměstské Náměstí 146
Prakash, Vikramaditya 48
Pritchett, V.S. 94
privatization 116, 144 *see also* corporations
private spatial needs 88, 106, 180, 188
Protzen, Jeanne-Pierre 58
public-private agreements *see* corporations
Pugin, A.W.N. 40

Quinones, Andreas Garcia de 158
Quinones, J. Garcia de 158

Ralston, Alexander 76
Rasmussen 32, 56, 88, 90, 92
real estate development 90, 122; Bath 18; Boston 34 ; Cairo 44; New York 90, 118, 122; Paris 134, 138; Tokyo 182; Trieste 186 *see also* amenity
religion 160; role in shaping urban space 42, 58, 68, 80, 100, 160, 162, 188; as primary role of space 20, 80, 180
Renaissance architecture 24, 30, 34, 46, 100, 110, 146, 170, 178
Renaissance urban form 110, 148, 152, 166, 174, 1989
Reps, John 62, 76, 112
residential squares 12, 18, 90, 94, 106, 120, 166
Richardson, H.H. 34
Richelieu, Cardinal 130
Rogers, Richard 26
Rohe, Mies van der 26, 50
Roman architecture, as model 18; remnants of 98, 152
Roman colonial planning 18, 32, 98, 170, 194; underlying pattern 82, 98
Rome 42, 64, 86, 98, 138, 148, 150, 152, 154, 156, 158, 192, 194, 198; Piazza del Campidoglio 148; Piazza Navona 98, 104, 150, 152, 156; Piazza San Pietro (Vaticano) 152, 154, 156, 160, 192, 198
rond-point 132
Rossi, Karlo 156
Rothstein, Fritz 42
Rouse, James 36
Rowe, Colin 66, 130, 134
Rowe, John Howland 58
RTKL 52
Ruskin, John 40

Saarinen, Eliel 74
Sabastiao José de Carvalho e Melo 86

Sagalyn, Lynne 122
Saint Petersburg 108, 156; Dvortsóvaya Plóshchad 156
Salamanca 100, 158; Plaza Mayor 100, 158
Salzburg 160, 194; Domplatz 160; Kapitalplatz 160; Residenzplatz 160
San Francisco 34, 52, 96, 162; Union Square 34, 52, 96, 162
Santiago 164, 170; Plaza de Armas 164
Sasaki, Dawson & DeMay 34
Sattler, Christoph 26
Savannah 88, 120, 166; Historic District 166, 168; Johnson Square 166; Oglethorpe Square 166; St. James Square 166; Warren Square 166; Wright Square 166
scale 12, 14, 20, 38, 66, 94, 110, 142, 170, 188; modulation of in architecture 28, 56, 88, 90, 112, 140, 142, 148; modulation of urban space 14, 42, 82, 134, 160, 170
Scamozzi,Vincenzo 160, 166
Scharoun, Hans 26
Schaubert, Eduard 10
Schinkel, Karl Friedrich 24
Schumacher, Thomas 50
Seattle 168; Occidental Park 168; Pioneer Square 144, 162, 168
security: impact on urban space 20, 116, 202, 204
Semper, Gottfried 64
Seville 170; Patio de los Naranjos 170; Plaza del Triunfo 170; Real Alcázar 170; Santa Cruz Quarter 170
Siena 172; Piazza del Campo 172
Sitte, Camillo 72
Smedsvig, Arne 22
society 26, 30, 32, 74, 88, 140; response to needs of 16, 32, 38, 140, 146; role of in shaping urban space 20, 28, 30, 42, 44, 68, 74, 82, 162, role of in shaping urban space in English cities 88, 94, 112; role of in shaping Asian cities 20, 180; role of in shaping French cities 112; role of in shaping Islamic cities 80, 188
social life in urban spaces 20, 28
Solari, Santino 160
Sorkin, Michael 44
Spanish colonial town planning 58, 102, 164
see also Leyes de Indias
spatial experience 6, 8, 18, 28, 50, 68, 86, 134, 154, 192, 194, 198
spatial sequence 6, 18, 30, 56, 68, 70, 72, 110, 166
spatial layering 130, 134, 188, 204
Speer, Albert 20
Speer, Robert 60
Saint Louis, Missouri 114
Stockholm 174; Slottsbacken 174; Stortorget 174
streets, pedestrianization of 168
subtlety, role in urban form 52, 68, 70, 134, 154, 192

Takayama, Masami 50
Tallinn 176; Raekoja Plats 176
tartan 166
Telč 178; Náměstí Zachariáše z Hradce 178
terminal plazas 182
Thompson, Benjamin 36
Tokyo 74, 122, 180, 182; Asakusa Nakamise Dori 180; Hachiko Square 122, 180, 182
Toledo, Ohio 62
topography, role of in urban design 10, 12, 22, 42, 70, 172, 178, 200
Torino 184; Piazza San Carlo 184, 198
Traub, James 122
Trieste 86, 186; Canal Grande 186
Tunis 74, 170, 188; Medina 188
Tuttle, Richard 30
twentieth century urban design 24, 36, 54, 60, 70, 80, 126; management of 116 *see also* corporations; modernist 38, 48, 64
twenty first century urban design 26, 62, 122; models for 66, 182; challenges of 92, 126, 140, 196
Tyler Davidson fountain 52

University of Virginia 56, 198
urban fabric 142, 154, 188, 192; demolition of 36, 44, 80, 82, 92, 132, 154, 196; insertion into 134, 138, 192; reweaving of 26, 36, 66, 196
urban rooms 66, 122, 150, 160, 172, 190, 202; as part of a spatial experience 92, 110; within a square 96

Valdivia, Pedro de 164
Vancouver 190; Robson Square 190
variety: of groups 12, 162, 200; of uses 12, 16, 52, 124, 164, 170, 190, 200; within order 56, 148, 188; *see also* American urban spaces;
Venice 40, 72, 86, 186, 192, 198; Piazza San Marco 72, 192, 198; Piazzetta di San Marco 192
Venturi Scott-Brown and Associates 94
Verona 194; Piazza dei Signori 194; Piazza delle Erbe 194
Vicenza 12
Vienna 36, 46, 84, 186, 196; Rathausplatz 196; Ringstrasse 36, 196
view, role of 8, 10, 50, 72, 114, 152
Vigévano 192, 198; Piazza Ducale 192, 198
Ville Radieuse 140
Vittozzi, Ascanio 184

Washington, DC 38, 60, 76; Daniel Patrick Moynihan Place 202; Dupont Circle 62, 132, 200; Grand Plaza 202; Judiciary Square 204; Logan Circle 200; Washington Circle 200; Woodrow Wilson Plaza 202
weaving of the urban fabric 66, 134
Webb, Michael 42, 82
Wines, James 96
Wittlesbach, Otto von 10
Wood, John, Jr 18
Wood, John, Sr 18
Woodward, Augustus Brevoort 62
World's Columbian Exposition in Chicago (1893) 60
Wycherley, R.E. 10

Zähringer, Dukes of 28
zoning 8, 40, 118, 122, 142
Zucker, Paul 8, 12, 18, 54, 64, 70, 86, 98, 138, 152, 154, 158, 176, 194
Zurich 28

Plan index by country and city

ARGENTINA
Buenos Aires, Plaza de Mayo 42

AUSTRIA
Salzburg, Domplatz, Residenzplatz and Kapitalplatz 160
Vienna, Ringstrasse 196

BELGIUM
Bruges Grand Place and Burg 40

BRAZIL
Brasília, Praça dos Três Poderes 38

CANADA
Montréal, Place d'Armes 106
Vancouver, Robson Square 190

CHILE
Santiago, Plaza de Armas 164

CHINA
Beijing, Tiananmen Square 20

CROATIA
Dubrovnik, Placa 68

CZECH REPUBLIC
České Budějovice, Náměstí Přemysla Otakara II 46
Prague, Staroměstské Náměstí 146
Telč, Náměstí Zachariáše z Hradce 178

DENMARK
Copenhagen, Amalienborg Slotsplads 56

EGYPT
Cairo, Midan al-Tahrir 44

ESTONIA
Tallinn, Raekoja Plats 176

FRANCE
Arras, Grande Place and Place des Héros 8
Bordeaux, Allées de Tourny 32
Nancy, Place Stanislas, Place de la Carrière and Place Général de Gaulle 110
Paris, Palais Royal 130
Paris, Place Charles-de-Gaulle/Place de l'Etoile 132
Paris, Place des Vosges 134
Paris, Musée du Louvre 136
Paris, Place Vendôme 138
Paris, Voison Plan 140

GERMANY
Berlin, Museumsinsel 24
Berlin, Potsdamer Platz and Leipziger Platz 26
Dresden, Zwinger and Theaterplatz 64

GREECE
Athens, Syntagma Square 10

INDIA
Chandigarh, Capitol Complex 48

IRAN
Isfahan Maidan-i-Shah 78

IRELAND
Dublin, Temple Bar 66

ISRAEL
Jerusalem, Western Wall Plaza and the Temple Mount 82

ITALY
Bologna, Piazza di Maggiore 30
Florence, Piazza Uffizi and Piazza di Signora 72
Genoa, Piazza de Ferrari 74
Lucca, Piazza dell' Anfiteatro 98
Milan, Piazza del Duomo 104
Rome, Piazza del Campidoglio 148
Rome, Campo dei Fiori 150
Rome, Piazza Navona 152
Rome, Piazza San Pietro in Vaticano 154
Siena, Piazza del Campo 172
Torino, Piazza San Carlo 184
Trieste, Canal Grande 186
Venezia, Piazza San Marco and Piazzetta di San Marco 192
Verona, Piazza delle Erbe and Piazza dei Signori 194
Vigévano, Piazza Ducale 198

JAPAN
Tokyo, Asakusa Nakamise Dori 180
Tokyo, Hachiko Square 182

MEXICO
Mexico City, Zócalo/Plaza de la Constitucíon 102

MOROCCO
Tunis, Medina 188

NETHERLANDS
Amsterdam, Dam Square 6

NORWAY
Bergen, Fisketorget and Torgalmenningen 22
Oslo, Rådhus Plassen, Kronprincess Märthas Plassen and Eidsvolls Plass 128

PERU
Cuzco, Plaza de Armas 58

POLAND
Kraków, Rynek Główny 84

PORTUGAL
Lisbon, Praça do Comércio 86

RUSSIA
Moscow, Krasnaya Plóshchad 108
Saint Petersburg, Dvortsóvaya Plóshchad 156

SPAIN
Barcelona, Barrio Gòtic 14
Barcelona, Eixample 16
Madrid, Plaza Mayor 100
Salamanca, Plaza Mayor 158
Seville, Plaza del Triunfo, Patio de los Naranjos and Real Alcázar 170

SWEDEN
Stockholm, Slottsbacken and Stortorget 174

SWITZERLAND
Bern, Alstadt 28

TURKEY
Istanbul, Yeni Cami and Misir Çarsisi 80

UNITED KINGDOM
Bath, Royal Circus and Crescent 18
Edinburgh, St. Andrew Square 70
London, Belgrave Square and Wilton Crescent 88
London, Cavendish Square and Hanover Square 90
London, Park Crescent and Park Square 92
London, Trafalgar Square 94

UNITED STATES
Balitmore, Mount Vernon Place 12
Boston, Copley Square 34
Boston, Faneuil Hall Marketplace and Quincy Market 36
Chicago, Federal Center 50
Cincinnati, Fountain Square 52
Cleveland, Public Square 54
Denver, Civic Center 60
Detroit, Campus Martius 62
Indianapolis, Monument Circle 76
Los Angeles, Pershing Square 96
New Haven, The Green 112
New Orleans, Jackson Square 114
New York, Bryant Park 116
New York, Rockefeller Plaza 118
New York, Stuyvesant Square 120
New York, Times Square 122
New York, Union Square 124
New York, Washington Square 126
Philadelphia, Rittenhouse Square 142
Portland, Pioneer Courthouse Square 144
San Francisco, Union Square 162
Savannah, Historic District 166
Seattle, Pioneer Square 168
Washington, DC, Dupont Circle 200
Washington, DC, Grand Plaza, Woodrow Wilson Plaza and Daniel Patrick Moynihan Place 202
Washington, DC, Judiciary Square 204